ECONOMIC PROGRESS
AND SOCIAL SECURITY

By Allan G. B. Fisher

THE CLASH OF PROGRESS AND SECURITY (1935)

ECONOMIC PROGRESS
AND SOCIAL SECURITY

BY
ALLAN G. B. FISHER

LONDON
MACMILLAN & CO. LTD
1945

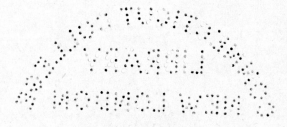

PRINTED IN GREAT BRITAIN
BY R. & R. CLARK, LIMITED, EDINBURGH

PREFACE

IN 1934 I wrote a book, *The Clash of Progress and Security*, " the rather simple theme " of which, as one reviewer put it, was that " economic progress was impeded by resistance to change ". The ideas which I there attempted to elucidate had their origin in a conviction that the belief at that time almost universal in " new " countries such as Australia and New Zealand, that statesmen there should plan for an indefinite expansion of rural population engaged in agricultural and pastoral production, ran directly counter to the requirements both of material progress and of social security for these economies. Further reflection upon this problem suggested the usefulness of a study of the causes and consequences of the widely varied influences which everywhere from time to time impede the adjustments in our economic structure without which the attainment of higher standards of living is impossible.

Whether or not this examination was well done at the time, the urgency of the problem does not, ten years later, seem to have appreciably diminished. Many, perhaps most academic economists have not been unaware of the importance of the issue involved, but the influences of fashion, which are sometimes scarcely less noticeable in the realm of economic theory than in ordinary commerce, have had the unfortunate effect that after the existence of the problem has been formally recognised, it has often been pushed on one side, and no serious attempt made to do anything about it. It therefore seemed worth while to attempt a re-statement in the light of current events and trends of thought. In so doing particular attention has been paid, first to the unhappy tendency displayed in many of the excited discussions of the new world which planning offers to us to neglect the overwhelming importance of flexibility in our economic structure, and, secondly, to the impediments placed in the way of the development of orderly and harmonious international relations by the stubborn and short-sighted determination of national economies to protect themselves from the necessity for structural adaptation. The task

v

of restoring the world's productive capacity after a long and destructive war will tax to the full our powers of far-sighted organisation, and unless we pay much more serious attention than in the inter-war period to the damaging effects of the powerful influences which try to keep the structure of production as it is, our efforts will fall far short of the measure of success which otherwise might reasonably be expected. For no economy, moreover, is this truth more important than for Great Britain. I am, I hope, under no illusion that action based on the principles outlined in this book would by itself be sufficient to ensure the solution of our post-war economic problems. Many issues of first-rate importance are here almost entirely neglected, and many other things, not here referred to, also need to be done. But the utmost skill and care in dealing with these other things will, it is believed, be ineffective, unless we also provide more effectively than in the past to ensure that the forces which resist structural changes are kept under control.

I owe much to my friends with whom I have from time to time discussed many of the issues under consideration, though they might not in every case easily now recognise the stimulus which their observations have afforded. I am particularly indebted to my former colleague, Mr. Barnard Ellinger, and to Professor Eugene Staley, both of whom have read a large part of the manuscript at one stage or another, and whose comments and criticisms have been most valuable. Professor Staley also kindly allowed me to profit from the perusal before publication of his *World Economic Development : Effects on Advanced Industrial Countries* (International Labour Office, Montreal, 1944).

My greatest debt is, however, to the Royal Institute of International Affairs, and to Sir Henry Price, whose generosity made possible the establishment in 1937 of the Price Chair of International Economics, of which it has been my privilege to be the first occupant. The broad-minded and enlightened policy of the Council of the Royal Institute has made the period of my association with it as a member of its staff an educational experience of the utmost value which it would have been impossible to enjoy by any other means. In particular, during the last twelve months, at a period when with straitened personnel resources the Institute was engaged in many other current activities of great importance, it generously allowed me to devote practically the whole of my time to the preparation of this book, and also took the trouble to facilitate a visit to the United States, where the further experience gained has also been of great value in attempting to look at the broader issues of international economic policy in a clearer and more accurate perspective. In its own publications it is customary to state that " The Institute, as such, is precluded by its rules from expressing an opinion on any aspect of international affairs ; opinions expressed in this book are, therefore, purely individual ", and it is perhaps proper to state here formally that the same principle applies to the present work.

Much of the analysis in the present work is concerned with matters which on a superficial view might appear not to fall within the province of a specialist in international economics. No apology, however, is needed for this extension of the range of our interest. Both experience and general reasoning have by now demonstrated with abundant clearness the intimate organic relations between internal and international policy. Strictly speaking, there is no such thing as International Economics. There is only Economics, one and indivisible. And if anyone preferred to revert to the terminology of an earlier generation and describe the present work as an essay in International Political Economy, its author would raise no objection.

ALLAN G. B. FISHER

CHATHAM HOUSE
May 3, 1944

CONTENTS

ix

CHAPTER XVI

These ye ought to have done, and not to have left the other undone.

Matthew xiii, 23

If anyone asks me if I am a socialist, and demands an answer, yes or no, in the rude way ill-informed people have, I say no. But if anyone asks me if I am an anti-socialist or an individualist, I say no with equal readiness. I am not an anti-socialist, because I think progress involves a great extension of conscious organisation, and I do not object to that extension and try to hinder it as much as possible. . . . On the other hand, I refuse to call myself a socialist, because . . . I am not prepared to take the line of advocating or opposing things simply on the ground that they seem to be in accordance with a general principle.

EDWIN CANNAN, *The Economic Outlook* (1912), pp. 281-2

If anybody asks whether there should be more socialism or Government planning or more free enterprise, my answer is that there ought to be a great deal more of both.

MR. OLIVER LYTTELTON, April 26, 1942

CHAPTER I

INTRODUCTION

1. THERE can be little dispute about the necessity for radical changes in economic policy when once the war has been brought to a successful conclusion. But this necessity once admitted, the task of reducing to some kind of order the rich and bewildering profusion of plans and policies now offered from all quarters at first sight seems almost hopeless. The plans themselves are often contradictory, because there is no consistency in the foundations upon which they are built. The real purposes lying behind the policies which we are asked to approve can often be identified only after a careful examination of their details, and not infrequently the purposes so disclosed differ in important respects from what some of their supporters believe themselves to have in mind. The author of the present study cherishes no confident hopes of being able to elaborate a blue-print which will commend itself at once to everyone as being so obviously and sweetly reasonable that wrangling and controversy about principles will forthwith cease, to be replaced by the quieter discussions of technicians, agreed about what they want and uncertain merely about the most efficient way of getting it. The issues involved, economic, political, social and even philosophical, are far too complex to justify any such naïve expectations. A fallible mortal may, however, perhaps be permitted to entertain the more modest hope of helping to clarify our present confusions by an analysis of some of the fundamental notions which, though implicit in much of the current controversy about post-war economic policy, are nevertheless seldom brought to the surface by controversialists too eager to establish their points with the least possible delay. We cannot always delay the search for a satisfactory technique until we have formulated precise ideas about the ends the technique is designed to achieve, and even when we have apparently made up our minds about what we want,

we often express our intentions in phrases which do not clearly reveal the underlying implications. Careful examination often shows some of the details of our policies to rest upon assumptions inconsistent with the wider ultimate objective to which we believe that we have pledged our devotion. In such circumstances the common unhappy experience of well-intentioned plans coming to naught should occasion little surprise. We can make this painful experience salutary if it compels us to face our hidden inconsistencies and makes us determined to avoid their repetition in the future.

2. In periods of confusion and disturbance it is natural to look back at the golden days when, as we may now imagine, the machinery for the mere routine of ordinary living could more or less be left to run itself, and confident that the foundations were secure, we could concentrate our energies upon the cultivation of the cultural elements, whose quality and development, it might have been supposed, were the true tests of civilisation. At all times, however, the solution of nearly every important problem demands some adjustment of social machinery and habits of thinking to inexorable changes in the background of conditions of our life, and nostalgic longings for a (probably imaginary) Golden Age, the foundations for which no longer exist, are unlikely to be a satisfactory starting-point for new policies. We are perhaps less liable now to errors of this kind than we were at the conclusion of the war of 1914–18. To condemn the short-sightedness of those who then yearned for " normalcy " and a return to the pre-war *status quo* is now indeed so much a matter of course that our thinking is more likely to be infected by the opposite error of supposing that nothing that was done during the inter-war period was right. We too easily forget the remarkable improvements in standards of living which were registered during that period (for both employed and unemployed), and are apt rashly to conclude that by following the simple course of enquiring what was done after 1918 and then deciding in favour of exactly the opposite, we shall have a sufficiently safe rough practical guide for action when the war is over. It is easy to gain universal assent for the proposition that " we must avoid the mistakes we made after the last war ", but unanimity here

will not carry us far along the right road unless we take more trouble than many people care to do to examine the nature of the mistakes then made, and the extent to which differences in the backgrounds of the two sets of problems may make simple comparisons inapplicable.

CHAPTER II

THE ECONOMIC PROBLEM

1. OUR first task then must be to enquire whether the foundations of the pre-1939 discussions of economic problems have so far changed that economists are no longer justified in making the same fundamental assumptions as at that time seemed appropriate. In principle our enquiry should lead to substantially similar results whatever country the enquirer happens to have particularly in mind. As many of the subsequent illustrations will suggest, the greater part of the analysis which follows was worked out with special attention to the problems and controversies of Great Britain. The author was indeed not unaware that for other countries the emphasis might appropriately be placed somewhat differently, and in even a brief contact with the United States the inappropriateness for other countries of part of the provisional framework in which current British problems are most conveniently studied becomes quickly apparent. Nevertheless the most lasting impression left by a hasty comparison of the economic and social problems of the two countries comes not from the contrast between " the British " and " the American points of view ", upon which nervous propagandists are apt to concentrate so much of their attention, but from their fundamental identity. Sometimes apparent contrasts are little more than matters of timing. Some British interests are, for example, now disposed to commit the same mistakes as the Americans experimented with in the 1930's.[1] For the time being the Americans have lost interest in these experiments. But the fundamental conditions from which they emerged have not changed much, and so long as the root problems remain the same, the same impatient responses may well be forthcoming again in face of some slight and transitory change in the manner of their presentation. If our analysis is not to be repellently abstract, it must be worked out in terms of real economies. In the present study the

[1] Cf. *infra*, X, 16.

British economy inevitably looms larger than any other, but it is believed that the adaptations necessary to apply the analysis to other economies will be neither violent nor difficult.

2. Up to 1939 economists took it for granted that the main economic problem for any society with facilities at its disposal for expanding the volume of its production was that of allocating its resources, its labour and capital, so that its members could with the least possible delay enjoy as much of the larger and more varied volume of goods and services which expanding production would bring with it as was compatible with the cultivation of the non-economic values regarded as important by the society in question. This process demands changes from time to time in customary habits of employment and of investment, changes in relation to which a lead must be given by an " entrepreneur ", in the person of either an enterprising individual, or the servant of a business firm, or of a government instrumentality. If the advance of science makes possible the large-scale production of cheap motor-cars, this possibility can become a reality only if some people who earlier would have found employment as farmers or blacksmiths or textile operatives are trained for work in motor factories or garages, and if some capital which earlier would have been invested in agricultural improvements or railway construction is made available instead for those engaged in the production of automobiles. These changes have frequently brought with them serious embarrassments for both labour and capital ; the more surprising thing is the ease with which they have frequently been carried through and on quite a considerable scale. Many people have quite failed to realise the significance and extent of the silent revolution in the relative importance of different kinds of employment which has been quietly going on everywhere during our own lifetime, and had indeed begun much earlier.

3. If we adopt the convenient classification of economic activity into the three types of primary, secondary and tertiary production, primary including agricultural and mining activities, devoted directly to the production of food or raw materials of various kinds, secondary including manufacturing in all its forms, and tertiary a vast miscellaneous residue of activity devoted mainly

B

to the production of " services ", ranging from transport and commerce through amusements and education to the highest forms of creative art and philosophy,[1] we may say that in every progressive economy there has been a steady shift of employment and investment from the essential " primary " activities, without whose products life in even its most primitive forms would be impossible, to secondary activities of all kinds, and to a still greater extent into tertiary production.[2] It has become common form in certain circles to decry some modern types of tertiary production, alleging that we could very well do without them, as mere excrescences competing unfairly with the true " producer " in the distribution of income. But while waste is just as possible in tertiary production as it is elsewhere, and too much labour or too much capital may be diverted into tertiary channels, war-time experience should have taught us how important tertiary services have been in building up the standard of living even of people with modest incomes. When an economy is really hard pressed it more readily dispenses with them than with some other things, but the considerable contraction of their volume in war-time ought to have brought home to us how much we lose in terms of convenience and otherwise when they are not available, losses whose real significance may be out of all proportion to their money cost.

4. In a progressive economy there are thus inevitable and continuous changes in the outlook of everyone with any responsi-

[1] Cf. Allan G. B. Fisher, *The Clash of Progress and Security*, pp. 25-31 ; " Production, Primary, Secondary and Tertiary ", *Economic Record*, June 1939.

[2] This is by no means a recent phenomenon, nor even a phenomenon of the twentieth century. More than fifty years ago, in 1887, Giffen directed attention to its significance for economic development. " An increasing part of the population ", he said, " has been lately applied to the creation of incorporeal functions. . . . If a nation chooses to produce more largely in this form as it becomes more prosperous, so that there is less development than was formerly the case in what were known as staple industries, it need not be becoming poorer for that reason ; all that is happening is that its wealth and income are taking a different shape " (*Economic Inquiries and Studies*, vol. ii, pp. 139-40). And in 1890 it was pointed out that " nearly and probably fully one-half of all those who now earn their living in industrial pursuits, do so in occupations that not only had no existence, but which had not even been conceived of, a hundred years ago " (D. A. Wells, *Recent Economic Changes*, p. 336). The only modification which we should now feel disposed to make in Giffen's statement would destroy his implication that nations had much freedom of choice in the matter. If they are to become more prosperous, they must be prepared for a relatively rapid growth of " incorporeal functions " or " tertiary production ".

bility for either the investment of capital or the training and direction of labour. Forty years ago the prudent investor had no need to compare the attractiveness of share holdings in motor-car, radio or aviation companies, nor did the wise father ask whether it would be advantageous to train his son as a scientific researcher, an employment manager or a motor mechanic. All these and many other similar possibilities are now commonplaces. Their influence is visible in the census statistics of nearly every country, and certainly of every country which has been able to register economic progress. Nor is it a matter of chance that they are most clearly visible precisely in those countries where progress has been most rapid, for the two things are connected in the closest possible way. The shifts of employment towards secondary and tertiary production revealed by the census are the inescapable reflection of economic progress. If we do not have the one, we cannot have the other. Anyone who dislikes the shifts or tries to prevent them, or even fails to encourage them, is in effect announcing that he dislikes economic progress and prefers that average incomes should not rise above their present level. For if the average income level rises, some money will certainly be spent on things different from those now purchased. If these things are to be purchased, they must first be produced. They cannot be produced on any adequate scale without shifts of employment, and to prevent these shifts is therefore to prevent improvement in the average income level.

5. The economist's view of the definition here suggested of the essential character of the main economic problem certainly did not command unanimous assent. Many insisted that attention should rather be directed towards the provision of an adequate volume of purchasing power, or towards its equitable distribution. The essential problems of a dynamic or growing economy often received too little attention, and even some economists who formally addressed themselves to dynamic issues took too narrow a view of their task.[1] The importance of many

---

[1] Not even a third-rate economist could go so far as formally to deny the importance of these issues. But in the ebb and flow of fashion, from which even the most austere theorists are not entirely immune, many English economists in recent years have tended to leave them on one side and pass on to other things which happened to excite them more. There have indeed been excellent and pressing reasons for giving the closest

of the questions which aroused more public interest cannot be questioned, but there is little difficulty in showing that their solution could not be carried far without a recognition of the necessity for orderly transfers of resources of production from relatively old to relatively new uses. The practical results of many of the policies adopted by governments before the war were often disappointing precisely because this necessity was ignored or in some cases deliberately denied. The solution even of the problem of the trade cycle, which at first sight has the strongest claim to independent status and treatment, can be shown itself to require careful attention to the task of transferring factors of production to new uses, in response to changes in the technique of production or in consumers' demand.

6. A simple definition of the central economic problem in any event obviously by itself provided no solution for the specific economic problems of the inter-war period. Even if the nature of the problem had then been more widely understood, effective solutions were sometimes difficult to discover, or their application hindered by various non-economic factors. The general definition suggested was, however, useful in helping to construct an intelligible general framework within which more immediate current problems could be seen in proper perspective, and therefore with better hope of finding a solution ; it was accordingly an important part of the economist's task in inter-war days to examine the difficulties which impeded desirable transfers of productive resources, to study the consequences of failure to deal with them, and even to suggest practical means for overcoming them.

attention to the problems of the trade cycle and of recovery from depression, but it is unfortunate that in their zeal for what they believed to be new approaches to this subject some writers seem to have convinced themselves that the basic influences making structural adjustments necessary are now less powerful than they were, and that the problem of structural adjustments therefore has little immediate urgency. The future economic historian, bearing in mind the far-reaching technical changes affecting almost every sector of production in our generation, and which still show no sign of slowing down, may well be astonished that an economist of the highest standing should in 1937 have declared that " a new age of invention comparable with the nineteenth century is scarcely to be hoped for " (Joan Robinson, *Introduction to the Theory of Employment*, p. 123) ; the influence of such views as this is certainly relevant for an understanding of the lack of balance which has characterised much English thinking on economics during the last twenty years, even among those who pride themselves most on paying careful attention to practical affairs.

CHAPTER III

POST-WAR ECONOMIC PROSPECTS

1. A STUDENT who had busied himself particularly in this field before the present war is naturally reluctant to believe that the principles which he was then able to elaborate may have no relevance to the new post-war world in which in due course he will have to live. Nor is his reluctance in any way diminished when he observes that many of the essential economic problems of war-time are still those which formerly interested him. For though the purposes of a war economy are quite different, the problem of the appropriate and speedy reallocation of productive resources is still the central problem in the light of which the efficiency of policy must be judged. But while all genuine economic problems are problems of dynamics, the economist cannot safely reject without further investigation the possibility that the movements of the future may differ so fundamentally from those to which he has been accustomed in the past that the elaboration of a new set of principles may be an essential condition for his continued usefulness as an economist. Before attempting, therefore, any further detailed analysis of the principles which he had earlier worked out, he will, if he is wise, ask himself whether changes in the factual background of the post-war period may not compel him to take a new starting-point and abandon his former prejudices in favour of economic progress ; he will be the more careful in this preliminary examination if he recalls that, even before the present war, there were not lacking influential dissentient voices who questioned his fundamental presuppositions. There are at the present time at least two powerful currents of thought, one of which has an obvious intellectual ancestry in much of the ferment of discontent of the inter-war period, whose strength makes such an examination desirable. Neither has so far been expounded so systematically as to justify referring to them as " schools of thought ", but the study of dynamic economics as applied to probable post-war conditions cannot

9

profitably proceed far without defining our attitude to these two currents.

2. There have always been some to whom it has been distasteful to find the effective realisation of material progress put in the forefront of economic and social studies. To them the importance attached to this objective suggests the primacy of base materialist notions, inconsistent with the cultivation of higher values. Many of the manifestations of the urge towards material progress are not indeed very gratifying to anyone of finer sensibilities, and the reprobation meted out to those who think of little else but their own material gain is thoughtlessly transferred to those who, though steadily refusing to regard material progress as anything more than a means to other ends, nevertheless insist that the current standards of large masses of the population are discreditable to even the most advanced and wealthiest economies, that higher average standards for the community as a whole will be at least useful aids for the attainment of other values, and that the processes of material progress are therefore a subject to the study of which a civilised man may justifiably direct his attention.

3. The cultural standards and much less the moral standards of different communities are of course not always closely correlated with their standards of material wealth ; while art, literature and other cultural activities have often flourished under the patronage of wealth, the absence of independence due to such associations has also frequently led to gross abuses which a more civilised society would strive to avoid. But though material progress is no guarantee of cultural progress, the latter will seldom be carried very far unless the community which strives to attain it has adequate access to resources which only material progress is likely to make available. It would no doubt be a grave error to think of education, for example, solely or mainly as an instrument for making higher incomes possible, but that the expenditure needed to carry out far-reaching educational reforms is much more easily managed in a wealthy than in a poor community is an obvious truth not to be neglected even by those who prefer to discuss education on a more lofty plane. Nor is it entirely pointless to remark that many (though not all) of those

who profess to take such high-minded views of the grossness and vulgarity of material progress are themselves already in a position where they can easily enjoy a high level of economic prosperity. For them to suggest, now that they are free from material cares, that others who have been less fortunate need no longer worry about improving their position, is a less convincing manifestation of a generous and self-sacrificing mind than some who are contemptuous of material progress would like us to suppose. At least the abuses of which an uninstructed public taste may be guilty will be more rationally remedied by the education of consumers' demand than by keeping incomes at an unnecessarily low level.

4. More significant for our purposes is a variant form of the argument which maintains, not that economic progress is a base materialist objective the pursuit of which leads people astray from the cultivation of higher things, but rather that it is not something which the ordinary man really wants. The thing which really interests and excites him, it is argued, is security ; the primary end of wise economic policy in the future should therefore also be security. This thesis has been widely supported by statesmen and writers of many otherwise divergent schools of thought and may properly be regarded as part of, to use Lord Keynes's phrase, " the contemporary climate of economic opinion ".[1] It may be suspected that a phrase such as this is often little more than a pretentious excuse for deference to a mere dictate of fashion ; while the practical statesman would be unwise entirely to ignore current fashions of thinking, he will, however, also recall that fashion is often an unsafe guide to anyone seeking rational solutions for difficult problems. Some of the ideas propounded in our subsequent analysis, it is to be feared, will not be very congenial to those who are peculiarly susceptible to climates of opinion. But it is sometimes a prudent course to swim against the tide, for tides have a habit of turning. It is certainly much more foolish to kick against the pricks, to pretend that things are other than they really are, for the harsh logic of events will in the end upset our plans if we ignore realities and attempt to achieve objectives which are inherently contradictory.

[1] *Proposals for an International Clearing Union* (Cmd. 6437, 1943), p. 5.

At least before we too enthusiastically throw ourselves on the side of those who ask for security and nothing but security, it is important to discover precisely what they mean.

5. We shall, however, endeavour first to dispose of the second current of thought to which we have referred. This is a little more grim, for in effect it argues that it matters little what people may want after the war ; whether they like economic progress or not, they will be unable to get it. Some of the pessimists are obsessed by the destruction, both material and non-material, imposed by war ; others are overwhelmed by the obvious difficulties of reorientation on an unprecedented scale necessary when war-time demands are replaced by those of peace. In either case it is suggested that far-seeing men should begin now to attune their minds to a prolonged and perhaps permanent condition of poverty for the world as a whole. Many of those who believe security to be the primary objective nevertheless think that we shall have some freedom of choice in this matter. The school with which we are now concerned believes that there will be no range of choice of any importance at all. At best it will be only a matter of choosing between more poverty and less poverty. The influence of these views and the manner in which they affect public thinking naturally varies from country to country. They naturally command most attention where the war has been most destructive. One hears less of them in the United States than in Great Britain, though no country is entirely free from pessimism on this score. If they are correct, much of the analysis in the subsequent parts of this study would be rendered useless, and we must therefore at the outset attempt to ascertain whether there is any justification for these gloomy forebodings.

6. To embark upon such an enquiry is indeed the same thing as to ask what are the fundamental conditions of material welfare, and how far after the war these conditions are likely to be fulfilled. Before the war the conditions were obviously present which made possible, at least in the more advanced countries in every continent, a standard of living substantially higher than had prior to the nineteenth century been anywhere within the reach of any but quite numerically insignificant minorities, and which moreover had been substantially improved even after the disasters

of 1914–18. The question we now have to ask ourselves is whether the course of the war is likely so to affect these fundamental conditions that for an indefinite period it will be impractical to contemplate the resumption of pre-war trends.

7. Real incomes are invariably dependent upon the volume of current production, and the conditions which determine this volume will inevitably be affected in many important ways by the course of the war. If war seriously or permanently damages the basic elements upon which current production must depend, post-war standards of income may have to be permanently reduced. If not, we may indeed have to be content for a time with lower standards, until the difficulties of transition from a war to a peace economy have been surmounted. But after a period of recuperation we can then confidently look forward to a resumption of the trend of economic progress which we had come to regard as normal, or even to an acceleration of the trend, provided that we take full advantage of the opportunities offered for new inventions, increased rationalisation and the speeding-up of obsolescence.

8. We can get a clearer idea of the probable importance of the economic destruction wrought by the war if we examine its impact on the four principal elements determining the volume of current production, the efficiency and volume of labour, the existing standard of, and the prospects of extending scientific and technical knowledge, the accumulation of capital inherited from the past and the efficiency with which current supplies of capital of all kinds are maintained, and, finally, the maintenance of adequate machinery of organisation and co-ordination, which must include proper provision for risk-taking. We shall examine these four elements in turn.

9. Important as they are, the economic significance of losses of life during war can easily be exaggerated, for though the supply of labour is thereby reduced, the demand for its products is reduced almost *pari passu*. The really important economic problems connected with war-time losses of life, leaving aside that of the maintenance of the permanently or partially incapacitated, arise from the distortions introduced into the age distribution of the population, and the relatively heavier losses which

war often inflicts upon the potential leaders of the community. Even when these are taken into account, however, it is not improbable, even for the actively belligerent countries, and much more for the world as a whole, that the average standard of labour efficiency will at the end of the war be higher than ever before, except perhaps in quite recent years. This conclusion may require modification in varying degrees in countries where military operations and occupation have seriously affected standards of nutrition and health ; the extent to which during the war we allow the machinery for technical and other forms of education to rust is also an important factor, but the war itself has compelled the acquisition of new skills by many people, and the proportion of the labour force able to command more than one skill has probably been increased. If, therefore, after the war we show sufficient energy in raising further the standard of efficiency of our human capital, there is little occasion to fear that defects in the labour supply will keep standards of living low.

10. In the widest sense the efficiency of labour may also be taken to include the efficiency with which the tasks of organisation are performed. For, whatever the shape of the political and economic machinery adopted after the war, the responsibility for solving problems of organisation must in the last resort rest with individuals. Problems of organisation will occupy much of our attention at later stages of our analysis. Here we need only refer again to the relatively heavy toll taken by war from among those who in the ordinary course of events might have been expected a little later to play an active part in business and administrative life. The general decline in initiative and in willingness to take risks which was an unfortunate feature of the history of 1918–39 is probably to be explained at least in part by the fact that a disproportionate number of the men endowed with these qualities had been killed by the war. Reconstruction was accordingly left too much in the hands of war-exhausted old captains of industry. A similar problem will have to be faced at the end of this war, and the necessity of utilising in the best possible way all the human capacity still at our disposal is therefore especially urgent. Partly as a result of short-sighted educational policies and social prejudices, a substantial fraction of those endowed with these and

other socially valuable qualities have hitherto had insufficient opportunity of using them for the general benefit. More than ever after the war, we shall be unable to risk the waste of even a single such individual.

11. The most important cause of the impressive improvements in standards of living which with some interruptions have gone on throughout the last century and a half is, however, without any doubt the growth and application of our knowledge of our material environment which went on continuously throughout that period. In normal times we are better off than our great-grandfathers, mainly because our collective knowledge is now so much greater than theirs ever was. At the stage in the world's history which we have now reached, even the most destructive war cannot cause any serious damage to these stores of accumulated knowledge ; in some directions indeed war itself gives an active stimulus to further scientific advance, which, however lop-sided and distorted, leaves an important positive residuum for use in peace-time development.

12. The post-war prospects in relation to these two elements in productive capacity are therefore favourable ; the position in regard to capital equipment will, however, in certain important respects be entirely different. On the one hand war inflicts extensive physical destruction and damage on existing capital equipment of all kinds, while the maintenance of much equipment which does not suffer direct damage is at the same time allowed to fall into arrears. Stocks also fall far below the normal peace-time level, so that many goods which in normal times consumers are in the habit of purchasing without difficulty will still for some time after the war is over be abnormally scarce or even quite unobtainable. In an important sense the consequences of these capital losses are irrevocable. Until they are made good either directly, or as a result of making more effective use of the other elements in productive capacity, we shall be obliged to content ourselves with more modest standards of living than were customary in many countries before the war. On the other hand, however, modern war demands the construction of certain types of capital equipment on an unprecedentedly gigantic scale. It would be rash to exaggerate the ease with which this equipment

can be adapted to meet peace-time requirements, but a substantial proportion will not lose its value when war demands are contracted. Especially if we exercise a reasonable measure of foresight, we may be able to fill some of the gaps left by war-time destruction and deterioration more speedily than pessimists might fear. Provided therefore that our immediate expectations are not pitched too high, there is no reason why, from the stream of post-war current production, we should not, with the aid of the adapted equipment which the war will have bequeathed to us in embarrassing abundance, divert without great difficulty and within a comparatively short period of time a fraction sufficiently large to restore our capital equipment to a level adequate for re-establishing something at least no worse than our old standards of living, and later for substantially improving them.

13. The proviso that our immediate expectations must not be pitched too high is of great importance, and must not be brushed aside as a merely formal reservation. The rate at which after 1918 the level of real incomes rose in many countries, despite the destruction of the war of 1914–18, was a surprising achievement. Recovery might, however, have been based on surer foundations had it not been for exaggerated hopes that the termination of the war would at once make possible the enjoyment of standards of living higher than those usual before 1914. After the present war we shall be in a position comparable with that of an able-bodied and well-educated man, in effective contact with the growing accumulation of scientific and technical knowledge, who finds that, as the result of a series of unfortunate and devastating accidents, a large proportion of his investments has gone wrong. If he attempts to maintain the manner of life to which he had become accustomed before these accidents occurred, he will soon be irretrievably ruined ; if on the contrary he adapts himself to the new conditions, and temporarily adopts a more modest mode of life which enables him to build up his capital equipment again, the inconvenient interruption to his prosperity to which he has had to submit need be no more than temporary. In forecasting post-war economic conditions a prudent observer may indeed be somewhat embarrassed in picking his way between the errors of excessive optimism and excessive pessimism which

dog his footsteps everywhere, and the tone of his exposition may properly be affected by his knowledge of the preconceived prejudices of his audience. It is sometimes his duty to arouse from their lethargy those who believe that we are faced with universal and irreparable ruin, from which the only consolation to be drawn is that our characters may be purified by suffering ; in so doing he must, however, avoid the opposite error of unduly encouraging those who believe that, if only the world could be persuaded to adopt their ingenious devices, in the field of finance or elsewhere, for scattering prosperity everywhere, we could at once, as soon as the war is over, and without the necessity for much hard work and careful reallocation of the resources of production, inaugurate a Brave New World. It is often not easy to be sure which is practically the more important task, to counter currents of thought, which from the standpoint of economic recovery are fundamentally defeatist, or to damp down the injudicious enthusiasm of those who believe that the economic problem has been solved, and that after the war we need concern ourselves only with the distribution of the bountiful fruits which the solution of the economic problem has placed within our grasp.

14. In some directions indeed war destruction of capital equipment makes possible certain incidental positive and not altogether remote advantages. Some at least of the demolition now being achieved by enemy action is in fact a saving of subsequent trouble for us. The problem of obsolescence is a constant source of anxiety in a normally developing economy, and it has been argued with some plausibility that the risk of loss through obsolescence may sometimes increase the reluctance of business men to invest in new plant liable to have its earnings reduced at short notice by subsequent inventions. The solution offered by war, though ruthless, is often highly effective. The business man whose plant has been completely destroyed by war has thereby had one of the alternatives between which he would otherwise have had to choose entirely removed. It was for this reason that war-devastated areas in some instances were found some years after 1918 to be more efficient productive agencies than competitive areas which had escaped more lightly. Provided that devastation had not gone so far as to render the task of

reconstruction quite hopeless, the equipment of the industries concerned with the most up-to-date machinery was the only course to receive any serious consideration.

15. The fourth element, efficiency of organisation, is also of the most far-reaching importance. The primary task immediately after the war will be to repair the dislocations imposed by the war itself. The war will have distorted the allocation of productive resources so that the speedy attainment of the optimum allocation necessary if potential high standards of living are to become realities may be very difficult. Highly complicated transitional problems must be faced, and failure to solve them may render vain the somewhat optimistic hopes which, as has here been argued, are in themselves well founded.

16. When people observe the rapidly mounting war debts, they are sometimes afraid that the intolerable burdens imposed by the necessity of " paying for the war " after it is over will make the task of reorganisation quite hopeless. We are perhaps in some danger of underestimating the difficulties involved in preventing the nominal purchasing power now accumulating for the use of short-term lenders after the war from driving us into a dangerous inflationary situation. So long, however, as we are thinking strictly in terms of available resources of production, there is little justification for these fears. If we neglect the question of foreign indebtedness, the worst embarrassments arising from which it is intended to avoid by the ingenious invention of lend-leasing, payment for the war in the true sense is made by each belligerent country as the war proceeds ; it is merely a matter of convenience (or, of inconvenience, as those who criticise current methods of war financing would prefer to call it) that to ensure prompt control of certain means of production during the war the government promises to continue certain payments to certain people after the war is over. The existence of these promises may diminish or increase the willingness of people to make their appropriate contributions to the national income after the war ; essentially, however, the transfer of income from taxpayers to bondholders does not itself diminish the efficiency of the basic elements upon which national income and real standards of living depend.

17. The basic conditions essential for solving problems of organisation will thus again be present after the war ; the widespread economic destruction of war-time does not condemn the world to perpetual poverty. To argue that solutions are possible is, of course, quite a different thing from arguing that solutions are certain. In many fields, political, social and economic, there are numerous baneful possibilities of obstruction and misunderstanding, but just because such possibilities are so numerous and some of them likely to be so important, it is an urgent matter to attempt to get more fundamental issues clear in our minds.

18. Even, however, if we are unconvinced by this analysis and persist in taking a much more gloomy view of the possibilities of post-war recovery, we are not by that fact absolved from the duty of studying the processes of adaptation in a dynamic economy. It is a commonplace that among the most knotty immediate post-war problems will be the orderly transfer of labour now employed in the armed forces or in industries expanded for war-time purposes far beyond the requirements of any conceivable peace-time situation.[1] Nor will transfers be needed merely as part of the first immediate transition from war to peace conditions, when demand for shells and guns and torpedoes and bombs is replaced by demand for all the things which during the war we have been obliged to forgo. At many subsequent stages still more transfers will be necessary, and some on quite a substantial scale. It is scarcely possible to contemplate such a slowing-down of rehousing programmes in air-raid devastated areas as would ensure anything approximating to perfect regularity of employment in the building industry ; we may properly take some steps to check any too exuberant over-expansion of the shipbuilding industry after the war, but it is inconceivable that the demand for ships should so far be smoothed out as to avoid

---

[1] In the United States it has, for example, been estimated that " the enormous volume of new plane capacity, combined with the switch-over from automobile manufacturing, has led the present aircraft industry to expect an employment of 1,700,000 workers in 1943, more than 70 times the 1937 employment. In contrast, the American Aeronautical Chamber of Commerce has estimated that less than 200,000 men can be employed in the post-war industry, even if we were to maintain an air force of 24,000 planes to police the world, produce flivver planes for those who will have learned to fly during the war, and transport all Pullman and cabin-class ocean passengers by plane " (Mark S. Massel, *Business Reserves for Post-war Survival*, p. 2).

the necessity for a considerable contraction of employment there within a few years. Similar fluctuations in the volume of employment are equally inevitable in other industries. Whether our expectations about post-war standards of living are gloomy or cheerful, these adjustments will have in any case to be made. Moreover, the war itself has vastly accelerated the application of certain technical processes which scientists had previously been slowly perfecting ; to these it has added new techniques formerly almost unknown, and all on a scale which in some directions may completely alter our conventional views of the boundaries separating industries and produce entirely new competitive relations between them. These new techniques will not be abandoned after the war, and their wider application will necessitate further large-scale shifts in the allocation of factors of production. Whether therefore we are optimistic or pessimistic about the future trend of standards of living, the problems of a dynamic economy will insistently demand attention after the war ; from whatever low level we may in our darker moments think it prudent that we should prepare our minds to start, the impact of technical change will in any event demand the most careful attention. If, whatever we do, we cannot avoid this difficult problem of the transfer of productive resources, it seems more sensible deliberately to regard it as at the same time offering an opportunity for the attainment of rising average income levels. By thus widening our view of the problem we can scarcely make it more difficult ; we may even make it more tractable by seizing the opportunity to clear out and widen the channels of employment and investment in industries capable of producing the goods and services which people with rising incomes will want to buy.

19. Actually the very complexities of the present war, as contrasted with any of its predecessors, carry with them, paradoxically enough, some hope that we may be able to tackle this thorny problem rather more effectively than we did after 1918. The magnitude of the shocks sustained by the industrial structures of all countries, belligerent or neutral, has made the impossibility of restoring the pre-war allocation of factors of production so obvious that the most casual observer cannot fail to note it. Those who have a vested interest in returning to their old occupa-

tions will be relatively less numerous than after the last war, and though in the process of economic development we are never presented with a complete *tabula rasa*, the widespread weakening or in some cases complete destruction of traditional ideas and traditional customs and institutions, which is inherent in total war, will enable us after the war to draw our picture of a new industrial structure on something much more closely resembling a clean sheet than we have ever had before. We cannot be certain that we shall make the best use of our opportunities, but the opportunities will certainly be there.

20. If this analysis is correct, we may therefore proceed to examine the problems of dynamic economics without any uncomfortable doubts that in preparation for the post-war world such a study would be a waste of time because it was unrelated to the hard facts of the real world in which we shall then be living. The difficulties of realising the high living standards which will then potentially be at our disposal may be very great ; they were great enough, in all truth, before the outbreak of war, and the dislocations of the war, while breaking down some of the rigidities which previously checked essential adjustments, will also have created some new vested interests and stimulated many new desires which it will be impossible immediately to satisfy. International feeling may be embittered to such an extent that many of the co-operative policies necessary if the high standards of living which will be theoretically possible are to be attained will not be adopted unless national leaders display unprecedented capacity for statesmanship. On balance, therefore, the practical difficulties are unlikely to be less than they were. But a solution of the problem with which we are concerning ourselves will not be intrinsically impossible.

CHAPTER IV

SECURITY

So far as security permits an expansion of power it is " good " ; so far,
however, as it induces stagnation it must be damned. Man must avoid not
only the evils of the jungle, but also those of Lotus Land.

F. D. GRAHAM, *Social Goals and Economic Institutions*, p. 23

1. WE turn back, therefore, to the alternative view which holds,
not that material progress will be beyond our reach after the war,
but that public sentiment is now so strongly in favour of economic
security, that it would be idle to think of post-war economic
problems primarily in terms of the adaptations necessary for
material progress. While people will welcome material progress
if it happens to come their way, they have been, it is argued, so
profoundly impressed by the risks of inconvenience and suffering
in the form of unemployment which conscious effort to ensure
progress is believed to threaten, that they will insist, and are indeed
already insisting, that governments and statesmen should, after
the war, concentrate their efforts instead upon the attainment of
security, or, to use the phrase which has become popular in recent
years, though its meaning is seldom sufficiently clearly defined,[1]
the assurance of " full employment ". Some go so far as to hold
that if any conflict arises between the two ends, security and
material progress, the latter must be sacrificed to the former, or
at least postponed until a reasonable degree of security has first
been assured.

2. This view, we shall endeavour to show, is erroneous and
misleading. The widespread failure, of which these views are a
reflection, to understand the inevitable interrelation in the modern
world between security and material progress constitutes the
gravest threat at the present time to the realisation of either of
them. If we go about it in the right way, we may be able to enjoy

[1] It is surprising to find, for example, that in a popular pamphlet, *After Defence —
What ?*, published by the National Resources Planning Board in 1941, the conditions
of full employment are discussed without any trouble being taken to explain that its
meaning is not what at first sight the words would suggest, *i.e.* that everybody should
always have work.

a substantial measure of both ; the dual defect of some of the approaches to security which are now widely popular is that they not only involve the sacrifice of progress, but are also likely in no very long run to mean the loss of their own immediate objective, security itself.

3. Many of the points raised in this discussion are by no means novel.[1] Long before the war, " stability ", a concept closely related to security, was quite a familiar idea ; it was quite common to insist upon " the importance of maintaining a reasonable measure of economic stability relatively to that of securing the largest development of international trade ",[2] or of some other objective whose claims had to be weighed against those of stability. The urgency of the claim for security is now, however, it is widely believed, much greater than before, and the compilation of an impressive and lengthy list of official and non-official declarations placing the attainment of security in the forefront of the programme to which we are invited to address our minds in preparing for the post-war world would be an easy task. A few typical illustrations will be sufficient for our purpose. Most weighty and authoritative is Article V of the Atlantic Charter, to which the representatives of the United Nations have subsequently given their approval, and wherein " social security " is set forth as one of the objectives justifying the signatories' " desire to bring about fullest collaboration between all nations in the economic field ". Mr. Ernest Bevin, the British Minister of Labour, went further than this in suggesting that " at the end of this war and indeed during the war we accept social security as the main motive of our national life ",[3] while Mr. Eden has also declared [4] that " social security must be the first object of our domestic policy after the war ". Or, as the Netherlands Minister of Social Affairs put it,[5] " after the final triumph we will

---

[1] In their eagerness to press their remedies upon our attention, propagandists often imply that problems which are quite old are entirely unprecedented. " Instead of controversies about political freedom, the fight for economic security became the focus of public discord " might at first sight pass as a comment on the history of the 1930s. It refers in fact to the Political and Social Consequences of the " Great Depression of 1873–1896 in Central Europe " (Hans Rosenberg, *Economic History Review*, 1943, p. 64).

[2] H. D. Henderson in *The Improvement of Commercial Relations between Nations and the Problem of Monetary Stabilisation* (International Chamber of Commerce, 1936), p. 161.

[3] *Manchester Guardian*, November 21, 1940.

[4] In London on May 29, 1941.   [5] In New York on October 27, 1941.

face the gigantic task of building a new and better world in which
the problem of security for the masses will be pre-eminent ".
Mr. Beneš too lays " greater stress on the ' social security ' of
every member of the nation " than on international trade and the
access of all nations to raw material resources.[1] Somewhat more
elaborate and at the same time more cautious is the view of Mr.
Edward Phelan, Acting Director of the International Labour
Office, who suggested " that future policy is to be directed to
ensuring for the individual not only an improvement in conditions
of labour but economic security without which, it is now recognised, there can be no fully effective implementation of social
justice ".[2]

4. The primacy now accorded to security, the argument often
proceeds, is justified by the belief that " our most urgent economic
problem is no longer to expand production ",[3] and therefore
demands an entirely new approach to economic problems. This
claim, if justified, is clearly of the utmost importance, but before
we can assess its merits, some preliminary questions must first be
cleared up. Before we agree that stability, or security, should be
accepted as our primary objective, we should take care that we
understand the meaning of this concept. Misunderstanding on
this point may easily cause misconceptions about the nature of
the steps most likely to ensure security.

5. It would no doubt be unreasonable to deny anyone the
right to place security in the forefront of his post-war economic
programme until he had first equipped himself with a complete
and water-tight definition of the term. For it might well be urged
that while security, like many other ideas of great importance,
was difficult to define precisely, it was not in practice at all difficult
to recognise its absence, and that for practical purposes, therefore,
its meaning was sufficiently clear. There is some measure of truth
in this, but it is equally true that it means different things to
different people, and that a too ready assumption that everyone
knows what security means, and uses the term in the same sense,
and that there is therefore no need for its careful definition, has led

---

[1] *Journal of Central and Eastern European Affairs*, April 1941.
[2] *Towards Our True Inheritance* (Montreal, 1942), p. 6.
[3] E. H. Carr, *Conditions of Peace,* p. 80.

to much confused thinking, which, if not cleared up, will lead to equally confused action, and probably to unnecessary insecurity.

6. No one would seriously expect even the most perfect economic and social system to provide for everyone at all times that "freedom from care, apprehension, anxiety or alarm", which is the literal meaning of security, such freedom, in any absolute sense, lying outside the reasonable range of expectation for ordinary mortals. Usually we contrast the insecurity which made such a profound impression upon the public mind during the inter-war period with something much less far-reaching than this. At that time the wage-earners of all countries suffered in varying degrees from widespread and persistent unemployment, and the position of the small farmer, the shopkeeper, the so-called independent artisan or business man was often not much better. A man who enjoys security has an assured position in the economic structure, which was beyond the reach of these victims of depression.

7. Any such assured position has, however, two aspects, related but distinct. The secure man has a job, the character of which may, however, change from time to time. More important, he also has an income, not absolutely fixed, but without variations of such magnitude as to compel drastic adjustments in his customary mode of life. As the most obvious method of securing such an income is to hang on to the job which one already happens to have, it has been widely assumed that a security policy must enable anyone who is embarrassed by the temporary loss of his place in the economic structure to get back to precisely the same place as he had occupied before and to no other, though security in a real sense will also be his if he gets back into a different place where he can earn an income not too different from his former one. These two alternatives, getting back to one's old place or taking up a different type of work, correspond to two fundamentally divergent interpretations of security, and two equally divergent policy approaches to the problem of insecurity.

8. We ought indeed to distinguish with the utmost sharpness between stability for an economy as a whole, with individuals from time to time changing their places in it, and the situation which would develop if we extended indefinitely the process of

securing to each individual the job which he already happened to have. The former is compatible with both progress and security ; the latter, if universally applied, would make progress of any kind quite impossible, and security in the end highly improbable. Stability in the true sense is something quite different from this stagnation or freezing of economic conditions. For it implies rather that the economy as a whole is capable of adjusting itself promptly, without violent upheavals or slumps, to the shocks of technical change and the variations in consumers' demands which are an inevitable feature of a changing world. It is not surprising that many individuals, stunned by the shock of these unexpected changes, should suppose the attainment of security to mean their restoration to the jobs from which they have been ejected. It is no more surprising that groups, each member of which finds himself affected in much the same way, should use their political influence to induce the State to ensure that not merely some kind of employment but their old employment will be restored to them,[1] thereby threatening to freeze existing economic conditions. But even if such purposes could be realised, security, which in a truer and more profound sense can only be attained by other means, would not be assured. These other means not only have the incidental advantage of not sacrificing material progress, as the former method threatens to do ; the security which they would achieve is also likely to have a permanence which tends to be absent from the other type. An attempt to stabilise an organism piecemeal by stabilising successive parts of it would not ensure a healthy organism capable of steady and vigorous growth, but would tend rather to immobilise it and prevent its fruitful develop-ment. If, as in a modern economy, with the immense powers con-ferred by the expansion of knowledge, the forces of growth were strong, any policy which implied a high degree of immobilisa-

---

[1] The remarks of Mr. Frank Longworth, President of the Manchester Chamber of Commerce, at the 122nd Annual Meeting of that body on February 8, 1943, illustrate how the uncritical use of the concept of full employment encourages confused thinking on this issue. " Some people ", he said, " advance the view that we should give more attention to the production of those types of textiles which would not be in competition with the products of countries with lower standards of living. I see the importance of this point, but I think we should only delude ourselves if we thought that such a policy would result in anything approaching full employment for our vast productive machinery and large labour force ", an observation which clearly implies that for a textile operative full employment can only mean employment in the textile industry.

tion would soon lead to breakdown and disruption more violent
and more disturbing to its members than that from which they
were seeking to escape.

9. To many, however, the associations which first come to
mind when social security is mentioned would at least superficially be of quite a different kind from the ideas which we have
so far been discussing. For it would be assumed to mean those
measures of insurance, health, unemployment and old age, which
are now part of the social organisation of most modern states,
designed to protect individuals who have lost their assured
positions. There is still some disagreement about the most convenient terminology for describing the various activities which
fall under the category of social services or social insurance.[1]
The details of this discussion are not relevant to our present
purposes, and here it is sufficient to point out that if social security
is interpreted to mean nothing more than more elaborate and
efficient and far-reaching systems of social insurance, the idea
does not introduce into our economic thinking any fundamentally new or revolutionary principle. There have been, and
there are always likely to be, disputes about the organisation of
social insurance ; its details should not be worked out without
reference to probable repercussions on other parts of the economic
structure, and as in the past many people have taken an unduly
short-sighted or unimaginative view of its proper scope, policies
based upon such short-sighted views ought from time to time
to be reformed and liberalised. But however reformed and
liberalised social insurance policy might be, it would not necessitate any fundamentally new approach to economic problems such
as is often asked for by those who are most insistent upon the
claims of security. As has indeed very properly been pointed
out by many leading statesmen in recent discussions on this
subject, the greater our success in assuring social security in a
wider sense, the less need will there be for resort to stopgap and
supplementary measures of social insurance. As Mr. Herbert
Morrison has said, such social security schemes are " at best
nothing more than ambulance and salvage work ".[2] They are

---

[1] Cf. Harry M. Cassidy, *Social Security and Reconstruction in Canada*, pp. 13-16.
[2] *Looking Ahead*, p. 196

no doubt important and necessary, but the frequency with which we are obliged to call out the ambulance is itself a measure of the inefficiency of our social organisation.[1]

10. If the State's obligation to provide social security were to be interpreted so widely as to involve the assumption of a duty " to guarantee to every individual a sufficient quantity of food, clothing, shelter and the acknowledged necessities of life ",[2] — a policy which has recently been strongly supported, — more far-reaching changes in social and economic policy would be necessary. But even this probably does not correspond very accurately to popular anticipations of what a secure economic life would mean, and the level of real income thus assured would probably be disappointingly modest.[3]

11. However interested he may be in social insurance, the ordinary man undoubtedly thinks of security much more in terms of getting a job.[4] And he also has a lively interest both in the kind of work he will be expected to do and the rate at which it will be paid. He may not always think the matter out very clearly, but he certainly does not picture himself as deliberately sacrificing his standard of living for the sake of security. It is quite easy to provide work for everyone, if no one minds how low his pay is. But quite rightly most people do mind a great deal, as wage-earners showed when during the depression they insisted upon the maintenance of customary rates of pay. Any dispute about their wisdom in so insisting is not now very profitable, but the virtual disappearance of unemployment during the war is no proof that those who criticised them were wrong. The fillip to investment arising from preparations for war made

---

[1] For a more detailed discussion of the bearing of social insurance on the problem of a dynamic economy see Chapter X (c).

[2] *Economist*, July 6 and September 7, 1940.

[3] Cf. F. Zweig, *The Planning of Free Societies*, p. 71 : " This National Dividend, if practicable, could only be fixed at a very low level, practically the level of a dole — just enough for mere existence. This is not what is meant when social security is put forward as the goal of planning."

[4] As Sir William Beveridge has put it, " income security, which is all that can be given by social insurance, is so inadequate a provision for human happiness that to put it forward by itself as a sole or principal measure of reconstruction hardly seems worth doing. It should be accompanied by an announced determination to use the powers of the State to whatever extent may prove necessary to ensure for all, not indeed absolute continuity of work, but a reasonable chance of productive employment " (*Report on Social Insurance and Allied Services* [Cmd. 6404, 1942], § 440).

possible in many countries for some time after September 1939 a considerable expansion of employment without any serious inroads upon standards of living, especially so long as the accumulated stocks of goods which were not being renewed could be drawn upon. In wealthy countries such as the United States and Canada,[1] this process could be carried a long way, but even there, where the high level of productive capacity has made it possible to continue in war-time the enjoyment of considerable quantities of butter without in the slightest degree impairing capacity to turn out guns on a quite unprecedented scale, — and at the same time to send abroad large quantities of essential consumers' goods for the benefit of allies less favourably situated, — and much more in countries with less productive capacity, the maintenance of " full employment " by war-time methods would have been impossible without a considerable degree of willingness to accept declines in real income of exactly the kind which the critics have been reproached for approving as a useful temporary stimulus to recovery from depression. Some of the resistance to the control of inflationary tendencies in the United States has indeed arisen precisely because this association has not been universally understood there. Elsewhere there has been some tendency to minimise the decline in living standards which the industrial hyperactivity of war brings with it. It is a matter of some delicacy, testing to the utmost the ingenuity of statisticians, to balance the relative importance of the war-time gains and losses accruing to different sections of the community, but it remains true that war-time experience throws light upon peace-time policy in this connection, only if we can assume that after the war the ordinary man will not regard the maintenance of customary incomes as a major objective of economic policy.[2]

12. It would clearly be very rash to make any such assumption. The ordinary man, it is frequently alleged, would in the interests of security be prepared to sacrifice everything else. It would be of interest to make this the subject of a Gallup Poll enquiry,

[1] According to one Canadian writer, " on a straight, arithmetical calculation it would appear that, as a nation, we purchased and consumed, at the close of 1943, some 20 per cent. more of the good things of life than we did at the close of 1939 " (Gilbert Jackson, *Facts in the Case*, p. 43).

[2] For a more detailed discussion of the economic lessons of the war see Chapter IX.

though the framing of questions to elicit the full truth would be a delicate matter, and some of the discoveries of any ingenious statistician who applied his talents to interpreting the results might be surprising. For people do not invariably get most excited about the things which they value most. Excitement is at least as likely to be aroused by things which they seem to be in greatest danger of losing. A valued possession may in the course of time come so much to be taken as a matter of course that it ceases to arouse violent emotions. The maintenance of customary standards of living of those in work is no doubt in modern industrial communities not yet quite so assured as this, and we have created elaborate institutions for their protection. But their maintenance is felt to be a natural and, on the whole, provided that employment is assured, a probable thing. The risks of a decline in standards of living so long as one is employed seem much less threatening than the risks of unemployment, and the latter problem therefore arouses the more lively interest. But even those who are most afraid of the consequences of unemployment, for themselves and for their dependants, would not necessarily, if they fully understood the implications of their choice, gladly accept anything which promised to remove their fears, if in so doing their standard of living had also to be sacrificed. We may easily get a wrong idea of the attitude of the ordinary man to standards of living for the same reason as we may misinterpret his attitude to political and social liberty. In some quarters to-day it has become customary to scoff at these ideals as obsolete relics of the despised nineteenth century. Men, it is said, no longer care for these things. The truth, however, is that we seldom get very excited about things which we take for granted, and where there is a long-established tradition of liberty, and it seems inconceivable therefore that liberty should ever be sacrificed, men do not get excited about it. That issue they believe to be settled, and it is natural to be more excited about issues believed still to be open. The danger in both cases is that, without realising what has happened, we may later find to our dismay that we have lost something, standards of living or political or social liberty, which was still cherished, but, because it was believed to be assured, no longer aroused violent emotion.

13. However this may be, many who now urge us to embark upon a " social security " programme are certainly not indifferent to the levels of remuneration to be associated with the work to be performed, and some even insist that they should be above the old customary levels. " Economic security for the individual ", according to Mr. Phelan,[1] ". . . implies more than ' the prevention of unemployment ' by such economic measures and policies as may produce that result and thereby eliminate economic insecurity from the life of the average worker. It aims in addition at enabling him to secure, for himself and his family, all that is necessary to enable him in youth, through his working years, and in old age, to enjoy a place of dignity in the life of the community and to make to it whatever contribution his gifts and capacities may render possible." The attainment of economic security in this wider sense is clearly a formidable task ; however inspiring it may be as an ultimate objective — Mr. Phelan agrees that to some it may seem utopian — we need not reproach ourselves unduly if after the war we can realise it only slowly and by gradual stages.

14. In Mr. Phelan's mind the attainment of economic security therefore by no means implies the abandonment of hope for further and very considerable material progress, and many leaders of the United Nations have spoken in similar terms. The authors of the Atlantic Charter itself did not, in Article V, limit their approval to social security in any narrow sense. Their declared object was to secure for all " improved labour standards, economic development and social security ". As Mr. Cordell Hull put it on July 23, 1942, " with peace among the nations reasonably assured, with political stability established, and with economic shackles removed, a vast fund of resources will be released for each nation to meet the needs of progress, to make possible for all its citizens advancement towards higher living standards ". " Continuous self-development of nations and individuals ", he added, provided " the sound and logical road to the higher standards of life which we all crave and seek ". " We are determined ", said Mr. Atlee on October 30, 1941, " that . . . questions of the universal improvement of standards

[1] *Op. cit.* p. 7.

of living and nutrition shall not be neglected as they were after the last war." " Governments everywhere ", said Dr. Pasvolsky, Special Assistant to the Secretary of State, in March 1942, " will have to make good their present promises to create conditions of economic security and higher levels of individual well-being." " Each country ", declared the first Inter-American Conference on Social Security at Santiago de Chile in September 1942, " must create, conserve and build up the intellectual, moral and physical vigour of its active generation, prepare the way for its future generations, and support the generation that has been discharged from productive life. This is social security : a genuine and rational economy of human resources and values." [1]

15. But if this *is* social security, it clearly goes very much further than some current discussions would lead us to expect, and it might be thought that the interests of clear thinking would be better served if it were to be described by some other name. For the programme outlined by Mr. Phelan, and in varying forms of words endorsed by many of the leaders of the United Nations, is in fact a programme for far-reaching and extensive improvements in standards of living. Its attainment necessitates careful attention to precisely those principles which many of those who have greeted social security as a new and inspiring slogan declare to be old-fashioned and irrelevant. Its study is identical with that study of material progress which an economist could reasonably regard before the war as among the most important of his tasks, for the improvements desired will be impossible without substantial increases in production. If this is the meaning of economic security, the suggestion that more emphasis should be placed upon the concept than used to be customary does not require the economist to adjust his mind to the consideration of a new set of problems, and he may confidently expect to find his pre-war work still of some value.

16. The dilemma between security and progress is thus rejected as unreal by the authorities we have quoted, for in their view the two ends are not regarded as incompatible. Whether we ought in some indefinitely remote future rest content with stable standards of living, the provision of " all that is necessary "

---

[1] *International Labour Review*, November 1942.

for the purposes outlined clearly necessitates a great improvement upon the standards customary in the recent past. On even the most cheerful interpretation of recent economic progress no one could seriously maintain that all that was necessary to ensure a place of dignity in the life of the community had been generally available to people in employment in even the most prosperous countries ; the realisation of this end is impossible unless we resume the progressive movement which has been interrupted by the war, and all hope of which, according to some current thought, must now be abandoned.

17. As we shall see, there is no essential reason why Mr. Phelan's ideal should not be progressively realised. In a sense the whole of our subsequent argument might be regarded as an analysis of the implications of his definition. Our analysis will, however, also suggest that the effort to achieve all that he aims at necessitates the abandonment of certain popular approaches to the narrower security problem. For as we recognise the necessity of combining with assured employment a satisfactory level of remuneration, we are obliged to return to the question what kind of work is to be given the man who seeks security, and this question inevitably drives us back to the fundamental issues of the dynamics of a progressive economy. This question is particularly troublesome for anyone seeking a precise definition of " full employment ".[1] A literal interpretation would suggest employment of any kind whatever sufficient to occupy fully the normal working time of every individual capable of working. If no other qualifications were admitted, it would not matter what

---

[1] Some recent typical definitions may be quoted. According to an American writer, full employment means " a state of affairs in which all men and women willing and able to work will always have the opportunity to do so, at prevailing rates of pay and under prevailing hourly specifications and working conditions generally " (John H. G. Pierson, " An Economic Policy to Insure Permanent Full Employment ", *Antioch Review*, 1942). In the view of a more cautious British group " by ' full employment ' is meant a state of affairs in which the number of unfilled vacancies is not appreciably below the number of unemployed persons, so that unemployment at any time is due to the normal lag between a person losing one job and finding another. ' Full employment ' in this sense cannot be completely attained as long as there exist structural maladjustments needing to be put right. Indeed, it can probably never be reached completely in normal times, but . . . it is the correct object to aim at, and a reasonably near approach to it can be actually achieved " (Nuffield College, *Employment Policy and Organization of Industry after the War*, 1943, p. 10 n.). Cf. " By social security is meant full employment at fair wages, *i.e.* wages sufficient to support family life at a traditional standard " (F. Zweig, *The Planning of Free Societies*, p. 71).

a man was working at so long as he was employed, and some of the proposals for ensuring full employment seem sometimes to imply that this is not a matter of any great moment. But in the view of the ordinary man in the street who is believed to attach so much importance to security and " full employment ", it is certainly not a matter of indifference. He is, quite rightly, much concerned about the kind of work he is expected to accept. Work is important not only as a means for ensuring an income ; it also affects the individual's sense of self-respect, and not every kind of work will satisfy this test. Work must be recognised as being useful ; otherwise there are the same objections to being obliged to perform it as to the treadmill. Digging holes and filling them up again will not do.

18. Many people, moreover, also have a deeply rooted and quite natural prejudice in favour either of work to which they are already accustomed, or at least of some kind of work which is not too widely different. Many of the disappointments which attended efforts at " work creation " during the depression were the result of this prejudice. The ordinary man tends to assume that social security means not only a job for him with wages which safeguard his customary standard of living but also a job of the same kind as he has been accustomed to. The two assumptions are closely related, for we shall fear a change of work still more if it also threatens to diminish our income.

19. The attempt to assure to everyone undisturbed and continuous employment in his customary occupation and at the customary rates of pay would, however, be no guarantee of security. For every change in conditions of production would necessitate some change in the allocation of employment, and probably in rates of pay as well.   On the other hand, we could go a long way towards assuring general income stability, but only on condition that we maintained production by appropriate changes in the structure of employment. Some changes of this kind might well be found an essential preliminary condition without which even a provisional equilibrium would be impossible. For no existing structure of employment is likely ever to be exactly right. Even if our interest is confined merely to giving employment, we should first examine the existing structure, with

a view to discovering how far it diverges from the shape necessary to assure the highest standard of living compatible with existing technical conditions. The removal of such divergencies is the key to any permanent solution of the unemployment problem. To establish " the right to work " and to correct distortions in the structure of production are therefore not independent tasks either of which can properly be given priority over the other. The two are organically related. We cannot get very far in regard to either of them unless we act simultaneously in regard to the other.

20. Some sceptics who recall the profound disturbances which have often attended the course of technical development may still have ·some doubts about the compatibility of progress and security. That material progress and widespread unemployment have sometimes been found side by side is an indubitable fact ; even if we reject the hasty hypothesis that unemployment is normally due to technical changes which displace labour, the number of instances is impressive where such changes and unemployment have apparently been associated as cause and effect. What, however, still remains doubtful is how far the association is inevitable. If we decide to plump for security, must we, the question may still be asked, by that very decision at the same time abandon any hope of material progress ? Or, to put the question in another way, if our votes are cast for progress, are we thereby implicitly committing ourselves to a course which destroys any reasonable prospect of security ? " How to get economic security without stagnation and decline ", it has been said, is " one of the unsolved problems ".[1] Is it also one of the insoluble problems ?

21. We may anticipate the general course of our subsequent analysis by suggesting that we shall probably find here, as so often happens also in other fields of controversy, that an ill-judged decision to discuss the problem in terms of priorities inevitably condemns us to futile and pointless bickering. If we take it for granted without serious examination that we might conceivably attain either one of the two ends which we happen to prefer without at the same time taking the steps necessary for the attain-

---

[1] *Manchester Guardian*, October 20, 1942.

ment of the other, we thereby preclude ourselves from any fruitful and hopeful approach to the solution of our problem. If we want security, our efforts for that purpose must in the modern world be frustrated unless at the same time we strive hard for progress. And similarly, though for different reasons, our efforts to achieve progress may be frustrated unless at the same time we provide at least a greater measure of security than was commonly enjoyed during the inter-war period, the failure to satisfy the desire for security now widely felt encouraging a stubborn resistance to the changes without which progress will be impossible.

22. A consideration of these questions thus brings us back to the two conflicting interpretations of security or stability which have already been mentioned. On one interpretation the individual is secure if he is left undisturbed in or restored to the possession of his present job ; on the other, stability is a characteristic of a constantly developing and growing economy in which changes in individual employment are regarded as normal, though associated as far as possible with arrangements to ensure that customary incomes will not be unnecessarily disturbed. A general sense of income security is quite compatible with modest and indeed sometimes with substantial fluctuations in income. Business men are quite accustomed to this, and do not necessarily regard such fluctuations as synonymous with insecurity. The second of our two interpretations is the correct one, and policy should be based upon it rather than upon the interpretation too hastily read into the fact that the most obviously effective way of maintaining one's income intact is to keep one's customary job.

23. If it is believed that undisturbed possession of his present job constitutes security for a single individual, to many the conclusion seems to follow that security for a social group or for society as a whole involves the assurance of the same thing to each individual member of it. This is, however, impossible for society as a whole unless we contemplate a more or less indefinite freezing or ossification of the *status quo*, or at least of the situation established when first a reasonably close approximation to general security is assured. It might be objected that this makes no allowance for the normal course of promotion, and that a rigorous interpretation of the idea as outlined would make the absurd

assumption that not only could our economic structure be permanently ossified at some point of time, but also that none of its individual members would ever grow older. This objection might with some plausibility be set aside as a niggling debating point ; for, especially when the rate of population increase is so slow as to approximate closely to stability, a society is quite conceivable in which there would at successive points of time be practically identical distributions of employment and income, although the individuals falling within each employment or income class might be constantly changing as they grew older, passed on to positions requiring more skill and experience, and subsequently died, leaving their places to be filled by the newcomers who were constantly being drafted from school to take their places in the economy.

24. Such a state of affairs would doubtless have merits of its own ; it is attractive to many people, who would be quite satisfied if their position in real life corresponded to the place which they regarded as suitable in the hypothetical economy which we have sketched. Whether after careful examination we should regard its merits and attractions as so overwhelming in comparison with those of other conceivable (and real) societies that we should unanimously prefer the static ideal is much more doubtful ; it is still more open to doubt whether in the real world in which we live, with a lively interest in scientific research which shows no signs of declining, and which few people would seriously wish to curb, even a remote approximation to such a static ideal is at all possible. But whatever answers we might give to these interesting questions would not affect the fact that the state of affairs which has been described does not accurately correspond to what most people have in mind when they talk about security. Unfortunately just because these issues are seldom squarely faced, and the exact meaning of the term security is accordingly left somewhat misty in our minds, we are often in danger of adopting policies designed to ensure security which, when they have produced their full consequences, will turn out to be something quite different from what we had expected.

25. The popular but erroneous interpretation of security which we have been criticising has had important consequences

in colouring the terms in which many people seem naturally to start their thinking about unemployment. Taking it for granted without much careful consideration that the existing structure of production is, broadly speaking, satisfactory, they think first of getting people back to their old jobs. In itself this is quite sensible, but when difficulties are encountered along that path, they still think of restoration to one's customary job as the only " natural " course, and turn in the meantime as a stopgap measure to the organisation of opportunities for work which on the whole is ill paid and results in the production of goods and services about which the rest of the community does not feel very strongly either way. Those who, on the contrary, are prepared to question the existing structure of production, and to take seriously the re-allocation of resources necessary for raising standards of living, will concentrate their attention mainly on the discovery of suitable niches in the economic structure which would provide relatively well-paid jobs for those to be placed in employment, and earning incomes as a result of producing goods or services which the rest of the community was eager to enjoy. On the former hypo-thesis we would prepare well-thought-out programmes of " public works ", to which displaced labourers could be swiftly transferred, to take up jobs to which would certainly be attached quite modest remunerations. With the other bias in our mind we should also think well ahead, but either by reforms in our education system, or by other suitable measures, try to ensure that increasing numbers of people could seize the opportunity of performing work at a high level of skill and with a corre-spondingly high income. The subsequent analysis of this book is intended to elaborate this distinction, and to examine the implications of a preference for the second alternative, which on the face of it seems much more attractive, especially for those who feel the persistence of inequality to be one of the most glaring defects of the present economic system.

26. Curiously enough, in practice the former alternative has in recent years received most attention, and in this respect there is no clear distinction to be drawn between thinkers of the right and thinkers of the left. It may well be that during the Great Depression and the years which immediately followed it there

was excessive scepticism in many countries about the extent to which public works of various kinds could assist the recovery of economies suffering from severe shock ; emergency measures were then sometimes necessary without much careful consideration of their ultimate effects. The interest aroused in emergency or crisis measures seems, however, to have left in many minds the impression that similar action should in all circumstances be the normal objective of economic policy. We are now familiar with the unfortunate consequences of efforts to win a past war when attention should be concentrated exclusively upon a current war. If the many enthusiastic workers who now seem anxious to persuade us after this war to carry out more thoroughly and systematically the policies which in their view ought to have been adopted, or more vigorously applied, during the depression of the thirties get their way, the consequences may be no less unfortunate, for in many important respects conditions then will be entirely different. " The school of economists who are still fighting the depression of the early 1930s " [1] enjoys an extraordinary prestige and influence to-day ; we shall find ourselves ill-prepared for the new post-war problems which will confront us if we do not curb the power of this unimaginative school. It may often be better to employ men on more or less useful public works than not to have them employed at all,[2] but undue interest in this possibility may easily induce us to forget that in a growing economy genuine stability demands the organisation of opportunities for normal employment. If we can do that, we shall indeed be able to combine three substantial benefits. Those who are incorporated in the growing economy will have a reasonable prospect of more satisfactory income levels than if they were employed as an emergency measure on public works, they will have the further satisfaction of knowing that their fellow citizens will be eager to enjoy the contributions they are making to the welfare of the community, and moreover, though in the nature of things there can be no absolute certainty here, there is at least a high degree of probability that their employment will be per-

[1] Melchior Palyi, *Review of Politics*, January 1943, p. 134.
[2] It seems, however, to be going a little too far to enunciate as a universal truth that " it is better to employ a man on digging holes than to leave him without any work at all ", as is done by a writer in *Planning*, No. 206, May 11, 1943.

manent. Employment on public works must for most of those
who are offered it be an avowedly temporary expedient, with
another and, at the moment, unknown change still to be faced
in an unknown future. If possible, it is surely better to get a
change of employment over once and for all rather than follow
a course which at an early date must inevitably necessitate another
change. The main purpose of this book is to examine the
circumstances which make the provision of relatively high-paid
posts for individuals seeking a place in a growing economy both
possible and desirable, the difficulties which attend such provision,
the dislocating effects of failure to surmount the difficulties, and
the most effective methods of grappling with them.

27. It may perhaps be objected that, whatever the value or
significance of the points raised in our analysis so far, it is still
defective because the standpoint we have adopted is too individualist or atomistic. We are thinking first, it may be argued,
of security for individuals ; even when we insist that economic
stability is an idea which can have meaning only in relation to a
working economy as a whole, and not in relation to certain
selected parts of it, we are paying insufficient attention to the
growth and preservation of distinctive social values, as expressed
by social groups and cultures of different kinds. We may even
be charged with falling into the habit of thinking of human beings
as mere pawns, to be shifted about here and there in accordance
with the dictates of economic forces, which, if not quite impersonal,
sometimes seem to pay scant respect to the personalities of those
upon whom they impinge, and not, as they clearly ought to be
regarded, as living and responsible members of living societies.
Among the varied meanings which can be attributed to the protean
phrase, social security, it might well seem reasonable to include
the security of a society, the preservation of its characteristic
ways of life and thinking, and of social relationships whose value
has been proved by experience.

28. Even if we ignore altogether the violent shocks of war,
the world in recent years has frequently observed social insecurity
in this wider, and as some might think, deeper sense. Communities in the Pacific, in Africa and elsewhere, which ignorant
westerners are sometimes pleased to describe as " primitive ",

have had their customary modes of life completely disrupted by the clumsy impact of the western world, and even westerners with the best intentions can have little confidence that they have found the secret which will quickly place these societies again on a secure and stable foundation. The whole development of modern mechanical industry has brought with it quite unintended changes in social structure, which are constantly presenting problems all the more difficult because their content and character are themselves constantly changing under our hands. Our approach to the problem of security may be criticised by those who quite rightly are most concerned by such problems as these, because our analysis might appear to an uncritical reader to assume, without question, that the only sensible thing to do is to adapt our economic structure as speedily as possible to the requirements imposed by technical change, ignoring as merely incidental any changes thereby imposed upon cherished social structures properly regarded as having an independent value of their own.

29. It may be difficult to define precisely the meaning of " the American mode of life ", or " the peasant way of life " or " French culture ", but the things indicated by these and many similar phrases are real and significant, with equally real and significant marks of differentiation. The Yugoslav peasant leader to-day may be a little timid about whole-hearted acceptance of the proposals of eager world-planners for grandiose schemes of industrialisation in his region, for, apart from any other ground of legitimate scepticism, he may feel in his bones that, for him at least, the Yugoslav peasant way of life is much to be preferred to the American industrialism which he fears will be his lot if the world-planners get their way, just as André Siegfried showed quite clearly in *America Comes of Age* that he much preferred the French to the American way of life. And who can say with confidence that these sceptics are not right? In the last resort there is no one better qualified to pronounce judgment on these wider issues than the individuals directly affected.

30. The assumption which we have here allowed our imaginary critic to attribute to our analysis has, however, not in fact been made. The issues which he raises are of the utmost importance,

and even if the economist were disposed (which, to do him justice, he seldom is) to ignore them, he would find that his analysis of the problems with which this book is concerned could not proceed far before he was compelled to admit their existence. If he wishes to understand the process of economic change, these considerations, among others, must be fitted into the picture. He may, however, it is submitted, reasonably claim that his critics are no more entitled to make these so-called " social " considerations the pivot around which all decisions of policy must be made to turn than he would be to insist that none but what are popularly but erroneously described as " economic " considerations need be taken into account. If it is of the essential nature of an " economic " problem to be concerned with situations where we are confronted with alternative choices not all fully realisable at the same time, then in that sense the balancing of these " social " considerations against others, including those popularly labelled " economic ", as is itself a fundamental economic question. If changes in the background and structure of our society are inevitable, if indeed they are so intimately rooted in the texture of our social life that a refusal to attempt adjustment to change would itself be a denial of some of our own most cherished social values, then no one has the right to claim that, whatever may happen elsewhere, the type of society which he happens to prefer either for himself or for other people must be preserved absolutely intact. Changes in social structure are not to be made lightly, or without due consideration of their effects upon the traditional foundations upon which in the past social values have been built up. It may sometimes be quite proper to slow down the process of economic change in the interests of social stability in the sense in which we are here using the term, but equally when we decide in favour of such a course we should have as clear a picture as possible before us of the probable consequences of our decision ; our subsequent argument is intended as a contribution to this end.

31. The economic historian is perhaps likely to have a keener sense of the inevitable transitoriness of such things than some of the devotees of particular types of social structure, and he may accordingly sometimes be a little too impatient of what he is

inclined to regard as the romanticism of those who paint idealised pictures of the social structures they are so eager to preserve. For whatever may have been the value of the social structures of the past, there is no single one of them which has not been subject to constant change, sometimes no doubt for the worse, but sometimes also for the better, and unwise efforts to resist change have frequently led to ossification and subsequent decay. Even universal past experience does not, of course, prove conclusively that an indefinite continuance of the same trend is inevitable, but it does create a powerful presumption in favour of that view which cannot easily be rebutted. And however much the members of a particular society may be determined, so far as this depends upon their own efforts, to preserve the social forms which they prefer, any claim that the rest of the world is under an obligation to impose considerable inconvenience and loss upon itself in deference to their wishes is much less convincing. There are even to-day some scattered nomadic societies who, if they were sufficiently vocal and expressive, could no doubt make out an excellent case for the view that their mode of life provided such a fertile soil for social virtues of the highest value that in no circumstances should they be disturbed. No one would or should propose to disrupt nomadic societies merely for the sake of doing so ; the rest of the world cannot, however, be easily convinced that changes, otherwise desirable, should be held up altogether merely because they happened to impinge inconveniently upon nomadic traditions. Similarly, other societies, whose members (or their ancestors) have already made the violent social and psychological adjustments required when a nomad is obliged to live a more settled life, are in no position to demand that, whatever the consequences for the rest of the world, they must be allowed to preserve without any significant modification the form of society which they now happen to prefer.

32. As we have already seen, our problem of security is fundamentally the problem of the organic growth of a society, and the elements embraced in the concept of organic growth [1]

---

[1] Some instructive parallels can be worked out between the automatic self-balancing mechanisms of an adult organism and the social adjustments needed to ensure social stability. There is, however, some danger that biological analogies may encourage just that static view of social and economic processes which we are here most concerned to

include both the narrowly economic, the social as well as other aspects of human life. We should not make the mistake of supposing that change is in itself " a good thing ", something to be desired for its own sake. The wider repercussions of many changes, gratifying to those who make them, and even at first sight perhaps quite harmless from a broader point of view, are so disturbing that, on balance, they deserve to be condemned. Many changes are based on little more than fashion, and the dictates of fashion are often irrational. But while it is a matter of some difficulty to distinguish clearly between changes which are worth the incidental dislocation they cause and those which are not, some changes, and indeed changes of a fundamental character, there are certain to be ; any efforts to check those rightly condemned as undesirable may themselves fail if at the same time we do not remove the obstacles in the way of other changes both desirable and inevitable. And though there can be no complete assurance that growth must invariably mean improvement, we have already seen that there are adequate grounds for the belief that in the post-war world the possibility will at least be open for raising average standards of living. No absolute validity can be claimed for the view that improvements in standards of living are desirable, but the most superficial observation of the lives of large masses of our fellow men suggests that for a considerable period of time, and not least from the point of view of the provision of conditions favourable to the development of higher and non-material values, such improvements may properly be given a prominent place on the agenda for a civilised society, whether national or world-wide. We shall, therefore, endeavour to analyse in broad outline the conditions to be satisfied if these

combat. " The adult organism . . . is the equivalent of an adjusted population. It has no provision for any process which would be the equivalent of immigration into the social community. Nor has it any provision for unlimited growth either as a whole or in its parts. . . . Any wisdom which the human organism has to offer to the social organism would be based on the proviso of a population which is adjusted to reasonably assured means of subsistence and which is undisturbed by large increases from either local or foreign sources " (Walter B. Cannon, " Relations of Biological and Social Homeostasis ", in *The Wisdom of the Body*, p. 301). The most difficult and important problems of social and economic adjustment arise thus in circumstances to which the normal biological processes of an adult organism present no parallel. If we speak of the organic growth of an economy, we must think rather of the growth of an organism which is constantly moving towards adult status, but never actually reaches it.

possibilities are to become realities. We shall keep in mind throughout the ever-present and pressing problem of unemployment, and if the difficulties of finding employment for some members of our society are very great, methods which seek a way out by means of relatively low-grade employment, by producing things which the community as a whole is not particularly anxious to have, may sometimes have to be adopted in default of anything better. We shall not, however, endeavour to conceal our bias in favour of the view that this should always be regarded as a third-rate compromise, and that for the problem of labour displacement solutions in terms of higher grade employment, producing things that other people will wish to buy, are much to be preferred.

33. The view to which we have already referred, that economic problems now require quite a different approach from that customarily adopted by economists before the war, is frequently expounded in terms of an alleged contrast between the economics of production and the economics of consumption.[1] Economists in the past, it is alleged, paid too much attention to problems of production ; these no longer present any serious difficulty, and their attention should therefore in the future be directed more to problems of consumption and distribution. It is a curious paradox that many of those who make much of this contrast often show in the details of their concrete proposals that they have little intention of paying much serious attention to the preferences of consumers. Professor Carr, for example, appeals to the natural susceptibilities of the consumer, who may well feel that his interests were unduly neglected in the inter-war period, by announcing that " we must begin by firmly setting the consumer, not the producer, in the centre of our economic system ".[2] Any hopeful anticipations by the consumer that, having once been placed in this honourable position, he will then be allowed to

---

[1] Even the admirable Report of the League of Nations Delegation on Economic Depressions (*The Transition from War to Peace Economy*, 1943, p. 10) defers to this fashion by suggesting that, during the three or four years preceding the outbreak of war, " the fundamental assumptions of economic thought came to be questioned. The economics of consumption began to replace the economics of production ", though the subsequent analysis of the Report is in no way inconsistent with the general character of our argument.

[2] *Conditions of Peace*, p. 135.

have what he likes, are however at once rudely dispelled, for we must also begin, he is told, " by making planned consumption the starting-point of our policy ", and in the most striking illustration quoted of such " planned consumption ", that of Nazi Germany, it is quite obvious that the spontaneous wishes of consumers played a relatively unimportant part. We are urged to follow President Roosevelt's wise advice " to think more about the consumer ", but our thoughts, it is clearly implied, are not to be directed to letting the consumer have what he wants.[1] Economic problems in the true sense are always at the same time problems both of production and of consumption, and so long as we think it proper to pay attention to consumers' demand, it is difficult to see how the two can in fact ever be disentangled. Economists in the past have concentrated their attention upon the conditions likely to be most favourable to the optimum distribution of productive resources, but the criterion by which the optimum was to be judged was always consumption, the satisfaction of consumers' demand. Economic policy in the inter-war period was indeed unduly dominated by the supposed interests of producers' groups, a fact which lies behind a great deal of our subsequent analysis. But whatever their other shortcomings may have been, economists have seldom been indifferent to these errors of policy. They insist, however, that in a growing economy the problem of production is incapable of any " final " solution. Technical problems of production may be solved in relation to particular goods or services, but the economic problem of production is essentially the problem of the appropriate distribution of resources for the production of a wide and constantly changing variety of goods and services : every time there is a change in production, in the technical sense, this economic problem has to be " solved " afresh. This insistence, moreover, is primarily in the interests of consumers themselves, who often seem now to need most protection against those who profess to make consumption the cornerstone of their policy. Consumers may reasonably become alarmed if either economists or statesmen lose their interest in problems of production, for the fear would then be justified either that they would be unable to get what

[1] *Ibid.* pp. 94-7.

they wanted or that they would get it only in inadequate quantities.

34. There are great advantages in postponing in our analysis any specific reference to the character of the economic system and institutions most appropriate for realising our objectives. Much of the confusion of thought which characterises many discussions of rival economic systems, and in particular of planning, arises because many people have too hastily committed themselves to approval of one system or another, without having first taken the trouble to understand the nature of the changes in economic structure which, under any system, must in any event be faced if economic and social life is to develop in a satisfactory way. An understanding of these changes is therefore a prior condition for intelligent speculation about changes in our economic system.

CHAPTER V

THE DYNAMICS OF A PROGRESSIVE ECONOMY

1. OUR enquiry has thus brought us back very close to our original starting-point. Up to 1939, the background of material conditions within which our economy was developing justified the expectation of rising standards of living. In those days, therefore, although other issues were often more immediately pressing, the fundamental economic problem was that of ensuring the smooth transfer or adaptation of resources of production, of labour and of capital, to those fields of employment where goods and services could be turned out likely to be demanded by a community with rising standards of living. The advance of science indeed made it essential that, even if there had been no eagerness for rising standards of living, such transfers should be made. This problem, many have suggested, might now, however, be thought to have lost its practical significance, either because in the future we shall be obliged to adjust our minds to poverty rather than to increasing wealth, or because the pressure of public opinion in favour of security is now so strong that, until this prior objective has been assured, plans for further increases of wealth will necessarily have to be set aside. We have seen that neither of these reasons is sound and that, in the future, as in the past, the great practical economic problem will be the efficient organisation of appropriate transfers of productive resources.

2. By a convenient shorthand expression this problem is sometimes described as one of structural adjustment. Already, without troubling to define it, we have used the word structure in our argument, but something further should be said about the sense in which this metaphorical term is here used. It is intended to suggest the relations between the different types of productive activity in an economy, visualised more or less on the model of a building, with its rooms and storeys, or a town with its regions, its industrial and residential areas, open spaces and the like. We

make a structural change in a building when we knock down a wall between two rooms or erect a partition to screen off a portion of a larger room. We make a structural change in a city when we extend or rearrange its factory area or increase the space reserved for playing-fields. Similarly, we make a structural change in an economy when we alter the relative importance of the parts played in it by the various industries and other economic activities which together constitute the economy as a whole. A structural change occurs, for example, when the relative importance of agriculture as a field of employment declines, or when the relative importance of aircraft production as a field for investment increases. The term economic adjustment or economic adaptation has been frequently used in a wider sense of which these structural changes form only one, though a highly important aspect. It is, however, a little unfortunate that more care has not as a rule been taken to stress the essential role of such structural changes. Many writers have no doubt had them in mind, but so far as any popular views have developed on the subject, it may be feared that economic adjustment more naturally suggests unpleasant things like wage-cuts or scaling down debt charges. In this study we shall frequently use structural adjustment as a convenient general shorthand term to describe the shifts in the relative importance of different fields of employment and investment which are an essential part of the life of a growing economy, but we should not be misled by its abstractness into forgetting that it is always the redistribution of concrete resources of production which we have in mind.

3. The immediate causes demanding structural adjustments are often very varied. The development of the potentialities of hitherto neglected areas, political decisions affecting barriers to trade, and other similar factors from time to time necessitate adjustments in various national economies. In the last resort, however, all these factors can be classified under two main headings : changes in the technique of production and changes in consumers' demand. The practical importance of the latter is overwhelming in the transition from either peace to war or from war back to peace, when the whole world economy has to be adjusted to the most violent changes in the character of the goods

and services which it is called upon to produce. But in more normal times the effects of changes in consumers' demand, though sometimes of great importance, are usually less fundamental than of changes in the technique of production. The responses demanded by changes in consumers' demand are, moreover, not essentially different from those demanded by changes in productive technique, and we shall therefore endeavour to elucidate the nature of our problem further by examining in more detail the kind of adjustment (in the sense just defined) needed in any economy liable to changes of the latter kind. It is at least theoretically conceivable that changes in consumers' demand might be prevented, or so effectively discouraged, as to lose much of their present importance. The regimentation of the human mind necessary if in the present state of our scientific knowledge changes in the technique of production were to be made impossible would, however, demand such a radical revolution as would completely transform our habits of thinking and of social intercourse, and therefore scarcely deserves serious consideration. Changes in production technique are, in fact, going on at varying rates of speed all the time. New methods are constantly being discovered, or methods already discovered are being more widely applied. Sometimes for various reasons efforts are made to check or prevent these changes. But whatever measure of success these efforts may have,[1] at the worst they only slow down somewhat the movement towards greater productive capacity which has been characteristic of all modern societies, and which, so far as

---

[1] There has, for example, been a sharp controversy about the extent to which businesses who believe it profitable to do so buy up patent rights with a view to suppressing a new invention, and on this matter active industrialists themselves have recently expressed quite contradictory opinions. According to Mr. Samuel Courtauld, " industrialists sometimes take out patents not in order to exploit them seriously, but with the deliberate intention of preventing others from trying new and improved methods which may render their own methods obsolete, and endanger their invested capital. A large number of good inventions are thus deliberately stifled. The buying-up of existing patents in order to suppress them has exactly the same effect " (*Economic Journal*, April 1942, p. 15). The author of *Patents and Licences of Right*, a pamphlet issued by Imperial Chemical Industries, with a foreword by Lord McGowan (and to which a vigorous reply, with a preface by Lord Trent, has been published by Boots Pure Drug Co. Ltd.), maintains, on the contrary, " that there is little evidence that suppression exists even in the U.S.A. . . . In this country, the suppression of patents in the sense of taking out or acquiring a patent and then not working the process even though it possesses economic, technical or commercial merits over existing processes, may . . . be treated as virtually non-existent " (p. 11).

one can see ahead, is likely to continue to be characteristic at least for several generations.

4. As an immediate effect of improvement in the technique of production, goods or services can be placed upon the market which give better value to their purchasers, because either their price is lower or their quality higher. The subsequent reactions upon the economy as a whole depend first upon the character of the demand for the cheaper product. If it is sufficiently elastic, *i.e.* if consumers are induced by the fall of price to increase their purchases on a sufficiently large scale, the change may not necessitate any ejection of labour from the industry affected. In the nature of things, changes in the productive process will usually demand some rearrangement of resources of production within each of the industries directly concerned, but on the whole these industries will not, in these circumstances, themselves be gravely troubled by problems of insecurity or by unemployment arising directly from technical change. Historically large-scale technical improvements in the production of goods or services with an elastic demand have always attracted into these fields a larger share of the community's or of the world's working population than was employed there before their products came within the reach of consumers with modest incomes. There are important problems, both " social " and economic, associated with the concentration of large masses of wage-earners in the employment of, say, motor manufacturing firms, some of whom have been reproached with paying insufficient attention to the evils of irregular employment. The transfer of productive resources into these industries has not, however, in itself presented any great difficulty. The expansion of industries whose technical efficiency is improving has sometimes been hampered by shortages of certain types of skilled labour, but, broadly speaking, if the forces of change are in their first impact " attractive " to labour, and not " ejective ",[1] the readjustment problem is comparatively easy to handle.

5. The position is rather different when the impact of change falls first upon industries for whose products demand is relatively inelastic. For the " ejective " power upon labour then gets to

---

[1] Cf. Guy Chapman, *Culture and Survival*, p. 57.

work first, and the problem at once arises of organising with the least possible delay opportunities for generating at least a corresponding " attractive " power in other directions into other fields of employment. The consumers of goods with an inelastic demand will be very pleased when they observe that their price has fallen, and may even buy more of them. They can, however, now get all they want of these things with a smaller expenditure of money ; preferring to spend on other things part of the free money now placed at their disposal, they will not maintain at the old level the demand for labour in the industries affected by technical change. The producer may accordingly find that his services are no longer needed in the old field, and he must therefore discover some other occupation which in principle must be in an industry which can offer the additional goods demanded by the consumer who has discovered that he now has more free money to spend. Problems of displaced labour created by such technical improvements are, of course, very familiar. These sectors of agriculture where goods are produced for which demand is inelastic are peculiarly susceptible to such changes. Elsewhere crude man-power has often been displaced by more elaborate machinery, especially when, even if we include all the labour needed to produce the machinery and prepare the raw materials, mineral and otherwise, necessary for this purpose, the amount of labour required per unit of output falls more rapidly than any extension in demand. Indeed sooner or later, wherever the first impact of technical change may fall, demand for the goods and services which are thus more cheaply produced always tends to become inelastic. The ultimate benefits of improvements in the efficiency of production are enjoyed partly in the form of larger supplies of the goods and services directly affected, but often even more in the form of larger supplies of quite different goods and services the conditions of whose production may not have altered at all.

6. Even, however, if the first impact of change falls upon industries for whose products demand is elastic, there is another side to the picture. Output may then expand rapidly with an insistent call for the services of workers who can without much difficulty see where they are needed. But there may also be

important repercussions elsewhere, which may be all the greater the wider the opportunities for new employment offered by the expanding industries. For simple references to elasticity of demand may in this connection be misleading. Price elasticity is a convenient concept for describing the responsiveness of demand to changes in price, assuming that other things remain unaltered. But the inevitable and proper consequence of the changes with which we are concerned is a general increase in consumers' income ; we must therefore also take into account income elasticity, the responsiveness of demand to changes in consumers' income. The effects of expanding demand may also be differently described according as we are thinking of a single commodity or service by itself, or of a group of commodities or of services, each one of which may within quite wide limits be a convenient substitute for any of the others. If, for example, any particular form of transport becomes cheaper, the consequential redistribution of employment will be different, according as the cheaper form is merely substituted for others, or stimulates an expanding demand for transport as a whole. The invention of bicycles probably did little to diminish the demand for other forms of transport, but the invention of the motor-car has had profound effects upon employment in both horse-drawn transport and railways. Increased employment in the motor and ancillary industries has been accompanied by decreased employment in horse and other older forms of transport, or at least by a slowing-down in the rate of their expansion, and the effects of this can be traced back through several stages in the productive process. The demand for petrol has risen, while the demand for oats fell ; there are accordingly more opportunities for employment in the petroleum industry and fewer for oats-growing farmers. In the last resort, indeed, there are practically no goods or services which consumers would in no conceivable circumstances think of dropping from their expenditure programmes in favour of something else which had become more attractive to them. If the general level of incomes were kept rigidly stable, an expansion of demand for any single commodity must be at the expense of diminishing expenditure on something else. In the circumstances with which we are concerned, the general level of incomes will not, or should not, remain

E

rigidly stable ; *ex hypothesi* technical improvements make higher income levels possible, but even then the demand directed towards the newer goods or services which can now be purchased more cheaply will probably to some extent become effective at the expense of a diminished demand for something else. Assuming the ideal situation to be one where the volume of resources to be transferred is a minimum, we should approximate to it more closely if technical change were to occur only in industries for whose products consumers' demand was so delicately balanced as to expand in response to a fall of price just so far but no further than was necessary to keep at work in the industries affected everyone already employed there. This is unlikely often to occur, and where the expansion of demand goes beyond this, the " attractive " power exerted upon labour in the industries where technical efficiency is increasing always operates alongside a corresponding " ejective " power operating in other industries whose products are neglected by consumers in favour of the newer and cheaper things now offered to them.

7. The significance of the contrast between industries for whose products there is an elastic demand and those for which demand is inelastic may therefore seem to have been somewhat exaggerated, for at best we are likely merely to shift the position of the problem of displaced resources but not its essential character. Nevertheless, it is of considerable practical importance whether the " attractive " or the " ejective " power gets to work first ; if by some remarkable accident all technical changes were confined to industries for whose products there was an elastic demand, our thinking about practical economic issues would probably not be so much dominated as it is by the difficulties of people who find that, as a result of changes for which they have no responsibility and over which they can exert little control, their services are no longer wanted. Such people would still present a problem, but the prospects for fitting them into a new place in the structure of production would appear more favourable if at the same time the industries upon whom the first impact of changes in technique had fallen were rapidly expanding.

8. To state the problem of technological unemployment and of structural readjustment in this way and to solve it are obviously

two quite different things. The statement which has been offered might, moreover, with some reason be criticised as inadequate because by referring to " the consumer " in general it skates too lightly over a matter of considerable practical importance. We have said that, in the circumstances described, the problem of economic organisation is the problem of transferring resources of production which have become superfluous in their original fields of employment to new fields where the things can be produced which the consumer, with more free purchasing power at his disposal as the result of the fall of price of some of his former customary purchases, will now wish to buy. But who actually is *the* consumer ? In an abstract analysis it may be permissible to reason along lines which suggest that at any given point of time there is only one answer to the question, Where should we apply the productive resources released by technical improvements ? In point of fact there is normally a wide variety of possible answers, and in a changing world it could scarcely be otherwise. The consumer may hesitate about the relative attractiveness to himself of the alternative purchases which his new-found effective purchasing power now brings within his grasp, and his ultimate decision may also be affected either by pressure from competing salesmen or by public policy expressing itself in a variety of ways. There is an important sense, the implications of which have so far been inadequately studied, in which, quite apart from any policy of State control of industry or subsidisation of special types of activity, an economy has a real freedom of choice in creating conditions to encourage the production either of things most likely to be of service to the wealthier sections of a community, or of things within the range of purchasing power of those with small incomes. Fastidious objections to the vulgarities of material wealth, of which earlier we found little cause to speak with respect,[1] may perhaps be judged somewhat more favourably if they can be interpreted as being founded on a dislike of the quite unwarranted belief that material progress inevitably means nothing more than the aimless accumulation of unnecessary luxuries for wealthy people. Institutional factors may sometimes canalise too large a fraction of the stream of increasing wealth to serve merely

Cf. *supra* III 2-3.

this limited purpose, but the process is by no means inevitable. In making suggestions for the solution of the general problem of the speedy reallocation of productive resources, we shall therefore at the same time endeavour to take account of their relevance to this choice.

9. The unpredictability of consumers' demand in an expanding economy deserves to be noted, but its importance should not be exaggerated. The practical problem before us, if we wish to facilitate the smooth and rapid development of an expanding economy, is to identify its growing points, for if movement is hampered at these points, the whole economy is in danger of being thrown out of gear. But while the probable character of consumers' demand in response to a situation which offers larger real incomes may in any single case be difficult to predict, we are not entirely in the dark as to the location of these growing points if, as often happens, several changes occur simultaneously, and we have to forecast the responses of large numbers of consumers to such changes. We can then make fairly precise statements about the probable future course of their demand, and therefore about, what is indeed the same thing, the lines along which a reallocation of productive resources would most usefully be attempted. Both general reasoning and observation of the course of events in a large number of countries over long periods of time justify the conclusion that normally in any economy which is growing wealthier there is a relative decline in the importance of primary production as a field of investment and employment, and a relative increase in the importance of tertiary production ; [1] this general trend, moreover, is observable not only if increases in real income fall into the hands of those who are already wealthy, but also when they are more widely distributed, having perhaps the effect of diminishing inequalities in income distribution. Importance is rightly attached to the reality of the choice between economic change which accrues mainly to the advantage of those who are already well off, and economic change which mainly benefits those whose income standards are below the average, but whatever the choice actually made, the general character of the trend in the relative importance of different types

[1] Cf. *supra*, II, 3.

of employment will in any progressive economy be much the same, though the details will naturally vary in accordance with variations in the division of the increase in national income among the different income strata. Poor people spend relatively more on food than rich people, but as poor people become better off they will tend, just like rich people in similar circumstances, to spend relatively less on food ; the relative importance of industries concerned with food production tends to decline as soon as quite a modest average level of income has been reached. Rich people tend always to spend relatively much more on services and intangible goods than poor people are able to do, but as their incomes increase poor people also tend to spend more on these things, though the services selected in the two cases may be entirely different ; practically always when the average level of income is rising we must, therefore, be prepared for a relative increase in the volume of tertiary employment. As time goes on, indeed, an increasing proportion of inventive capacity is devoted to directly exploring new types of consumer demand, with close affinities to tertiary production. Instead of technical change impinging first upon primary or secondary production, and releasing resources which later must, as it were, be mopped up in the tertiary sector, it may get to work at once in the tertiary field, creating there demands for productive resources which in some sense anticipate their release elsewhere.[1]

10. The same point may be put in a slightly different way, perhaps more useful as a guide for the direction of policy. If we are slow to take the steps necessary for facilitating increases in the volume of tertiary employment, and much more if we take positive steps to hinder these increases, we are *ipso facto* sabotaging economic progress and thus condemning ourselves and our fellow men to a standard of living lower than that to which we and they could reasonably aspire. Unless the declarations to which so many statesmen from all countries have committed themselves in recent years in favour of higher standards of living imply a willingness

---

[1] Of the 120 most important inventions of the last generation, it was estimated that 45 per cent were in the field of consumers' goods, and not directly either capital saving or labour saving. See G. Chapman, *Culture and Survival*, ch. viii, for an interesting account of the significance of inventions such as produced the roller-skate, the bicycle and the gramophone.

to encourage and facilitate these structural changes, these shifts in employment, they mean precisely nothing. Nor, if our subsequent argument is sound, can we console ourselves, if this encouragement is not given, and higher standards of living are thereby sacrificed, with the hope that our sacrifice will enable us to confer greater stability upon our fellow men.

11. Much of the economic friction of recent years is to be traced back to sheer ignorance of the nature of this problem, and some quite solid advantages might therefore be anticipated from merely stating it. It may be difficult to find a solution to cover all cases ; it will be almost impossible if we do not first know what the problem is for whose solution we are painfully groping.

12. So far we have considered only the case where improvements in the technique of production are reflected with the least possible delay in the offer of goods at a correspondingly lower price. Such prompt reactions to technical improvements are frequently delayed by monopolistic influences of one kind or another, and the next stage in our analysis must be to examine the effects of these influences. The distinction between goods for which the demand is elastic and goods with an inelastic demand still has some significance here, but for a different reason, a prudent monopolist tending to keep this factor in mind in determining the price policy likely to be most profitable to himself. In general, however, the effect of monopolistic influences must be in the direction of maintaining output at a lower level than would be attained if competition were freely operative. Prices may fall, but not so far as is warranted by the technical improvements which have been made, and in an extreme case they may be held at exactly the old level. An expansion of output may, however, go so far as to involve the employment in the industry affected of a larger volume of resources than before, but even in this case the " attractive " power of the impact of technical improvement will be weakened by monopolistic or quasi-monopolistic control, and the chances that technical improvement will result in an ejection of productive resources are considerably increased.

13. The monopoly gains accruing in these circumstances will not necessarily all pass into the hands of the monopolist himself.

He may be obliged to share them in varying proportions with some of those who get their incomes by selling their services to him. Equilibrium can, in any event, be re-established only if the labour rendered superfluous, either in the monopoly-controlled industry or in other industries whose products compete with the cheaper goods now being offered, again finds employment, directly or indirectly, in the production of the additional things which those who enjoy the benefits of monopoly gains are in consequence in a position to buy. In its essential outlines, the problem of transfer of productive resources which here arises is therefore not different from that already described. But the solution, however arrived at, is likely to prefer unduly the production of things for the use of wealthy people to the production of things purchasable by people with small incomes. Under monopoly or quasi-monopoly control, the chances are in favour of the former being the main beneficiaries of improvements in productive efficiency, and at the same time the possibility of easing the transfer situation through the operation of forces " attractive " to labour in the fields of employment directly affected by technical improvements is limited. And what is still more important, the difficulties of adjustment will be greatly increased if monopoly influences are also at work in the fields of employment towards which the ejected labour should be directed. Structural change, at least on any considerable scale, is seldom quite easy. In a world where scientific invention is actively pursued, the problem cannot, however, be evaded. The gratuitous addition to its magnitude, through the influence of monopoly controls, whether in the industries directly affected by technical change or those into which displaced resources should move, is a powerful reason, quite apart from anything else, for regarding counter-monopoly measures as an important task for modern economic policy.

14. It is now a commonplace that any attempt to draw a sharp dividing line between monopoly and absence of monopoly is unlikely to give satisfactory, and may give misleading, results. To some extent this is merely a question of definition. Monopoly means literally the organisation of an industry under the control of a single seller ; it is not easy to discover many cases in which

formal monopoly control is so complete as this, and some people
have therefore been disposed to underrate the importance of the
monopoly problem. The principle of monopoly implies, however, the unified or concerted discretionary control of the prices
at which purchasers are allowed to obtain a monopolised good
or service, and therefore of the supply which they can secure.
Such concerted action may be far from complete, but the absence
of formal completeness from any organisation which effectively
limits supply does not mean that the monopoly problem may not
be present there in a quite acute form. We need not elaborate
all the complications associated with the complex of devices now
available for limiting output or for earmarking quasi-monopolistic
gains. One variant of the case just outlined deserves, however,
to be mentioned. It has a special importance in relation to the
international side of our problem, though in the ordinary sense
of the term it might not be regarded as monopolistic at all, tending
to occur instead in industries where there is a large number of
small independent producers. The attempt has often been made
to mitigate the impact of falling prices upon such industries,
especially when the fall reflects technical improvements by foreign
competitors, by maintaining prices by governmental or other
action at what is regarded as a " reasonable " level. This policy
has been frequently adopted in relation to certain agricultural
prices, and a consideration of its effects upon employment and
structural readjustment raises issues similar to those already discussed. Such efforts at price stabilisation are in the long run
usually found to be unsuccessful unless something is also done to
limit production. If, at the same time, it is assumed to be necessary to maintain in their original employments everybody previously concerned in the production affected, the monopoly gains
which accrue are in effect redistributed among all the producers
so that, even if no one is worse off, no one is better off than
before. By imposing a certain measure of concealed unemployment upon each producer, the intention to free resources of
production which is implicit in the invention of technical improvements is, for practical purposes, defeated. He is, in effect, obliged
to take out the benefits of technical improvements in the shape of
more leisure or less intensive work. In principle there can be

little objection to distributing some of the benefits of technical progress in this way, but except in some special cases, there seems no reason for confining the benefits of increased leisure to a single group of producers. But if, in limiting output, employment in the industry must also be contracted, the problem of extruded labour is exactly the same as before.

15. The illustrations of our difficulties which most readily come to mind are naturally those where shifts of labour are involved. Shifts of capital are, however, at least equally important, and may sometimes be more difficult to organise. When we spoke earlier of the search for security being naturally interpreted as a search for security in one's ordinary and normal employment, a more complete statement would also have included the effects of the natural desire to keep one's capital intact. It was, for example, at least as much the amount of capital invested in the Lancashire cotton trade as the fear of large-scale unemployment there which, after the last war, induced the leaders of the trade to try to preserve it on its original scale. Especially when we are discussing shifts of labour, however, we should not be misled by an over-simplified presentation of the argument into supposing that we were asking of the ordinary man or woman a quite impossible degree of versatility. How, it might be asked, can anyone possibly seriously think of insisting that a displaced coal-miner or textile operative, whose labour is no longer needed in his old industry, because oil has become more economical than coal, or because the Japanese can now supply more cheaply the goods formerly exported from this country to West Africa or the West Indies, should apply his mind to acquiring the skill needed for one or other of the types of tertiary production which, if the economy is to function smoothly, are now needed in increasing quantities? Some productive resources, whether labour or capital, already crystallised in a specialised form not or not easily adaptable for other uses, seem to be quite incapable of transfer elsewhere. In such cases insistence upon structural adjustments in our economy may threaten crippling losses for some owners of capital equipment, or some workers with specialised skill.

16. Fortunately, however, the position is normally not quite so difficult as that. " Very great changes in the distribution of

labour are continually being slowly made without hardship to anyone by diversions of the stream of young recruits." [1] Instead of thinking in terms of the redistribution of a crystallised and static labour force, we should think rather of a constant redirection into the proper channels of a stream of labour which is constantly being replenished. If the demand for coal-miners, for example, is falling off, the situation will largely be met if the sons of coal-miners are encouraged to seek some employment other than that of their fathers. The prominence of educational policy in our practical programme is largely due to the significance of this factor, though a new industry can obviously not be recruited exclusively from the ranks of young people entering industry, and some changes of occupation on the part of those who have already found employment will therefore always be desirable.

17. Moreover, while the presentation of our problem is for some purposes conveniently simplified if we think first of the impact of change upon single individuals, the actual situation is always more complex, and for that very reason in some respects easier to handle. The transfer of any given displaced individual to the new niche which a growing economy needs to fill may be literally impossible, but if at the same time other individuals are similarly affected, the chances are somewhat increased that some other person, with a different set of natural aptitudes, may be set free to occupy this niche, leaving another vacancy to be filled by someone else, by a method not unlike the normal process of promotion. This process may be repeated several times until at last a vacancy is discovered suitable for the capacities and experience of the displaced man who constituted the original problem. In general even the most sluggish economy usually displays a certain amount of fluidity ; there are always some changes going on. The simultaneous occurrence of a number of heterogeneous changes increases the chances for any single individual that there may be among the new places which ought to be filled something suitable to his capacity and at the same time conforming to the general requirements of a growing economy.

18. The smoothness of adjustments in the capital structure also depends, perhaps more than in the case of labour, upon the

---

[1] E. Cannan, *Review of Economic Theory*, p. 110, and *Economic Scares*, p. 26.

rate at which change is imposed upon the economy. Much of
the capital equipment in existence at any moment of time is
crystallised in forms which do not readily admit of adaptation to
other purposes. But even large disturbances will seldom require
a radical transformation of the whole of the capital structure. To
maintain equilibrium in a growing economy all that is needed is a
certain measure of interchangeability at the margins, and it is
easy to underestimate the size of the fraction of the capital available in various forms at any moment of time which can without
undue difficulty be diverted to some relatively new field of investment. The practical problem is first to divert into the fields of
investment where expansion is needed an adequate proportion
of the new stream of savings which is continuously becoming
available. This does not, however, exhaust the opportunities for
relatively smooth adjustment. Provision against depreciation and
replacement of existing items of capital equipment is an important
item which offers business men ample opportunities of changing
the forms in which their capital is temporarily crystallised. It was
estimated that in 1928 the depreciation and depletion charges
against the current income of American corporations amounted
to 4·1 billion dollars, a sum equal to about two-thirds of the new
capital issues of corporate securities in that year. The normal
amortisation period varies a good deal from industry to industry,
and for the United States it has been estimated that the average
life of capital equipment is not less than ten years. But this
average conceals a wide range of variety. The prevailing forms
of capital and the prevailing business practices in the United
States " are such that a very considerable diversion of capital
from one industry to another is constantly taking place through
ordinary business transactions, without the intervention of
banking institutions, and often without the formal decision of
those whose capital is affected ". " A large part of business
inventories consists of primary industrial materials — mined
coal, pig-iron, steel ingots, lumber — which, because of the great
variety of their alternative uses, are effectively unspecialised ;
and the capital which they represent is to that extent highly
mobile." Even of the " fixed capital ", embodied in buildings
and industrial and agricultural equipment, a larger proportion

than might at first sight be supposed is capable of diversion from one use to another, and therefore possesses a substantial measure of mobility. " New or growing industries may readily divert to their products an increasing proportion of the current output of steel, coal, copper, electric power, transportation service. In doing so, they are in effect obtaining the services of an increasing proportion of the capital equipment of the primary industries. And in this very real and practical sense, the fixed capital of the latter may be said to possess a substantial measure of mobility." The most important forms of capital in an industrial society are relatively unspecialised, and may without serious inconvenience be diverted from the use of one final consumer to another within a short space of time.[1] Even when the fullest allowance is made for these considerations, the problem of capital mobility does not indeed entirely disappear, but they enable us to examine it in a better perspective.

19. Our argument so far has been directed towards establishing the point that if we are to realise the higher standards of living made possible by technical improvements in production, we shall be obliged continuously to reallocate our resources of labour and capital between the various industries and occupations in which they are employed. If we refuse to make this reallocation or are too slow in carrying it out, protestations of devotion to higher standards of living are worthless, because by such a refusal we make certain that standards of living will not rise. At a later stage we shall examine some of the special conditions which in our own time make or appear to make the difficulties of such structural adaptation more acute than they used to be. Our main purpose is to discover suitable means for diminishing or removing the difficulties, or, where difficulties still remain, to avoid the imposition of unfair hardships upon innocent individuals or social groups. We must, however, first establish the further point that if the necessary transfers of resources are not made, not only will the average level of income fail to rise as improvements in the efficiency of production would justify us in expecting, but the failure to make them will also mean the loss of the individual or

---

[1] L. H. Seltzer, " The Mobility of Capital ", *Quarterly Journal of Economics*, May 1932. Cf. C. Iversen, *Aspects of the Theory of International Capital Movements*, p. 503.

group security which is usually the avowed object of resistance to adjustment. By refusing to adjust our economic structure, we shall have sacrificed the potential additions to real income which technical progress offered to us, and at the same time the security which we misguidedly made our main objective will have eluded our grasp.

CHAPTER VI

CYCLICAL UNEMPLOYMENT AND ADJUSTMENT
TO TECHNICAL CHANGE

1. An exhaustive analysis of the relation between resistance to structural readjustment and the risks of instability would demand a full-dress consideration of the whole problem of the trade cycle, a task clearly beyond the scope of this book. Much of the controversy that has raged around this theme clearly illustrates the unfortunate propensity of the human mind to waste time in arguing whether *the* cause of some phenomenon is A, B or perhaps C, whereas in fact A, B and C, and probably many other factors as well, are all contributory partial causes ; a realistic theory which is to cover *all* the facts, and not merely some of them, must pay due attention, but no more than due attention, to each one of these contributory causes. Eclecticism is often repellent to those who like simple solutions, but if, as so often happens, simplicity in these matters is purchased at the cost of accuracy, we must be prepared to abandon it, and to rest content with the complexities of eclecticism.

2. The following analysis therefore in no way pretends to give an exhaustive account of the trade cycle, or necessarily to involve rejection of other theories which also contain part of the truth. There is, however, abundant justification for enquiring whether there may not be a close connection between the risks of unemployment and undue delay in making the structural adjustments demanded by improvements in technical processes.

3. In discussions of unemployment in general it is now a commonplace to make a preliminary distinction between its several types, the main and legitimate purpose of the distinction being to show that for different types of unemployment different remedies are needed and that a complete solution of the problem therefore demands a combination of all these remedies. With certain types of unemployment we are not here concerned. We need say nothing, for example, about seasonal unemployment or

about the casual unemployment which affects dock labourers. For our purpose the more important distinction is that commonly drawn between technological or structural unemployment and cyclical unemployment. The first impact of the former, due mainly to changes in the technique of production, such as we have been discussing, or to fundamental changes in consumers' preferences, falls upon the industries where technological changes occur, and can in the long run be avoided only by transferring resources of production to suitable new fields of activity. The latter type is more diffused, affecting in varying degree all sectors of the economy. Its causation has been variously interpreted, and a correspondingly varied range of remedies proposed. But while the interrelated consequences of these two main forms of unemployment are readily recognised as combining in the creation of a social and human problem of the utmost importance, it is not so universally understood that they may also have a significant common cause. It is agreed that, as a matter of practical politics, action ought to be taken simultaneously to deal with both types, but the two are still often thought of as distinct and separate problems, so that, theoretically at least, either might be dealt with, and its unfortunate effects removed, even though nothing of importance was being done in regard to the other.

4. This view of the relationship between the two types of unemployment we are here concerned to show to be erroneous. If large numbers of men are already unemployed, it is no doubt right to pursue simultaneously policies designed to impinge separately upon each. Cyclical unemployment having once made its appearance, we should attempt by means of wisely directed credit policy or by properly planned public works to check the otherwise cumulative effects of the vicious deflationary spiral, and these steps may rightly be represented as important, irrespective of whether we are at the same time taking steps to diminish technological unemployment by facilitating the expansion of the new types of production of goods and services which alone will deal with this side of the unemployment problem. The enthusiast for public works is not indeed entitled to obstruct the efforts of those who aim at other remedies which they believe to be more fundamental and permanent, but neither is the man who

thinks mainly in terms of structural change entitled to decry, as being inadequate, the efforts of those who are more interested in the maintenance of cheap money or in the organisation of public works. In the midst of an unemployment crisis it is highly probable that each one of these efforts will, by itself, be inadequate, but that is no reason for refusing to make it.

5. If, however, as at the present time, we are not troubled by any pressing problem of unemployment, but are looking to the future with, it is to be hoped, a view to preventing the recurrence of large-scale unemployment, our attitude should be somewhat different. Those who think mainly in terms of cyclical unemployment are very apt to postulate some general situation, a decline perhaps in the general level of demand, or a decline in the demand for capital goods, as the starting-point of their problem, and too often fail to ask themselves what lies behind this general situation. Why should there be any falling-off in the general level of demand ? This question needs to be asked, and, if possible, answered ; the search for an answer suggests that structural and cyclical unemployment are not properly to be regarded as two co-ordinate types, each with its own set of causes, but that the failure to effect the redistribution of productive resources in face of technical change, which is the obvious and immediate cause of structural or technological unemployment, is also, though perhaps not so directly, one important cause of cyclical unemployment itself. When we are actually confronted with both types simultaneously, we may properly apply remedies to cyclical unemployment with little or no relation to its ultimate causation. But in planning for the prevention of unemployment, the emphasis is wrongly placed, and we may unwittingly subject ourselves to unnecessary disappointments later, if our thinking about cyclical unemployment is too much coloured by the necessity of preparing beforehand remedial measures to be used if unfortunately the problem should again present itself in the future as in the past. For this encourages the tendency to wait for unemployment to come along, for general demand to fall off, and to suppose that it will be enough then to check or reverse the downward movement by dealing with its symptoms. Even if we are certain that action initiated at this stage would be successful, — and that

point is still far from being completely established, — the more sensible course would surely be, so far as was possible, to take preventive action beforehand, so that general demand will not fall off ; if this method of approach is adopted, which means turning our attention to the problem of structural change, we will probably find that we are at the same time diminishing the risks of cyclical unemployment. In that event cyclical unemployment is shown to be not a co-ordinate or independent type of unemployment, but, to quite a significant extent, a by-product of the same causes which produce structural unemployment, and therefore removable by the same steps as are taken to deal with structural unemployment.

6. There is, of course, nothing novel in suggesting a connection between technical progress and cyclical fluctuations in employment. The whole of Cassel's theory of the trade cycle is based upon this idea,[1] which also has obvious close affinities with the anti-depression policies now widely approved aiming by one means or another at stabilising the volume of capital goods production. Our thesis is, however, somewhat different. We are less interested in the dependence of cyclical unemployment upon technical progress, as such, than in its dependence upon the failure to reap the fruits of technical progress which is implicit in the failure to redistribute resources of production in response to changes in the technique of production.

7. From this point of view, therefore, we recall our previous discussion of the impact of improvements in technical efficiency upon an industry the demand for whose products is relatively inelastic. Such a change, we attempted to show, will exert an " ejective " power upon some of the resources of production employed in the industry, which, if equilibrium is to be re-established, must be countered by a contrary " attractive " power drawing the now superfluous resources into other industries which can supply the goods or services demanded by consumers with more purchasing power at their disposal in consequence of their reduced expenditure on the goods whose prices have fallen. If the " attractive " power works promptly, everything is satisfactory, the effective general level of demand is maintained, or,

---

[1] *Theory of Social Economy* (1932 edition), pp. 642-8.

in terms of real goods, actually rises, and there is no tendency for unemployment to grow. But if it does not work, *i.e.* if no one is prepared to take the initiative, or to face the risks involved in expanding productive capacity in some other field, or if those who are so prepared are checked by monopolistic counterforces or by the imperfections of the institutional machinery for organising the flow of productive resources into the proper fields, the displaced labourers and the owners of displaced capital are left without any income, and their normal demand for goods and services is correspondingly contracted. The effective purchasing power of those engaged in producing other goods and services is diminished to the same extent, with similar repercussions in still other parts of the economy, the cumulative effects of all of which may easily create a situation very similar to that of a cyclical trade depression.

8. Despite their delicacy, modern economic structures are often surprisingly tough, and it should not be supposed that the argument here outlined implies that balance will be irretrievably destroyed as a result of even the most trifling failure promptly to reabsorb any part of the productive capacity of an economy which some technical change may have left temporarily unemployed. Many changes of this and other kinds are in fact always going on at the same time ; the motives which induce people to expand or contract output are numerous and varied, and in real life the cumulative effects of such trifling failures may easily be overborne or indeed reversed by another set of decisions made by another set of people for another set of reasons. But if technical changes occur more or less at the same time in several important industries, and especially if other strong influences are also at work encouraging other industries to check so-called " over-production ", we then have to deal not with a mild disturbance of little practical importance because it is completely swamped by expansive activities elsewhere, but with much more far-reaching disturbances whose cumulative effects may easily outweigh those of any influences operating in the opposite direction, and ultimately produce something very like a general depression.

9. Until the displaced resources of production are again put to work, technical improvements will indeed produce no net increase of purchasing power. " The increased purchasing power

of other groups is exactly offset by the decreased power of the displaced worker. What these technological developments set free is not purchasing power but productive power ", and slowness in the proper use of released productive power will be all the more natural, and indeed from some points of view justifiable, if, as may easily happen, consumers are a little slow in deciding how to use the additional free purchasing power which the availability of cheaper goods leaves at their disposal. This time-lag means a temporary increase of hoarding, which, if on a sufficient scale, may generate a deflationary trend which, if unchecked, would lead to general depression. Those who determine the volume of output in the industries affected by technical improvement may, moreover, easily over-estimate the quantity which can be sold at prices which, though reduced, are still sufficiently high to assure a normal return. Prices may thus at least temporarily fall below the new equilibrium level, and though the free purchasing power made available for consumers will thereby be further increased, this may again encourage temporary hoarding, while those whose incomes decline because they have over-estimated the demand which they could profitably supply may also on that account prefer to conserve their resources, and postpone some of their normal expenditure until more prosperous times return.

10. Another subsidiary factor which may strengthen the tendency to generate general unemployment of the cyclical type by delaying prompt adjustment to technical change is the credit policy easily, and without any formal or conscious decision, adopted in such circumstances. An appropriate policy would offer credit on somewhat more liberal terms for use in industries which, in relation to the new situation which has arisen, are underdeveloped. If prices fall as a result of technical improvements, a smaller volume of credit will finance the production and sale of a given volume of goods, and the demand for credit should therefore also decline. Some credit, thus released or set free, should then be available for new uses, just as labour and capital are ; the reabsorption of these displaced resources of production may indeed be contingent upon the availability of this displaced credit. There is not necessarily any call here for credit expansion in the ordinary sense (though this might be desirable for other reasons)

but merely for the maintenance of the volume of credit at the old level, some, no longer needed in the older industries, being transferred to the new industries, without any change in general credit policy. In principle, however, such a transfer would tend to depend upon a reduction in the interest rate, and the habits of thought current in credit institutions might well encourage them to believe that this was identical with a credit expansion, which for other reasons they might feel reluctant to permit. So long, however, as they failed to make effective use of the credit now found to be superfluous in the industries affected by technical change, the general effect of their credit policy would be deflationary, and would thus reinforce the tendency towards cyclical unemployment. This tendency towards undue caution in making credit available might be further strengthened, if, as suggested in relation to an earlier point, some of the industries affected by technical improvement had as a whole over-estimated the volume of output of which they could dispose at profitable prices. This would mean that some business units operating within these industries would suffer losses, and if the losses were severe this might appear to impose the necessity for rather more than normal caution in credit policy in general. The outstanding characteristic of wise credit policy in relation to the needs of an expanding economy is a high degree of selectivity. One group of productive activities should be stimulated, while others are damped down. Banking policy in general has never been entirely insensitive to this requirement, but there is a widespread habit which prefers instead to think of *general* credit policy as the main banking instrument for dealing with the trade cycle. General credit policy is, however, an inadequate instrument for stimulating structural adjustments in an expanding economy, and if it were to be supplemented by a more discriminating attitude towards the requirements of relatively declining and relatively expanding industries, it would also have more beneficial effects in ironing out the fluctuations of the trade cycle.

11. We may not be so completely confident of our power to take adequate precautions for the prevention of any recurrence of cyclical unemployment as to deprecate the preparation by wise statesmen of some second strings for their bows to meet the

unhappy but by no means improbable eventuality, that their best preventive efforts may have only imperfect success. That obviously is one good reason for organising unemployment insurance funds, and it is also an adequate reason for working out beforehand plans for public works to be put into operation without the necessity for hasty improvisation. But if we only think of preparing remedial measures to be applied *after* the unemployment virus has infected our economy, we shall have failed to take full advantage of the lessons to be drawn from the experience of the past. If our argument above is sound, we should also, and even from the limited standpoint of the avoidance of cyclical unemployment and the assurance of security, apply our minds directly to the problem of ensuring an expeditious transfer of productive resources, and we should be the more eager to do so, for even a partial solution of that problem would, while it increased the chances of stability in the economy as a whole and of security for the individual, also at the same time facilitate the expansion of production upon which the attainment of higher general standards of living must depend. Unless there is a steady and continuous flow of resources into types of production which poorer economies have been unable to afford, any economy endowed with the capacity for progress will suffer from chronic instability. The search for stability itself thus demands that continuous and increasing attention should be paid to the production of the amenities of life, of things which poorer communities have been in the habit of regarding as luxuries.

CHAPTER VII

BARRIERS TO PROGRESS

1. At this stage of our argument a simple-minded reader might feel constrained to ask why, if the benefits to be derived from prompt adjustment to changing technical conditions are so uniformly good, affording us assurances both of greater stability and of higher average standards of living, the opportunities for enjoying such delectable benefits should not be embraced without hesitation or delay, and without all the pother commonly associated with these trends. The first provisional answer to this question is obvious enough. Prompt adjustment to change may be a condition of stability for the economy as a whole ; the assurance of greater stability for any individual is much less certain, and for many the risks are extremely high. Any man who has gone to a great deal of trouble to acquire valuable skill and experience is threatened with serious loss if he is obliged to undertake new work for which his acquired skill and experience may have little or no value.[1] The individual may thus naturally prefer, as he thinks, greater security for himself to a problematical wider security for the economy as a whole, in which he fears that he personally may not share. And his preference may be all the stronger and more deeply rooted if others are dependent upon him, for whose welfare he has a keen sense of responsibility. " If he followed the instructions of the economists he might indeed be a better member of the greater society, but he would probably be a worse husband and father ".[2] Similar risks, sometimes in an even more acute form, may discourage the owner of capital from facing the readjustments for which we have been asking. " It seems to be ", as a writer in 1890 put it, " in the nature of a natural law that no advanced stage of civilization can be attained, except at the expense of destroying in a greater or less degree the value of the instrumentalities by which all previous attain-

---

[1] " The peculiarities of labour in relation to readjustments form one of the main sources of injustice and hardship in an individualist economy " (Knight, *Risk, Uncertainty and Profit*, p. 346).   [2] Barbara Wootton, *Plan or No Plan*, p. 159.

ments have been effected ",[1] and whether this is properly to be regarded as a natural law or not, the process is inevitably unpleasant for many of the owners of the values condemned to disappear. In any event, for many human beings change of any kind is somewhat distasteful.[2] Moderns sometimes recall with an indulgent smile the alarm provoked in the minds of their ancestors by innovations such as the railway steam-engine or gas-lighting in public thoroughfares. But while we now take for granted innovations which have become traditional and part of our ordinary everyday life, our own attitude to new innovations which threaten to disturb established habits is not very different from that of our ancestors. There is not much to distinguish between the Paris guild of scribes who delayed the introduction of printing in that city for twenty years, the members of the medical profession in the United States who in the 1840s " warned against the bath tub as a producer of rheumatic fevers, inflammatory lungs and all zymotic diseases ", the printers who later led the opposition to lithographic and photographic processes that threatened to compete with them, and the modern bankers who in the United States opposed experimentation with pre-fabricated houses because they held mortgages on about 58 per cent. at 1933 values of all urban real estate, and feared that an influx of cheap modern dwellings would subtract substantially from the market value of existing structures.[3] Nor has such resistance been confined to those who would normally be described as conservative. Even those who pride themselves upon being most " progressive ", and therefore favourably disposed towards change in general, are often conservative in their judgment of the appropriate content of social change, and, as much as any ordinary unenlightened individual, dislike any change in circumstances which demands a revision of attitudes to which they have committed themselves.

[1] D. A. Wells, *Recent Economic Changes*, p. 369. A banker is said to have defined invention as that which makes his securities insecure.

[2] " That the history of inventions is replete with frustrations and protracted delays in the acceptance of innovations which subsequently have proven of inestimable value to mankind " is illustrated by Bernhard J. Stern in a lengthy record of " Resistances to the Adoption of Technological Innovations " in the National Resources Committee's *Technological Trends and National Policy* (June 1937), pp. 39-66.

[3] Bernhard J. Stern, *op. cit.* pp. 48, 49, 58, 59.

2. We should certainly be careful not to assume, as some have done, that the main factor in resistance to technological change is rooted in the ingrained conservatism of those who live by the sale of their labour. In Great Britain, " the hard core of unemployment ", which proved so intractable throughout the inter-war period, naturally attracted attention to the difficulties of large-scale labour transfers. Coal miners and textile operatives could not easily be moved in large numbers either to unfamiliar types of work or to an unfamiliar geographical environment. With this experience in mind many current plans take it as axiomatic that the first condition for post-war labour policy must be to avoid any large-scale geographical movements. Labour transfers create problems of social adjustment which deserve more attention than they have usually received, and no sensible person would, merely for the sake of moving people about, propose large-scale population movements. But even the experience of the inter-war period by no means establishes conclusively the impossibility of persuading more than a small fraction of the British working population to take up new work in new surroundings. Costs of movement are always an important factor, and their significance will naturally be rated all the more highly if, as was so often the case during the inter-war period, movement is not movement from insecurity to security, but merely from one insecure position to another. Any attempt to fasten exclusive responsibility upon one factor of production rather than another will almost certainly be misleading ; if a choice has to be made, responsibility should properly be placed upon the man whose duty it is to take the first step. In adjusting our economic structure, the first step must nearly always be taken by the man who controls capital, and the significance of this truth is not confined to so-called capitalist economies. The historical evidence in Great Britain at least, — and the experience of other countries would no doubt confirm this view, — suggests that the stickiness of capital rather than the stickiness of labour was most responsible for the rigidity of our post-1918 economic structure, interpreted in the sense in which we have been using this term. It is difficult to think of any important case where, provided capitalists were prepared to take the risks of new capital investment, their action

was seriously hampered by any reluctance on the part of labour to present itself for employment at the place where the capitalist wished to start his venture. There were no doubt often difficulties arising from inadequate supplies of certain types of skilled labour, but the removal of such " bottlenecks " called for action of quite a different kind, both in the sphere of education and technical training and elsewhere, which, as we shall see later, constitutes an item of first-rate importance in any programme designed to ensure the simultaneous enjoyment of material progress and economic stability.

3. In any case our problem is misleadingly presented if it is implied that we regard as either desirable or inevitable large-scale wholesale transfers of population. This may in extreme cases be difficult to avoid, and has, of course, frequently happened in the past. People who lived in Australia forty or fifty years ago can easily recall the spectacle of wooden houses being moved about on lorries from gold-mining towns, whose reason for existence had been destroyed by the working-out of the gold seams there, to other areas where the working population was increasing. A decayed mining town is not a pleasant sight, but the difficulties in the way of building up industries in concentrations of population which had come together for the exclusive purpose of gold-mining were often so overwhelming as to receive no serious consideration. It is difficult to believe that either those who were thus obliged to shift, or their children, are not to-day on balance much happier and better off than they would have been if at the time it had been assumed that at all costs employment must be found for them in the places where they happened to be when the gold-mines petered out ; nor, if a different view had been taken at the time, would they now have any reason to thank those who on their behalf were so sensitive to the inconvenience of change.

4. Gold-mining, it must be admitted, is an extreme case. In more normal circumstances adjustments to technical change will usually demand a geographical shift by only a small minority fringe ; modern power developments favourable to industrial decentralisation, moreover, make it easier than it used to be to bring new industries to the existing sources of labour supply, thereby avoiding some of the capital loss of empty houses and

ruined shops and factories. Especially if the matter is taken in
hand at an early date, it may therefore even happen that no one
will be obliged to move who does not actually enjoy the experience. The proportion of the population still influenced by some
of the instincts of the nomad is perhaps smaller to-day than it used
to be, though it would be rash to dogmatise upon this matter.
But even so, there are still many who would not like the prospect
of spending the whole of their working life in the same place and
who, provided that other circumstances were favourable, would
welcome an opportunity for occasional change. The pressure
for large-scale transfers, which quite naturally some people
find very alarming, is less likely to be felt if necessary structural
changes are not too long delayed. The number affected will
then tend to be smaller, and the probability increased that only
those will need to move whose roots are not too deeply embedded
in their native soil.

5. Even if the responsibility for prompt adjustments of
economic structure is agreed properly to rest more upon the
shoulders of the capitalist than of those who have only their
labour to sell, the latter being in general usually prepared to
accept any offers of employment at current wage rates which an
enterprising capitalist makes to them, it must also be admitted
that the capitalist who is quite prepared to take a risk is often
faced with a difficult choice in deciding in what direction an
expansion of investment is proper. The preservation of consumers' freedom of choice in an expanding economy inevitably
means a certain indeterminacy, producing here and there a definite
blind spot. We can confidently predict in general terms the goods
and services which people with rising incomes will wish to buy,
but we can never be quite certain that they will always slavishly
imitate the expenditure habits of those who had already attained
a higher income level.

6. We should not, however, take too gloomy a view of either
the number or the importance of these blind spots. Much work
has been done, both of an academic character, and by business
men concerned with the practical task of analysing potential
markets, which shows the limits often to be quite narrow within
which we can accurately estimate how people with rising incomes

will wish to use their additional purchasing power. " However capricious individual taste may be, the reaction of the major classes of consumption to income changes follow certain norms which make possible a vague forecasting of the responsiveness of future consumption to income changes." [1]

7. But even when such forecasts are carefully made, there is a natural tendency to imitate existing types of production, and if this is pushed too far it may check efficient development. If producers are merely imitative when changes in the structure of production are clearly needed, instead of taking care to make net additions to its volume, they may seek merely to replace goods and services, already satisfactorily provided by other people, a response all the easier and more speciously attractive if the other people happen to be living in other countries whose exports can be checked by tariffs or other restrictions. It is widely believed at the present time, for example, that after the war British agriculture will have to submit to some important structural changes, but the strong tendency to take it for granted that these structural changes naturally imply the exclusion from this country of agricultural imports which other countries have in the past and will certainly again in the future be prepared to offer in quite adequate quantities and at perfectly " reasonable " prices, is significant as indicating a standpoint from which the problem with which we are concerned is too often approached. The question is asked, for example, whether there are any fundamental reasons for the apparent competitive advantages enjoyed in the past by the New Zealand dairy farmer, with the obvious implication that to replace New Zealand butter by British butter might be a sensible course to follow. If it indeed could be shown that by an adaptation of customary British farming methods adequate quantities of dairy produce could be turned out at cost levels comparing favourably with those of New Zealand, there is nothing in principle to be said against so doing, but wherever we have a free choice in the matter, it seems normally to be more sensible to experiment with the production of new things rather than merely to displace existing products which have already reached a high level of efficiency. Where the imitative spirit is strong, the very attempt

[1] Cf. C. M. Wright, *Economic Adaptation to a Changing World Market*, pp. 28-48.

to make structural adjustments merely shifts the risks of relative over-production without diminishing them in the aggregate.

8. These are important considerations about which something further will be said later. They do not, however, go to the heart of the matter. A much more complex problem, failure to grapple with which must mean failure to realise to the full the already existing potentialities of higher standards of living, is presented by the fact that, although capitalists prepared to take the risks inherent in the types of enterprise which material progress demands will on the average usually find it advantageous to do so, to other important groups of capitalists investments of this type may be highly distasteful, because they threaten them with loss. Wherever such groups can exercise power, they will tend to obstruct the necessary structural adaptations, and by various devices check the flow of capital into the proper channels. Capitalists who fear that the competition of new enterprises may be disadvantageous to them will endeavour to prevent others from filling the gaps which the public interest demands should be filled.

9. Two groups are likely to exert an obstructive influence of this kind. Those already operating in the spheres whose expansion would harmonise with the trend towards material progress will naturally dislike inconvenient competition, which may bring their incomes below the customary level, and accordingly take such steps as existing institutions permit to keep competition at arm's length, and, if possible, destroy it altogether, by obstructing the flow of competing capital into their industry.[1] In this group should be included professional men and other purveyors of tertiary products, who also often desire to protect themselves from inconvenient competition by various devices for limiting the entry of new competitors.[2] A second group may find demand for their products falling off as technical change facilitates the cheap production of other things with a highly elastic demand.

[1] " Owners of stage-coaches were among the most active opponents of railroads. They were supported by tavern-keepers along the route of the roads, and by farmers who felt that the introduction of the railroad would deprive them of markets for horses and for hay. . . . In Alaska the drivers of dog teams and those that sold them fish were vigorous in their opposition to airmail service " (Bernhard J. Stern, *op. cit.* pp. 40, 47).

[2] Cf. F. W. Eggleston, *Search for a Social Philosophy*, p. 307 : " Professional codes are recommended to practitioners as ' ethical ', but their rules are often designed merely to conserve material benefits and to protect the members from competition ".

The expansion of this demand inevitably means a decline in the demand for other products, directly or indirectly competitive with them, and the risk of loss may induce the capitalists concerned to attempt to check this inconvenient trend.

10. Our argument thus brings us back to the significance of monopolistic restrictions on production for the growth of a progressive economy. When applied to an industry affected by technical improvements, such restrictions limit the operation of the " attractive " force, which, by maintaining or even increasing employment here, would sometimes keep the labour adjustment problem within manageable limits. These restrictions are, however, even more important when applied to the industries or occupations into which the ejected resources of production should be admitted if the promise of rising standards of living is to be fulfilled. It has become fashionable in many quarters in recent years to take a favourable view of " controlled " monopoly as a factor making for " stability ", but when we consider the immense power of monopoly influences in checking the structural adjustments necessary both for raising income levels and for assuring steady growth to an economy as a whole, the weight of the argument seems to be on the other side.

11. In the last resort responsibility for making or for failing to make the necessary readjustments rests on the capitalist. It would, however, be unfortunate if constant reiteration of his name were taken to imply some wickedness inherent in him which justified discussion of the problem in tones of moral indignation. His errors often have grave and far-reaching results, but we concentrate our attention upon him, not because he is more wicked than other men, but because when he stubbornly refuses to perform his proper function, he converts a characteristic, which in itself might be regarded as no more than a pardonable human frailty, into a grave threat to the effective realisation of the social and economic values which should be within our grasp. Some capitalists are no doubt no better than they should be. It is not, however, always they who are most dangerous. Our course would be much plainer than it is if all capitalists were wicked and justly merited severe moral condemnation. Unfortunately, if we concentrate our fire exclusively upon the obviously selfish and

anti-social activities of wicked men, we may easily overlook other obstructive activities which are morally less reprehensible, but are no less damaging to both economic progress and social stability. The "good" capitalist is sometimes unwittingly a formidable stumbling-block in the path which leads to these objectives. Actuated by the best motives, men of the highest integrity have formulated and supported some of the schemes put forward at the present time, which at best entirely ignore the fundamental economic problem here discussed, and at worst prescribe action of precisely the wrong kind. To place service in the public interest among their avowed objectives is now almost a matter of routine for many organisations which scarcely even attempt to conceal their monopolistic purposes. It would be unduly cynical to suppose that these protestations were not sometimes sincere. But when judged by the real test of their social value, the kind of control of production which they would justify, it often becomes clear that the ends which these schemes would in fact realise would be something quite different from anything revealed by an objective analysis of the public interest. Goodwill may be an essential condition for post-war economic recovery, but unfortunately goodwill is not enough. Certainly no man can safely be trusted to decide the volume of production, which it is in the public interest to maintain, of any goods or services in whose production he happens to be directly interested, and it would be still more rash to leave such decisions in the hands of any group of similarly interested individuals, among whom the average level of highmindedness will normally be lower than that of its most virtuous members. For, human nature being what it is, they will inevitably tend to make an estimate which falls below the appropriate level.

12. Superimposed upon the effects of these elements of resistance is another more general social fact of considerable importance. Even if structural amendments could be completed without any friction, the course of material progress must inevitably change in various ways, which to many will seem highly inconvenient, the relative positions of groups of people occupying different places in the income scale. People in the high income groups may approve in principle of changes which increase the

real incomes of people in the low income groups, especially if these changes at the same time make their own high incomes still higher. The more far-seeing of them may indeed not wish to make any such qualification, and will approve of upward movements of low incomes even if their own incomes remain unchanged, or are perhaps slightly reduced. But a steady supply of some services found very convenient by those who receive them depends on their price being kept quite low. Their price will remain low only so long as there are sufficient people unable to find more remunerative employment elsewhere ; as material progress must mean an increase in the opportunities for more remunerative employment in other kinds of work, the people who have hitherto had no choice but to perform these poorly paid services will become scarcer ; other people will then begin to complain about a " shortage ", *e.g.* of domestic servants, when what they really mean is that their incomes are not sufficiently large to pay the higher market price corresponding to the new supply and demand situation created by material progress, or that they are unwilling to permit the changes in working conditions which even more than wages may explain the shortage. In such circumstances, material progress demands some reordering of the customary modes of life to which people with high incomes have become attached. This prospect is often distasteful to them, and they accordingly tend to take an unfavourable view of the process of material progress itself.[1] It has been convincingly argued that " increase in wealth, and in the means of creating it, should increase purchasing power correspondingly, since human desires are indefinitely expansible and will continue so to be until the last Hottentot lives like a millionaire ". But long before the last Hottentot reaches this agreeable situation, a great many other people (and of them very few will be millionaires) will have dis-

[1] This attitude of mind is well illustrated by the fears sometimes expressed that the encouragement of native agriculture or other activities designed to raise colonial standards of living in Kenya or elsewhere would have inconvenient effects upon the labour supply available for other purposes, and in particular for the benefit of the white colonists, nor are the efforts of well-meaning people to convince the white colonists that their fears are groundless entirely convincing, at least in the short run (cf. H. W. Foster and E. V. Bacon, *Wealth for Welfare*, p. 92). Some inconveniences of this kind can scarcely be avoided ; the important question which demands an answer is whether the convenience of a small privileged group is an adequate reason for refusing to permit adjustments needed for higher standards of living for the economy as a whole.

covered that the improved economic position of the Hottentots and other depressed social groups makes it a physical impossibility for them to maintain unaltered their customary mode of life ; when this is realised, a movement against the further progress of the Hottentots may well be expected. The condition for the realisation of the end postulated that " the Hottentot must produce something that others want and find the purchaser before his desire can become 'effective demand'"[1] is an essential, but it is not a sufficient condition. It is also necessary that the non-Hottentot should be prepared to put up with the loss of some attractive goods and services, which with the new distribution of productive resources will be too expensive for him to buy.

13. This point is indeed the foundation of another criticism sometimes levelled to-day against the whole idea of material progress. " Our main preoccupation during the past 150 years ", it has been said, " has in a sense been with the gradual extension to the poorest members of the population of the luxuries and amenities enjoyed by the rich. . . . Such a method of progression necessarily tends to increasing congestion the nearer the rich and the poor respectively approach the middle of the ladder where the great middle class is already congregated. . . . Perhaps the poorer units after a reconstruction of this kind will still feel themselves to be at the bottom of the ladder, while those at the top will feel that they have been deprived of something which does not appear to have very obviously benefited anyone else. . . . It is scarcely realised how many of the advantages enjoyed by the rich have depended on such things as exclusiveness, avoidance of overcrowding, or rarity — on things the value of which disappears as soon as they become available to the many. At the present day a working-class family of good standing can, within the means at its command, obtain nearly all the ordinary luxuries of food, clothing and entertainment enjoyed by the rich. The main, almost the only, difference is that they must be enjoyed under more crowded conditions and with less personal service, and that they must be waited for until time has deprived them of that exclusiveness which they owe to being innovations in fashion or invention or to the fact of their being produced ' out of season '.

[1] Sir Arthur Salter, *Recovery*, pp. 28-9.

Practically the only luxuries which they cannot enjoy are those in which territorial limitations impose an almost insuperable barrier ",[1] such as garage accommodation and golf-courses. It is physically impossible for many of the elements which play an important part in the standards of living of people with incomes well above the average to be enjoyed by everybody, or indeed by more than quite a small fraction of the population. " We cannot all have motor-cars, because there is no room for garages. In large towns to house a motor-car is as expensive as to house a family." [2] Even if there is no obvious physical barrier, the expansion of output of some of these things on any considerable scale may necessitate such radical alterations in their content that they become something substantially quite different from what they were when other people were first anxious to enjoy them. The urge towards the improvement of one's economic position, it is argued, arises in part from the desire to imitate those who are already enjoying an income higher than one's own. It is not only, or perhaps even to any important extent, more money as such that people want when they aim at increasing their income. They want rather to be able to purchase the same goods and services as they observe those who already have incomes higher than their own are able to buy. The man who can afford only a week's holiday, organised on the most frugal basis, wants to be able to take his wife and family further afield for a fortnight or three weeks ; the man who cannot afford to pay school fees wants his children to enjoy the benefits of education readily accessible to those whose incomes apparently place them in a higher social class ; the man who lives in a crowded slum wants an income which will enable him to live in a residential suburb, and the man who is already living in a residential suburb wants a still higher income which will enable him to buy a week-end cottage in the country, or perhaps ultimately a large country house. But in the very process of raising incomes in general, it is pointed out, the conditions which permit a realisation of these ambitions may be destroyed. There are not, and never will be, enough country houses to go round, and indeed long before physical difficulties

[1] R. Glenday, *The Economic Consequences of Progress*, pp. 168-70.
[2] R. Glenday, *op. cit.* p. 174.

G

have finally checked any further addition to their number, their hopeful owners will discover that they are precluded from getting the same satisfaction from their acquisitions as their wealthy predecessors enjoyed, because the tendency described above will have so diminished the supply of people prepared to earn a modest livelihood by performing menial services in country houses that these structures tend to become white elephants.

14. This is, of course, an extreme case, and the march of material progress might go a long way before the country-house problem became really acute ; even when it did become acute, most people would probably think that its intrinsic importance was insufficient to warrant our attempting merely on this account to check further improvements in standards of living. It is, however, only an extreme illustration of a principle which in its milder manifestations has considerable importance. If everybody had an income which made it possible to enjoy long ocean voyages, the conditions under which the voyages would then have to be made would become much less attractive to many who are already ocean travellers. If everybody enjoys an income which facilitates access to remote beauty spots, such places cease to be remote and may even lose some of their beauty. A wide extension of educational facilities would demand some drastic changes in the customary mode of life of many people with quite modest incomes who, even in their most expansive moments, have never seriously contemplated the possession of a country house.

15. It follows from these facts that, in addition to the changes in economic structure which we have already shown to be necessary if material progress is to be realised, the process of adjustment also demands, especially if progress is on any considerable scale, further structural changes of a different kind in the expenditure schedules of many people who in the first instance have not been directly affected by the impact of technical change. But they in no way justify the view either that material progress is itself a mirage, or that efforts to attain it should be abandoned, as some have been disposed to believe, too much impressed by the possibility that persistent search for higher standards of living may, if too many are successful in the search, show up some of the

elements for which they are striving as mere wills-o'-the-wisp which elude their grasp just as they seem to be coming within reach. The measurement of differences in real standards of living involves some difficult, and perhaps in the last resort insoluble, problems, which are merely concealed when we calculate incomes in money terms, even if we remember to point out that in estimating the significance of changes in money income we must also take into account changes in the general level of prices. And these difficulties are especially great if comparisons are attempted between incomes earned at different periods of time. If, to take a fantastically simple illustration, effective steps were taken to ensure that everybody's real income rose by an amount which, converted into money, was equal to £100 per annum, those whose incomes had risen, say, from £300 to £400 would probably find that some of the things formerly available for people in the £400 income group had inevitably changed their content, and perhaps had disappeared altogether, and so on throughout the whole range of incomes. The real income actually enjoyed after the change had been effected would therefore not in all respects be identical with the income expected. But this certainly does not mean that they would not be better off than before the change was made. The same might not be true of all the higher income groups, but, despite the difficulties of balancing an increase of satisfaction for one man against a decrease suffered by another, it seems on the whole common sense to regard a change of this kind as a case of a higher average income level, even if no one of those concerned ever gets exactly what he has hoped for.

16. As we have seen reason to reject this line of argument as a merely sophistical objection to material progress, it might be thought that we were spending too much time over it. Why in any case, it might be asked, should we worry about the troubles of the owners or occupiers of country houses ? They are as a rule well able to look after themselves, and if they are inconvenienced in certain directions they can usually easily find compensation elsewhere. There is indeed, it may be agreed, no particular reason why we should be specially tender to the sensibilities of country-house owners, but just for the reason mentioned, that as a rule they are well able to look after them-

selves, we should be careful to bear in mind the existence of these apparent difficulties ; the fear of inconveniences of this kind is often another contributory factor tending to strengthen resistance to the processes of adaptation demanded if material progress is to be a reality.

17. We should, moreover, sadly deceive ourselves if we believed that it was merely with the irrational prejudices of the owners of country houses with which we had to deal. Theirs is an extreme case, but it is only one illustration of a widely diffused state of mind. This state of mind is often behind the lukewarm reception so frequently given to proposals for educational reform, and, as we shall see later, also has significant effects upon certain aspects of international economic policy. Striking manifestations of this human weakness might even be discovered in observing the conduct of some who believe themselves to be well to the left in politics, and therefore quite out of sympathy with the owners of country houses. The central fact from which our whole problem emerges is that material progress threatens loss to important groups, who accordingly take such steps as they think will be effective to protect themselves.[1] In so doing they power-fully reinforce any other forces which may be generating in-stability, and thus create additional risks of insecurity both for others and ultimately often for themselves as well.

18. We may repeat that, in pleading for policy consciously directed towards speeding-up the processes of structural adjust-ment, we have no novel or revolutionary ends in view. In these days it may to some people seem a tactical error to admit that our purposes are ancient and respectable ; we might do better to pretend that we had discovered some new and startling truth which in their blindness our forefathers had persistently and stupidly ignored. On the other hand, even for those who are most eager to build an entirely new world there may be some satisfaction in moments of quiet thought in the reflection that in certain respects at least they are not called upon to break abruptly

[1] Cf. P. H. Wicksteed, *Common Sense of Political Economy*, vol. ii, p. 701 : " We, the privileged, must remember that if we are in earnest we are endeavouring to curtail or to abolish privilege. We are throwing open the preserves, and in proportion as we succeed in our endeavours, we and our children will have to take chances in a world that has no special care for us."

the threads of continuity between past and future, which, if history can offer any lessons at all, have hitherto always been characteristic of even the most revolutionary periods. But, whatever we may think about tactics, changes such as we are now proposing should be more carefully organised in the future have in some form or other been a constant element in human history. They have sometimes been slow and almost imperceptible, but they have seldom ceased altogether. At other times they have been extensive and rapid. Judgments about their ultimate social value must depend on philosophical presuppositions which cannot be fully argued here. Romantic devotees of some bygone golden age sometimes deplore the changes which have occurred since their own favourite period. But even if they resent the imputation of sceptics that their nostalgic longings for the past ignore many of the most unpleasant features of life for the ordinary man during the period which they idealise, and that they would probably find the restoration of the past conditions which are so much admired an exceedingly uncomfortable experience,[1] they can scarcely deny that at certain periods the balance of advantage has been definitely on the side of change.

19. What, however, is perhaps even more significant for our purposes is the fact that not only have the changes which we are discussing been a normal feature of human history at almost every stage, but that they have also been taking place on quite an extensive scale throughout the very period when many have been agitatedly discussing whether they were still possible. To judge

---

[1] As a recent writer has put it, " it must not be presumed that ", because markets and prices had little interest for him, and he was spared our contemporary griefs of booms and slumps, " the life of the medieval peasant was either happy or prosperous. Famine sickness occurred at short intervals. Between 1066 and 1322 there are recorded forty-five years in which pestilence was sufficiently widespread to be noted by the chroniclers. . . . In each decade in the century from 1350 there were grave outbreaks of epidemics. Each successive century discovered its own peculiar scourge, the fourteenth bubonic, the fifteenth influenza and the ' English sweat ', the sixteenth smallpox. In the seventeenth century plague flitted to and fro about the country. . . . The medieval countryman, overworked, hungry, ragged, a prey to disease, had little pleasure from existence " (Guy Chapman, *Culture and Survival*, p. 19). " Had industrialisation not taken place, it is possible that, given the improvements in medical science and the consequent fall of the death-rate, England and Wales might have developed in like fashion to twentieth-century Poland, parts of which, owing to the minute parcellation of the soil, have been reduced to a state no better than that of an agricultural slum " (*ibid.* p. 39), to which the author adds the footnote, " It is, of course, improbable that medical science would have improved without the presence of industrialisation ".

by the alarm frequently expressed or implied when the importance of flexibility in our economic structure is emphasised, it might be supposed that a change of occupation was a terrible disaster to be avoided at almost any cost. Casual observation of our circle of acquaintances drawn from any income level reveals, however, a surprisingly large number of people who have changed their occupations, and sometimes more than once, with results which on balance have been highly satisfactory to many of them. Such changes are not indeed to be undertaken lightly, but the number of people who have adjusted themselves in this way during the inter-war period has in every country been quite large. Not all of them have thereby achieved happiness, but the average of both happiness and physical welfare for their children is certainly higher than it would have been if the parents had refused to risk making a change. On balance the troubles of the inter-war period, measured by reference to their effects upon either economic welfare or happiness, have been greatest for those to whom a change of occupation was indicated as a necessity but who for various reasons were unable to make it. Sometimes indeed there is something a little repulsive about the disingenuous sympathy accorded to the unfortunate victims of economic change, for those who are most effusive in such expressions often forget that, by refusing to contemplate any adjustment in their own position which might threaten some of their customary privileges, they may themselves be making much more difficult the position of those to whom they offer their sympathy. If they were prepared to submit to change themselves, the necessity of change for others would often be less pressing, and the changes, when made, would be less burdensome and alarming. Certainly, if we can help in formulating a policy for making such changes easier in the future, we need not fear that materialistic preoccupations are leading us astray from the humane task of providing the conditions necessary for human welfare and happiness.

20. We may note in passing that the validity of this analysis is in no way affected by the prior existence of unemployment in our economy. It has been strongly urged in recent years that the truth of certain economic principles depends upon the prior full employment of the productive resources available. Certain

principles applicable in a state of " full employment " may, it is
argued, properly be ignored if that condition has not been
attained. Whether or not this is ever true, it is certainly not so
of the principles which we have been enunciating. The prior
existence of unemployment may facilitate or make more difficult
the adjustments which are needed, and much of the labour
mobility which is characteristic of a depression is of quite a
different kind from that with which we have been concerned.
The existence of unemployment does not, however, affect the
general character or direction of the adjustments which are
needed, however much it may sometimes influence the adjustments which actually occur. Whether there is already unemployment or not, the presumption is always in favour of directing
productive resources into those channels where they will be able
to produce the goods or services which people with rising incomes
will wish to buy. The resistances to such redirection of resources
will be of much the same kind in either case, and the general
effects of failure to overcome the resistances will be equally detrimental to both material welfare and to economic stability.

21. So far our analysis has for the most part been in quite
general terms, without any attempt to distinguish between
adjustments of economic structure which are purely internal in
both origin and effect and adjustments which become necessary
as a result of changes in other economies, or which have effects
upon other economies elsewhere. In the last resort the problems
of national and of international economic policy are not fundamentally very different, and though there are certain important
and well-known distinctions which justify the special treatment
often accorded to international economic questions, it is always
worth while to press the analysis as far as it will go in general
terms before making any such distinctions. In relation to our
problem indeed, the distinction has great practical importance,
for the increasing power of the machinery of modern states
creates the impression that it is correspondingly easier for separate
states to set in motion action designed to assure security to their
citizens by protecting them from the effects of disturbances
generated elsewhere. States sometimes go so far as deliberately
to attempt to impose upon other less powerful economies the

necessity for structural changes any benefits accruing to the economies which make them being purely incidental. Some of the most significant and disruptive efforts to resist the necessity for change have been made by using the power of the State in these ways.

22. The power of the State is obviously very great, but, even for the most powerful of states, there are limits to it. Those who observe its possibilities from close range, however, easily deceive themselves about its limitations, and it is most notably in international economic relations that the illusion has been widely cherished that stability for one part of an interlocking economy may be maintained irrespective of the impact of instabilities elsewhere. National policy has frequently been directed at the " insulation " of national economies from the effects of world fluctuations, and it will be an important part of our subsequent task to show how such efforts are almost certain to be self-frustrating. It is as true of the world as a whole as it is of any given national economy that ultimately stability in its various parts can be attained only by paying proper attention to the conditions of stability for the whole. It is sometimes assumed that any appeal to this principle must be based primarily upon moral foundations ; we are told that " we must be prepared to make sacrifices " in the interests of the inhabitants of countries other than our own. There is nothing to be said against placing international policies upon a securer moral foundation than has hitherto been usual, nor is there any pre-established harmony to bring the interests of the people of each state inevitably in the long run into accord with the interests of the people of every other state. For the most part, however, discussion of this problem in terms of " sacrifices " does not at all closely fit the facts, and is therefore inappropriate. These so-called " sacrifices " are often nothing more than adjustments which, though slightly inconvenient at the moment they are made, may at a later date and in no very long run give an adequate return in terms of both higher national income and greater income stability.

CHAPTER VIII

THE INTENSIFICATION OF THE PROBLEM OF STRUCTURAL ADJUSTMENT IN THE TWENTIETH CENTURY

1. WE have already seen that the story of both adjustment and adaptation along the lines for which we have been pleading, and of resistance to change with its inevitably stultifying consequences, is both ancient and lengthy. It is, however, often believed that in our own time some special factors are operating with such unusual intensity as to make the whole problem much more acute than it ever was before.

2. In the first place, our very success in providing standards of living much higher than were known in previous centuries has probably at the same time made us more sensitive to the risks of insecurity, both for ourselves and for other people. The more people have, the less willing are many of them to run serious risks of losing anything. In any event, in a poor community fewer difficult transfers of the resources of production will usually be needed, for the proportion of goods and services for which demand is elastic will then tend to be large, so that, without occasioning any very serious inconvenience to anyone, increased productive capacity can advantageously be applied in large measure to producing more of the same things in roughly the same proportions as before. In a wealthy community the importance of relatively inelastic demands tends to increase, while the range of choice is often bewilderingly wide, and as a larger proportion of income is devoted to expenditure upon non-essentials, the scope for fluctuations in demand under the impact of fashion and the influence of advertising in all its forms is correspondingly increased.

3. The improvements in the average income level which have occurred in recent years have, moreover, increased the relative importance of small savings, and this, too, has helped to tip the

scale too far in the direction of preference for " safe " investments.
The orderly growth of an economy is dependent upon the
maintenance of appropriate and changing relations between the
fraction of the community's savings allotted to safe investments
and the fraction in relation to which the investor is prepared to
take a risk. The small investor is seldom in a position where he
can prudently take a risk, and this fact, in combination with others
which have been mentioned, means that there tends to be a disproportionate demand for fixed interest-bearing securities as
compared with equities. The consequences of this chronic disequilibrium in the capital market further intensify the tendency
for necessary adaptations in economic structure to be undertaken
too slowly. If economic activity slows down and prices fall as a
result of delays in making the new investments demanded by
technical change, transfers of income for the benefit of the rentier
who derives his income from fixed interest-bearing securities may
occur on a considerable scale. The distorting effects of these
transfers upon income distribution are well known, but their
effects in further slowing down the process of adjustment are at
least equally important.   " The rentier is likely to be less conscious
of an increase in his income when that increase comes about
indirectly through a fall in prices, than when it is due to a direct
increase of his money income. He may in consequence be less
inclined to increase his consumption and thus automatically save
more.   But the willingness to invest tends to weaken when
commodity prices and profits are falling and the demand for goods
shifting uncertainly, so that the savings may lie idle and prices be
still further affected." [1]

4. The urgency of the problem of structural adjustment also
depends upon the speed and the radical character of the improvements made in the efficiency of production. Where changes are
slow the diversion of resources required may be no more than
corresponds to the normal wastage of labour and capital, so that,
without any direct transfers, it is merely a question of seeing that
the new supplies of labour and capital coming forward each year
are directed into their appropriate channels. The problem will

---

[1] A. Loveday, " Financial Organisation and the Price Level ", in *Economic Essays
in Honour of Gustav Cassel*, p. 410.

be much easier if there is no need for any large number of individuals to change their job.

5. Any statement about the average rate of technical change must in the nature of things be only approximate, but there appears to be no convincing reason for the view sometimes put forward that in future its relative importance is likely to be much smaller than in the past.[1] This suggestion has usually been made in discussions of probable movements in the demand for capital ; if it were sound, it would mean that the rate of economic progress was likely to slow down for " natural " reasons, without any interference or obstruction on the part of human or institutional factors. In the aggregate the volume of technical change in our own time has probably been at least as far-reaching in its influence as all the changes of the early nineteenth century, whose effects have often been dramatised by economic historians. The so-called Industrial Revolution undoubtedly speeded up the tempo of adjustment in a way which, compared with the leisurely pace of most earlier centuries, might fairly be described as revolutionary. But though the pace of change has fluctuated from time to time, it has not on the average perceptibly slackened since then, nor does the evidence at present available suggest that it is likely to slacken for many years to come. There is scarcely a single field of economic activity which has not been and is not being subjected to frequent and rapid changes of technique ; to this fact probably more than to anything else we owe the surprisingly rapid recovery after the waste and destruction and dislocation inflicted by the war of 1914–18. In agriculture, for example, the resources of chemistry, botany, biology, bacteriology and other sciences have been and are still being mobilised to produce new and improved methods of production, which in many directions have entirely transformed the character of agricultural work. Many of the scientific discoveries on which improvements in technique depend were, moreover, in the past almost fortuitous, the result of the uncoordinated work of individual researchers. This has already become increasingly less common ; to-day scientific research is highly organised, and technical improvements are everywhere the object of deliberate and systematic search.

[2] Cf. *supra*, II, 5, note.

6. Much of the scientific work of the past has also not yet found anything like its full range of practical application. The work of popularisation often lags behind the work of discovery, but here too there has in recent years been a marked acceleration. Even if scientific invention were to enter a period of inactivity or quiescence, the stimulus already given to technical change by the knowledge already accumulated would take many years to exhaust itself.

7. So far from the war interrupting the development in technical conditions which will necessitate further structural changes in our economy, we have already seen that in many important directions it is likely to speed it up. There is no reason to suppose that the urgency of the problem of structural adjustment will in any way be diminished at least during our lifetime by any tendency to return to the less exciting technical stability of the sixteenth or seventeenth century.

8. In one other respect, however, the rate of population growth, the conditions of our own time contrast sharply with those of the previous century. It is now so much a commonplace as to be the subject of parliamentary debate that the age structure of the populations of most western countries is now such that, even if there were a quite sharp increase in the birth rate, accompanied by a further decline in the death rate, the rate of population growth in these countries is certain for a lengthy period to be much slower than our fathers were accustomed to, and there is even in some countries an imminent prospect of actual decline in the size of the population. Recollection of a period not so far distant, when we were invited to become alarmed about a trend of exactly the opposite kind, may make us disinclined to share to the full all the alarms which have been widely expressed concerning the probable secular decline of population. Nevertheless the slowing-down of the rate of our own population growth in contrast to the rapid rate of growth still characteristic of countries like India, Japan and the U.S.S.R. does significantly increase the practical difficulties of adapting our economies to the requirements of technical change. For one thing, it diminishes the chances of making all the adjustments that are needed merely by redirecting the new annual flow of productive resources, so that it is unneces-

sary actually to shift labour or capital which has already built up a vested interest in employment or investment of some other kind. " If in the first decade of the present century the number of workers in a given industry became excessive, it sufficed, as a rule, to abstain for a few years from engaging new workers in that industry, leaving the young people entering the labour market to seek their first employment in other industries. The natural expansion of demand from a growing population could be relied upon to bring about equilibrium almost by itself. . . . At present conditions are in many respects different. As far as the increase in demand is concerned, it will not be brought about in the same degree as previously by an increase in population but will rather be the result of a rise in the standard of living. A gradual increase in the demand for more or less the same kind of goods can no longer be expected, but there will be considerable shifts in the direction of the demand ",[1] and this necessitates shifts of labour too on a considerable scale.

9. Errors of investment are also less important if population is growing rapidly. Many " new " countries have at certain periods pushed ahead with railway development, the provision of harbour facilities, of irrigation works and other public utilities, far in excess of anything justified at the time by the size of the existing population. As population increased rapidly, however, it soon caught up with the too rapid growth of capital equipment which had preceded it, and no irreparable harm was done by errors of judgment whose effects happily turned out to be merely temporary. With a slower rate of population growth this safety-valve is removed, and greater care will therefore be needed in the future to maintain the proper relationships between rates of expansion in different fields of capital investment.

10. Through its effects upon age distribution a decline in the rate of population growth may also affect detrimentally the psychological attitude of the community as a whole towards

[1] Ninth Annual Report of the Bank for International Settlements, 1939, p. 12. Similarly, it is stated that in the United States the introduction of automatic looms into the textile industry was so gradual and occurred at a time when the demand for textiles was so increasing that no unemployment resulted, though the saving of labour was much more radical than in the later multiple-loom system, which created serious displacement problems (E. D. Smith, *Technology and Labour* [1939], p. 43).

transfers of productive resources. A rapidly increasing population normally has a relatively low proportion of old people, and though flexibility of outlook and willingness to experiment with new things are by no means a monopoly of the young, on the average old people are naturally somewhat more resistant to change ; their minds tend to be less receptive to new ideas, they acquire new manual skills with greater difficulty, and they will accordingly dislike more the alterations in habits of work and life involved in embarking on some new and comparatively unknown undertaking. A partial explanation of the contrast between the economic history of the U.S.S.R. and of France during the inter-war period is to be found in the fact that in the former country in 1920 only 6·7 per cent. of the population were over the age of sixty, whereas in France the percentage was 13·7. The intensification of this difficulty by the losses of war has already been mentioned.

11. This factor cannot safely be ignored in any realistic analysis of the economic problems of the modern world. It should nevertheless not be supposed that their character is fundamentally changed thereby. The unfilled wants and the unsatisfied desires of a stationary population are just as real a source of potential demand, to which the structure of production must be adjusted, as would have been the elemental needs of those who might have been born but in fact were not. The structural adjustments needed will indeed be different. "Instead of additional bread and potatoes for more hungry mouths, we should provide a greater variety of food for a population receiving better nourishment. Instead of additional hovels, shacks and tenements, we should build houses and apartments of improved design. Instead of bare floors and walls and the most meager household equipment, we might have attractively furnished homes equipped with adequate labor devices." [1] But while from certain points of view

[1] Moulton, Edwards, Magee and Lewis, *Capital Expansion, Employment and Economic Stability* (1940), pp. 168-9. The same authors quote a statement made in 1886 by Carroll D. Wright, then Commissioner of Labor, which indicates the existence of similar alarms about " economic maturity " more than fifty years ago   " The rapid development and adaptation of machinery have brought what is commonly called ' over-production '. . . . The nations of the world have overstocked themselves with machinery and manufacturing plants far in excess of the wants of production. . . . The day of large profits is probably past " (*op. cit.* p. 194).

a slowing-down in the rate of population growth makes structural adjustments somewhat more difficult, it certainly does not make them impossible. Even France, mentioned as illustrating particularly the effects of an unusually high proportion of total population in the older age groups, also shows that standards of living can be raised without rapid increases of population. Its population has been practically stationary for a long time, but during that period the French standard of living has on occasion registered quite substantial improvements. The sluggishness of more recent years is attributable at least as much to other factors as to the stationariness of the population.

12. There is still, however, another and more fundamental respect in which it has been widely believed that our own time so far differs from its immediate predecessors as to demand an entirely new approach to economic policy. The nineteenth and early twentieth centuries, it is argued, was a unique period of expansion for the world economy, because at all times untapped resources were calling for exploitation and development, and virgin country held out attractive prospects to emigrants from the overcrowded western world. Now, on the other hand, it is said, areas available for development on the nineteenth-century model are no longer available ; especially in the more advanced and wealthy economies a stage of " maturity " has been reached, with an inadequate supply of suitable investment outlets. The period of expansionism, in which, moreover, rapid increases of population played an important part, has come to an end, and economic policies which may have been quite suitable when expansion was easy must be replaced by something quite different and better adapted to the new conditions which have arisen.

13. Adaptability to changing conditions is clearly a mark of wise economic statesmanship ; the whole of our argument might be described as a plea for such adaptability on the part of those responsible either for the allocation of productive resources or for constructing and keeping up to date the institutional framework within which this allocation must proceed. It is, however, misleading to suggest that our problems are different from those of our grandfathers because the fundamental character of the economic task before us is something quite different from that

with which the nineteenth century attempted to grapple. Economic development is no doubt a little easier if we can see with our own eyes natural resources visibly waiting to be developed, though it might be observed in passing that the theory that all the world's available natural resources have now been organically linked with the world economy as a whole is difficult to reconcile with the existence of countries like Brazil and the U.S.S.R. But even if there were literally no areas available for further development, the thesis of economic maturity would still be unsound. The real basis of development is always and everywhere to be found in the capacity of human beings to increase production ; this capacity is no less now than in the nineteenth century, when the wheat lands of Argentina and Canada were awaiting cultivation, and migrants streamed forth to the goldfields of California and the Witwatersrand. The practical problem of development is invariably the problem of organising production in response to the probable demand of people with expanding incomes. If population is growing rapidly, there can be little doubt about the wisdom of increasing production of the same kinds as previously satisfied the demands of a smaller population, and supplies of these things will more easily be obtained if new territory is available for exploitation. Great expansion in the production of wheat and wool, of cotton and rubber, was desirable in the nineteenth and early twentieth centuries because the rapidly expanding world population at that time would certainly wish to purchase greatly increased quantities of these things ; happily the resources of Australia and New Zealand, of the United States and Malaya, were waiting to be used for precisely this purpose. Now that there is a less urgent necessity to expand the production of wheat and wool, the direction of wise world development, and with it the place in our production programme where emphasis is most needed, have shifted a little. The resources needed to permit movement in the right direction are, however, available in abundance, so that the fundamental character of world development has not changed, though types of production, in some respects different from those of the past, are now more urgently needed. The scope for what may somewhat inaccurately be described as " horizontal " or " extensive " development has narrowed, and development of this kind is no longer so necessary as it was. There is still, however, practically unlimited scope for " vertical " or " intensive " expansion,[1] and so long as that is so, the theory of economic " maturity " fails to harmonise with the facts.

14. There is indeed one difference of some practical significance between our own time and the preceding two or three generations. Expansion during the nineteenth century was relatively easy because for the most part the newer types of production which it was then generally advantageous to develop did not threaten much serious inconvenience to well-established vested interests.[2] The " vertical " expansion which is now more necessary does, however, threaten a good deal of such inconvenience. While therefore there was no particular reason why vested interests should resist expansion in the nineteenth century, they have tended more and more to be mobilised against the developments demanded by the conditions of our own time. But while important adjustments thus become necessary in the tactics of those charged with responsibility for working out wise economic policy, the fundamental character of the problem with which they are concerned is not altered. The contrast between our own time and its predecessors may therefore be usefully emphasised, if it helps us to identify with greater precision the enemy upon whom, if the ends of further material progress and greater economic stability are to be jointly realised, our attacks should now be directed. It is highly misleading if it suggests that the ends of the earlier period are no longer realisable, and that we must take the victory of the forces of resistance for granted, as something which is in the nature of things and therefore not to be questioned. The geographical frontier towards which the pioneers of the nineteenth century moved has disappeared, or

---

[1] " Extensive " and " intensive " are the words used by Professor Alvin Hansen (*Fiscal Policy and Business Cycles*, pp. 42-6), whose conclusions, however, differ from those defended above.

[2] There were, however, many important exceptions to this. The rapid expansion of cheap wheat production in the New World imposed the greatest inconvenience upon many European farmers, while, in the opinion of one writer in 1890, the opening of the Suez Canal in 1869 " was probably productive of more immediate and serious economic changes—industrial, commercial and financial—than any other event of this century, a period of extensive war excepted " (D. A. Wells, *Recent Economic Changes*, p. 29).

H

become of little practical significance. The frontier of rising standards of living remains, and always will remain ; at all times this much more significant frontier has, so to speak, lain behind the geographical frontier and justified geographical expansion. The changes introduced by the decline in importance of the geographical frontier are not insignificant ; they are, however, trifling as compared with the unbroken continuity in the fundamental character of the economic problems with which we still have to deal.

15. Another characteristic of our own time to which much attention has been paid in this connection is the increasing rigidity of wages and other production costs. At bottom this is only another aspect of our central problem of monopolistic and quasi-monopolistic resistances to structural changes ; in the last resort costs can be kept rigid only if those responsible for charging them can exert some control over the supplies of the services they render or of the goods they produce. The problem of rigid wage rates has often been discussed in terms of the effects upon purchasing power of changes in the general wage level. It is not, however, this aspect which is most important for our argument. We are concerned rather with rigidity in the relations between particular wage levels. Too rigid adherence to customary wage differentials has sometimes checked appropriate transfers of labour from one set of industries to another, and sometimes its repercussions may be far-reaching. The maintenance of wages in the building industry, out of relation to the prices of other kinds of labour, would, for example, seriously limit the effectiveness of a building programme as a measure for smoothing out the fluctuations of the trade cycle.

16. Our analysis has, however, already suggested that in this connection wages should be interpreted in the widest possible sense, to include payments for every kind of work, and undue rigidity in the relative incomes of those who sell their labour by means other than wage contracts may have much more serious consequences than rigidity of wages in the more popular sense of that word. The most important infusion of flexibility needed in our wage structure would affect mainly the relative advantages at present enjoyed by the most highly paid labourers (interpreting

that term too in the widest possible sense), for flexibility here would loosen the general structure of production precisely at the point where the risk of congestion impeding progress and threatening instability is greatest. Nor should we always conclude, if any part of the supply of a particular type of labour remains unsold, that it is necessarily the price of that type of labour which is unduly rigid. Its inability to find a market at the current price may be the result of the maintenance at too high a level of the cost of some other element, whether of labour or of capital, equally necessary for production. Undue conservatism in the practices lying behind distribution costs are perhaps the most practically important illustration of this point.

17. Rigidity in the structure of interest rates creates problems of a somewhat different character. The question of the maintenance of an appropriate relationship between the reasonable expectations of investors prepared to take risks and the returns accruing when risks are small or negligible has already been mentioned. There is, however, another and wider problem arising from the expectations of return from capital investment, which, though sometimes presented in a different way, in fact, as we shall see, leads us back to the theory of a "mature economy", which we have already seen reason to reject. Leaving aside a number of important qualifications, we may say that in a wealthy economy, and still more in a wealthy economy which is rapidly growing still wealthier, a secular downward trend in the equilibrium rate of interest is probable. Despite any abnormal demands for new capital equipment associated with large-scale extensions of new industries, the supply of savings which accumulate more or less automatically, through the medium of insurance companies or otherwise, will then often tend to outrun the demand for capital, if the price paid for capital continues to conform to current standards. A new equilibrium can be re-established only if the normal return on capital investment is allowed to fall, and some would go so far as to claim that in circumstances which are not entirely improbable the equilibrium rate would sometimes even fall to zero or become negative. There are various institutional rigidities, including the prejudices of bankers, which are believed to prevent recognition of this fact,

and the consequence, it is argued, is that the community as a whole endeavours to accumulate savings on a scale larger than investors are in practice able to use. Even where there are no institutional checks on a fall in the interest rate, investors accustomed to something higher refuse to believe that the downward trend will not be reversed. They prefer to keep their money on short term in the expectation of something better being offered later ; the inevitable consequence of such chronic shyness is a chronic tendency to deflation and depression, the price of capital being maintained by methods analogous to those used by the people who kept up the prices of coffee or wheat by burning surplus supplies, or the price of fish by throwing surpluses back into the sea.

18. In discussions of the trade cycle in recent years this approach has been widely adopted. It is largely responsible for the belief that the best method of dealing with cyclical unemployment is to counteract the depressive effects of " over-saving " by stimulating and encouraging consumption. This raises many issues which cannot be fully examined here. It is, however, relevant to question the hypothesis that in a wealthy community there is an inherent tendency for voluntary savings to outrun the limits of investment opportunity. The reluctance of investors to accept downward trends in the normal rate of return which upset their customary expectations is important, and attention to its effects is an obvious corollary from our general analysis. Until, however, we can estimate more accurately the volume of potential investment at present stifled before birth by monopoly and quasi-monopoly controls, as well as the volume which might with advantage flow into fields of activity where the institutions for capital investment are at present lacking or at best highly deficient, it would be premature to assume any chronic disharmony between voluntary savings and real investment opportunities. In both cases the volume is substantial, and if reformed institutions could remove these blockages in the investment stream, we should probably, for as long a time as it is worth while for us to consider, find useful outlets for all our savings.

19. Our argument here is not to be interpreted as a rejection of the entire case for direct action to increase consumption.

There is much to be said for income transfers which have this objective in view. The dangerous consequence, however, of rash generalisation about the significance of " under-consumption " for the trade cycle is that the important contrast between the background of the economic problem with which we shall have to deal immediately after the war and the background of the period when under-consumptionist doctrines were most fashionable, is thereby too easily concealed. The very success upon which we may legitimately congratulate ourselves in controlling the more glaring symptoms of war-time inflation means the piling-up in all countries of large masses of purchasing power which is only temporarily sterilised, and we have not yet discovered any infallible solution for the problem of controlling this purchasing power which will arise when the powerful social and psychological restraints of war are relaxed. The existence of this purchasing power will for some time after the war make any talk about stimulating consumption grotesquely out of touch with the realities of the situation. Hard necessity will demand the much more difficult course of continuing to keep consumption in check, at least until the capital structure of war-scarred economies has been repaired. Already indeed there are some signs of embarrassment observable in the utterances of some who pressed hard for increases in consumption during the last depression, as they realise that the post-war situation will for several years be entirely different, but a full appreciation of this fact is still far from being universal.[1]

20. Leaving aside, however, this special though important case, closer examination suggests that the belief that it is now impossible to convert the voluntary savings of a highly developed economy into appropriate investment forms rests upon little more than a reluctance to grapple with the problem of structural adjustment. Appropriate structural adjustments would remove the alleged discrepancy between savings and investments, and at the same time provide a more stable foundation for permanent

---

[1] The most glaring recent illustration of this dangerous misunderstanding is to be found in J. R. Bellerby's *Economic Reconstruction*, vol. i, *National, Industrial and Regional Planning*, the whole argument of which is built up around the theme that the methods needed to assure full employment " are possible only in a community which has learnt to believe in lavish expenditure " (p. xi).

improvements in the standards of living of the more poorly paid sections of the community. Instead of being offered subsidised cheap goods more or less at the discretion of " authorities " with imperfect knowledge of what the consumer really wanted, they would be able to choose for themselves between the various goods and services offered at the cheaper prices corresponding to the conditions arising from a more abundant supply of capital for all purposes.

CHAPTER IX

THE LESSONS OF THE WAR

1. EXPERIENCE of a war-time economy has naturally raised in many minds the question whether useful lessons might not be drawn from it for application in the different circumstances of peace. Many are not satisfied merely to apply incidental lessons here and there, but look hopefully for more far-reaching programmes of general reconstruction based upon methods similar to those which have been tested as valuable for war. Mr. Henry Wallace, Vice-President of the United States, told us some time back that for the average man the economic problem of the peace was summed up in the question : " If everybody can be given a job in war work now, why can't everybody have a job in peace-time production later on ? " Or, as Mr. Herbert Morrison, the British Home Secretary, has put it, " I can see no sharp distinction in nature between the economic problems of war and the problems of the strenuous difficult peace that lies before us. If control is right and useful to-day, no one can assume that it will be wrong and dangerous to-morrow." [1] One of the incidental benefits apparently conferred by a war economy is " the virtual disappearance of unemployment ",[2] and therewith of industrial insecurity, and it is natural to ask why, if during a war we allow nothing to stand in the way of providing full and often over-full employment for everybody, insisting on using every scrap of our productive capacity, we should not be able, when the war is over, by an adaptation of the methods of war economy, to achieve a similar purpose. In war-time there is no question of an insufficiency of aggregate demand. The government needs much more than it can possibly get of everything essential for the successful prosecution of the war ; its unremitting pressure to increase output of anything regarded as essential keeps aggregate demand up, and thereby also ensures full employment. Why

[1] *Looking Ahead*, pp. 199-200.
[2] H. W. Singer, " Some Disguised Blessings of the War ", *Manchester School*, October 1941.

should it not do the same when the war is over, but with employment directed towards other kinds of production ? The question is not unreasonable, but as it is also in many respects highly misleading, it is important to get as clear a picture as possible of the profound differences between a war and a peace economy.

2. We shall merely mention one vital characteristic of our present war economy, the applicability of which to peace conditions is extremely doubtful, the Lend-Lease principle, whereby many belligerents have been enabled to secure stocks of various essential materials without any question of payment being immediately raised. The significance of this institutional invention will be more conveniently treated when we come to deal with the international side of our problem. In the meantime, attention should be directed to the more general aspects which may make analogies drawn between a war and a peace economy misleading.

3. We may note in passing that it is quite wrong to suppose that in a war economy we find full employment for *all* the factors of production at our disposal. There are large masses of capital equipment which we allow or indeed compel to lie idle, because their output has lost its peace-time importance. Such enforced idleness is properly regarded as an essential condition for the success of the war effort. If this equipment were utilised, other more essential things would have to be sacrificed.

4. There are two other more fundamental differences. The experience of the war entitles us to conclude that if we select a group of commodities, accepted for the time being as of such overwhelming importance that any conceivable output could scarcely satisfy our requirements, we can by making effective an inexhaustible demand for these things, ultimately ensure full employment for everybody. But, — and this is an essential proviso which is frequently overlooked, — we can do this only on condition that no strong resistance is provoked when it is discovered that the production of other things has slackened off and perhaps ceased altogether, and that consumers therefore must go without them. This discovery is certain to be made before very long. It may be delayed for some time while consumers use up the stocks already accumulated of certain products. It may

be further delayed if war activities begin from an abnormally low level of employment, and the allocation of resources to war purposes is not pushed ahead so vigorously as to prevent some parallel allocation of hitherto unemployed resources to the production of other things. But neither of these escapes can remain open indefinitely, and even for an economy like that of the United States or of Canada the primary condition for success in modern totalitarian warfare is comparative indifference to what happens to standards of living.

5. This indifference can never be absolute. To maintain morale some attention must be paid to people's feelings about the sacrifices imposed upon them ; the organisers of war economies never have a completely free hand in lowering the standards of living of the people under their influence. The fact that they invariably feel obliged in their propaganda to elaborate upon the virtues of tightening one's belt suggests, however, the practical importance of the issue. Some people have gone so far as to pretend that war proves that we do not really mind very much the loss of our customary peace-time amenities and comforts, and that our ideas of what constitutes a satisfactory standard of living are thereby shown to need a radical revision. For the immediate purpose in view this line of argument may have a value. If we have to make the best of a bad job, it is no doubt helpful if we can, for the time being, persuade ourselves that things are not so bad as they seem. It may, however, be doubted whether this stoic austerity will survive the return to more normal conditions of production after the war. The necessity for rigid restriction of consumption in the interests of speedy victory is obvious enough, and the ordinary man has no difficulty in understanding it. But while he is prepared for every necessary sacrifice, and may even sometimes be impatient because, in deference to his supposed ignorance of the realities of the situation, sacrifices are imposed too slowly and too timidly, he will not easily be persuaded that it would not be advantageous, when the pressure is relaxed, gradually to get back the goods and services which he has sacrificed ; in other words, that he has not really made any sacrifices at all. Accurate measurement of movements in standards of living is difficult at all times, and never more so than during a

war ; while, however, the losses imposed on different sections of the community vary widely, and some sections, especially of those formerly unemployed, may even be better off than they were before the war, common observation suggests that everywhere war, on a large scale and especially for any prolonged period, inevitably means an uneven, but very real decline in the general standard of living. Where the standard is already high, the losses may to a considerable extent be of products which an austere critic might regard as unimportant, and many who experience such losses dislike making very much of them when they recall the much more serious sufferings being borne in other countries more directly affected by the war. But if the main lesson which war-time experience teaches us about maintaining high levels of employment is that work can easily be provided for everybody, provided that the sentiment in favour of maintaining customary standards of living is not so strong that it cannot be overborne, this is not a very helpful or even relevant conclusion for post-war policy, when our objectives will include the maintenance or raising of standards of living.

6. If we cared to do so, we could, in time of peace, select a different collection of commodities from those which absorb our attention during war, and by again bringing an unlimited demand to bear upon them, again assure full employment for everybody. But just as before, we should have to be relatively indifferent to what happened to the production of other things excluded from our collection. We could get ideal housing at the expense of clothing or transport, or perfect nutrition at the expense of household equipment and education. But if we attempted to include everything regarded as essential for a civilised standard of living, we should destroy the analogy with war-time conditions. If the problem to be solved is the maintenance of aggregate demand, war-time experience shows what can be done by concentrating a practically unlimited demand upon a comparatively restricted group of commodities, and by neglecting the consequences for the production of other things. It does not show how aggregate demand can be maintained if, as in times of peace, we must also take these consequences into account.

7. The confusion in the minds of many popular writers on

this subject frequently finds expression in unhelpful discussions of " sacrifices ". Sacrifices are often desirable and necessary, but general talk about them is not very useful, unless we get answers to the questions, sacrifices by whom ? and sacrifices for what ? It has been argued that the fallacy underlying schemes for the full utilisation of available labour and resources in peace-time by producing armaments and dumping them in the sea, or by building castles and pyramids, is moral rather than economic. " The end in view is not worth while, and people will not be prepared to make sacrifices to attain it. . . . The unemployment problem can be solved in time of war because war provides an aim deemed worthy of self-sacrifice. It cannot be solved in time of peace only because modern civilisation recognises no peace-time aim for which people are prepared to sacrifice themselves in the same way. . . . The economic crisis is in essence a moral crisis." [1] It is, however, by no means easy to determine the exact meaning of " sacrifice " in such a context as this. In time of war we sacrifice, *inter alia*, our standards of living ; and it is largely by so doing that we can under war conditions get rid of unemployment. The argument therefore seems to suggest that if in time of peace we were equally prepared to sacrifice our standards of living, then too we could avoid unemployment by producing castles and pyramids, or other things which no one really needed. The logic is sound, but completely sterile. The ordinary man does not in times of peace want to sacrifice standards of living. Happily there is, as a general rule, no convincing reason why he should ; on the contrary, one of our main and perfectly legitimate peace-time purposes is to maintain and improve standards of living, and as we have seen, we need not fear that large-scale unemployment will be an inevitable by-product of the attainment of this purpose. To talk about sacrificing standards of living in order to avoid unemployment makes sense ; to talk about sacrificing standards of living in order to raise standards of living does not.[2] Anyone who believes that after the war we ought to

[1] E. H. Carr, *Conditions of Peace*, pp. 100-101.
[2] Except so far as the postponement of present in favour of future satisfactions involved in the accumulation of capital equipment may properly be regarded as a sacrifice of current standards of living. But this is usually quite clearly not in the minds of the writers who are here being criticised.

sacrifice standards of living again as an insurance against unemployment should say clearly what he has in mind ; he should not, however, pretend that there is anything particularly " moral " about a policy whose only excuse would be an incapacity to think out clearly the implications of rising standards of living, and to take the steps necessary to clear obstacles out of the way. " Sacrifices " on the part of some individuals and groups are indeed necessary if this purpose is to be realised ; the main object of our analysis has been to show that reluctance or refusal to make these " sacrifices " (which may indeed often turn out to be illusory, if we screwed up our courage and took the plunge) has been a main factor in preventing the attainment of higher standards of living and hampering effective policy for the prevention of unemployment. Vague talk about sacrifices in general, or about the essentially " moral " character of the economic crisis, does nothing to direct attention to the precise points in our economic structure where these so-called " sacrifices " are needed. It unfortunately often has the opposite effect of diverting our thoughts from these unpleasant subjects, and thereby preventing us from seeing things as they really are.

8. The second point in relation to which war and peace conditions are sharply contrasted is that in time of war successful results are (again within limits) dependent upon the success of the authorities in persuading or compelling substantial sections of the working population to change either the character or the location of their work, and sometimes of both, and in imposing a similar degree of mobility upon capital. Industrial mobility on a quite unprecedented scale is a striking characteristic of every modern large-scale war economy. Transfers of working population have created many difficult problems, but the thing has been done, and a careful study of the process would no doubt reveal many highly useful lessons capable of adaptation to different circumstances. But if we could always assume a high degree of mobility of both labour and capital, it would be quite unnecessary to write this book, because the problems with which it deals would almost have disappeared. War-time experience can throw no useful light on the impossible problem, which many people are still setting themselves, of providing remunerative employ-

ment for everybody in the occupation or locality where they happened to be before the war, because the problem which has been solved during the war is something entirely different ; it is quite misleading, — and a harsh critic might even add, a little dishonest, — to suggest the contrary. If people are to be told that by maintaining the institutional inventions of a war-time economy they will all be assured of " full employment ", they ought at the same time to be informed that the " full employment " thus assured will be something entirely different from anything they are believed to be so eager to establish.

9. The importance of this point is indeed realised by some who are anxious to maintain war-time economic institutions, and who accordingly propose to add to the financial and other devices believed to be necessary further machinery for compulsory transfers of labour. But if labour and capital can be either persuaded or compelled to be sufficiently mobile, the case for maintaining the financial devices of war is much weakened. It is moreover mainly the stringent shortages during war-time of urgently needed materials of nearly every kind which make these devices necessary. So long as the period of shortage continues after the war, many of them must be maintained in some form or other, but as soon as the shortages disappear we shall need institutions suitable for dealing with a situation of plenty rather than of scarcity.

10. There is one other significant contrast of a rather different kind which has special relevance in any attempt to assess the real significance for economic policy of the experience of totalitarian economies, by which many people have been unduly impressed. In relation to certain specific limited issues indeed this experience may be of considerable value. A study of war-time experience should reveal much, for example, which is relevant to the conditions making labour mobility easy or difficult ; it has thrown some useful light upon the organisation of distribution, and upon the advantages and limitations of standardisation. But if our interest is wider than this, and we wish to work out general principles of organisation for an economy as a whole, the experience gained is much less relevant, not only for the reasons already mentioned, but also because the nature of peace-time

demand is such as to require the application of tests to the results
of our decisions of a kind which, except within a rather limited
range, is impossible for war-time demands. In an important
sense the people of a belligerent country, united in support of a
war, get what they want, when their governments organise on
their behalf the production of guns, aeroplanes, tanks, submarines,
battleships and other instruments of war. But this sense is something significantly very different from that in which they hope,
when the war ends, to get from a peace economy the things
which they will then want. Broadly speaking, the taxpayers want
the war effort, and pay for it by means of taxes and in other ways.
But very few taxpayers are in a position to express any useful
opinion about the relative merits of different types of gun, or
about the best way of allocating resources as between, say, aeroplanes and submarines. These things are inevitably left to experts,
in whose decisions there must even at the best be a good deal of
trial and error. In the last resort, indeed, no other test than the
arbitrament of battle can decide whether the experts' decisions are
right or not, and speaking quite strictly, neither victory nor
defeat itself can settle the question. For the country which is
defeated may have been so intrinsically weak that no conceivable
allocation of its resources could have provided a war equipment
sufficient to ensure victory, and no one can ever test the hypothesis
that the victorious country might have won the war more quickly
if its resources had been allocated in different proportions. The
task of a government at war is indeed essentially an economic
task, for in choosing between aeroplanes and tanks, for example,
the relative scarcity of all the elements needed for their construction has to be considered, and at the same time the minimum
amount of resources needed to maintain the minimum standard
of life for the civilian population consistent with efficiency must
also be calculated with the same facts in mind. But in the last
resort there is, except under certain limited conditions, no
economic test which can ever tell us the appropriate proportions
in which we ought to have distributed our available resources
between the different types of equipment or production necessary
for war. Totalitarian economies bent on unremitting preparation
for war may indeed enjoy considerable advantages when war

breaks out over other economies who have been less eager to equip themselves for this purpose, just as a man who devotes all his attention to scientific research is likely to be a more efficient scientist than one who devotes most of his time to sport or poetry. For general peace-time economic policy, however, economic tests are essential, as otherwise we are unable to tell how far consumers' demands have been satisfied ; just because in the nature of things there can be no final economic test of the effectiveness of totalitarian preparations for war, experience drawn from this source can have little value for the broader issues of peace-time economic policy, though in relation to certain more or less technical questions we may get a few useful incidental lessons.

11. If we want to win battles, it is obviously essential to establish as nearly as possible the right proportions between, say, the number of fighter pilots, the number of naval gunnery officers and the number of parachute troops. There is, however, no economic means for determining whether the actual proportions are correct or not. If we want a higher standard of living, it is equally essential to have the proportions right between, say, the number of electrical engineers, the number of journalists and the number of dairy farmers. But here we have an economic test at hand to tell us whether the proportions are correct or not. In the last resort consumers' demand, expressing itself through the price mechanism, shows whether we have produced too much or too little of any particular skill or any particular good or service. The experience of an organisation which by its very nature is precluded from applying any such test can afford little help in a situation where success or failure can be judged only in the light of this test.

12. It is indeed not surprising that many of those who are most eager to maintain the general structure of a war-time economy in times of peace are, in fact, often quite contemptuous of consumers' demand. Some attention, they would admit, must no doubt be paid to it, as is indeed necessary even in time of war, but to a significant extent they contemplate making independent decisions, which consumers will have to accept, whether they like them or not. We have already made some references to the

desirability in certain circumstances of controlling or directing consumers' demand, but even the most far-reaching interpretation of the principles which have been suggested in that connection would still fall far short of what often appears to be contemplated in adapting war economies to peace-time purposes.   During a war consumers are in general quite prepared to accept what the authorities think will be good for them ; they grumble sometimes, and even on occasion agitate vigorously for bigger supplies of types of war equipment which they think have been unduly neglected.   But for the most part they are well aware that, on account of the inevitable limitations of their knowledge, their opinions on such subjects can have little value.   Their attitude to what they would like to consume in time of peace may reasonably be expected to be rather different, and it would, therefore, be dangerous to assume that machinery which is acceptable and even essential when practically all demand must necessarily be controlled, and sometimes controlled in great detail, will be equally acceptable under entirely different circumstances.

CHAPTER X

A PROGRAMME FOR STRUCTURAL
ECONOMIC ADJUSTMENTS

1. CAN we now attempt to outline a policy for making structural adjustments easier and less burdensome than they have sometimes been in the past, and especially in the recent past ? No such policy is likely to be simple. There are no simple panaceas in this field ; we should seldom go far wrong in writing off at once as a charlatan anyone who pretended to have an infallible simple solution for our problem, and charlatans are not always less dangerous because their intentions are good. The problem is complex, and complex problems seldom have simple solutions. But many of the elements of the solution may be quite simple, and though complete success may demand coordinated action all along the line, a partial, but still useful, success might nevertheless be registered by applying independently some of the more simple elements. Nor should we dissipate our energies in futile discussions as to which of a number of remedies should first be applied, if all of them would in varying degree be useful. Probably we all have our own particular hobbies in this connection, and to press strongly the hobby which happens to appeal to us most will cause no serious harm. But we should be careful in so doing to avoid sabotaging the efforts of others, if they too can make useful contributions to a comprehensive policy.

2. It is unlikely that we can expect a great deal from mere changes in the habits of thought of important social groups, much as such changes would help. In the broadest sense some kind of " intervention " is necessary. It may take the form either of direct action by the State and its various instrumentalities, or of changes in the institutional framework which, consciously or unconsciously, will influence the decisions made by the individual members of the economy. The value of intervention of either kind should be judged by its suitability for encouraging structural changes in conformity with the requirements of a growing and

expanding economy. We have in recent years become familiar with intervention of both kinds, but too often their effects, and sometimes even their deliberate purpose, have been to facilitate effective resistance to the structural changes. In contrast with intervention of this kind, each of the proposals suggested below is designed to reverse the too common practice of the recent past by creating conditions which will make change and structural adaptation easier instead of more difficult.[1]

3. With some slight but not misleading inaccuracy, we may suggest an analogy here with the path pursued in recent years in the treatment of certain diseases. In the more remote past, unfortunate individuals just contracted these diseases, went to hospital, were cured or died. By itself this was clearly not a very satisfactory procedure, and later the hospital treatment was sometimes made more effective by the invention of some kind of injection which more or less ensured recovery. At the next stage it seemed more prudent to anticipate hospital treatment by precautionary immunisation, and those who submitted to it did not contract the disease at all, or suffered from it only in a mild form. For many diseases, however, whether or not immunisation was wise or effective, the most important predisposing cause was found in bad housing, primitive sanitation, tainted water supply or impure milk. Where this is so, the most sensible starting-point for a campaign against disease is direct action against these evils. Much the same story might be told of the social diseases of poverty and unemployment. We are no longer satisfied with mere hospital treatment of the unfortunate, and many of the suggestions now being actively canvassed are in effect equivalent to proposals for general immunisation. Without in any way decrying the value of immunisation, our interest in this study is, however, much more with strictly preventive measures directed rather towards the improvement of the social water-supply and

---

[1] The English language is unfortunately not well equipped with adjectives for conveniently describing this contrast. The Germans are rather better off in this respect, for Professor Röpke has labelled the two types as *gleichsinnig* and *gegensinnig*, terms for which no concise translation seems to be available. Professor Staley has suggested "adaptive" and "anti-adaptive". Or, alternatively, we may contrast *Anpassungsintervention*, intervention designed to facilitate adaptation to changing conditions, with *Erhaltungsintervention*, intervention designed to facilitate the maintenance of the *status quo*. The programme outlined in this chapter is a programme of *Anpassungsintervention*.

sanitation system. We shall not entirely ignore immunisation, but our interest in that subject will be mainly to determine how far ill-considered immunisation runs the risk of holding up improvements in the water-supply. We are entitled to ask any reader who may be disappointed that we do not pursue this subject further to reflect that in practice there is likely to be ample room for both types of policy, and that it would be short-sighted to suppose that either was necessarily competitive with the other.

(a) DIRECT CONTROL OF TECHNICAL CHANGE

4. The various elements to be combined in such a policy might be expounded in a wide variety of orders. The order suggested by our previous analysis of the nature of the problem is probably as convenient as any. We saw in the first place that the problem of adaptation was likely to be most difficult when technical changes first affected parts of the economy where an " ejective " influence upon labour was generated before the counterbalancing " attractive " factors got properly to work. This suggests the possibility of directing policy first towards the point where the motive force stimulating technical change is generated, *i.e.* towards the scientific discoveries upon which technical change is based. New discoveries in science, which to the scientist may appear of equal interest, may often have quite divergent economic implications, and this fact perhaps offers us a more promising field for fruitful co-operation between " natural " and " social " scientists than those in which scientific leaders with vague yearnings for such co-operation have hitherto rather fumblingly and ineffectively made their preliminary surveys. It is, of course, by no means easy to predict the directions in which scientific discovery is going to break out in either the near or the remote future ; even those most eager for the " social control " or direction of scientific research will probably agree that some spontaneous outbursts are both probable and in the general interest. But equally those who insist on maintaining freedom for scientific research must admit that scientific discovery, whether pure or applied, is not like the wind, blowing where it listeth. It has frequently been subjected to powerful influences

eliciting a growth of knowledge of certain kinds or in certain provinces of science more rapid than in others.[1]   These influences can scarcely be rendered entirely impotent, nor can they safely be ignored, but there are good reasons for modifying them, or supplementing them by taking conscious account of the extent to which the alternative choices presented to scientific researchers are likely to affect the production of commodities or services for which demand will probably be elastic.   Already, and not only for purposes of war, the State exerts considerable influence upon the distribution of the available supplies of scientific inventive capacity.   Hitherto neither the State nor the other organs and institutions which provide the finance for scientific research have taken much account of this economic factor.   If they could be induced to do so, the problem of structural adjustments in our economy would still be far from being completely solved, but it would certainly become more manageable.   Entrepreneurs who themselves engage in large-scale research already no doubt take this factor into account, for it is obviously to their interest to encourage invention in connection with products for which an elastic demand is likely to be forthcoming.[2]   But in so doing there is seldom much inducement to extend the range of their vision beyond the particular products in which they are directly interested.   As we have seen, an elastic demand for some particular product is quite consistent with an inelastic demand for a group of substitutable products of which any given entrepreneur's is only one.   From a broader point of view, and especially from the point of view of a rational redistribution of productive resources, the reactions upon other substitutable products should also be taken into account.   Both the social and the economic effects of labour-saving inventions will be quite different according as their impact falls mainly upon particular employments where unskilled labour is already over-plentiful, or operates more generally within an economy where unskilled labour is, on account of other technical and social changes, already becoming scarce.[3]

[1] Cf. J. Huxley, *Scientific Research and Social Needs*, pp. 211-15, 254-9.

[2] This factor was obviously in the mind of Henry Ford when he abandoned his early interest in watches and turned his attention to cheap motor cars.

[3] The effects of inventions designed to create or expand new types of consumers' demand are also relevant to a discussion of this point. Cf. *supra*, V, 9 and note.

(b) DISCIPLINING CONSUMERS' DEMAND

5. We have so far paid little attention to such structural changes as may be called for in response to spontaneous changes in consumers' demand. They have much the same character as those already discussed, but for reasons already outlined it is not necessary for our purposes to give them special attention. A practical programme should not, however, ignore the possibility of influencing these changes in ways which might diminish the risks of instability. If we belonged to a race of robots, it might even be possible entirely to eliminate structural changes due to this cause by compelling consumers to take what the authorities thought good for them, and thereby keeping changes in their demand within such limits as were unlikely to create any problem of structural adjustment. Happily the human race is not·a race of robots, and even where consumption is most rigorously controlled, at least some slight attention must be paid to what people themselves really want. Change is not, however, necessarily a good thing in itself. Human welfare was not appreciably diminished when motor-car manufacturers abandoned the practice of producing a new model every year, and we could with no serious loss do without many of the fluctuations of demand which occur in response to the allurements of advertisement. The capriciousness of demand which satisfies a mere whim, rather than the genuine desires of consumers with well-grounded standards of taste, is a de-stabilising factor with which our economy could with great advantage dispense. To discipline tertiary consumption (which is by no means the same thing as restricting it) with a view to a wider appreciation of genuine cultural values is an educational task which would at the same time bring substantial economic gains.[1]

6. While, moreover, it is a mark of a well-ordered economy to offer consumers a wide range of choice, circumstances are easily conceivable, and may be practically important, where some narrowing of this range would actually on balance make more effective the freedom of consumers to get what they really wanted. To say that " undue change and an undue variety of products

[1] Cf. G. Chapman, *Culture and Survival*, pp. 231-43.

impede production more than almost anything else " [1] is perhaps an exaggeration, but a greater measure of standardisation, especially in, though not necessarily confined to, some of the instruments of production which do not themselves directly satisfy the final consumers' demand, would lower production costs and tend to remove some of the instabilities in the productive process. There is already a considerable literature on this subject,[2] which need not be pursued further here except to point out that an inevitably complex problem of structural adaptation might be handled more effectively and expeditiously if some of its less necessary complications could be removed.[3]

(c) THE SOCIAL INSURANCE APPROACH

7. The next item on our agenda for treating the problem of structural change contemplates no action directly designed to affect either the direction of the reallocation of resources or the actual process of reallocation itself. Here we merely endeavour to soften the impact of change for those upon whom otherwise it might fall unfairly with devastating effect, so that they shall not be innocent victims blindly sacrificed for the general good. This, the so-called " social insurance " approach to the problem of social security, is probably the most familiar. Much attention has been devoted to it in many countries in recent years, and the controversies centring around the Beveridge Report have placed it in the forefront of the public consciousness.

8. The chances of a changing world have often plunged many inoffensive people, who cannot reasonably be asked to assume responsibility for the changes of which they are the victims, into a position where it is a matter of the utmost difficulty to find employment in the trade or occupation to which they are accustomed or for which they have been trained, or indeed sometimes

---

[1] Sir Thomas Barlow in Julian Huxley, *Scientific Research and Social Needs*, p. 128.

[2] See, for example, the bibliography at the end of George Soule's article on " Standardisation " in the *Encyclopaedia of Social Sciences*, vol. xiv, pp. 319-22.

[3] " Standardisation in many commodities is a liberating force, and does not impoverish life aesthetically. In other commodities it does, and there we must avoid it. . . . Even with products where variety is desirable, you may need standardisation of raw materials and processes ; the variety emerges in the manufacture " (J. Huxley, *Scientific Research and Social Needs*, p. 130).

in any trade or occupation at all. Left to such meagre resources as they may have accumulated in better times, or to the generosity of their friends, or to public charity, the situation of these people would be a standing reproach to any civilised society, which obviously has at its disposal resources for producing in adequate supply most of the things needed for at least a modest standard of living for them. Faced with this reproach, many modern societies, though often in an unduly niggardly and cheeseparing fashion, have created institutions designed to ensure to the victims of economic change the means for maintaining at least a minimum level of subsistence for themselves.

9. This principle is now admitted in most of the more advanced economies of the world and even in some whose average standard of production is still well below the higher levels attained by the more wealthy countries. Sir William Beveridge has proposed for Great Britain considerable extensions of this principle to cover the numerous cases who hitherto have fallen outside the defined limits of the beneficiaries of insurance funds, and to ensure that payments, while still far from lavish, should be on a somewhat more generous scale.

10. For our purposes it will be most useful first to look at social insurance in a wider perspective, which may help us to relate fluctuations in the working activity of individuals with fluctuations in the aggregate volume of economic effort. Caution is necessary in drawing analogies between the activities of individuals and the activities of societies ; nevertheless, the intrinsic nature of social problems may sometimes be illuminated by using them. Cautious people are sometimes a little hesitant about according whole-hearted support to vociferous demands for " full employment ", for occasional personal experience of what, on the face of it, seemed to be full employment in its most obvious meaning suggests that it is not a very comfortable condition, nor one that it would be pleasant to prolong indefinitely.[1] Even a man fortunate enough to find complete satisfaction in the pursuit of a task chosen for its own intrinsic interest does not

---

[1] Some aspects of English life in the latter months of 1943 have suggested that it might be prudent, in the interests of a low death-rate, to postpone the permanent attainment of any exaggerated form of full employment until we were better equipped to deal with influenza epidemics.

usually want to be tied down to it for every hour of his working life. In an ideal situation an individual would combine work which can be enjoyed for its own sake, but can also be dropped when it is found convenient to do so, with an income so distributed over time as not perceptibly to vary in any close correlation with the degree to which the income-receiver is in " full employment " or is enjoying his relaxation. He is thus able to enjoy periods of slackness, without any risk that they would also be periods of abnormally low income. Whether or not the organisation of work is ideal, many are obliged for many practical reasons to vary the intensity of their work from time to time, or sometimes to drop it altogether ; such periods of partial or total " non-employment ", whether enforced or voluntary, need cause them no inconvenience or embarrassment provided that their incomes are continuous, as for most salaried persons they usually are. Indeed one of the great attractions of the better paid posts is the opportunity they usually afford for " non-employment " of this kind.

11. The organisation of work in a society is far from ideal, but there too we might visualise conditions where it accorded with the general convenience to permit or even to insist upon substantial fluctuations over time in the volume of work performed. Except in relation to certain well-established social habits, such as the week-end cessation of work in most industries, the enforced leisure which is a by-product of such fluctuations unfortunately tends to be concentrated disproportionately upon a comparatively small section of the population, and concentrated, moreover, in such a way that those who cease work usually at the same time cease to have any income. Unemployment insurance may be regarded as an attempt to assimilate the condition of a society in such a situation to the condition of a more fortunate individual. At the best it will do so very imperfectly, because for a variety of reasons the income assured to unemployed persons is likely to be substantially below the average income level of those still at work. The principle is nevertheless important. Fundamentally there is no more sense in insisting that everyone should be busily engaged in work than there is in insisting that any individual should remain hard at work the whole day and

every hour of the day. But just as a sensible individual may properly aim at getting work on terms which assure him a steady income despite the occurrence of periods when he is not actually working, so there is sense in insisting that people temporarily deprived of work by changes generally accepted as in the public interest shall not on that account be deprived at the same time of their incomes. An individual in this happy position redistributes his own income, transferring for use in the periods when he is not at work part of what he has earned while at work. By social insurance a society aims at doing much the same thing, except that here the enjoyment of income while not at work is by an individual different from the one who earned the income, part of which is redistributed.

12. Social insurance is essentially an instrument for income redistribution. The extent to which this process can safely be carried depends on the extent to which it may affect the willingness of the various groups or individuals concerned to continue the efficient performance of their appropriate functions in the economy of which they are members. Two main groups must be considered : those who on balance are contributors to the funds, and those who on balance are beneficiaries. The reactions of the former are clearly in large measure a part of the wider question of the general effects of taxation ; further examination of the problem may therefore be postponed until we deal more specifically with that issue. In any event, the extent to which taxation can be used for social insurance purposes is closely tied up with the average level of income from which taxes have to be drawn. Even if, as has been suggested earlier, a relatively high average income level may in certain respects make the problem of structural adjustment more difficult than it used to be, by increasing our sensitivity to the risks of insecurity, it also at the same time makes it easier by means of income redistribution to provide adequate insurance against these risks.

13. The danger that net contributors to social insurance funds will be discouraged by their obligations from the efficient performance of their functions is usually less than they think, and nearly always less than they say. The human race has a remarkable resilience and capacity for adapting itself in the long run to

new conditions ; within limits we may trust to the beneficial effects of the gradual disappearance in the course of nature of those who cherish fond memories of the times when taxation was lower. To anyone who enjoyed a large income when income tax was only 1s. in the £, a tax of 10s. may appear an intolerable imposition to be removed at the earliest opportunity. A younger man with a similar income who has never paid less than 6s. 6d. is unlikely to feel such genuine deep indignation. As a consequence of our unfortunate preference for old and middle-aged politicians, the proportion of those with whom the immediate responsibility for political decisions rests who can actually remember the " good old days " when taxation was relatively low is much higher than the proportion of the population as a whole with similar lively memories. But though the limit is elastic, it is also real. If we push too far, we may discourage the efficient performance of essential economic functions, and thereby incur a risk of decline in national income. In the interests of assured incomes for the victims of change or unpredictable hazards, some of us might be prepared to run the risk of decline in the aggregate volume of production. It would, however, be rash to apply this principle too energetically ; if production fell too far, some who were formally assured a share in a redistributed but smaller aggregate income, might nevertheless find themselves on the whole worse off than before.[1]

14. One further aspect of the contributory principle deserves mention. Starting with the pioneer Wisconsin unemployment insurance law of 1932, United States practice has tended to favour a system which aims not only at providing for the payment of benefits to unemployed persons, but also at giving employers a direct stimulus to regularise employment. Employers' contributions were accordingly varied in accordance with their experience in stabilising employment within their own firms, and in thirty-nine states this principle of " merit rating ", or " unemployment compensation experience rating ", was adopted in a variety of forms. Usually the whole or a part of an employer's contribution was credited to his account, and the ratio of the excess of con-

---

[1] For a further discussion of this issue in its relation to international competition see *infra*, XVI, (*d*) (v).

tributions over benefits paid to his employees to his average annual pay-roll was to be used as the basis for modifying his rate of contribution in a subsequent period. Most of the United States unemployment insurance laws are of too recent date to permit the accumulation of much experience of the actual working of this principle, for by the end of 1940 adjustments of employers' contributions had occurred in only four states. On the whole the experience appears to have been disappointing ; [1] the adoption of the principle necessitates elaborate record-keeping and complex administrative operations, and the administrative complications have apparently seemed likely to be such as to discourage British expert opinion on unemployment insurance from giving the idea much serious consideration. To some extent, however, the same principle is involved in proposals for extending the practice of relatively long-term wage contracts. " The State ", it has been suggested, " could intervene . . . by imposing financial sanctions, such as a double rate of social insurance contributions in respect of all workers not on long-term contracts, and penal taxes on fluctuations in numbers employed in the preceding three years, always saving cases where this was conditioned by such unavoidable causes as climate." [2]

15. The position remains to be considered of those who are on balance beneficiaries. Opposition to unemployment insurance or other forms of relief on a generous scale has frequently been based on a fairly widespread fear that, if even quite modest incomes were made available without the necessity of performing any work in return, large numbers of people would at once seize the opportunity to live in idleness. It was believed, in other words, that the fear of poverty was an essential condition for the efficient performance of work. Human nature is extraordinarily varied, and there are certainly some people of whom these fears may be justified. But, and especially if certain precautions are taken, which are a normal part of most efficient unemployment insurance systems and are retained and strengthened in the Beveridge plan, the abundant evidence now available of the working of these schemes suggests that in general the fears were

---

[1] Cf. *Security, Work and Relief Policies* (National Resources Planning Board, 1942), pp. 335-7.   [2] *The Times*, March 2, 1943.

grossly exaggerated,[1] though the maintenance of a fairly wide gap between the most generous unemployment relief payment offered and the average income level of people in employment is mainly, and perhaps rightly, due to the feeling that it might be dangerous to tempt people too far in this connection. When, moreover, one takes also into account the incidental favourable reactions upon productive efficiency in general, which, especially in the long run, may be very substantial, of the assurance of higher standards of health and education, and of the disappearance or at least the contraction of fears of unforeseen disasters, the conclusion seems reasonable that the net effect of an inclusive unemployment insurance system upon the productive efficiency of the beneficiaries, actual or probable, is likely to be good.

16. These considerations, however, bear only indirectly upon our main problem. We suggested at the outset that the " social insurance " approach, as ordinarily understood, was not directly concerned with facilitating changes in economic structure, and merely attempted to mitigate the impact of change upon its more unfortunate victims. This, of course, is not wholly true, for a well-contrived insurance scheme usually also makes some provision for the " reabsorption " of its beneficiaries in ordinary remunerative work. Even, however, if it were wholly true, it would still be of interest to examine the indirect consequences of unemployment insurance upon the redirection of the resources of production indicated to be desirable by the course of technical change. Is it likely to impede desirable transfers, to accelerate them, or might its effects in some circumstances be entirely neutral ?

17. The distinction between those who are mainly contributors and those who are mainly beneficiaries is again useful here. Little, however, need be said about the first group. The risk which we have to examine in this context is less that they may altogether abandon the performance of their normal functions, than that their standard of efficiency will be low, because the rewards likely to accrue, in the event of taking a successful

---

[1] " Actually reluctance to undertake work has been due to the difficulty or expense of moving to new employment rather than to a preference for idleness " (A. L. Bowley, *Journal of the Institute of Bankers*, April 1943, p. 57).

chance, seem to them, after deductions for income redistribution have been made, so unattractive that, taking into account the risks of loss if a venture fails, they will on the whole tend unduly to avoid risky enterprises and follow always what appears to be the safe path. If too many business men follow the safe path, an inadequate proportion of the community's savings will be applied to the more risky enterprises which are a condition for rapidly rising aggregate incomes. The discussion of this point will be taken up again at a later stage.[1]

18. The question remains of the probable effects of unemployment insurance upon the willingness of the beneficiaries to change their occupations in response to the requirements of an expanding economy. In estimating the wisdom of facing the risks inherent in a new employment, a man will naturally take into account not only the relative attractiveness of the money incomes offered in return for the old work and the new, but also any incidental benefits in the way of pension rights, security of tenure, unemployment benefit or the like, which may be associated with either. If a change of employment involves the sacrifice of substantial benefits of this kind, labour mobility will almost certainly be impaired. Mobility, of course, is not necessarily a good in itself. In certain circumstances there may be too much of it ; Soviet propaganda against the " grasshoppers " who wandered irresponsibly from factory to factory had no doubt much justification, and firms which have established pension schemes with the object, among others, of reducing wasteful labour turnover, were often quite right in so doing, both from their own point of view and from that of the general welfare. But schemes of this kind may also tend to keep attached to the particular firms or industries for which they are set up a number of people whose employment somewhere else would, especially in times of rapid change, be more in the general interest. This was one reason justifying an expansion as rapidly as possible of experimental unemployment schemes which had applied in the first instance, as in the original British experiments, to only a few industries. If there is already any undue reluctance in any industry to seek new employment elsewhere, that reluctance will be intensified by any insurance

[1] Cf. *infra*, X, 36.

scheme which does not include, in addition to the industry in question, any other industries to which transfers of labour ought to be encouraged.   An unemployment insurance scheme which covers even all wage-earners may be a deterrent to some who would otherwise face the risks of working on their own account, for by working on their own account they deprive themselves of the protection afforded by unemployment insurance, so that in this respect too the Beveridge proposals mark an advance on previous British practice.   The practical importance of this point may not indeed be very great.   If the employments excluded from the scope of unemployment insurance are such that there would normally in any event be little inducement to enter them, this particular check to mobility might be regarded as negligible, and this was probably for the most part true of the pre-Beveridge British system.   A good deal might also depend on the details of administration.   A nominally all-inclusive scheme might still be so administered as to penalise in certain circumstances men or women who changed their employment, by obliging them to sacrifice certain accumulated rights which had accrued to them in a previous employment.   There are advantages in removing even the slightest check of this kind to mobility, especially when the forces operating in the other direction are strong.

19.   The same principle applies to the effects of unemployment insurance schemes which are geographically limited.   A United States investigation found that " persons with initiative who through circumstances beyond their own control have fallen on relief in one state are afraid to leave such assistance in search of employment elsewhere for fear of losing their settlement rights ",[1] and this fact has been used to support the plea for a federal policy in that country.   Similarly there was much discussion during the last twenty years of the discouraging effects of differences in social insurance benefits upon emigration from Great Britain to the Dominions, and the same point has been made in discussions of the Beveridge proposals.[2]

---

[1] Report of the Select Committee to Investigate the Interstate Migration of Destitute Citizens (House of Representatives, Washington, 1941), p. 4, cit. *Security, Work and Relief Policies* (National Resources Planning Board), p. 355.

[2] *E.g.* by Lord Barnby, who suggested in the House of Lords on May 25, 1943, that it would be difficult to get people in Great Britain to consider migration to the Dominions

20. The more inclusive an unemployment insurance scheme is the better it is, therefore, in reference to its effects upon mobility, and judged by this criterion also the Beveridge proposals are ahead of the pre-Beveridge practice. Upon some indeed the effect of the rather more generous benefits proposed may be to encourage them to settle down just where they happen to be without any thought of change ; there will, however, certainly be others whose doubts about the wisdom of change may be mitigated by the knowledge that, even if things go wrong, the Beveridge benefits will still in any case be available for them. It would be rash to trust to the automatic working of such influences, and Sir William Beveridge has not in fact proposed that such a course should be followed. " The correlative of the State's undertaking to ensure adequate benefit for unavoidable interruption of earnings, however long," he argues, " is enforcement of the citizen's obligation to seek and accept all reasonable opportunities for work. . . . Men and women in receipt of unemployment benefit cannot be allowed to hold out indefinitely for work of the type to which they are used or in their present places of residence." [1] The right to benefit for an unlimited period, it is accordingly proposed, should be associated with an obligation to undergo suitable training. The proposals have been criticised as being unduly timid,[2] but for our purpose it is sufficient to establish the principle. If the principle is properly applied, a well-administered all-inclusive unemployment insurance scheme need have no detrimental effects upon transfers of labour, and could be made into an instrument for facilitating them.

21. In view of the widespread enthusiasm with which schemes of social security are now being studied, it may be worth repeating

unless the problem was solved of transferring the benefits accruing from contributions to social security schemes. It might be supposed that, to the extent to which the alarms now widely expressed about the dangers of a rapidly declining population in Great Britain were justified, the urgency for giving a stimulus to emigration had been much weakened, but this special consideration does not affect the general validity of the argument that the geographical limitation of a social insurance scheme will tend to check labour mobility.

[1] *Social Insurance and Allied Services* (Cmd. 6404), pp. 130-31.

[2] For example, by Mr. A. D. K. Owen, who fears that " minimum standard benefits, in the absence of positive counteracting measures, may encourage large numbers of men and women to ' hang on ' in the unjustified hope of re-employment in old jobs in familiar neighbourhoods ", and declared that " the new conception of Training Benefit is welcome, but it is disappointing that even greater emphasis has not been placed on measures designed to increase mobility " (*Economic Journal*, April 1943, p. 9).

that even on the most favourable estimate their value is limited because avowedly they claim merely to deal with symptoms. We have seen that under a wise administration the incidental effects which they may have upon the more fundamental forces directing the allocation of productive resources may on balance be favourable. They are, however, still strictly incidental, and it would be dangerous if an excessive concentration of interest upon the details of social insurance policy and machinery encouraged us to forget that they left the fundamental questions of economic policy unanswered. Genuinely radical reforms usually require a long time before their effects are fully realised. Redistribution of income is no doubt an instrument of policy whose usefulness will continue for many generations. Instead, however, of allowing quasi-monopolistic positions to generate large incomes, part of which is then by taxation transferred to other people, it would seem more sensible to attack the quasi-monopolistic positions directly, so that as far as possible the structure of income distribution which is socially approved should emerge at once from the payments made to the different factors of production, instead of seeking to patch up an unsatisfactory structure by subsequent redistribution.[1]

(d) Inducements to Flexibility

22. We now turn to more direct methods of making the process of structural adaptation itself smoother and less troublesome. Here we may conveniently adopt the provisional, if not absolutely watertight, distinction suggested by our earlier analysis, between policies designed to make things easier for those who want to move, and policies designed to make things more difficult for those who, fearing that their privileged positions may be impaired, want to prevent movement. In organising war-time evacuations, suitable preparations were needed in both the evacuation and the reception areas. Similarly inefficiency in the allocation of productive resources may be due either to bad organisation in the industries from which resources should be

---

[1] " For the idea of taxation as a palliative for more general and basic reforms there should be no quarter " (Frank D. Graham, *Social Goals and Economic Institutions*, p. 236).

moved, or bad organisation in the industries where expansion is needed. Any shortcomings in either respect would receive attention in a well-ordered economy.

(i) *Family Allowances*

23. We have seen above that one incidental effect of social insurance should be to make things easier for those who want to move. Family allowances, too, apart from any other merits, should also diminish the difficulties of the choice between taking risks and thus being a good member of the great society and avoiding risks in the effort to discharge the responsibilities of a good husband and father. It is on account of its obviously cramping effects upon labour mobility that the organisation of family allowances on an industrial basis, and much more on the basis of single firms, is now generally agreed to be inferior to its organisation on a wider basis. The point has less importance where the employer-employee relationship is normally expected to last a lifetime. But even for the civil service, the most obvious illustration of this category, whose members sometimes enjoy the benefits of special family allowance schemes, efficiency might be increased, with incidental benefits for the efficiency of other sectors of industry, by a more frequent interchange of personnel, which such schemes must check.

(ii) *Housing Amenities*

24. A detailed examination of the significance for industrial mobility of the careful preparation of housing and other amenities wherever industrial expansion is probable would make disproportionate inroads upon our space, and a few illustrations must suffice. In Great Britain the subject has received most attention in relation to the unattractiveness of agricultural employment, but more broadly the efficient organisation of housing and general living conditions in the appropriate areas is likely to diminish the hesitation and thus to increase the mobility of those who might otherwise be deterred by the risks of discomfort in their ordinary daily lives for both themselves and their families. Useful evidence relevant to this question might be gleaned from the history of the rapid war-time expansion of industries in new areas in

K

belligerent countries, and of such large-scale industrial expansions as the Hermann Goering Works and the pre-war English exploitation of low-grade iron ore at Corby.

(iii) *A Bonus for Mobile Workers*

25. In ordinary wage contracts it is seldom possible to differentiate between the pay of those who rate continuity of employment highly and those who would gladly change their employment if they were safeguarded against risks of loss. Socially desirable mobility might be increased by differentiating between these groups, establishing, for example, " a paid reserve of versatile and mobile labour trained in several techniques, especially for newly developing jobs, and ready to go anywhere." [1] " Would it not be possible to introduce a scheme by which the State itself should become a third party to contracts of employment and carry the employee through intervals of unemployment at full pay ? He would then be in the position of a soldier waiting at his depot for posting orders, and not of one flung out of the service. . . . Such a scheme would have to be optional, since as a *quid pro quo* for the security provided, the worker would have to be willing, as occasion required, to change his trade and even the place of his home. . . . The worker clamours for more security ; the community needs more mobility. Both needs can be met if we give one as the price of the other. The worker who chose security would be carried by the State at full rates but he would have to be willing to change his trade and, if necessary, the place of his home. The worker who valued his independence too highly for this could remain outside, and, when unemployed, would fall back upon an insurance scheme, giving him benefits sufficient for subsistence but substantially below his normal rate of wage. By offering the alternatives we could obtain the necessary flexibility in our system without loss of individual liberty." [2] The voluntary industrial army, whose members would thus move under instructions, as do the members of the armed forces, need not be very large, for prompt adjustments of labour supply at the margin would in most cases be sufficient to prevent that

---

[1] Frank D. Graham, *Social Goals and Economic Institutions*, p. 175.
[2] *The Times*, March 2, 1943.

accumulation of difficulties which in the past has so frequently created intractable regional unemployment problems.

(iv) *Educational Policy*

26. The next item on our programme, the reform of educational policy, deserves more extended treatment, because, though this has for a long time been the centre of lively discussion and controversy, its broad economic effects are still frequently insufficiently appreciated. It suggests, moreover, the importance of taking action at the earliest possible date to ensure that the direction of labour supply later into the right channels will not be unduly impeded. The main objective of a civilised educational system should no doubt be the cultivation of a social sense and of a broad moral and philosophical basis for the good life, but many writers who have had this purpose chiefly or sometimes exclusively in mind, have neglected the more pedestrian but still highly important point that the size of the fraction of total resources which society decides to allocate to the cultivation of human capacity by suitable educational processes will itself directly determine its capacity for raising standards of living. If we wish to reach again as soon as possible our pre-war income standards, and thereafter to raise them further to levels more appropriate to the requirements of a modern civilisation, we cannot afford to neglect even the tiniest scrap of human capacity ; unless our educational practices are reformed much human capacity will be wasted. This need is, moreover, all the more urgent on account of the seriousness of war-time losses of material capital, the effects of which might be mitigated by more careful husbanding of our human capital.

27. Other aspects of educational policy are also important for the reallocation of people who have already found a place in the economic structure, but for whom a change in that structure makes it desirable to seek another place elsewhere.[1] In such circumstances facilities for acquiring new skills are an important part of any wise policy of readjustment. Often, however, we should do still better by taking thought before the necessity for reallocation had arisen, and doing our best to ensure that the

---

[1] R. W. B. Clarke, in *Social Security* (ed. W. A. Robson), pp. 277-81.

supplies of skill were prepared at an earlier stage.   As a nineteenth-century writer put it, " the problem of what to do to prevent a mass of adults, whose previous education has not qualified them for taking advantage of the new opportunities which material progress offers to them, from sinking into wretchedness and perhaps permanent poverty, is a serious one, and not easy to answer ".[1] A partial solution of this problem to be confidently pressed in the twentieth century is to take care that, so far as possible, their previous education will qualify them to take advantage of some of the new opportunities.

28. From the narrower standpoint of the prevention of industrial fluctuations, educational policy is also relevant, because the expansions of industry, which are needed if fluctuations are to be avoided, are often checked by the existence of labour " bottlenecks ".   Such " bottlenecks " might be avoided, or their significance much diminished, by an educational policy which gave a larger number of people an opportunity to acquire higher types of skill, or skills more likely to be applicable in a variety of situations without special or elaborate retraining.   The relatively new types of production necessary in an organically growing economy will not develop expeditiously and efficiently unless there is available in good time a sufficient number of people endowed with the knowledge and skill needed in the new types of work.   It may never be possible altogether to avoid the shortages which often slow down these essential processes of adaptation, but educational policies which widen the range of opportunity for acquiring skills would tend to bring the ideal and the actual distribution of knowledge and skill among the working members of the population much closer together than at present. We have become so accustomed to a chronic over-supply of unskilled labour that to suggest that a chronic shortage of such labour should be a normal characteristic of a healthy society may seem to many paradoxical and even fantastic, but it is no exaggeration to say that wise educational policy should be deliberately directed towards that end.   There is indeed little risk that in normal times the end would be fully realised, but, even if it were, the remedy for any incidental inconvenience would in principle

[1] D. A. Wells, *Recent Economic Changes*, p. 437.

be easy ; the situation could be adequately met if, reversing the practice of the past according to which mechanical inventions constantly brought in their train the problem of absorbing elsewhere the labour displaced by them, we directed our inventive faculties towards fields of production where increased opportunities for acquiring skill had made unskilled labour inconveniently scarce. Mechanical inventions would then solve instead of create a problem. The widespread use of household " gadgets ", which diminish the burden of dull domestic work, in countries like the United States is not unrelated to the scarcity of people who have no opening other than domestic service to turn to for a living.[1] Many other illustrations could be given of the close correlation between the availability of cheap labour and the invention or wider application of new techniques. The comparative sluggishness in applying mechanical techniques in the ancient world was, for example, no doubt in large measure a result of the foundation of slave labour on which society was then usually based. Despite the active intellectual effort sometimes, as in Greece and Alexandria, directed towards scientific speculation, there was little urge to give it much practical application. Conversely, in our own time, the extensive use of milking machines by dairy farmers in New Zealand, as compared with some other countries, is partly to be explained by the relative scarcity and dearness of labour in that country.

29. Proposals for more extensive facilities for education to render our economies more flexible often meet the objection that in many countries in recent years — and countries of widely divergent social and economic structure, including India, Roumania and Germany — the supply of the products of higher education apparently grew so much more rapidly than any possible demand that unemployment among black-coated and professional workers became an acute problem, providing a fertile breeding-ground for Fascist and near-Fascist movements.[2] Just as certain types of material capital equipment may be over-

[1] According to the 1930 Census there were 1·33 female domestic servants in the United States to every thousand of the population. In Great Britain in 1931 the number was 3·28.

[2] For a more detailed discussion of certain aspects of the extension of higher education see W. M. Kotschnig, *Unemployment in the Learned Professions* (1937).

supplied, so it is equally possible that investment in human capacity may fail to maintain a proper balance between the different types of skill. The attractiveness of certain fashionable types of professional work may induce an unduly large number of people to prepare themselves for such work. But at the same time the adjustment of the economy as a whole to changing conditions may still be hampered by a chronic shortage of other skills, and in that event the case for a properly directed extension of education is still valid. The proportions in which people ought to be trained for the performance of different kinds of work will usually be somewhat different, and in many cases markedly different, from those to which we have been accustomed in the past. In practice the error of providing inadequate supplies of the rarer types of skill is much more likely than the error of creating a superfluity. In any case we should always be slow in accepting at face value any claim put forward that changes in educational policy would threaten to create an over-supply of any kind of skill, professional or otherwise. These claims usually rest on the implicit hypothesis that customary relative standards of remuneration are sacrosanct, and that no change in them should be contemplated. There is nothing in the nature of things to justify this hypothesis. The differences in the average incomes accruing to people performing different types of work can in the last resort usually be traced back to differences in the supply of and demand for their various skills. Special factors often operate in special cases, but, broadly speaking, the market disparities in the prices at present paid for different kinds of work are mainly to be explained in terms of over-supply of the worst-paid labour and under-supply of the better paid. If we wish to reduce these disparities, and are not content with income redistribution through taxation and the provision of social services, we shall not get very far unless we diminish the labour supplies which are now over-abundant and increase the supplies where there is now a shortage ; the converse proposition is equally true, that if we substantially extend educational opportunities, a policy which is likely and indeed intended to have precisely this effect upon the distribution of labour supply, we must be prepared for corresponding changes in relative income distribution. There is indeed quite striking historical evidence to support this view. It is not a matter of chance that the margins between the wages of skilled and of unskilled workers tend normally to be smaller in countries where the average standard of at least primary education is high and much greater in countries where illiteracy is still not uncommon.[1] It does not of course follow that the absolute income of the more skilled man will necessarily fall as a result of an increase in the number of his competitors. The main economic purpose of extending educational facilities is to raise the general level of efficiency in production. In favourable conditions the aggregate of incomes may rise so fast that the skilled man is absolutely no worse off than he was before, though his relative advantages may be less. The skilled artisan in Australia or Great Britain is much better off than the skilled artisan in Yugoslavia, but his income superiority over his unskilled fellow countryman is much less than it would be if he were working in a poorer economy ; in general the income superiority of any group which drew its income from the performance of work demanding special skill might be expected to decline as educational facilities increased the numbers able to perform such work.[2]

30. Shortages of skilled labour of all kinds are a frequent war-time phenomenon, but even in normal times economic progress has constantly been hampered by the inadequacy of the supply of people with the skill and knowledge necessary for taking advantage of the opportunities constantly offered in a changing world for further advances in productive capacity. The same limitation also unduly restricts the range of choice for young people seeking employment, so that too many of them are obliged to prepare themselves for work for which, judged by the remuneration offered, the demand is subsequently discovered to be inadequate. In reply to criticisms of current educational policy,

---

[1] Cf. " Education and Income Distribution ", *International Labour Review*, June 1932, and " Industrialisation Overseas ", *Bulletin of International News*, June 27, 1942, pp. 562-4.

[2] According to a Danish calculation (by Professor Zeuthen), the rate of return on a capital of Kr. 10,000 invested over a ten-year period on an academic education was, assuming a working period covering the age of thirty to the age of sixty-two, between 30 and 50 per cent. (C. M. Wright, *Economic Adaptation to a Changing World Market*, p. 169). The steady prospect in any other field of investment of such an abnormal rate of return would undoubtedly, if no monopoly influences checked the entry of new capital, bring the return down to something much nearer the average level.

it is not enough to point to the high standard of technical skill which in many industries and professions can often be taken almost as a matter of course, or to claim that the quality of the education made available in the critic's country is in no respect inferior to that of other countries. Even if such claims were completely justified, they would not touch the essential point that, judged by the requirements to be satisfied if potential progress is to become a reality, the volume of such education has always been too small.

31. Some of the dominant social attitudes towards changes such as this are particularly relevant to our argument, for they illustrate the power of social monopolies whose influence is no less far-reaching because there is often no visible formal machinery to make them effective. It is indeed often just because they are already so effective that those who profit by them feel no urge to create such formal machinery. If educational limitations or social habits have already imposed a *de facto* restriction upon new entrants into any trade or industry, without the necessity for any formal recognition of the fact, those who are already there will be less likely to press for the statutory right to control new entrants which has been proposed in some recent discussions of post-war industrial organisation.[1] This is in effect the position of many types of professional work to-day. The form of freedom of entry is preserved, but the reality of quasi-monopoly control lies behind the form. The importance and extent of this problem are not always realised by those who quite sincerely insist upon the necessity of a " new spirit " in the organisation of our social and economic life, but the energy and persistence with which it is tackled may properly be regarded as one acid test of the seriousness of our proclaimed intentions to create a more stable and a more genuinely civilised social order.

32. Whatever the form of economic organisation preferred, the supply of effective entrepreneurial skill is also directly affected by educational policy. Whether we aim after the war at a system of undiluted private enterprise, or at complete State control of economic activity, or, as is probably more realistic, at some synthesis between these two methods of organisation, there will

[1] Cf. *infra*, XIII, 19.

without question be an urgent need for men and women with creative or organising and administrative capacity and with the power and will to take initiative. An inadequate supply of such people was among the reasons for the relative economic sluggishness of the inter-war period. Totalitarian war inevitably means disproportionate losses among those sections of the population whom we should naturally expect to display these essential qualities in the highest degree ; it is therefore a matter of the utmost importance that, having incurred such losses, we should be most meticulously careful that no one who possesses these qualities should, as a result of educational handicaps or for other reasons, be prevented from exercising them. This is not entirely a matter of education. Even the most elaborate education cannot ensure the growth of the qualities which are needed unless the seeds are already there ; there is no reason in the nature of things why people who have not had the proper formal educational training, but who are otherwise well qualified, should not ultimately find their way to the responsible positions which it is in the general interest that they should occupy. But the complications of modern industry and government make this more difficult than it used to be ; it is natural and, within limits, proper that those who recruit for administrative posts, whether in private or in public enterprise, should pay increasing attention to formal educational qualifications; in these circumstances it would gravely impede the processes of structural adaptation if the proper facilities for education were denied to anyone who had the necessary innate ability. " The waste of human ability which our educational and social system had permitted in the past "[1] inflicted injustice upon the individual ; it should now also be recognised as inflicting unnecessary and avoidable loss upon the community.

(v) *Clearing Away Obstructions at the Growing Points*

33. The smooth and healthy development of any organism is dependent upon the existence of a favourable environment at its growing points. Congestion or improper interference there will check the general processes of growth, and probably have damaging repercussions extending far beyond the area immedi-

---

[1] Sir Stafford Cripps, May 1942.

ately affected. This principle applies as much to an economy as to anything more strictly described as an organism. If the economic process as a whole is not to be congested and jammed, it is especially at the growing points, the points where new consumers' demands are to be satisfied, that it is most important to give adequate scope for development. If production there is hampered, so that its development is unduly retarded, there will be congestion and unemployment and an appearance of overproduction in other parts of the economy, some of which may seem to have little close connection with the growing points. The significance of appropriate action at these points will therefore often be much greater than a superficial examination of the number of persons likely to be employed or the volume of capital investment directly involved might suggest.

34. The significance of educational policy rests in part upon its usefulness in preventing such congestion. Development will be delayed if there is not a sufficient number of people qualified to work at the growing points, and wise educational preparation will diminish the risk of this happening. Greater freedom of movement at these points may, however, also be facilitated in other ways. We may attempt to influence consumers' demand with a view to increasing the probability that it will be directed towards satisfactions likely to elicit an elastic demand, and for which the expansion of production needed is therefore likely to be more stable. Or, accepting consumers' demand as a *datum*, we may examine the existing machinery for directing the flow of either labour or capital to see whether its historical development, with an eye mainly to the requirements of production of quite different types, may not have left it unduly sluggish in responding to the requirements of newer types of production upon whose development depends the maintenance of equilibrium for the economy as a whole, and which are for this reason now more urgently needed. If this machinery is unsatisfactory, the process of adaptation may, even in the absence of any definite resistance or opposition to the newer developments, slow down or stop altogether. Someone must take the initiative in reforming the machinery or in providing alternative devices for directing aright the flow of factors of production.

35. Both these issues arise if we enquire into the conditions most conducive to the development of " tertiary " production, which ought to emerge at many of the growing points of a progressive economy, and which are therefore required by such an economy on an ever-expanding scale.   For some of these tertiary products there is already an elaborate organisation to provide the necessary capital ; [1]   many others, however, lie outside the normal range of the capital market, partly because so much of the investment required is investment in human beings.   It is not, however, enough to educate suitable individuals for the practice of tertiary production.   Much more is usually necessary in the way both of organisation and of the provision of further material capital. There seems to be a case here for State intervention on grounds which hitherto have usually been neglected.   One conventional socialist argument, anxious to meet the criticism which imputes undue caution and lack of enterprise to State instrumentalities, has commonly urged that State control should be imposed upon some or all of the main industrial activities, responsible for turning out basic products, but has left the fringes or frills or, as we would prefer to put it, the growing points to the private entrepreneur. There is, however, it is suggested, a case for reversing this argument.   Leaving aside for later discussion the problem of monopoly, the State would often appear to have less reason to concern itself with the basic industries which, just because they are basic and well established, may be presumed already to have reached a reasonable level of efficiency, than with the newer untried types of production which, just because they are new, are, when the conditions for further growth are present, of more urgent importance to the economy as a whole than the basic industries which are already running fairly well.   If the private entrepreneur did handle these new things satisfactorily, all might be well, but our whole problem arises in practice very much because he often fails to do so.   State instrumentalities have indeed been far from inactive in this field.   State or municipal provision of parks, playgrounds, museums and the like are already a commonplace, and

---

[1] For an interesting account of the development of popular amusements, and of their economic significance in the latter part of the nineteenth century, see Guy Chapman, *Culture and Survival*, ch. iv, " The Exploitation of Leisure ".

in some countries the State is also an active entrepreneur, without any monopoly control, in the field of music and the theatre. Further extensions in these directions are, however, often frowned upon as involving the waste of public money upon extravagant and unnecessary luxuries. Instead, our argument suggests, it might more properly be regarded as an important stabilising element in the absence of which a growing economy would be more liable to violent fluctuations. If "in the long run, barring unforeseeable good fortune, the problem of stagnation will be the dominant preoccupation of government in relation to the economy ",[1] it would appear an obvious characteristic of prudent statesmanship to devote its attention in the first instance to those places in the economy where a clearing-away of obstacles would be most likely to allow the stagnant stream of development to flow once more. This policy moreover illustrates the point made earlier that more favourable conditions for the satisfaction of consumers' demand might in some circumstances be created by subjecting consumers' demand to a certain measure of control ; the case for this will be the stronger in a wealthy community where a large proportion of additional purchasing power will normally be directed towards goods and services with an uncertain and fluctuating demand and in connection with which a certain amount of education may therefore produce useful results.

36. Action of this kind need not involve any interference with the freedom of consumers' choice in the true sense. Consumers' preferences are always dependent upon the prices at which goods and services are offered to them. If an increase in productive capacity makes it possible to offer increased supplies of either A, B or C, but not of all of them together, and if consumers have not yet developed any strong sentiment in favour of any one of these things, we do not interfere with their freedom of choice by taking special steps to make available, say, A, at a price sufficiently low to make sure that consumers will, in fact, prefer it to either B or C, on the ground that there is good reason to believe that the demand for A will turn out to be elastic, and that conditions there therefore justify the expectation of a stable expansion of produc-

[1] J. M. Clark, " The Relation of Government to the Economy of the Future ", *Journal of Political Economy*, December 1941, p. 798.

tion. Consumers' immediate satisfaction in terms of real income will be no less, and the risks of instability will be diminished for the economy as a whole, and therefore also for consumers in their capacity as income-producers.

37. The general course of economic development has often been traced in terms of the effects of large-scale investments stimulated by new inventions, and the economic history of the last century or more cannot indeed be properly understood if we neglect the profound significance of the period of railway construction, of the stimulus subsequently given to investment by the development of electricity, or by the exploitation of other new discoveries of a similar kind. It should not, however, be supposed that economic expansion must inevitably slacken unless there are more inventions in the future with comparable far-reaching effects. We have already seen that the aggregate volume of technical change in our time has probably had at least as profound an influence as all the changes of the Industrial Revolution, and scientists promise us with the greatest confidence the continuance of this trend. But even if there were no further large-scale technical changes, it would still be important to visualise the effects upon our economic structure of the inevitable extension of the changes already made. It then becomes clear that in a well-ordered economy in such circumstances there would be ample opportunities for capital investment in tertiary production, and in the absence of suitable institutions for directing the flow of capital thither, there is a strong case for filling the gap by means of a suitable State instrumentality.

38. Where we have any choice in the matter, it is always wiser to give preference to such growing points in the economy as are likely to satisfy requirements for which demand will be elastic. For at such points it will be reasonable to anticipate an extensive growth, before any approximation to a satiated demand makes it necessary to start a new process of adaptation. This is one convincing reason for organising special facilities for the provision of improved housing, for there is a reasonable presumption that if the costs of producing houses and their furnishings are reduced the new demand thus stimulated will be fairly steady and permanent. Another suggestion which points in a

similar direction has been made by Professor Röpke, mainly, however, with an objective in mind somewhat different from that with which we are here concerned. He is especially anxious to provide conditions favourable to the work of independent artisans, and points out that the competitive advantages which industrial mass production appears to enjoy as compared with the work of independent producers are not always based upon a comparison of the costs of identical articles. The artisan product is often of better quality, and this not merely from the standpoint of individual taste, but also on account of its durability. Where consumers are in a position to weigh the advantages of the two products, they may therefore be obliged to prefer the mass-produced article, not because they really like it, but because, despite the knowledge that in the long run it will be dearer, they cannot afford to buy anything else. " Is there a case ", he asks, " in which organised consumers' credit would be so clearly legitimate as here ? Should not what is proper for the automobile, which next year may be a wreck or obsolete, at least be regarded as fair for the solid furnishings which the grandchildren may still be able to enjoy ? " [1]

39. State organisation of tertiary production is not, however, the only way of clearing away the obstacles which may clog the growing points of our economy. We have already seen that, even when he has decided to divert some of his savings from their customary channels, the best-intentioned business man may have some hesitation in deciding to which among a large number of competing claimants they should be allotted. There may apparently be several growing points with equally strong claims for attention. Some may seem to offer a small return, with little or no risk, others a moderate return with an appreciable measure of risk, while a third group may involve very great risks combined with a chance of very great gain in the event of success. If stable progress is to be assured, an adequate proportion of the community's savings must be made available for each group. At certain periods indeed too much capital may have gone into

---

[1] *Die Gesellschaftskrisis der Gegenwart* (1942), pp. 338-41. The significance of elasticity of demand will be mentioned again in the subsequent discussion of nutrition policy.

risky enterprises, with consequent loss and undue instability, but it is equally important that there should not be too little capital allotted to them.

40. In this connection the possible effects of high income tax, already referred to,[1] should be further examined. The effects of high taxation upon business activity in general have often been the subject of a good deal of unintelligent comment. It may be true that taxation which curtails the average return to the entrepreneur may sometimes induce him to slacken his activities, but the point would be more honestly and accurately presented if, instead of wrapping it up in general phrases about the limits of taxable capacity and the burdens placed upon industry, it were clearly presented in some such way as the following : " Further increases of taxation will inevitably decrease the consumption by taxpayers of certain goods and services. Already people with large or moderate incomes are obliged by taxation to curtail their expenditure on many pleasant but unnecessary things which if taxation were lower they would be able to enjoy. Most of them are still tolerably comfortable ; a good deal of money is spent under normal peace conditions on motor-cars and holidays, on amusements and entertainments of various kinds. But rather than curtail still further expenditure of this kind, they think it better to go slow on, for example, expenditure on education, and thus to perpetuate the handicaps under which the children of poor parents now labour, and to deprive the rest of the community of the benefits which would accrue to it if these people were permitted to develop their natural capacities." [2] Stated in this way the point probably sounds less convincing.

41. It is not, however, with this rather crude view of the effects of high taxation with which we are here concerned. The point which requires more serious attention is a more subtle one, but none the less of great importance. " A speculative stock, if it is to attract capital, must offer a return over and above the gilt-edged rate of interest such as to provide an adequate premium for the general and specific risks of the business. Income tax and super-tax, when heavily increased, may so cut into the rich

---

[1] Cf. *supra*, X, 17.
[2] Cf. " The New Zealand Economic Problem ", *Economic Record*, May 1932, pp. 86-7.

investor's return that the premium element is no longer sufficient, on an actuarial basis, to cover the valuation of possible loss. In such circumstances, capital from the wealthy class of speculators cannot in the long run continue to be attracted. Any taxation which unduly diminishes the reward of entrepreneurs for taking pioneer risks is in that respect a source of harm to the community." [1] Income tax rates have risen a good deal since this passage was written, but little progress has been made in applying a satisfactory principle for discriminating in income tax assessment in favour of the risk-taker, the man who is prepared to perform the experimental and exploratory functions needed by a growing economy at its growing points.[2] There is indeed reason to believe that some taxation reforms based in the first instance upon considerations of equity would also have desirable consequences from the point of view of stimulating enterprise. There is a strong case in equity for increasing the relative importance of personal income taxation, and avoiding direct levies on business units as such, and for the application of a simple averaging procedure to ensure that persons whose annual incomes fluctuated widely did not on that account bear a heavier taxation burden than others with the same average, but a steadier income. The argument in favour of these principles is equally strong if based on the desirability of giving adequate encouragement to risk-taking.

42. Professor Frank Graham, who also favours the remission of taxation on the profits of new, independent and still small concerns, has, by processes of reasoning similar to those used above, defended the view that if by other means, including in particular the practical confiscation of large inheritances, the distribution of income were made to conform more exactly with conditions of genuine equality of opportunity, the requirements of equity would be satisfied, and at the same time deterrents to investment in risky enterprise would be removed, by abandoning progressive taxation altogether and substituting proportional taxation, except so far as minimum exemptions might be main-

[1] Report of Colwyn Committee on National Debt and Taxation, p. 142. Cf. Henry Clay, *The Financing of Industrial Enterprise*, Manchester Statistical Society, March 9, 1932.
[2] The League of Nations Delegation on Economic Depressions has recommended that " the taxation of risk-capital should be overhauled after the war ".

tained, together with steeply progressive taxes on incomes above a defined upper limit, designed to skim off a large proportion of the windfall and quasi-monopolistic elements in individual incomes.[1] This proposal, however, seems to be one whose practical application must be postponed until the more drastic inheritance taxes upon which it depends have become a reality.

43. An adequate supply of entrepreneurs prepared both to undertake the supervision of enterprises of the kind needed in a growing economy and to risk their own money in them may not, however, be enough. Enterprise may still be unduly hampered unless the entrepreneur can add to the capital provided by himself a sufficient amount provided by other people. His difficulties may even be greater if his capital requirements are modest, for, especially when expert opinion is unduly impressed by the alleged advantages of very large-scale enterprise, the ordinary machinery of the capital market may be much more easily put in motion to provide capital on a large scale than to provide it in the moderate amounts needed for small and medium-sized experiments of the greatest importance in the development of a growing economy. Already in 1931 the Macmillan Committee drew attention to this defect in the English capital market.[2] " Great difficulty ", it was said, " is experienced by the small and medium-sized businesses in raising the capital which they may from time to time require even when the security offered is perfectly sound ", and the establishment of a financial organisation with special responsibility for the provision of intermediate credit for these types of business enterprise was suggested. In response to this criticism some interesting experiments were undertaken, notably by Credit for Industries, Ltd. and its subsidiaries.[3] These experiments met with a certain modest success, but any feeling of disappointment aroused by a study of their operations should be mitigated by the reflection that at best they were never intended to be much more than a subsidiary contribution to the solution of our problem. It is none the less worth while again to direct attention to them. The problem of an adequate provision of capital for such types of enterprise still remains, and while these

[1] *Social Goals and Economic Institutions*, pp. 220, 236-41.
[2] Report of the Committee on Finance and Industry, Cmd. 3897 (1931), pp. 161-74.
[3] Cf. B. Ellinger, *The City*, chs. xxxiv, xxxv.

L

organisations cannot by themselves guarantee to us either assured progress or lasting stability, they may, in combination with appropriate action in other spheres, provide useful assistance which cannot safely be ignored.

44. The importance of the small investor is unlikely to diminish in the future ; from many points of view it is desirable that it should increase. But his capacity to take risks is unlikely to increase very much. For him it will always be prudent to seek safe investments with fixed returns. At the same time it is desirable in the interests of both progress and stability that the relative importance of fixed interest-bearing investments should decline, and the importance of equities correspondingly increase. If income levels are sufficiently high, the small investor may find in small industrial units capable of producing quality or specialised articles under conditions where the investor's chances of accurate knowledge are fairly good, some outlet for his savings which combines a reasonable degree of safety with the flexibility assured by equity capital. This, however, is unlikely to provide anything like a complete solution. We need intermediaries to provide the small investor with the security for which he is naturally looking, and who at the same time are capable of taking a wider view of the needs of industrial development as a whole and allocating an appropriate share of the small investor's savings to the more risky enterprises without which progress will be damped down and genuine stability difficult to maintain. The insurance company and the investment trust have already made some contribution to the solution of this problem. At present there are serious limitations to be taken into account in assessing from this point of view the importance of their work. " The most appropriate form " of organisation for the purpose " is likely to vary from country to country ; but it is evident that in almost all countries some mechanism for spreading risks is required, and much educational work will have to be undertaken in order to persuade both the public and the banks that some change is essential and that facilities can be devised ".[1]

---

[1] For a more detailed discussion of this point see A. Loveday, " Financial Organisation and the Price Level ", in *Economic Essays in Honour of Gustav Cassel* (1933), pp. 409-18.

(vi) *The Control or Disintegration of Monopoly Resistance*

45. Our discussion of education has already shown our preliminary distinction between policies designed to make things easier for people who want to change, and policies designed to make things more difficult for people who want to prevent others from changing to be merely provisional. In discussing a proposal which at first sight fell into the first category we soon found it necessary to discuss also the chances of opposition from people in the second category. Any examination of the one type will indeed nearly always inevitably merge into an examination of the other. Educational policy has thus already brought us face to face with the problem of monopolistic resistances to structural adaptations.

46. Clearly it is neither possible nor desirable here to attempt even a bald summary of the main points which have emerged from the analysis by economists of monopolies and quasi-monopolistic activities. There has never been a time when it was not true that " everyone must from the standpoint of his own interest desire the maximum output of all goods, with the exception of those in whose production he has specialised, and by whose sale on the most favourable terms possible he gets his living ",[1] and the clash thereby generated between public and private interests has always attracted attention. " Natural " trends towards monopolisation have been made the ground for the most damaging attacks on modern capitalist economies, and some of the most ingenious refinements of modern economic theory have been those concerned with the phenomenon of " imperfect competition ". Here, however, our concern with monopoly is of a more specific and limited kind. Monopoly problems have frequently aroused popular interest on account of their obvious connection with inequalities in income distribution. Monopoly organisation offers opportunities for earmarking disproportionately large shares of the national income, and is indeed among the outstanding influences creating and perpetuating gross income disparities. But while the importance of this side of the problem should not be minimised, it is probably not the most important

---

[1] W. Röpke, *Die Gesellschaftskrisis der Gegenwart* (1942), p. 197.

side. The fundamental objection to monopolistic influences is less the fact that they distribute income badly than that they keep its aggregate size so much smaller than it need be. "A monopoly is not only socially intolerable ; it also constitutes a jamming of the economic process, and a drag upon aggregate productivity." [1] Even if it were possible to limit monopoly gains, or perhaps to destroy them altogether by means of taxation or otherwise, their evil effects in distorting the structure of production would still remain ; so long as these effects remain, the problem of monopoly has not been solved. The case against monopoly as an influence inimical to both economic progress and stability rests not merely or mainly upon the undesirability of strengthening the forces creating unequal income distribution, but upon the distortion of the normal structure of an expanding economy, which keeps the general income level lower than it need or should be.[2]

47. Strictly speaking, we are not concerned here even with the whole of this side of the monopoly problem, but only with the effects of monopolistic limitations of output when normal economic development demands, in response to improvements in the efficiency of production, an expansion in certain definite fields of economic activity. The practical problem is, however, much the same whether we are thinking of it in its widest form or from this slightly more limited standpoint. If we are to enjoy economic stability and rising living standards, elasticity and flexibility in our economic structure are prime necessities, which will not be forthcoming if large sections of our economy are controlled by the spirit of "not too much haste, not too much progress, not too much efficiency, not too many new ideas, not too many new men ",[3] which has been characteristic of many quasi-monopolistic movements of the recent past. Such movements mean inevitably an increasing rigidity, a diminishing capacity for adaptation, which keeps living standards low, while also increasing the susceptibility of our economy to the impact

---

[1] W. Röpke, *op. cit.* p. 359.

[2] " The issue is not just a question of whether prices are to be high or low, and output large or small, important as these matters are in a world as poor as ours still is. It is even more a question of opportunity. The spread of monopoly is the spread of privilege ; opportunity is denied to those who are outside the ring " (W. Arthur Lewis, " Monopoly and the Law ", *Modern Law Review*, April 1943, p. 104).

[3] Herbert Morrison, *Looking Ahead*, p. 125.

of economic fluctuations. Opportunities for increased production at lower prices are neglected, or actually destroyed, and barriers which check the growth of employment in monopolistically controlled fields of activity make the problem of finding suitable new places for those who have been ejected from their old employments by technical change more and more difficult to solve.

48. We have already insisted that the significance of monopoly is misconceived if the term is too narrowly interpreted. It covers the whole complex of devices whereby producers can either limit their output and thus maintain prices above the equilibrium level, or check the entry of would-be competitors who might offer goods or services superior, from the point of view either of price or of quality, to those already on the market.

49. We have already seen reason to criticise the current fashionable phrases which urge the abandonment of the habit of looking at things from the standpoint of production, and the adoption of an allegedly new habit of looking at them from the standpoint of consumption.[1] It might much more reasonably be argued that, so far from devoting too much attention to the art of producing, the main defect of inter-war economic policy was that it fastened much too avidly upon the art of not producing. Instead of making a misleading contrast between the economics of production and the economics of consumption, we must, if we are to avoid repeating our ancient errors, unwearyingly insist upon the highly significant contrast between the economics of production and the economics of non-production.

50. This might well be regarded as the most important lesson to be learnt from the experience of war-time economies. The objective of all belligerents is the full utilisation of every factor able to contribute to production to which priority is given for war purposes. The main justification of authoritarian controls is their success in realising this objective.[2] If after the war restraints upon the utilisation of productive resources can be removed by other means, the other " sacrifices " imposed by war-time methods may be largely avoided and the true " lessons " of war-time experience applied with rational discrimination.

[1] Cf. IV, 49.   [2] Cf. W. H. Hutt, *Plan for Reconstruction*, p. 90.

51. Every day we are reminded that the execution of sound policy " will demand courage and determination, and the road to success may prove a stony one ",[1] or that " it requires imagination and firm will on the part of each government and people to make use of " the knowledge already at hand for such far-reaching objectives as the organisation of adequate food production.[2] Courage and determination, imagination and firm will, are admirable, even indispensable qualities, but they can be used in the fight against any kind of enemy. If we fail correctly to identify our enemy, our courage and determination may lead us rapidly along the wrong path. In our case the enemies to be attacked are numerous, but if the fight is unremittingly directed against the forces which in the past have more and more hampered and restricted production, thereby creating the tragic paradox of " poverty amid plenty " and depriving large masses of the world's population of the natural fruits of scientific progress, the mopping-up of the minor allies grouped around these forces will not take much time. It is for this reason that institutions for the prevention or control of monopolistic or quasi-monopolistic influences should occupy a prominent position in our programme for practical action.

52. The trend towards monopoly control is likely to be most rapid in industries where technical or market conditions justify or even demand the organisation of production by large-scale units, and the discussion of monopoly is sometimes confused by being tied up with the discussion of large-scale business units. The two questions are in fact quite distinct, though they often come very close together, especially where technical conditions determine an optimum size of unit which at the same time is capable of meeting the whole of the requirements of the available market. Our subsequent criticism of monopoly organisation should not be interpreted as involving any neglect of the technical advantages of large-scale units, though one may also believe that popular thought has been far too ready to take at face value many of the claims made on their behalf. Their proper status in a well-

---

[1] *The Transition from War to Peace Economy* (League of Nations Delegation on Economic Depressions), p. 11.

[2] Resolution I of the United Nations Conference on Food and Agriculture, May 18 to June 3, 1943.

ordered economy should be determined, industry by industry, according to the conditions of production and demand in each case. The modern heresy of " megalolatry ", the worship of size for its own sake, has infected much of our thought on industrial organisation no less than on other subjects, and in many industries the expansion of large-scale units has probably been carried further than is justified by the ultimate test of the economic allocation of resources of production.[1] If conditions were created in which objective comparisons of efficiency could be made, the scope for relatively small units would probably be found to be greater than one might suppose from experience drawn mainly from times when the influence of economic institutions was too much on the side of the large unit. The technical advantages of large-scale units are in some cases very substantial. They have opportunities for research activity which for the most part are beyond the scope of the small man. But many of the advantages at present enjoyed are mere fighting advantages, which permit them to put the small man out of action irrespective of his technical capacity. If the two types of advantage were properly sorted out, and proper institutional protection afforded against mere fighting strength, we should be in a better position to form an objective judgment of the validity of claims of superior technical efficiency.[2]

53. If *laissez faire* is assumed to mean State inaction, the anti-monopoly programme here suggested has nothing to do with *laissez faire*. To carry out the tasks next to be discussed demands a powerful and active State machinery and a high standard of administrative ability and efficiency. In economic life as elsewhere, freedom is not possible without discipline, and this only a powerful and efficient State machine can provide. No approach to the conditions of free competition " will, in a complex society, ever be attained without drastic, though not ubiquitous, governmental action. Coercions of others, by private individuals, cover

---

[1] Popular thought often exaggerates the extent to which large-scale units in fact dominate industrial life to-day. Of more than five million persons employed in British factories before the war, 55·3 per cent. were working in units with a staff of less than 500, and 21·7 per cent. in units with a staff of less than 100.

[2] Cf. Lionel Robbins, " The Inevitability of Monopoly ", in *The Economic Basis of Class Conflict*, pp. 45-80.

much more than simple violence and it would be illusory to think of the State as other than an alert and active participant in the establishment of the conditions of freedom." [1]

54. In current discussions of the economic functions of the State, the usual practice is to concentrate attention upon two questions : the fields within which the State should itself undertake an active responsibility for production or distribution, *i.e.* the problem of " nationalisation ", and the provision of social services. Both are of great importance, but if the discussion is limited to them, there is a serious danger that the fundamental function of the State in economic life, the provision of a framework of laws and institutions, within which economic activity, whether by individuals, by companies or co-operative societies, or by State instrumentalities, must in any event be carried on, will be neglected and the necessity for fundamental and radical reforms in this field overlooked. For this unfortunate blindness the liberal thinkers of the nineteenth century are not without some responsibility. To a large extent they tended to take the existing framework of institutions for granted, and though not entirely unaware that the economic activity which they were concerned to analyse was invariably and inevitably conditioned by the legal and institutional framework of each particular economy, they seldom gave sufficient attention to the possibility of the framework getting out-of-date. This is not to say that our institutional framework is to-day quite unchanged as compared with a century ago. There have been many important innovations and reforms. In particular the recognition of the principle of limited liability in Great Britain in 1855 and 1862 provided machinery of great value for directing into productive channels savings for which otherwise it would have been difficult to find a satisfactory outlet. But we have been slow to realise that these very innovations might themselves create conditions which, instead of encouraging the further expansion of wealth and production, as they were originally designed to do, might in certain circumstances facilitate the accumulation of profits by contracting or limiting output. Broadly speaking, and no doubt

<hr/>

[1] Frank D. Graham, *Social Goals and Economic Institutions*, pp. 42-3. Cf. W. Röpke, *Die Gesellschaftskrisis der Gegenwart*, pp. 357-8, 388.

with some exceptions, the profit motive serves useful ends so long as it induces people to produce. Its effects are most noticeably anti-social if it encourages people not to produce, and even more to hinder others from producing. Many current discussions of the profit motive imply that this is now its normal effect. Such a generalisation would be hasty and inaccurate, but at the time when Company Law was first elaborated, and even in its subsequent amendments, it has not always been sufficiently appreciated that the new institutional invention would sometimes offer opportunities for the operation of the profit motive in this anti-social direction, and insufficient care was taken to ensure that the profit motive should then be denied the protection of the law.

55. Professor Cannan taught us thirty years ago that " a man's intelligent pursuit of his own interest generally serves others besides himself simply because the institutions of society provide hedges which are generally close enough to keep him on the road. When it is found that institutions fail to make it the interest of each man to serve the rest, society abandons or modifies them." [1] The first principle here enunciated was perfectly sound. In restrospect, the second now looks a little optimistic. It is indeed scarcely a legitimate ground for surprise that social changes should often get a little ahead of the rather lumbering movement of the parliamentary and administrative machine, whose duty it is constantly to adapt institutions to changing social needs. The process of trial and error is a normal human experience. The principle of business organisation within a corporate or company framework is very ancient. The extension of the privilege of limited liability, almost as an ordinary routine matter, is, however, a comparatively recent innovation, and some of the consequences of this important institutional invention were unlikely at once to make themselves fully apparent. Experience has shown the necessity for the application of discipline to limited liability companies, and we have not yet properly adjusted our institutional framework to the implications of unfettered freedom of enterprise for business units which enjoy this privilege. British Company Law has indeed been frequently revised since

[1] *The Economic Outlook* (1912), p. 25.

1862, but amendments have been for the most part directed towards the prevention of " abuses ", the protection of shareholders against fraud, or practices closely resembling fraud, and the prevention of obscurantism in company prospectuses and published accounts. These are legitimate concerns of the modern State, but they do not penetrate to the heart of the matter. The real problem is to create an institutional framework which will encourage a distribution of productive resources appropriate for the attainment of the highest possible average standard of living, and discourage or make impossible decisions which impede this distribution. We should not underrate the importance of " abuses ", but for the real significance of reforms of Company Law we must probe deeper.[1] We have been too slow to realise that the first experimental essays in creating a legal framework within which limited liability companies could operate freely, even with subsequent amendments designed to check abuses, almost inevitably failed to take account of all the possible situations which might arise.[2] Professor Cannan's hedges have been ill-tended and are now in a sad state of disrepair, so that the presumption which he enunciated has been subjected to more and more exceptions. The position is not unlike that which would have arisen if we had been satisfied with the first trials at new methods of traffic regulation which obviously became necessary when the horse and buggy era was replaced by the motor-car age. In that field no one has questioned the desirability of new types of road and of new types of traffic regulation, continuously adapted to rapid changes in transport conditions. The parallel problem in the field of industrial organisation has not been entirely neglected. But legislative activity here has been directed rather towards perfecting the new engine of industrial activity, the limited liability company, than towards regulating the new kind of traffic problem which arises when alongside the older type of independent entrepreneur the economic roads are crowded

[1] Judged by the criteria here suggested, the terms of reference of the committee to enquire into British Company Law, announced in June 1943, are unfortunately capable of much too narrow an interpretation.

[2] " Corporate Capitalism is a creature of a legal system, a product of company lawyers, an edifice founded on the thoughtless multiplication of privileges which at the outset the State was accustomed to grant only as a deliberate State act in a particular case and after the most careful consideration " (W. Röpke, *op. cit.* p. 363).

with new vehicles equipped with the new engine. Further legislative activity is now needed to take account of the risks revealed by experience that the new engine may sometimes be used for the contraction and limitation rather than for the expansion of production.

56. But if the liberal thinkers of the nineteenth century are in some degree to be blamed for failing to foresee the necessity for further institutional reform, they and their successors were certainly often energetic in protesting against the growing tendency for some of the traditional traffic guardians in this field to abandon any serious attempt to perform their functions. Judicial interpretation of the law on restraint of trade has changed so radically during the last century and a half as to constitute almost a complete reversal of attitude. The judges tended to confuse freedom to enter the market and sell with freedom to prevent others from doing the same,[1] and believing it to be their duty to protect the latter, they have often in fact destroyed the former. No analysis of the alleged inevitability of the growth of monopoly in our own time can be convincing if it fails to pay attention to this fact. For the law is always susceptible of amendment, and under the direction of the legislature, the judges could speedily construct a new institutional framework in which more rational interpretations of freedom would have their chance.

57. The direction in which this analysis is intended to point may be indicated in a slightly different way. There is in many quarters to-day a tendency to appease monopoly controls,[2] but this tendency itself shows a growing recognition of the reality of the problem. To this problem there are at the present time, broadly speaking, two fashionable lines of approach. One group, believing that monopoly trends are likely to grow in strength,

[1] W. Arthur Lewis, " Monopoly and the Law ", *Modern Law Review*, April 1943, pp. 99-100.

[2] Even " advanced " reformers seem prepared to give them another chance. " Monopolies or near-monopolies or well-organised Trade Associations ", says one recent writer, " should have the chance of proving that, given certain safeguards, they are capable of operating in the public interest and that the advantages of large-scale organisation can be made to outweigh the disadvantages of imperfect competition. The proof of all their puddings will be in the eating. If they fail to produce the right sort of pudding and enough of it, then and only then the Government machinery must intervene " (Charles Madge, *Industry after the War : Who is going to Run it ?* [1943], p. 57).

looks to some form of direct State control as the only possible way of dealing with them.   Others, impressed by the evils of bureaucracy and the practical difficulties of adapting the traditional civil service structure for the performance of an entirely different task, and believing in the virtues of the " practical man ", propose that the monopolistic tide should be harnessed by formal recognition on the part of the State, which, while giving a *de iure* status to the *de facto* powers of monopolist organisations, would at the same time place some overriding disciplinary powers, not always clearly defined, in the hands of the State.   Both approaches agree, however, in accepting a trend towards more and more monopoly as inevitable.   The second approach we shall later see reason for entirely rejecting.   The first should be judged on its merits in particular cases.   There is no valid reason for rejecting direct State control out of hand in all cases.   But equally there is no valid ground for the assumption that wherever monopoly influences are now powerful, and threaten to become still more powerful, it is quite out of the question to check or reverse or even entirely to destroy them.   There is a third line of approach, which while recognising the genuine economies of large-scale organisation, and not ruling out on any doctrinaire grounds State control where that should be shown to be suitable, would also seriously enquire how far the *de facto* monopoly positions which have grown up were the result, not of any inevitable technical trend, but of legal and institutional accidents, the results of which might without great difficulty be removed, leaving a freer field for expansive enterprise.   As one recent writer has put it, we need to-day " a systematic revision of the system of property ".[1]   We should investigate the conditions under which Professor Cannan's hedges have fallen into decay, and the best methods of repairing them or of supplementing them by new hedges more suitable for the conditions of a twentieth-century economy.

58. The institutional reforms suggested by this analysis have, on the whole, received inadequate attention in Great Britain, though they have been much more widely discussed in the United States.   Here we can do little more than sketch a brief

---

[1] W. H. Hutt, *Plan for Reconstruction*, p. 219.

outline.[1] The main concrete issues to be dealt with are the following : (i) legislation to reverse the trend of judicial decisions which favour price-fixing agreements and boycotts which in an earlier age were regarded as conspiracies. The experience of the United States has shown that it is not sufficient in these cases to rely upon private parties themselves initiating litigation against monopolies. " The maintenance of free markets is a positive task to which the police power of the State should be applied ; this requires a special department, amply staffed " ;[2] (ii) an examination of the status of holding companies and the right of companies to own the shares of other companies ; (iii) reform of the patent law, to preserve the right of inventors to a royalty on any use of their inventions, but to destroy the power to purchase such rights and withhold the use of patents from other users ; (iv) extension of the principles of public utility regulation to all industries where the economies of large-scale production necessarily result in market control by a few large firms ; (v) the provision of more adequate and accurate information as a guide for those who have to face the responsibilities of investment.

59. The last-mentioned point deserves more detailed notice. We have already mentioned the difficulties which face the enterprising investor who is prepared to take a risk but is obliged to choose between a wide range of alternatives in relation to many of which only the most imperfect knowledge may be available. Errors, with consequent waste of capital, are more likely to be avoided, and enterprise itself stimulated, if more effective machinery is created for collecting and disseminating information in the absence of which even approximately correct decisions may be almost impossible for investors. The main objective of institutional reform in relation to monopolistic influences is " to expose profitableness ",[3] and when once profitableness has been exposed, to remove as many of the obstacles as possible which otherwise hinder the response of investors to the facts thus

---

[1] For an admirably succinct but unfortunately not very accessible discussion of the whole problem see W. Arthur Lewis, "Monopoly and the Law", *Modern Law Review*, April 1943. For a more comprehensive, perhaps too comprehensive programme, the reader may be referred to Professor W. H. Hutt's *Plan for Reconstruction* (1943).

[2] W. Arthur Lewis, *loc. cit.* p. 111.

[3] W. H. Hutt, *Plan for Reconstruction*, p. 253.

revealed to them. " Private enterprise and business privacy are incompatible in a defensible social order ",[1] and, it might be added, most of the information in mind here is obviously equally essential in any planned economy, whatever form it might take. If the grosser errors of judgment are to be avoided, such information is in any event indispensable.

60. These proposals still leave quite open the question of the fields of production or distribution for which the State should itself assume direct responsibility. But even those who contemplate a very wide extension of public enterprise in the ordinary sense would be ill-advised to under-estimate their importance. For on any realistic view of probable future developments, any practical programme of nationalisation is certain to leave wide sectors of industry and trade to so-called " private " enterprise. Even the most ardent socialist would do well to insist that in these sectors enterprise should not fall into the hands of privileged groups, and that the rights of competitors to serve the public interest should be fortified by a reformed institutional and legal framework.

61. The question of direct State control should, in any event, be settled in each particular case on grounds of expediency or practicability. It is commonly believed that the case for direct State control is particularly strong in relation to industries where monopoly control is already well entrenched. Whether or not this is true of so-called " natural " monopolies, or of industries where technical conditions, in relation to the size of the market, make the existence of more than one unit of production uneconomical, we should certainly not be too ready to assume that the mere existence in any industry of monopoly or something closely approximating to it justifies the conclusion that monopoly there is either " natural " or inevitable. There are no doubt some fields within which monopoly should be controlled, or converted into a State instrumentality. But interest in this subject should not induce us to forget the importance of the neglected problem of monopoly prevention. It is sometimes truly said that business men cannot be compelled to compete if they do not want to ; this, however, is only one side of the question. Some business

---

[1] W. H. Hutt, *op. cit.* p. 173.

men who do not wish to compete themselves are still more anxious to prevent other potential competitors from having the opportunity to compete. The anxiety displayed in some industries where large units are already powerful to foster monopolistic trends by granting statutory recognition in some form to the organs at present in control of a large part of the industry suggests that these potential competitors are real beings. One of the alleged " disadvantages " attaching to voluntary trade associations, in the view of the Federation of British Industries, is " the emergence of new firms which, for one reason or another, do not wish to co-operate but rather, in competition, to take advantage of the position built up by an integrated industry ".[1] There would be no desire for statutory powers if these firms were entirely imaginary. In such cases monopoly is clearly not " natural ", and, given a more favourable institutional framework, the opportunities in many industries for would-be competitors at present excluded would probably be quite attractive, and equally beneficial for the economy as a whole.[2]

62. An anti-monopolistic policy might also include State enterprise of a different kind, as a competitive corrective to private enterprise tending to crystallise in a monopolistic mould. In the nineteenth century this played some part in countries such as Australia and New Zealand, where a *socialisme sans doctrines* was pragmatically applied without much attention to theory. In fields such as insurance, for example, governmentally controlled units were established to compete with privately owned units and thus to counter any tendency towards unduly high charges. The practical results were sometimes a little disappointing, partly because after a time the State enterprises themselves grew weary of taking an independent line, and were sometimes charged with following the monopolistic leadership of their rivals.

---

[1] Report on Reconstruction, para. 61.

[2] Mr. Herbert Morrison's programme for post-war economic policy, which would, however, go much further in the direction of direct " full and effective public control " than our argument suggests to be necessary, includes several of the items listed above. A return to free competition might in some instances, he maintained, be assured " by legal changes, by careful public supervision, and by fiscal policies which encourage enterprise ", while public action might " sometimes take the form of direct, unsubsidised competition by those Government plants with which the end of the war will leave us so plentifully provided " (*Looking Ahead*, pp. 127-8).

63. The anti-monopolistic activities of the Swedish co-operative movement have had a similar objective. For a variety of reasons the Swedish economy has succeeded in maintaining a considerable degree of immunity from monopolistic influences, and to this the policy of the Swedish Co-operative Federation, which has regarded itself " less as a wholesaler to the retail societies than as a watchdog of consumers' interests in general ", has made an important contribution. On several occasions during the last forty years, when a price-raising monopoly appeared in industries producing consumers' goods with an elastic demand, the Federation has established, or, what was sometimes as effective, threatened to establish a competing factory ; this has checked or reversed the upward price movement, and thus maintained a more economic distribution of productive resources.[1]

[1] Cf. R. W. B. Clarke in *Democratic Sweden* (ed. M. Cole and C. Smith), pp. 131-4 ; C. M. Wright, *Economic Adaptation to a Changing World Market*, pp. 261-3.

CHAPTER XI

BLIND ALLEYS

1. HAVING thus discussed some positive suggestions which in combination might be expected to provide a solution for our problem, we may appropriately turn to a number of other proposals which have attracted a good deal of public attention, but which, whatever their intrinsic merits, have sometimes had the unfortunate effect of diverting attention from the real issue. Some of the ideas upon which these suggestions are based are quite sound, but unless their application is combined with action of the kind which we have suggested, they are likely to be ineffective even for their own immediate purposes. From the standpoint of maintaining the flexibility of economic structure necessary both for higher standards of living and for stability, they may therefore not unfairly be described as blind alleys.

(a) THE "SCIENTIFIC" POINT OF VIEW

2. The first illustrations that come to mind are two important currents of thought with considerable influence in recent years, whose net practical effects in relation to our problem, however, it is difficult to regard as other than unfavourable. Those who have been most subjected to their influence have thereby almost uniformly been encouraged to neglect, and almost to refuse to admit even the existence of the fundamental problem of structural adjustment. Many scientists have quite rightly been troubled about the common neglect of the social implications of their work, and, repelled by the economic disorders of recent years, have further urged that they would be cured by a wider application in all fields of human activity of " the scientific point of view ". A similar faith in " the scientific point of view " and its power to dissolve economic difficulties helps to explain the upsurge of interest from time to time in the views of the techno-

crats, and the impatience of engineers with what they believe to be artificial and unnecessary economic restraints. The adoption of the scientific point of view demands from us, however, a rigorous analysis of the nature of the means required for the attainment of our ends. If our end is either the attainment of higher standards of living or of greater economic security, and if we further postulate, as we should, that the advance of science places the attainment of these objectives more nearly within our reach than before, we have still not carried the application of the scientific point of view to its proper conclusion, unless we further insist that the attainment of these ends demands a continuous reallocation of the resources of production, and that this continuous reallocation will not take place unless we pay proper attention to all the forces which stand in its way. This is, in the strict sense of the term, an elementary scientific fact, but the scientists and engineers who reproach us for neglecting the scientific point of view too often give little evidence of being aware of it. In their incursions into economic or social theory they usually refrain from making any reference to this central problem, and fall ready victims to the propaganda of the various popular movements which equally refuse to face it, because they have been led astray by the fashionable delusion that problems of production are no longer important. To some of these solutions we shall refer later. At best they provide only supplementary remedies. They are not radical, in the true sense of the term, because they fail to get to the heart of the matter, which must be sought in an analysis of the conditions which require or check appropriate transfers of productive resources. We have already shown that in a growing economy the problem of production can never be finally " solved ".[1] Improvements in standards of living may even make the economic problem of production more and not less difficult. It is relatively easy when poverty narrows the effective range of our choice in allocating our resources of labour and capital. Growing wealth greatly widens this range, and thus makes the problem of allocation correspondingly more complex. It cannot be expected that " natural " scientists who do not take the trouble to familiarise themselves with this elementary

[1] Cf. *supra*, IV, 49.

economic principle will be able to make contributions of much value to the solution of economic and social problems.

(*b*) The Religious and Moral Appeal

3. In recent years claims have also been frequently made for an entirely new consideration of economic problems upon religious and moral grounds. To question the immediate relevance to the problems of economic organisation of the arguments used in such contexts as these may appear unnecessarily ungracious, but without questioning the fundamental value of the principles enunciated, an economist who refrained from pointing out that they still leave his fundamental questions entirely unanswered would be creating and not avoiding misunderstandings. The radical significance of changes in economic structure is not to be grasped merely by appealing to religious and moral principles, any more than by adopting the " scientific " approach which we have just criticised. It is only quite rarely [1] that the pronouncements of leaders in this sphere reveal any understanding of the central economic problem, the problem of the allocation of productive resources, and more often than not it is entirely ignored. So long as this is so, their appeals, however eloquent and bold, seem unlikely to point us along the right path. Reluctance to face this problem may perhaps itself be rooted in the quite worthy sentiment that it is improper to regard a human being as a mere convenience to be moved hither and thither in accordance with the whims of an impersonal economic process. But at least in its more exaggerated forms this sentiment itself is based upon a misapprehension. The economic process is not nearly so " impersonal " as at first sight might appear, if it is interpreted as being, as clearly it is in many of its most important aspects, a means for ensuring reasonable standards of living for other people. It might seem a little paradoxical, but it could plausibly be argued that in some circumstances mobility was a positive social duty. For people who refuse to change their

---

[1] As, for example, by the Archbishop of York, who told the House of Lords on July 21, 1943, that " there must be greater flexibility of labour. . . . Labour ought to be moved much more freely from place to place than it is at present."

jobs or to move from one place to another will frequently, by such a refusal, be unwittingly condemning others to a lower standard of living than otherwise they might have enjoyed. Much of our previous analysis has been designed to establish the thesis that resistance to change often positively increases the risks of instability for other people, and if the objective of higher standards were thought unpleasantly materialistic, the claims of stability should be much more persuasive.

4. There is indeed no necessity that people should be *compelled* to move, but if they refuse to do so when the general interest demands it, they should have a clear understanding of the significance of their action, both for other people and for themselves. If, to take an extreme case, some people prefer a hermit existence, abstaining entirely from any kind of economic activity, and trusting to the charity of others, there may be no convincing reason why they should not be allowed to make their own choice in the matter. But by so doing they are certainly depriving others of contributions to a fuller life which may be valuable or even almost essential. If in a less extreme case they are content to engage in economic activity, but insist that it shall be activity of their own choosing, and not that which would contribute most to social income and stability, there may still be no convincing reason why they should not be allowed to do as they please. But it is difficult to maintain that in such circumstances the rest of the community is under any obligation to maintain them at the average standard of level attained for the community as a whole. For this level is itself the resultant of numerous past individual adjustments, in the absence of which something simpler would have constituted the customary standard. A correct interpretation of the relation of the individual to society would preserve the right of the individual to direct his economic activities as he thought proper, but in so far as his choice failed to conform to the best interests of society as a whole, would also limit the obligations of society to make available to recalcitrants the benefits which were only available because others had taken their social duties more seriously.

5. From a strictly religious and moral standpoint, therefore, as also from a strictly scientific standpoint, the case stands for

careful examination of the conditions necessary for structural adjustment in our economy. Unfortunately many of the remedies to which we have referred, and which have so much attracted both scientists and those who demand " a new spirit " in our economic and industrial life, receive much of their support precisely on account of the belief that by adopting them we can evade this problem and avoid the necessity for any awkward redistribution of productive resources. This hope is founded on an illusion. So far, therefore, as the two currents of thought referred to above encourage this illusion they deserve to be described as " blind alleys ", for the central problem for a growing or expanding economy is and must remain the problem of continuous redistribution of the resources of production. Supplementary policies should be given their own proper place, but as most of them have already received abundant attention, while the central problem has been sadly neglected, there is some justification for attempting here to redress the balance by directing our thought almost exclusively to this fundamental issue.

(c) Leisure

6. Many of the more concrete and detailed notions which for our purpose deserve to be described as " blind alleys " are very much a matter of fashion, and the amount of attention reasonably devoted to each may therefore vary from year to year. Ten years ago it would have been necessary to say a good deal about, for example, the suggestion that awkward transfers of productive resources might be avoided by a more generous distribution of leisure, through a diminution in the normal number of working hours, by a lowering of the normal age of retirement or in other ways. We may easily exaggerate the extent to which our war experience has finally removed prejudices on this subject ; we may after the war again have to combat the curious notion that economic welfare is best served by preventing a large fraction of the female population from making any contribution to the national income. For the time being, however, nothing more than a summary treatment is needed. Sir William Beveridge has rejected the notion that post-war economic reconstruction might

be facilitated by withdrawing from active employment as large a fraction as possible of the older sections of the population, arguing rightly that on the contrary it will for some considerable time be a matter of importance to assure to the community the productive services of all who are competent to make any useful contribution,[1] and this part of his analysis has so far met with little criticism. Provision of more adequate leisure may be a proper end of post-war policy, but it is not so widely supposed as once it was that by so doing we would make any change of importance in the fundamental character of the economic problem of allocating productive resources and finding employment for everybody. The saving of time which new technical devices make possible in different industries must, in the nature of things, be very uneven. In many types of production technical change is quite unlikely ever to make possible much significant saving of time. A decision, therefore, to take out the benefits of increased production potential exclusively in the form of increased leisure and not at all in the form of an increased supply of material goods and services would still leave the necessity for considerable transfers of resources from industries where technical change had diminished the demand for labour to industries where this demand remained much as before. We should then have merely changed a little the character of the transfers of productive resources which were necessary, but would not have much affected their aggregate volume.[2]

[1] " Giving to each individual an incentive to continue at work as long as he can, in place of retiring, is a necessary attempt to lighten the burden that will otherwise fall on the British community, through the large and growing proportion of people at the higher ages " (*Social Insurance and Allied Service* [Cmd. 6404, 1942], p. 59. Cf. also p. 96).

[2] The whole of this question is discussed at greater length in A. G. B. Fisher, *The Clash of Progress and Security*, pp. 120-25. See also " Technical Improvements, Unemployment and Reduction of Working Hours ", *Economica*, November 1937, and " Shorter Working Hours and Industrial Transfers ", *Economic Record*, June 1937. The argument here is, of course, only remotely connected with the different question of the optimum number of working hours. There is good reason for believing that, strictly from the standpoint of productivity, the average or normal working week or working day is still often longer than the optimum. Adjustments of working hours in the light of such facts would, however, be motivated by a different purpose from that considered here, for they would be associated with the maintenance and sometimes with an increase of output in the industries affected.

(d) BACK TO THE LAND

7. Could greater stability be achieved by checking the world-wide movement of population away from agricultural pursuits, or even by reversing it ? This idea is still very powerful, though in many countries where, fifteen or twenty years ago, it was a widely accepted article of faith, it is now being more and more abandoned in favour of the view that in countries which have hitherto been mainly agricultural both economic progress and stability now require more rapid progress in the direction of industrialisation.[1] Despite this, many people still apparently believe in a " natural " ratio to be preserved between the number of people engaged in primary production and the numbers engaged in other kinds of work. The principles by which this ratio is to be calculated are seldom explained, but they seem usually to lead to the conclusion that in any given country the number engaged in primary production is smaller than it should be, despite the frequently lamented fact that food prices have for several years tended to be unduly low, and that those who get their living by producing food are therefore often much worse off than those who get their living by producing other things.

8. An exhaustive analysis of the influences behind the public opinion which deplores the so-called " Drift to the Towns " would carry us far beyond the limits of this book. For the purposes of our argument we merely insist that any attempt to maintain the agricultural population at its present level, and much more any attempt to increase it, is the same thing as attempting to check the further raising of average production levels, of standards of living.[2] Inadequate preparation for the extension of non-agricultural employment has sometimes had unfortunate social consequences, but this error could be remedied without attempting to reverse the occupational trends with which it has been associated. Some are prepared to follow the logic of this

---

[1] In New Zealand, however, it was still possible in 1943 to say that " the idea of receiving large drafts of migrants to find employment in factories and workshops rather than to people empty rural spaces is a novel one for this part of the world " (*New Zealand Herald*, February 26).

[2] One of the most interesting by-products of war-time experience is the light which it has thrown on the possibility in many countries of simultaneously increasing the production of food, and diminishing the number of food producers.

argument, and in view of the high value accorded by them to rural modes of life, to accept without complaint the threatened damage to standards of living. Not all, however, who wish to increase the agricultural population see this so clearly, and they should not be allowed to delude either themselves or other people into the belief that the policy they wish to pursue does not inexorably impose a check upon rising standards of living. If we wish to make the readjustments of economic structure which we have been discussing easier, we shall have nothing to do with policies which aim at stabilising or increasing the agricultural population. We shall not necessarily condemn all proposals for subsidising certain forms of agriculture, and it will be an appropriate purpose for our policy to avoid as far as possible any unreasonable hardships which might otherwise overwhelm those formerly employed in agriculture for whom a different place in the economy is now indicated as more appropriate. But in so doing we should be careful to make quite clear, from the point of view of the development of the economy as a whole, what exactly we are doing. We shall raise no objection to policies designed to make agriculture more efficient, and thus to expand the volume of agricultural output ; reforms of land tenure or of agricultural credit which would give efficient farmers a more stable prosperity should also receive due attention. But we should point out that such policies are inconsistent with the maintenance of agricultural population at its present level, and may indeed fail to achieve their avowed objective unless the agricultural population is allowed to decline. Improvements in the efficiency of agriculture must mean a capacity to produce the same volume of output at the cost of a smaller expenditure of labour and other productive resources.[1] Except for agricultural products with an abnormally high elasticity of demand, expansions of output should normally be accompanied by some contraction in the volume of labour employed in their production. If ten years

[1] " Wheat, the production of which required 57.7 man-hours per acre a hundred years ago, and 8.8 hours as recently as 1896, is now produced on the open plains of the United States (and probably of Canada) with less than 4 hours of man labour. The production of milk which consumed 55 man hours per 100 gallons in 1890 now takes only 37 hours. Few, if any, farm products are not produced to-day with substantially less labour than was required a generation ago " (J. E. Lattimer, " The Problem of Surplus Agriculture ", *International Journal of Agrarian Affairs*, October 1939, pp. 55-6).

after the war the proportion of the world's population engaged in agriculture is found to be greater than in 1939, we shall be obliged to conclude that the gloomy predictions of those who insisted that the war would cripple our economic activity and make the restoration of pre-war standards of living impossible were right.

(e) THE NUTRITIONAL APPROACH

9. There has been the strongest resistance to the acceptance of these views, a resistance fortified moreover in recent years by appealing to the apparent contradiction between the claim that the world already has as many farmers as it needs, and probably rather more, and the obvious fact that everywhere large numbers of people are not getting enough to eat. The great importance for human welfare of adequate supplies of food, based upon sound nutritional principles, is now generally understood, and the arguments and illustrations upon which this belief is founded need not be elaborated here. Upon this foundation, however, a more doubtful hypothesis is based that the most useful starting-point for a practical policy to assure both progress and economic security is the organisation of the supply of more adequate supplies of food. The fact that this current of thought was probably first set in motion by people with a particular regard for the welfare of farmers, who saw that farmers would be better off if other people were enabled or persuaded to consume more food, is no reason for refusing sympathetic examination to their views. When we find particular groups of producers earnestly pressing upon the rest of the world reforms which they claim will be in the general interest, but which are quite indubitably profitable for them, we are justified in examining their claims with a certain cautious reserve. Happily, however, we need not push caution so far as to believe that anything which can be shown to be favourable to some particular group must necessarily be harmful to the general interest. It is rather a point in favour of any policy which is generally advantageous if it can also be shown to confer special benefits upon the farmers. We may prudently discount a little the arguments put forward by the representatives of wheat producers elsewhere in favour of a reform of the con-

sumption habits of the Roumanians and Hungarians, but we should not go so far as to suppose that there is any intrinsic disharmony between changes demanded in the name of better nutritional standards for South-East Europe and changes initiated in the interests of the Australian or Canadian wheat farmer.

10. The general purposes of those who regard nutrition as the most important avenue of approach to post-war economic problems are so reasonable and humane that it may be difficult to cast doubts upon the wisdom of making everything turn upon this point " without arousing irritation and appearing to be a destructive critic or even an opponent of social progress. For ' adequate nutrition ' is clearly more than a scientific concept nowadays. It is also a slogan in social reform, a shining banner borne at the head of a marching regiment." [1]   But while the demand for many of the protective foods which figure so largely in modern nutritional programmes has the elasticity which gives some guarantee of the stability in expansion which is so desirable in a growing economy, such serious dangers are involved in exaggerating the importance of this approach that, even at the risk of provoking the resentment of ardent crusaders, we should insist upon giving the whole subject the most careful scrutiny before enrolling ourselves under the same banner.

11. The possibility of conflict between the policies suggested by our analysis of the dynamics of a progressive economy and policies based upon the nutritional approach may be indicated as follows. The former analysis suggests, broadly speaking, that equilibrium demands a steady contraction in the proportion of the community's resources devoted to food production. This, the nutritionists urge, is absurd, so long as many people are without adequate supplies of the right kinds of food. By adopting the nutritional approach we may therefore avoid the contraction alleged to be necessary and incidentally enable farmers to enjoy incomes which they will feel are not too far out of proper relationship with the general income structure.

12. The implications of this view should become clearer if we distinguish four general methods which might be adopted for

[1] M. K. Bennett, " Essential Food Requirements in War-time ", *Journal of Farm Economics*, November 1943, p. 835.

improving the economic conditions of the agricultural community. First we might restrict agricultural production with a view to raising prices to the point where they will be profitable for all producers. This has been widely attempted in a variety of ways, but apart from general objections naturally raised against the restriction of production, any attempt to allocate production quotas to farmers tends to keep the least efficient units in production, and is therefore unsatisfactory for consumers, while as time goes on it is also attended by all the obvious difficulties which arise in connection with the admission of new entrants to an industry. It is indeed largely in reaction against policies of restriction that the nutritional approach has been so widely acclaimed.

13. Agricultural production may indeed be adjusted to the volume indicated as desirable by the existing price situation by the transfer of the least efficient or the least favourably situated farmers to other occupations. This process which is going on all the time is ultimately the only satisfactory solution, but such transfers are unusually slow in agriculture, the farmer's reaction to sub-normal prices often being to increase rather than to curtail output, so that an incipient depression is thereby easily intensified. Such transfers also appear to be unreasonable in face of widespread inadequacy of food supplies, and are therefore distasteful to those who adopt the nutritional approach.

14. The second method is to subsidise farmers so that, even if market prices for food are low, it will still pay them to produce it in large quantities. Whether there is any justification for such a policy is a matter for each economy to decide for itself. It was increasingly adopted in pre-war years, as, for example, through the provision of free or cheap milk for school children. It has been still more widely extended during the war, and Resolution XXVI of the United Nations Conference on Food and Agriculture has recommended to the governments there represented " some form of direct action to make protective foods available free, or at low prices, to groups with inadequate diets ", as well as " special attention to assisting such groups as pregnant women, nursing mothers, infants, children, aged persons, invalids and low-paid persons ". The apparent interference with the freedom

of consumers' choice involved in the offer of goods at low subsidised prices can easily be defended in such cases on the ground
that the subsidies are likely to be paid in large part by the rich,
and further that, especially where children are affected, nutritional
science affords firm ground for the direction of consumers' choice.
However this may be, this method is essentially a device for
income redistribution, and from the broader point of view of a
stable economy is therefore to be judged by similar criteria to
those already suggested for social insurance. If the members of
any economy believe the prospects for ensuring to everyone in
the ordinary course of their economic activity an income sufficiently
large to permit the purchase of everything needed for a civilised
life or for productive efficiency to be so remote that to wait for
the attainment of this ultimate objective would condemn many
people to inefficiency and poverty, it is for them to decide what
additions to the smaller incomes are to be provided, directly or
indirectly, out of public funds. Action of this kind is already a
commonplace, and, especially if the general level of efficiency is
maintained or raised after the war, it is likely to be further
extended. But however justifiable or indeed essential it may be,
it has little to do with the problem of structural adjustment. It is
theoretically possible that the taxes from which ultimately the
subsidies must be paid might be deducted from taxpayers' income
just as they were about to decide how to spend the additional
purchasing power accruing to them as a result of the offer of
cheaper goods based upon technical improvements ; in that case
the diversion of this additional purchasing power to the coffers of
the State might " solve " the problem of reallocating resources of
production by destroying the necessity for any such reallocation.
In practice, however, it is more probable that the payment of
such taxes would mean a reduction of certain types of customary
expenditure by the taxpayers, so that increased security for farmers
would be purchased at the cost of increased insecurity for people
employed in other industries.

15. Similarly the third method, education or propaganda
designed to persuade consumers to buy more food rather than
other things, however justifiable if their failure to realise the
importance of food damages their welfare and efficiency, will

tend merely to shift the problem of unremunerative prices from agriculture to other branches of production, and is therefore also normally irrelevant to the problem of structural readjustment.

16. The fourth, and in the last resort the only effective method of ensuring stable prosperity for farmers, is by means of a general increase in consumers' income, and this can be done effectively only by increasing production in general. But in any well co-ordinated plan for increasing production in general food should play its part only in appropriate relationship to other consumers' needs, and in certain circumstances its role will be quite subordinate. For the outputs of the various commodities ought then to be increased as nearly as possible in the same proportions in which any general expansion of purchasing power would be devoted to their purchase. The proper position of food in the programme would then depend on two main factors ; firstly, on the fraction of additional income which consumers were likely to allocate to food, and secondly, on the extent to which there was already a tendency for the supplies of various commodities to exceed or to fall short of the current demand. Judged by the first criterion, the relative importance of food would naturally depend upon existing average income levels. In poor countries the production of food would properly occupy a larger proportion of public attention than in wealthy countries. In countries like Great Britain and the United States, on the other hand, the fraction of any small general increase in real incomes likely to be devoted to the purchase of extra food would probably be rather less than a third.

17. An estimate of the significance of the second criterion involves much the same considerations as those already raised in our discussion of the " growing points " of an economy. Important modifications are no doubt introduced into the picture by the effects of war-time destruction and distortion, which especially in many parts of Europe clearly for a time place food in a much higher position on the priority list of requirements than it would normally occupy. But after these transitional diffi-culties have been overcome, there seems no reason why we should not anticipate a return to a structure of agricultural production not very different fundamentally from the structure

of the few years preceding the outbreak of war. The outstanding feature of this structure was the comparative ease with which increased supplies of food could be made available ; this fact indeed explained in large measure the normally weak competitive position of agricultural producers. As compared with other producers they always tended to be a little worse off, precisely for the reason that their products were relatively abundant. In the normal development of a progressive economy there should be a relationship, which will vary from time to time, between the rate of expansion in each part of it. If any single part gets a little out-of-step, and expands too rapidly, those who are working there will find themselves in a worse position than other producing groups, and the fact that this was the fate of which agriculturists complained so much suggests that they had got a little out-of-step. There is a considerable danger that a similar situation will recur, and may even be made more difficult by injudicious propaganda about nutrition. In the same process of normal development pressure is most usefully applied to those parts of the economy which are lagging behind ; an examination of recent history suggests that for the world economy as a whole this does not include the agricultural sector. There are indeed good reasons for believing that the range of application of Engel's famous " Law ", which postulated that " the poorer an individual, a family or a people, the greater must be the percentage of income necessary for the maintenance of physical sustenance, and again of this a greater portion must be allowed for food ", is not so wide as was once believed. Investigations at very low income levels, as, for example, in China, Siam and India, have shown that there at least small increases in income may be associated with an increase in the fraction of income spent on food, and not a decline, as is the normal experience in wealthier economies ; bearing in mind the intense poverty which still afflicts large areas throughout the world, it is not surprising to find it estimated that for about 50 per cent. of the world's population Engel's Law does not apply.[1] Where therefore nutritional standards are still grossly and almost universally deficient, as in certain colonial areas, there may be good reasons quite in harmony with our present line of

[1] Cf. C. M. Wright, *Economic Adaptation to a Changing World Market*, pp. 33-5.

argument for putting food production in a prominent, and perhaps in the foremost, place in a programme of economic development.[1] But these are special cases ; if we are taking a wider view of the relative needs of the world economy as a whole, we should, instead of agreeing with Resolution II of the United Nations Conference on Food and Agriculture that action " in the field of production, distribution and consumption of food and other agricultural products in the post-war period will be the most important prerequisite for the achievement of freedom from want " (freedom from want having already been distinguished from freedom from hunger, the problem of the period immediately following the war), rather support the alternative view that the most important prerequisite was appropriate action in the field of the production and distribution of things other than food.[2] A still more accurate analysis would perhaps differentiate between different types of food. The demand for many of the " protective " foods is probably elastic even at relatively high income levels, so that in this case the direct requirements of nutritional science harmonise with the requirements of adaptation in a progressive economy, provided that a reasonably high income level can be assumed. But as social workers have often pointed out, it is little use urging a man in receipt of no more than the basic wage to drink more milk, unless one can at the same time show how his income in general can be increased. And a substantial part of the expansion of demand for " protective " foods is often offset by some decline in the demand for other types of food.

18. Increased production in appropriate proportions of things other than food will benefit farmers, for part of the additional purchasing power thus generated will be used to purchase farm products. It will also tend to raise the nutritional standards of those responsible for such increased production, unless farmers

---

[1] Cf. H. W. Foster and E. V. Bacon, *Wealth for Welfare*.

[2] The Conference did indeed also draw attention to the importance of these other things. Resolution XV affirmed that " a secure, adequate and suitable supply of food ... can be achieved only as part of a world-wide policy of industrial and agricultural expansion ", and Resolution XXIV pointed out that " the sound expansion of industry in undeveloped and other areas, with equality of access to materials and markets, serves also to expand production and purchasing power, and is therefore indispensable to any comprehensive program for the advancement of agriculture ".

are sluggish in responding to the additional demands placed upon them. There is, however, much evidence to suggest that, at least in the case of certain agricultural products, there is an inherent tendency to over-produce,[1] and recent experience confirms the view that, given favourable price conditions, farmers will quickly adapt the volume of their output to an increasing demand. But if increased production of food comes first, farmers may not be any better off, for the tendency to sub-normal prices for their products will be strengthened, and can only be dealt with by various subsidy devices at the expense of other parts of the economy ; while moreover the provision of cheap subsidised food may be a useful and indeed an essential device for maintaining the welfare and efficiency of other poor sectors in the economy, it fails to raise these sectors to the assured position of prosperity which ought to be theirs in a smoothly developing progressive economy.

19. There is indeed no reason why in practice the policies of expanding production in general and of distributing cheap subsidised food for the benefit of the poorer sections of the population should not be combined. The former, while more radical and permanent in its effects, will also probably be rather slow, and if we wait for its full development, we may condemn substantial sections of the population to conditions discreditable to our civilisation. Measures of the second kind should, however, be clearly recognised for what they are, mere stop-gaps, worth undertaking no doubt, but dangerous if there is any tendency to regard them as adequate substitutes for more radical treatment of the situation, and there are good reasons for fearing that exaggeration of the value of the nutritional approach may encourage just this tendency.

20. It is indeed for this very reason that there is some justification for discussing the nutritional approach in close association with our criticism of " blind alleys ". For it may be suspected that among the attractions which this approach has exerted is the vague and perhaps scarcely conscious feeling that the inconveniences inherent in the structural adjustments which

---

[1] Report of the Delegation on Economic Depressions, Part I (1943), *The Transition from War to Peace Economy*, p. 104.

we have been examining are so great that it would be very agreeable if some easy way out could be found which would absolve
our consciences in declining to wrestle with the many formidable
enemies who seem to block the path to progress. A nutritional
programme seems to promise substantial benefits for farmers and
for poor consumers, without at the same time imposing any serious
inconvenience upon other people. This hope, for the reasons
given, is unfortunately based upon an illusion. The inconveniences of progress are real, and if we turn aside from them
because the task of removing them looks unpleasant and awkward,
the benefits likely to accrue from the subsidiary methods which
look easier, though worth having, will not carry us very far. As
the United Nations Conference on Food and Agriculture pointed
out, " the first cause of hunger and malnutrition is poverty ". In
the war against poverty provision must be made for larger supplies
of food ; this, however, is a relatively easy part of the task. The
much more difficult thing is to remove the barriers which impede
the production of larger supplies of other things, and difficult
tasks ought to take precedence of easy tasks. Food is undoubtedly
in one important sense primary, but it is not, on that account,
" the best starting-point for all other joint activities ".[1] The best
starting-point for a joint programme of production is surely a
field where in the past production has been unduly hampered,
and not one where production has normally tended to be even
over-abundant.

(f) CREDIT REFORM

21. Another extensive and important field of reform which in
our generation has received even more attention, both expert and
popular, than nutrition is currency and credit policy. It is widely
believed that more progress has been made in understanding and
controlling the monetary mechanism than in any other sector of
our economic life, and though it would be rash to overestimate
the extent to which all the important issues can now be regarded
as beyond dispute, there is much to be said for this view. Nevertheless while one is obliged to agree that a wise monetary and
credit policy is a matter of quite first-rate importance, the lively

[1] *Sunday Times*, June 6, 1943.

N

interest which the whole subject has aroused and the satisfaction so frequently expressed at the advances in wisdom upon which we can now congratulate ourselves as contrasted with our ignorant predecessors, have also had the unfortunate effect of encouraging the neglect of still more radical issues, for grappling with which even the wisest monetary policy merely prepares the way.[1]

22. There is indeed a much closer connection between monetary policy and the solution of the problem of structural adjustment than there is between that problem and nutritional reform, for general movements in the level of prices are among the most important factors complicating the task of structural adjustment at any time, and exerting a powerful influence upon the willingness of investors to perform their appropriate functions. Monetary policy cannot by itself determine that economic conditions in general shall be " good ", but it is often quite enough to ensure that they shall be bad, and ordinary observation fully justifies the opinion that " wise is the management and fortunate its employees, which puts its full energies into the problem of developing labor-saving technology at times when economic conditions are good ".[2]

23. Credit theorists, however, as well as those who have the practical responsibility for directing credit policy, should be constantly reminded that, however important their work may be, it is merely an instrument for attaining other ends, and not an end in itself. Bad credit policy may create an impossible situation for the appropriate and expeditious redistribution of productive resources. Good credit policy may create a situation more favourable for this purpose. But it will not by itself automatically produce the ultimate end aimed at. Given a sound credit policy, it is still necessary independently to initiate the steps needed for structural adjustments. This fact is indeed happily widely recognised by credit theorists, and in support of the particular proposals put forward from time to time, say for

---

[1] Professor Hutt even goes so far as to maintain that " the problem of unutilised valuable resources is capable of solution, even if not of the ideal solution, under the crudest monetary system with which any country is burdened to-day " (*Plan for Reconstruction* (1943), p. 141 note).

[2] E. D. Smith, *Technology and Labor*, p. 56. The whole question is further examined in *The Clash of Progress and Security*, ch. vii.

exchange depreciation, or for the creation of a new international credit mechanism, they are accustomed to say that these things are designed merely to provide a breathing-space within which the more fundamental adjustments can be attempted in better order and with greater hopes for success. Unfortunately the need for a breathing-space is often and naturally most keenly felt when people are somewhat weary, and when one is weary it is fatally easy to grasp eagerly at the breathing-space offered, using it merely as an opportunity for doing nothing more, or at best merely for endeavouring to maintain one's customary and familiar activities. Unless the breathing-spaces which ingenious monetary and credit devices offer us are made periods of intense activity within which structural adjustments are pushed forward with the utmost energy, monetary reform, in even its most admirable shapes, deserves also to be described as a blind alley.

CHAPTER XII

SOME THIRD-RATE SOLUTIONS

1. We have already agreed that especially in times of emergency we must sometimes be prepared for imperfect solutions which do not closely accord with the principles we have here outlined. We may prefer a policy which will facilitate the performance of relatively well-paid work likely to produce things which the rest of the community will be eager to have, but we shall not be able in all cases to get this, and we must therefore then put up with the provision of poorly paid stopgap work. And as this itself can seldom be easily improvised at a moment's notice, it is sensible to look ahead and have some plans ready as a precautionary measure of insurance. We live in an imperfect world, and if we expect that everything will work out without friction or waste of effort, we shall certainly be disappointed. Human nature, too, is often surprisingly tough, and we can and do adjust ourselves to almost anything. We are neither asking nor expecting that everyone shall order their lives exclusively in the light of the principles here enunciated ; we shall be quite satisfied, and would indeed have made solid progress, if we could ensure that the obstacles which at present impede action in accordance with them were removed for a comparatively small proportion of the population, for it is probable that a quantitatively small fringe of flexibility may turn out to be as much as is necessary, at the same time incidentally benefiting many who have no desire to figure actively in it.

2. It is, however, always dangerous to pay too much attention to mere insurance devices. We cannot always count on making our dreams come true, but it is often fatally easy to make our bad dreams come true, and excessive preoccupation with insurance against all possible risks may greatly increase the chances of risks becoming realities. Those who have carefully prepared the insurance devices then proudly display them, demanding congratulations upon their skill and foresight, but quite forgetting

184

that their own activities, and in particular their indifference to other problems, may in large measure have generated the very difficulties against which they can offer an inadequate protection.[1]

3. With this idea in mind we shall comment briefly upon a number of proposals, each of which has received attention as an insurance device designed to ensure greater stability. The list includes public works, controlled construction of capital equipment and international raw material controls. A characteristic common to all of them is that they rate very low the importance of producing what consumers are likely to want. To this extent those who regard the satisfaction of consumers' requirements as the most important end for economic policy will therefore class them as third-rate solutions.

4. As a subsidiary element in a more radical policy, public works no doubt deserve to maintain their place, but we should be careful to safeguard ourselves against the ever-present risk that they may deteriorate into the provision of public amenities and services which, however laudable in themselves, no one particularly wants to have. Some fringes in the areas normally covered by public works can in the general interest advantageously be filled in by otherwise superfluous labour in times of depression, but such solutions merely touch the surface of our problem.

5. It is a little curious that public works still occupy such a prominent place in the programmes of many who energetically press the need for expansionist policies in sharp contrast, as they insist, with the bad old ways of the past. The central problem of an expansive economy, it might have been supposed, was the problem of producing new things, or more adequate supplies of some of the things which many consumers had to do without when their incomes were smaller. The tone of much of the current discussion of expansionism almost gives the impression that the expansionists have despaired of any substantial addition to the volume of the goods and services which ordinary people would be glad to have, and therefore in what is fundamentally a defeatist spirit turn their thought to public works.

6. There has indeed in recent years been some growing uneasiness lest the popularity of old-style public works should be carried

[1] Cf. *supra*, IV, 3, 4.

too far. The spectacle during the Great Depression of policies designed to stem the tide by converting a substantial fraction of the working population into unskilled labourers, obliged to work with the most primitive capital equipment, was not at all inspiring. It was with good reason felt that a civilised society should do better than this. There has accordingly been a tendency recently to take a more sophisticated view of public works, a development often closely tied up with the view that the key to the trade cycle is to be found in the maintenance of an even level of activity in the industries producing capital goods. The demand for capital goods is clearly greatest in certain key industries, and with a view to stabilising this demand, it is accordingly argued that " an application of the Public Corporation principle to cover a number of the industries and services which are among the largest consumers of capital goods, both for extensions and for replacements, would give much more scope for the pursuance by the State of an investment policy calculated to promote ' full employment ' ".[1]

7. It would not be relevant to attempt here any exhaustive examination of the implications of this view. The importance of a balancing factor for stabilising the demand for capital goods may or may not be an argument of first-rate importance for deciding whether a particular industry should be placed under some kind of public control, though it may be suspected that this question ought mainly to be determined by reference to other criteria. It is, however, relevant to indicate the similarities between this proposal and the more old-fashioned public works. We used to be urged to fill in the gaps in employment in times of depression by planting trees, building new roads and bridges and repairing old ones, providing water supplies for rural districts, and the like. It was, however, increasingly difficult to believe that these were " exactly the projects, the need of which would have first struck a visitor from another planet who had been asked to look over our economic system and suggest enterprises which he thought might usefully be set on foot to meet genuine public needs ".[2] We are accordingly now urged to prepare for the

---

[1] *Employment Policy and Organisation of Industry after the War* (Nuffield College, 1943), p. 28.   [2] Barbara Wootton, *Plan or No Plan*, pp. 35-6.

production, beyond what would normally be demanded in times of depression, of all kinds of capital equipment, which might be found useful for the construction of railways or ships, or for the modernisation of electrical equipment and the like. These things will often be quite useful to have, just as it was useful to have better bridges and more roads, but we should not ignore the danger that we may again discover that we have been attempting to solve our problem by producing things which no one very much wants. Instead of having a rather over-elaborate equipment of roads, we may instead saddle ourselves with an unnecessarily elaborate equipment of machinery which we may never be able fully to utilise. And as the maintenance and upkeep of these things will require more effort than the maintenance and upkeep of the old-style type of public works, the risks of finding that we have produced a large herd of white elephants to trouble us at a later date will be correspondingly increased.

8. The maintenance of employment in the heavy industries is also a motive attracting support for industrial development in the so-called backward areas after the war. Such development certainly deserves a prominent position in post-war reconstruction programmes, but there is some danger of regarding it primarily as a measure for easing the difficulties of transition from war to peace for the over-developed heavy industries of some of the Allied states. In that event development may be pushed in directions different from those most likely to meet the really pressing needs of the inhabitants of the more backward countries. If we discover that what they need will also incidentally mitigate our own difficulties of transition, we shall have a legitimate ground for rejoicing. That, however, is a different thing from regarding industrial development elsewhere primarily as a means for assuring security to some of our own industries.

9. Our third and last illustration of third-rate solutions which, whatever their value for other purposes, may actually impede structural readjustments, is taken from the field of international raw material control. This too is a subject a full analysis of which would take us far beyond our present field of enquiry. Nevertheless there is an important sense in which these controls too are in some danger of being converted into an elaborate form of inter-

national public works, which, like other public works programmes, would be open to the criticism that they set out to provide opportunities for the increased production of things which consumers do not particularly want. In discussions of the deliberations of the United Nations Conference on Food and Agriculture of May–June 1943 a good deal of attention was paid to the organisation of buffer stocks as a stabilising price factor. The subject is important and complicated, but at first sight it was a little curious that a body presumably concerned with the task of ensuring that people had more to eat should have been asked, and not merely for immediate post-war relief purposes, to include in its list of practical proposals action designed to ensure a larger production of foodstuffs which then, just because the increased production was to be placed in a buffer stock, people would not be permitted to eat. There is, of course, a great deal more which deserves to be said on this subject, but in our eagerness to fall into line with the favourable attitude towards raw material controls which is now so fashionable, we should not be allowed to conceal from ourselves this important aspect of the problem. Instead of building roads and bridges which no one particularly wants, or storing further quantities of unnecessary gold, the world may find that in approving these controls it has committed itself instead to producing further unnecessary quantities of wheat or cotton. For the analogies sometimes adduced in defence of this policy are not very convincing. The policy adopted by Joseph as a safeguard against famines in Egypt was no doubt wise in his day, and a similar policy might equally wise to-day in countries such as China and India where famine is still a real risk. But taking the world as a whole, any difficulties experienced in recent years in getting enough food to eat have not as a rule been the result of any serious physical deficiency in the supply of food.

10. The obvious risks involved in the maintenance of buffer stocks have often been pointed out. The knowledge that large stocks are waiting to be sold may keep prices unduly low, and thus be disadvantageous to producers, while on the other hand the maintenance of prices in times of over-supply may encourage over-production and retard the processes of adjustment for which the situation calls. This point too has been clearly realised

by some supporters of these schemes, who defend themselves by pointing, like the monetary reformers, to the desirability of having a " breathing-space " within which high-cost producers can be gently directed into other fields of production. Their case is not lightly to be rejected, but as we have seen in the parallel case of credit policy, the risk remains that during the breathing-space thus provided the producers who ought to move will continue to do little more than breathe, and instead of seizing the opportunity for orderly readjustment, may treat it as an excuse for staying where they are.

CHAPTER XIII

PLANNING

Those who would give up essential liberty to purchase a little temporary safety deserve neither liberty nor safety.

BENJAMIN FRANKLIN

1. PLANNING is such a protean concept that some careful analysis of its content seems necessary before deciding whether it provides the solution for which we are seeking, or perhaps is merely a " blind alley " or a " third-rate solution ". No word has been more popular in recent discussions of economic policy ; many warnings have been given that we must " plan or perish ". But judged even by the current deplorably low standards of precision in definition, there is probably also no other word which is used so loosely as is " planning ", and which therefore has such little value as an aid to clear thinking. When one observes the same word being used to describe Mr. Bellerby's post-war proposals,[1] Professor Hutt's intensely liberal programme of institutional reform,[2] and Mr. Winston Churchill's sketch [3] of a four-year legislative programme for a post-war parliament, the conclusion can scarcely be resisted that it has now been so debased as to become practically meaningless.

2. Partly for this very reason an appearance of unanimity in favour of planning can easily be established. There is such an attractive common-sense sound about the word that whatever we propose we are naturally disposed to describe as a plan. But if everybody does this, the only possible definition left for the word is " whatever the writer or speaker using it happens to like ". If planning means forethought, the avoidance as far as possible of hit-or-miss methods, the careful adaptation of means to ends, no rational person can do other than approve it. " In this sense everybody who is not a complete fatalist is a planner, every political act is (or ought to be) an act of planning, and there

[1] *Economic Reconstruction*, vol. i, *National, Industrial and Regional Planning* (1943).
[2] *Plan for Reconstruction* (1943).
[3] In a broadcast speech on March 21, 1943.

can be difference only between good and bad, between wise and foresighted and foolish and short-sighted planning." [1] Whatever the department of human activity with which we are concerned, if we want to achieve anything, we must have clear ideas both of the ends at which we are aiming and of the means most suitable for their attainment. Approval of this obvious and indeed platitudinous proposition does not, however, carry us very far, and those who, dissatisfied with the results of economic planning in this broadest sense, now urge us to " plan " on new lines, usually intend us to go a good deal further. In any event general approval of forethought still leaves undetermined in any particular case the nature of the ends in view, the aptness of the instruments proposed for attaining them, and the methods to be used in balancing and co-ordinating the manifold divergent purposes which in real life motivate our activities. We are entitled to seek assurances on each of these points before we permit general approval of forethought to commit us to approval of any specific " plan ".

3. Curiously enough, however, while the " scientific " setting in which " planning " is often presented accounts for much of its popular support, the widespread approval which the idea commands in certain intellectualist circles is actually based on their reluctance to admit the necessity for any rational balancing of the relative advantages of alternative economic choices, and too often when planners urge us to neglect economic considerations and pay more attention to social considerations, they give no hint of any kind to show how in their opinion the various ends, agreed by all to be important, are to be compared or balanced. In effect they urge us to abandon the use of any rational standard for determining the relative advantages of different kinds of employment or investment, substituting for the admittedly imperfect methods of the past nothing better than the arbitrary decisions of the " planners ".

4. Many who feel that " socialism " is not quite respectable have also preferred to talk about planning, in the more or less conscious belief that approval might more easily be won for socialist programmes if they are given a more innocuous name.

[1] F. A. Hayek, *The Road to Serfdom*, p. 26.

To their credit, a good many avowed socialists have not found this devious procedure altogether attractive, and partly no doubt for the excellent reason that, while they rejoice at seeing others rallying around them in the attack on competition, they have an uneasy half-conscious feeling that there is a fundamental clash between the ultimate purposes which socialists have usually had in mind and the motives which often lie behind the modern criticisms of competition.[1]   And while the positive content of socialism is still much less clearly defined than the intensive labours of analysis and exposition which have now for several generations been devoted to the subject would have entitled us to expect, this fundamental divergence of outlook among the " planners " means that the ideas of socialism are crystal-clear as contrasted with the confusion which emerges from a study of the proposals which are now put forward as " plans ".

5. In this connection the Germans have been more precise in their use of terms than the English. *Planwirtschaft* means the centralised direction of economic activity by an overriding authority, and if " planning " is to mean something more precise than general foresight and willingness to look ahead, one would expect that it would be defined in similar terms. Some writers justify this expectation, but others use the term much more loosely, often mixing its meaning up with the complex of ideas suggested by the once popular phrase, self-government in industry, where centralised control may become very shadowy, or even apply it to any sort of policy programme, irrespective of the extent to which it happens to embody either of these two elements. In our subsequent analysis planning will be assumed to involve some measure of centralised control of economic activity, the precise form taken by such control being dependent upon various practical considerations, or sometimes upon the individual tastes of the planners. By their own lack of precision in definition, the planners have indeed presented their critics with a very awkward problem. Limitations of space forbid any attempt at exhaustive classification of all the ideas which are implicit in recent proposals,

---

[1] It may be significant that a correspondent in a left-wing journal has recently thought it worth while to observe " that in these days of monopoly capitalism, *laissez-faire* Liberalism no longer meets the situation, though the Liberal idea is not to be lost sight of " (*Tribune*, January 21, 1944).

which have been described as planning programmes, and any general observations such as are made subsequently in this study may only with difficulty avoid the accusation of unfairness to certain schools of planning, whose members may feel that certain charges at least do not apply to them. If, however, any are disposed to cherish resentment on this account, they are earnestly adjured to reflect whether there may not be others, no less influential, who call themselves by the same name, to whom our criticisms are directly relevant. It may even be that if they searched their own souls in moments of calm reflection they would recognise in some of their own ideas at least the seeds of notions which, when fully grown, would not be easily distinguished from what we are outlining here.[1]

6. The individual's own judgment upon the matter will moreover be much influenced by non-economic considerations. He will often be concerned to enquire whether centralised control of economic activity necessarily involves also centralised direction of all the other significant activities of human life. The issue becomes finally a political or philosophical issue, and a discussion here, which would inevitably be brief, of these profound questions would also serve no very useful purpose. It is common form nowadays to insist that planning *must* be reconciled with individual liberty, and with the preservation of all the social values which we believe to be characteristic of the best in our civilisation. Such issues cannot, however, be determined by mere reiteration, however emphatic or eloquent ; so far the practical experience of planned economies has not on this point been altogether reassuring, and our own war-time experience has not been entirely free from episodes which illustrate the natural tendency for fallible human beings endowed with power to use it for purposes other than those immediately in mind when the power was first entrusted to them.[2]

7. There are, however, certain aspects of the current dis-

[1] If Julian Huxley is right in supposing that the choice between " to plan and not to plan " is identical with the choice between " to go forward or to hold back " (Introduction to Michael Straight's *Make This the Last War*, p. 10), the author of this book is certainly to be classed among the planners. It is, however, difficult to believe that expressions of this kind are more than mere playing with words.

[2] For a stimulating general discussion of the implications of planning, the reader should refer to Professor F. Zweig's *The Planning of Free Societies* (1942).

cussions of this problem to which attention may usefully be directed here. The conclusions reached are unlikely to be decisive one way or another for answering the question, Should we or must we plan ? The analysis will, however, be worth while if it makes it clear that questions presented in that way are not as a rule very helpful. It is in fact almost impossible to pass any sensible judgment on planning in general as an abstract idea. We must first ask in each concrete case what the planners propose to achieve ; secondly, how they propose to achieve their objective ; and, thirdly, whether instruments are likely to be available for carrying out the proposed plan. And as a corollary to our second question, we should enquire particularly if the planners have taken into account, whatever their objective may be, higher income levels, greater economic security or more equal income distribution, the necessity for continuous change and adaptation in the structure of production as a whole. Few of our modern planners stand up very successfully in face of the analysis implied in these questions. We may accordingly find it quite consistent to combine hearty approval of the idea of planning in general, and properly interpreted (for such approval commits us to nothing at all definite), with a profound scepticism about most of the proposals put forward to-day by avowed " planners ".

8. We have already discussed the broad objectives which most modern " planners " put forward in justification of their proposals. We saw good reason for denying that the over-whelming importance now attached to security now demands an entirely new approach to economic policy, and for affirming that in the modern world security could not be attained unless we applied our minds with at least equal pertinacity to the continuous redistribution of productive resources which is necessary for rising standards of living. Too many of the planners appear, however, to imagine that emphatic repetition of the desirability of combining security with improvements in living standards absolves them from any duty to examine more closely the problem of structural adjustment, and accordingly push ahead with immediate measures which have security alone in view without pausing to consider whether in so doing both objectives may not be sacrificed.

9. This apparent unanimity conceals, however, a considerable divergence of opinion about the special objectives which arouse the enthusiasm of different planning groups. Planning derives much of its support from enthusiasts who implicitly assume that the plan will give priority to some often highly laudable objective for which they happen to have a special regard.[1] "It is the frustration of his ambition in his own field which makes the specialist revolt against the existing order."[2] It is, however, an obvious delusion to suppose that all such ends can be fully and immediately realised at the same time. We have an economic problem whose solution demands continuous readjustment precisely because compromises are necessary between conflicting purposes, and general talk about the virtues of planning affords no guidance whatever as to how the compromises are to be made. "The effect of the people agreeing that there must be central planning, without agreeing on the ends, will be rather as if a group of people were to commit themselves to take a journey together without agreeing where they want to go : with the result that they may all have to make a journey which most of them do not want at all."[3]

10. One of the justifiable grounds upon which severe criticism has often been levelled against the existing economic order is its tendency to view its human members quite impersonally, as mere means for the attainment of ends, rather than, as appropriate reforms in policy might make it easier to do, as ends in themselves. But judged even by this test, much of the work of modern "planners" must be condemned. Carried away by the specious beauties of a neat and allegedly "scientific" programme, they far too easily slide into a position where it is taken for granted that human individuals must be compelled or induced to adapt themselves to the plan, rather than that the plan must be adapted to the

---

[1] "The lover of the countryside who wants above all that its traditional appearance should be preserved and that the blots already made by industry on its fair face should be removed, no less than the health enthusiast who wants all the picturesque but insanitary old cottages cleared away, or the motorist who wishes the country cut up by big motor roads, the efficiency fanatic who desires the maximum of specialisation and mechanisation no less than the idealist who for the development of personality wants to preserve as many independent craftsmen as possible, all know that their aim can be fully achieved only by planning — and they all want planning for that reason " (F. A. Hayek, *The Road to Serfdom*, p. 40).

[2] F. A. Hayek, *op. cit.* p. 41.   [3] F. A. Hayek, *op. cit.* p. 46.

widely varying purposes of individual human beings. " To scorn
delights and live laborious days " is something from which a
far-seeing human being should not shrink, but to do this in a
spirit of devotion to an ideal, clearly understood and consciously
accepted, is something entirely different from doing it as a task
imposed upon passive human instruments, obliged to place themselves without reserve at the disposal of a planner's preconceived
notions of what is good for them.[1] Uneasiness about plans which
appear to postulate such passivity is in no way diminished when
sometimes even the same " planners " seek popular approval for
their schemes by quite unwarranted claims that a utopia might
thereby be speedily attained. Some who are attracted by such
utopias would be sadly disillusioned when they discovered in
more detail what the " planners " had in store for them.

11. One attractive side-aspect of planning to which importance
is often attached is the working-out of precise targets to be
attained within a declared period of time. If, by so doing, we
can arouse enthusiasm and ensure more steady attention to the
matter in hand, there is much to be said in favour of this device.
We should not, however, overrate its importance or exaggerate
its novelty. Every student who undertakes a university course
is obliged to examine with some care the successive steps prescribed for the progress of his studies which may be spread over
a long period of years, and in less formal ways we often find it
helpful to set out a co-ordinated programme of activity which
will lead step by step somewhere near our final objective. But,
especially as applied to many-sided economic activity, it is often
little more than a propaganda device, and the mere elaboration

---

[1] It is often insisted that the planners' objective will not be achieved without the
powerful aid of propaganda. According to Professor Zweig (*The Planning of Free
Societies*, p. 86), " good propaganda is the second condition for the proper working of
planning ", the first condition being good administration. As a social instrument propaganda can obviously be used for all sorts of purposes, good and bad, and there is no
convincing reason why its potentialities should not be fully used by beneficent statesmen.
In our own time, however, its long-run effectiveness has been much exaggerated. Many
clever people seem to have a boundless confidence in the power of propaganda to bluff
the ordinary man, and the influence of such views represents perhaps the most remarkable
of the victories upon which, even after defeat in war, totalitarian dictators may possibly
be able to congratulate themselves on scoring over certain sections of opinion among
their enemies. The cautious observer will prefer to wait a little before he allows the
peculiar experience of totalitarian states in recent years to convince him that clever propaganda will always be able to persuade people that things are other than they really are.

of the details of a target is no guarantee that its essential objectives will be attained. The position is rather like that of the importance attached at a cricket match to the strokes whereby the captain of the side approaches the century, or the total score reaches some neat round figure, such as 300. The process excites the spectators and may increase the keenness and efficiency of the players. The really important thing, however, is to win the match, to which the cricketers' targets may make a subsidiary but usually quite unimportant contribution. We know indeed much more about the " targets " publicised from time to time for the period plans of the various countries which have adopted this device than about the degree to which the results actually registered correspond to the prepared plan. There is, of course, no reason why we should on this account think any the worse of these plans, but an objective study of their history should find much more of interest in the trial-and-error methods often adopted than in mere propaganda devices.

12. It is, however, the test implied in the second of our three questions which most of the modern planners fail to pass, and many of them do not even see what the question means. By what means, we enquire, are the ends envisaged by the planners to be achieved ? In reply, we are often given an elaborate account of institutions and administrative machinery, of boards and government departments and tribunals, of public corporations and trade associations. The account may or may not be consistent and convincing. But at best the answer is as inadequate as an account of a new transport agency which confined itself to explaining the structure of the steam-engines or the aeroplanes which were to perform the work of transport, and entirely neglected both the power which was to work the engines and its relation to their structure. It is interesting to know about the form of any National Development Board to which it is proposed should be entrusted authority to control and direct capital investment throughout an economy. But before we approve of any such proposal, we prudently enquire about the principles to be applied by the members of the Board in granting or withholding assent to any specific investment proposal put before them. Such questions cannot be evaded. No Investment Board will

ever be in the happy position of being able to do everything for
which a plausible and attractive case can be made. It must
choose ; it must say, we shall do A and B, but we shall not do
C and D, even though C and D are highly meritorious projects
which we should dearly love to encourage. Unfortunately to
such questions we seldom get even a pretence at a satisfactory
answer ; sometimes there is a little irritation if the question is
merely asked. We may even be told that decisions will be based
on " common sense ", an answer which somehow does not seem
quite adequate. Some of the more sophisticated planners, when
pressed, confess that the planning authorities will apply the
ordinary tests of profit and cost ; there is an elaborate socialist
literature designed to show how such tests could in a refined form
be made effective in a properly planned economy, though there
is not a great deal of evidence to show whether or how they have
so far actually been applied in real planned economies. But they
are often a little shamefaced in offering this explanation, for much
of the strength of the popular drive in favour of " planning " is
based upon the denigration of the profit system, and it is felt with
some reason that many of their supporters might feel somewhat
shocked and disillusioned if they discovered that, after vigorously
asserting the necessity for throwing overboard everything that
was tainted by profit, they were to be fobbed off with an allegedly
new system whose controllers were to guide their decisions in
accordance with this, as they had supposed, thoroughly discredited test. More full-blooded planners, it is true, will have
nothing to do with nonsense of this kind. Professor Carr, with
his unbounded contempt for the nineteenth century — for him
" nineteenth-century precedents are valueless and misleading " [1]
— sternly refuses to touch the accursed thing. In his view the
substitution of welfare for wealth as our governing purpose
demands " the consequent abandonment of considerations of
price and profit as the determining factor of production ",[2] and
anyone timidly enquiring what principles are in future to determine production is informed that " it is clear that the regulating
force of the economic system under which we live must more
and more be sought in the realm of ethics rather than in the

---

[1] *Conditions of Peace*, p. 174.   [2] *Op. cit.* p. 97.

operations of a price mechanism ".[1] " Nearly everyone agrees ",
it is added, " that the trend in this direction should be encouraged
and intensified ", though nothing is said to show how the harassed
official who has to choose between building a railway from A to B
and constructing a road from C to D, or his colleague who has
to weigh the relative merits of removing the unwieldy con-
glomeration of London to a more central site in the Midlands and
the investment needed to provide large numbers of people with
cheap houses all over the country, will have his task lightened to
any significant degree by investigations in the realm of ethics.
The views of still other planners may be slightly caricatured, but
without any gross unfairness, by saying that their reply to our
question is " Leave it to me ", their position being indeed not
unlike that of the celebrated company promoter of the South
Sea Bubble period who invited the public to subscribe to a highly
attractive proposition the details of which he promised to disclose
in due course.[2] If these planners get their way, consumers may
ultimately find themselves reflecting upon the interesting contrast
between the despised nineteenth century, when people talked
little about raising standards of living but pushed ahead with the
practical business of raising them, and the age into which we are
now invited to enter when there will be plenty of talk about
raising standards of living, but perhaps very little actually done
about it.

13. It is no spirit of excessive academic refinement which
induces critics to press these points. They are of the utmost
practical importance, as becomes quite clear if we attempt to
construct a composite picture by combining the specific proposals

---

[1] *Op. cit.* p. 79.

[2] It is probably significant, and certainly interesting, in this connection to observe
how many of those who profess themselves to be the most ardent devotees of planning
seem in real life to find the restraints normally imposed by the necessity of adapting our
activities and interests to those of other people even more irksome than other people do.
The criticisms outlined above are not to be interpreted as involving acceptance of von
Mises' view that rational allocation of resources would be impossible in a planned or
socialist economy. The weight of expert opinion is apparently against this view nowadays
(cf. A. C. Pigou, *Socialism versus Capitalism*, ch. vii, and J. A. Schumpeter, *Capitalism,
Socialism and Democracy*, ch. xvi). The point which we are concerned to make is the
different one that, whether such rational allocation is possible or not, the analysis of most
modern " planners " justifies no lively hopes that it will in fact be practised. Many of
them seem rather bored by the subject, and others in effect ask us simply to trust their
judgment.

of individual planners. For the impatience which induces them
to neglect the essential economic problem, the problem of allocating resources among a number of competing purposes, further
leads them to suppose that a genuine " scientific " approach
demands an elaborate calculation of what, according to some
arbitrarily determined ideal objective, ought to be done in some
particular field of economic activity which for the moment
attracts their attention. Once the objective has been determined,
it is not a matter of fundamental difficulty, though the statistical
complications may be considerable, to calculate the amount of
labour and capital needed for the particular purpose in mind.
The calculation completed in one case, the process may then be
repeated in others, in the expectation that a combination of the
results so obtained will ultimately constitute a " plan ". Long
before all the calculations have been completed, however, one is
likely to find that the aggregate of resources needed for merely a
selection of the ideal ends postulated greatly exceeds the total
which, on any rational hypothesis, will be available.[1] At once
two difficulties of great practical importance arise. In face of
such a situation the obviously sensible thing is to cut down the
original requirements. These were in the first place arbitrarily
determined, and the enforced reduction now imposed must be
equally arbitrary. The shortages of resources likely to be most
troublesome will probably be in the field of capital ; even when
capital requirements have been cut down, it is easy to persuade
one's self that a little forced saving and further belt-tightening
would be in the public interest, and the actual enjoyment of higher
standards of living, which is the most attractive bait held out to
induce people to submit themselves to the orders of the planners,
accordingly recedes further into the background. Old-fashioned
socialists were often sarcastic about the efforts of religiously-
minded people who attempted to direct their thoughts to higher
things. We are not much attracted, they said, by the promise
of pie in the sky when we die. Instead of this, the modern

---

[1] This is of course by no means a novel difficulty of which we have hitherto had no
experience. The deliberations of the Australian Basic Wage Commission, under Mr.
Justice Piddington, which in 1920–21 came to the conclusion that the Australian basic
wage-earner " ought " to have a wage which in the aggregate would have exceeded the
total national income, throw an interesting and useful light upon this problem.

planners often in effect offer their followers, or their followers' descendants, a somewhat hypothetical mundane pie but in an equally hypothetical and certainly remote future. The old allegedly impersonal economy sometimes chastised us with whips ; if some of the planners get their way, their new and highly personal economy will certainly chastise us with scorpions.

14. Secondly, the reductions in the original programmes must be not only arbitrary but also provisional, at least until the whole series of calculations, covering the whole range of economic activity, has been completed. And this is certain to be such a complicated and lengthy business, and the results so much infected with inevitable uncertainties, that there is a grave danger that in waiting until the " plan " is complete a great many useful and indeed indispensable activities will be held up on the plea that if they are not retarded the " plan " will be upset. It is so much easier to tell producers what they must not do than to instruct them as to what they should do, that an exaggerated revulsion against the disorderliness of *laissez-faire* may lead us to a perhaps orderly but certainly stagnant and poverty-stricken condition of general *défense de faire*.[1] The appearance of scientific precision given by elaborate statistical calculations unfortunately helps to conceal for many minds the deplorable results likely to follow if the place rightly to be assigned to economic principles, in the sense in which we have defined them, is ignored. Insistence on the importance of these principles is not, as seems sometimes to be supposed, the result of any foolish pride on the part of economists, who indeed are well aware that they may not always fully comprehend them. They are inherent in the very nature of the problem to be solved, and " planners " who in practice ignore them, even if they do not positively decry their importance, cannot expect their proposals to arouse much confidence. This criticism by no means implies that the statistical estimates are worthless or a waste of time. On the contrary they are often of the greatest value. What is, however, often insufficiently under-stood is the inevitable limitations upon their value. An elaborate

[1] Mr. Samuel Courtauld's approval of the principle " that no business venture should start without State permission, if there is the slightest danger of it creating new com-munities which may be left derelict if the business fades out " (*Better Business*, October 1943) suggests that this danger is neither imaginary nor remote.

set of statistical calculations, however careful and accurate, does not constitute a " plan ", unless proper attention has been given to the central economic problem of the allocation of resources between competing ends.

15. The piecemeal approach encouraged by an unhealthy appetite for elaborate statistical estimates is moreover dangerous for the additional reason that it harmonises so perfectly with the illusion, to which we have referred earlier, that " stability " in general can be most conveniently attained by imposing stability step by step upon successive parts of the economy. We may perhaps start off with a partial " plan " designed to provide an assurance of steady investment and steady employment over a stated period of years for, say, the building industry. We shall probably add to this another partial " plan " for stabilising over a similar period some other industry whose fluctuations in the past have given unusual trouble, and so on, as we fondly hope, *ad infinitum*. But in fact unfortunately we cannot proceed along this road *ad infinitum*. In an economy working under the conditions which we must contemplate as inevitable during both our lifetime and the lifetime of our children a considerable degree of flexibility in the allocation of both capital and labour between different industries must be allowed for. The more, therefore, we provide a formal stability in this way for selected industries, the more we concentrate the necessity for flexibility upon the other sectors of the economy left outside. Fluctuations which apart from efforts to impose partial stability in the selected industries might have been quite manageable are therefore likely to be converted into violent convulsions, the repercussions from which may completely disrupt the apparent stability elsewhere which has been so carefully prepared, and ultimately render the instability of the economy as a whole much more disturbing and devastating. We can no more assure stability for an economy as a whole by providing stability in successive steps for its several parts, than we could assure equilibrium for a delicate and complicated and rapidly moving machine by providing a partial stability for a selected number of its parts without taking into account their relations with all the other parts. The result of any such attempt would much more likely be a complete stoppage, if

not a disintegration, of the whole machine. This partial approach to stability is based on an atomistic rather than a genuinely organic view of the nature of economies or societies, and it is a curious paradox that so many of those who now profess to follow the " social " approach to economic problems tend in their concrete proposals to take this atomistic view. A genuine " social " approach would show us that, if we want a stable growing economy, we must view the economy as a whole instead of attempting by successive steps to stabilise particular parts of it.

16. Our third question raises some further serious difficulties. However " social " our outlook may be, in the last resort decisions have to be made by individuals, and both introspection and experience of the life and work of even our best-intentioned and most high-minded friends demonstrate conclusively how fallible and imperfect individuals usually are. Unfortunately the planners are sometimes induced to neglect this elementary but highly important fact by their habit of talking about abstract institutions instead of about the fallible mortals who will have to staff these institutions. " The State ", as Professor Unwin said long ago, " is not ' a something not ourselves making for righteousness ', but bald-headed gentlemen in offices, with strong class prejudices, an inclination to magnify their own authority, and a comprehensive ignorance of the lives of nine-tenths of those over whom it is exercised ".[1] If we are a little uneasy because we fear that some part of the planning machinery may abuse its authority, the planners often try to reassure us by pointing out that in the last resort decisions will require the consent of " the appropriate Minister ". Sensible people will, however, continue to ask, ' Who is or will be the Minister ? ' and they will recall that there are no abstract omniscient impersonal Ministers, but in fact only Lord A., or Sir X. Y. or Mr. A. B., who may already have been in office, and even while doing his best there, has not entirely succeeded in establishing complete confidence that his decisions on such vital matters will invariably be wise or far-seeing.

17. It is indeed another of the curious paradoxes of our time

[1] *Studies in Economic History : The Collected Papers of George Unwin.* Introductory Memoir by R. H. Tawney, p. lxix.

that many of those who most enthusiastically support planning,
and who display most ingenuity in working out detailed " plans ",
are at the same time, often with good reason, the sternest critics
of the unfortunate individuals upon whom, whether as Ministers
of the Crown or as civil servants, is at present laid the responsibility for taking decisions in the ordinary course of governmental
work. The more urgently the necessity for planning is stressed,
the more resounding are the criticisms which demonstrate the
unworthiness of the existing civil service to do the planning. As
one recent statement has put it, " it will be necessary to develop
a new kind of public administration to deal with the State's new
and expanding functions in the industrial field. This will mean
recruiting new types of men and women, and adopting an
essentially different technique of administrative team-work." [1]
Drastic reforms in the civil service may very well be an urgent
necessity in relation to the present tasks of government, but we
may be pretty sure that at the best the process of reform, whether
confined to its existing responsibilities or extended to wider fields,
will be a rather slow business ; as a considerable time is sure to
elapse before we have a civil service even moderately adequate to
perform all the new tasks envisaged, it would seem prudent to
contemplate the desirability of permitting for quite a long time
a quite wide range of activity in the " unplanned " sector, not
under the control of people who, it is admitted, will probably be
incompetent to perform adequately all the planning functions.
One might almost suspect that the emphasis now more and more
placed upon the dependence of efficient planning on reform of
the administrative machinery was really intended to be a *reductio
ad absurdum*. Ideally, people seem to say, we should have a
planned economy, for it would theoretically function much more
smoothly than anything we have known before. But the realisation of this ideal is dependent on the availability of a corps of
administrators entirely different from the existing civil service,
recruited, trained and directed on entirely new principles. But,
the argument ought to proceed, it will be impossible to fulfil this
important and indeed essential condition on any considerable

[1] *Employment Policy and Organisation of Industry after the War* (Nuffield College,
1943), p. 20.

scale for many years. In the meantime, therefore, it will be better to set aside grandiose ideas of a planned economy, and instead to see what practical reforms may be immediately initiated with only imperfect human material at hand, upon which in any event we shall be compelled to rely for quite a long time. If only people were different, how different everything would be, seems sometimes to be the half-concealed lament of many of the planners. The principle enunciated cannot be questioned. But in fact people are not different : they are what they are, and a plan which depends for its success upon the individuals who are to carry it out being quite different from what they actually are, seems to deserve the name of vision rather than of plan.

18. Many business men who have turned " planners " have, however, an obvious solution for this difficulty. They are rivalled by no one in their scorn for the civil servant and for parliamentary " interference " ; the essential quality in their view for the administrative tasks of the new planned order is practical business experience. Who is more likely to have this quality than those already engaged in business ? It therefore follows that the new administrative machinery must be staffed and controlled by those who already know the business with which they will have to deal.

19. Along this path we come to what is perhaps the most dangerous form of modern planning ideology, the form which has as its ultimate ideal the Corporative State. It is not necessarily a reproach to those who favour this ideology that their ideas are expressed in such a wide variety of forms as to make it difficult to offer a succinct summary which will do justice to all of them. The most systematic exposition will be found in the writings of Italian Fascist economists. Following the usual British practice, corporatists in this country have as a rule troubled themselves much less about formal doctrinal foundations. Their ideas are sometimes reminiscent of those of the mediaeval guilds, while also having some affinities with syndicalism. But without any clearly defined philosophical background, and often apparently in complete ignorance of the experience recently gained in the United States, where similar ideas were tried out in the administration of NIRA, in the first phase of the New Deal, and are in

consequence now almost completely discredited in that country, in the view of both New Dealers and anti-New Dealers, there has in recent years in Great Britain been a widespread and active movement for forming trade associations of various kinds, which have gradually assumed regulative powers over their members, including sometimes the imposition of a definite price policy ; the question has now been seriously raised whether this movement should not be placed on a more formal and permanent basis, and trade associations given a more definite statutory authority than has, except in some cases, hitherto been permitted. As 120 leading British industrialists put it in November 1942, " it appears to be an essential condition of progress that the relations between firms, between different industries and between industry as a whole and Government should be more fully and comprehensively organised in some form of permanent association ",[1] and they accordingly proposed the classification of industries into sections, each one of which " should set up a Sectional Association which would be charged with the duties of co-ordinating the activities and securing the collaboration of all producers in its own section ". A variety of functions was suggested for these Associations, including the discouragement of " wasteful and destructive competition ", and the whole structure was to be completed by the formation of a Central Council of Industry.

20. " Such a plan ", it was added, " would have a limited usefulness only, if a considerable number of firms did not join the sectional associations, or having joined accepted such privileges as might accrue from membership while declining to accept any corresponding duty to accept majority views. In particular it would be impossible in such circumstances to be sure of avoiding the waste involved in uneconomic competition, and impossible to be sure of securing a general application of the code which we have recommended in relation especially to labour and the Social Services. It is necessary for this reason to consider whether, and if so to what extent, the associations and the councils should be given specific powers (of course within prescribed limits) to make regulations and to enforce decisions, and whether membership of associations should be made compulsory." [2]

¹ *A National Policy for Industry*, p. 14.   ² *Ibid.* p. 16.

21. The suggestion of compulsory membership is here put forward with some measure of justified caution, but it is clearly intended that it should receive serious consideration. There are two fundamental and related issues to be taken into account here : firstly, the conditions under which entry into a trade or profession should be permitted, and secondly, the formulation and imposition of minimum price policies. Registration and licensing has been an inevitable device for administering the limitation of supplies in war-time, and experience of its effects has suggested to some industries that they should push further the movement already initiated before the war for insisting upon some formal qualification tests for new entrants. In 1938, for example, " funeral directors " endeavoured to secure such statutory protection for themselves. A bill for this purpose was withdrawn in the House of Lords, when it had been pointed out that such registration would convert the trade into a closed corporation and drive small men completely out of business, " since the professional body would have power to regulate entrance into it ". More recently a building trade journal enquired, " is it not high time that builders sought to protect themselves in the same way as architects have done, and try to establish the principle that all directors and managers should be qualified to some degree ? " [1] The crucial issue raised by such proposals is whether it would be in the public interest for any body of men, already actively interested in a particular trade or industry, to be put in a position where either directly or indirectly they could place obstacles in the way of new competitors engaging in the same business. As the reference to architects showed, great importance is often attached in this context to analogies with the professions, but however important we may think it to protect the public against the dangers of unqualified medical practitioners, or inefficient druggists and pharmacists, these very cases themselves illustrate quite clearly the inherent dangers of any organisation which leaves to interested parties the last word in determining how much competitition they will have to face. It is not unduly cynical to maintain that even the most high-minded professional body needs to be constantly watched lest, with perhaps the best of motives, it should succumb

[1] *The Times*, March 7, 1942.

to the temptation of assuming that the narrow professional
interests of its members are identical with the public interest.
Anyone who has closely observed their activities will agree that
" the ' planning ' of a trade under the flag of progressive efficiency
may well serve the policy of restricting competition for the benefit
of the *beati possidentes* ".[1]   Competition may sometimes be
" wasteful ", and new entrants into a well-established industry
may sometimes run the risk of establishing mere " mushroom
growths ", but on these matters the evidence adduced by those
who are threatened by competition can never be regarded as
conclusive, and the public interest will be best served the more
their power to enforce decisions can be limited.[2]   There is abundant
evidence to justify the fear that so-called " planning ", left in
the hands of business interests, will speedily degenerate into
" plotting ".[3]

22. It is curious that proposals of this kind are frequently
made by those who profess the most ardent devotion to " private
enterprise ".   " Modern industry ", according to the 120 industrialists, " has grown up under the system of private enterprise. . . . Its essence is the right enjoyed by all members of
the community, whether individual, corporation or co-operative
society, from the small saver to the big investor, from the small
craftsman to the large manufacturing combine, to employ or
invest their savings or property in any business of their choice ",
but while affirming their belief that " it is a necessary condition

[1]   *The Times*, March 7, 1942.

[2]   We should search a long time before we found a more effective statement of this
point than Adam Smith's.   " The interest of the dealers in any particular branch of trade
or manufactures is always in some respects different from, and even opposite to, that of
the public.   To widen the market and to narrow the competition, is always the interest
of the dealers.   To widen the market may frequently be agreeable enough to the interest
of the public ; but to narrow the competition must always be against it, and can serve
only to enable the dealers, by raising their profits above what they would naturally be,
to levy, for their own benefit, an absurd tax upon the rest of their fellow citizens.   The
proposal of any new law or regulation of commerce which comes from this order ought
always to be listened to with precaution, and ought never to be adopted till after having
been long and carefully examined, not only with the most scrupulous, but with the most
suspicious attention.   It comes from an order of men, whose interest is never exactly the
same with that of the public, who have generally an interest to deceive and even to oppress
the public, and who accordingly have, upon many occasions, both deceived and oppressed
it " (*The Wealth of Nations*, Cannan's edition, vol. i, p. 250).

[3]   " Plotting may be said to include all attempts to diminish the efficiency of the
economy in the interests of groups or individuals " (Henry Smith, *Review of Economic
Studies*, June 1936, p. 199).

of achieving efficiency that the system of private enterprise should continue ", any control by the proposed Sectional Associations, such as has been hinted at, of the right to enter an industry would clearly involve the destruction of the " essence " of private enterprise, as here defined. There is indeed no reason in principle why these rights should not be modified in accordance with changing conditions. We have already suggested that the right of corporations to " invest their savings in any business of their choice " needs some review, and that investments in patent rights with a view to limiting production are not in the public interest ; any such limitations of the freedom of corporations would, however, be designed to encourage expansion. The powers contemplated for the proposed statutory trade associations are intended for quite a different purpose, and it is difficult to believe that the " proper safeguards " to which they are to be subjected could prevent " the creation of an era of privilege " [1] and afford adequate protection against restrictive tendencies.

23. It is an incidental corollary to corporatist schemes, to which on other grounds many would have no objection, that their realisation would soon necessitate a radical reconsideration of the principles upon which large incomes are paid to business men. " It is not surprising that entrepreneurs should like to enjoy both the high income which in a competitive society the successful ones among them gain, and the security of the civil servant ",[2] and most plans for " self-government in industry " assume that entrepreneurs will be allowed in this way to get the best of both worlds. But " unless private enterprise is prepared to take the risks which are its historical function, then private enterprise has no function ",[3] and those who hopefully anticipate the preservation of the forms of private enterprise without any obligation to perform its only true function, cannot reasonably expect that the remuneration which society has hitherto been prepared to allow to risk-takers will remain undisturbed when risks are being shifted elsewhere.

24. In discussions of monopoly control there have frequently

---

[1] *The Problem of Unemployment* (January 1943), p. 14.
[2] F. A. Hayek, *The Road to Serfdom*, p. 145.
[3] Herbert Morrison, *Looking Ahead*, p. 127.

been animated debates about the actual facts in particular disputed trades. It is often difficult to establish these facts beyond any shadow of doubt, and over-eager critics may sometimes impute evil on insufficient evidence. Trade associations are perhaps not as black as they are sometimes painted. Much of the debate is, however, strictly speaking, irrelevant. Even if the past record of trade associations was perfectly white, — and the 120 industrialists admit that " it cannot be denied that Trade Associations can be operated merely for price maintenance, incidentally affording protection to the inefficient or high-cost producer, rather than for the general good ", — there would still be no justification for granting them statutory powers wider than any at present exercised by them. They are able in most cases now only to make it difficult for new competitors, but without any absolute guarantee that the competition they dislike will not appear. The protection thus afforded to the consumer is no doubt imperfect ; he would do still better if there were a real competitor working on his side. But if he cannot get this, a potential competitor may be better than nothing. The importance of the potential competitor is sufficiently established by the expressed desire to get rid of him.[1] The tendency to stagnation from which many modern economies have suffered has sometimes been described as the result of " a strike of entrepreneurs ". It would seem over-optimistic to suppose that the trouble can be remedied by handing over the situation to the control of the strikers' leaders.

25. One apparently incidental technical point in these plans itself illustrates very well the static view of industrial development which often lies behind them. The classification of industries into sections which is a necessary preliminary step at once raises all the difficulties familiar to the statistician who works with censuses of production, or the classification of population accord-

---

[1] It is significant that even during the war some Italian economists have published outspoken criticisms, exactly on the lines suggested above, of the corporative system as they have experienced it in Italy. Einaudi especially criticised the way in which decisions were made about proposals to establish new enterprises, frequently amounting to a monopolistic protection of existing undertakings by hampering new competitors, and Demaria pointed out that, in sharp contrast with the anti-trust legislation of the United States, Italy had consciously facilitated the growth of monopoly, by that means checking the development of production (Borgatta, Turoni and others, *Ricostruzione dell' Economia nel Dopoguerra* [Padua, 1942], cit. *Volksrecht*, December 5, 1942).

ing to industry or occupation. As a practical man the statistician has to make his decisions in accordance with the material available to him, but his classifications easily become out-of-date, as technical conditions change, and need therefore to be subjected to constant revision. We have already seen that some of the technical developments which the war is bringing into prominence may completely alter some of the traditional boundaries between industries. The present would scarcely seem to be a proper time to organise industry on a basis which could have no other effect than to crystallise and ossify a structure much of which would be unsuitable to the conditions of the immediate future. Human affairs are indeed seldom capable of reduction to neat statistical formulas, and statistical complications are not a sufficient reason for rejecting an otherwise sensible plan. Those charged with the responsibility for wage regulation also have to face the insoluble problems of occupational classification, but somehow or other they get their work done. With so many inescapable problems demanding attention, it would, however, be unwise unnecessarily to divert a further part of our limited time and energies to demarcation problems which would arise only because we had set ourselves such unattractive tasks as are here being discussed.[1]

26. Even if the limitations upon output in each industry were quite small, their aggregate effects upon both national income and economic stability might be serious. It is a matter of simple arithmetic that the more trades and occupations are placed in a position to control the volume of their output and therefore the number of people employed by them, the narrower will be the range of choice left for those who are excluded. The combined effect even of modest under-estimates of the proper volume of employment would leave a considerable volume of labour for which the discovery of alternative forms of employment would be increasingly difficult. We have already referred to the possi-

[1] The prompt and hostile reaction of the Council of the British Rayon Federation to the Cotton Board Committee's thesis that the problems of the cotton industry " cannot be successfully overcome unless the constituency of the proposed [post-war cotton] board includes firms wholly or partly engaged in spinning rayon staple fibre, weaving rayon yarns, finishing rayon goods and merchanting rayon goods " provides an illuminating hint of the confusion and conflict which would almost certainly quickly arise if or when the widespread application of the idea of " self-government in industry " made it necessary to deal with such demarcation issues (*Manchester Guardian*, February 8, 1944).

bility that some schools of planning may present us with the task of providing capital for specified purposes which in the aggregate will far surpass anything even remotely possible. If we leave planning in the hands of business interests, we shall probably be confronted with the converse difficulty that their aggregate requirements of labour will fall substantially short of the total available supply. In these circumstances we might look forward with some confidence to the permanent existence of a rather large " hard core of unemployment ". The wider the range of occupations entry into which is directly or indirectly controlled, the larger the number of people for whom it will appear hopeless to provide employment except by the unsatisfactory device of extensive " public works ".[1]

27. It has now become a part of " the contemporary climate of economic opinion " to counter the doubts which past experience arouses about the fate of consumers in face of quasi-monopoly controls of industry by proposing that the new controlling bodies should include in one form or another " consumers' representatives ". It is not always clear by what means consumers are to make their influence effectively felt on such bodies, and the term consumer itself is often interpreted quite narrowly to cover not the final consumer of the finished product, but only the manufacturer at an intermediary stage, *e.g.* the " consumer " of the steel products necessary in the motor-car industry is thought of not as the man who is going to drive the car or the passenger whom the car is to carry, but the manufacturer who is going to make it. The value of consumer representation devices is not

---

[1] Some enthusiastic members of the modern school which attaches so much importance to government spending policy as the dominant factor in modern economic life have thought that it warranted monopolists in asking for a verdict of not guilty of the charge of keeping production low and increasing the risks of unemployment. Mr. Schumacher, for example, concludes that " monopolistic practices are hardly the direct cause of unemployment ", because " the general level of business activity and employment . . . is determined by the totals of spending, investment-activity, consumption and saving ", which " can be wholly controlled by the credit and spending policy of the Government " (*Agenda*, February 1944, pp. 45-6). Whatever other demerits this analysis may have, it illustrates again the low regard which many members of this school have for the satisfaction of consumers' requirements, for essentially the argument amounts to little more than claiming that if monopolists limit employment by checking the production of things which consumers would like, the government can maintain the volume of employment by facilitating the production of things which consumers do not much want, and perhaps do not even want at all.

lightly to be disregarded, but in the last resort it is difficult to see how any consumer can get more adequate protection than is afforded by the knowledge that if his present supplier fails to satisfy him, there is someone else available upon whose services he can call in case of need. The great advantage of this method of protection is that it leaves the consumer free to apply his mind to other and more interesting things. In effect a potential competitor does his work for him. It is no doubt much to be desired that consumers in general should take a more lively and intelligent interest in the quality of the goods they purchase, but the comparatively slight response evoked by the activities of such bodies as the Consumers' Union in the United States, which set out to enable the consumer to form an objective judgment of the merits of the goods pressed upon his attention by salesmen and advertisers, is not to be explained exclusively in terms of reprehensible sloth and apathy. Some consumers, no doubt, who refuse to take any lively interest in the activities of such bodies, spend the time which might have been thus occupied in other activities of little social value. But this is not so of all of them. Life is short, and anyone who feels that the time available is inadequate for cultivating the interests which really excite him may well feel a little irritated when he is invited to spend his time in a close examination of the relative merits of rival tooth-pastes, underwear or breakfast foods. A similar point has relevance in relation to the complaints sometimes made about the apathy of small investors who refuse to busy themselves with any close examination of the fortunes of the concerns in which ultimately their savings are invested. Why should they, if they have other more interesting things to do, and provided that specialists, who in any event will be more competent than they, are given favourable opportunities for acting as efficient intermediaries ? Complaints are sometimes levelled against our age that too much thought and attention are given to money-making. If our institutions can be so moulded that the benefits incidental to this process can be enjoyed while leaving those whose interests point in other directions free to cultivate their interests, it would appear to be a matter for congratulation rather than regret.

28. To anyone anxious to find a simple catchword or slogan

P

in which a wise post-war economic policy can conveniently be summarised, the upshot of this discussion cannot be other than disappointing. In any event such simple phrases do not suit very well the English habit of non-doctrinaire opportunist thinking. There is indeed no convincing reason why English habits of thinking should not be revised, and opportunism has sometimes been pushed too far, and made an excuse for refusing to face vital issues. But in this particular instance it appears that a " mixed " economic policy, which refuses to fit neatly into any clear-cut logical classification, suits not only traditional English habits of thinking but also the actual facts of the case.

29. It should indeed occasion little surprise to find that the complex adjustments of economic structure constantly demanded in the interests of both progress and security are most likely to be achieved by a wide variety of techniques. It would be much more surprising if we were to discover a device which could suitably be applied in all circumstances. The catholic approach which encourages us to adapt our techniques to variations in the conditions with which we have to deal should also save us from the error of expecting too much from any one of them. English habits of thought indeed have often had unfortunate results more on account of their insularity than on account of their opportunism ; despite a wide range of interest and knowledge in well-informed circles, popular thought, and often expert thought too, pays too little attention to the experience of other countries, whether by way of warning or of encouragement. We have already referred to the comparative indifference displayed in this country to the experience of the anti-monopolistic legislation of the United States. Where any account at all is taken of it, it is often hastily written off as a failure without much trouble being taken to enquire how far in fact this judgment is justified by the facts, and what are the underlying causes of the frustration which has often been the lot of those charged with administering these United States laws. Similarly the confident expectations encouraged in many quarters about the results to be anticipated from the nationalisation of certain key industries often entirely neglect the wealth of experience already gathered in other countries where nationalisation of this kind is already a common-

place. An economist who has spent most of his life in Australia and New Zealand is unlikely to be unduly alarmed by proposals for the nationalisation of the railways, for example. But equally he will not be unduly elated, and he will certainly discount heavily some of the optimistic claims put forward in Great Britain on behalf of railway nationalisation. He will point out that a State railway system is just as capable as a private company of taking a narrow monopolistic view of the value for the community as a whole of alternative forms of transport. He will also be sceptical about suggestions that the problem of labour relationships will be made any easier by State ownership, for he knows by observation that the feeling of the average railway employee about a State-owned railway system is not very different from that of any employee of any other large-scale economic unit. While therefore having no doctrinaire disposition to rule out State enterprises as such, he will be the more inclined to insist that " the important thing for Government is not to do things which individuals are doing already, and to do them a little better or a little worse ; but to do those things which at present are not done at all ",[1] though their importance for the smooth working of our economy in the complex conditions of the modern world may be quite overwhelming. Not all the items suggested for our post-war programme are of this character ; for many of them, however, we have no real choice, if they are to be done at all, between individual action and the activity of a State instrumentality. They are things which only the State can do. Nor need anyone who is eager for more State activity in the economic sphere fear that our programme gives insufficient opportunities for it to busy itself there. There will be abundant employment for all the frustrated economists and statisticians who yearn to show their capacity as " practical men ".

30. The old controversy about the relative merits of State and private enterprise often missed the mark just because it diverted attention from those functions which by their nature could not be performed except by some public authority. The controversy centred around which of two possible methods of doing a thing was the better, and other things, which were

[1] J. M. Keynes, *The End of Laissez-Faire*, pp. 46-7.

sometimes more important but to which only one of the two methods was applicable, were neglected. And while the controversy was mainly one about machinery, it tended to become particularly sterile when the question of what the rival machines were expected to do was neglected. Ardent controversialists on either side are still often guilty of perpetuating these ancient errors.

31. Against planning in the sense of forethought and the careful adaptation of means to ends, we have already seen that there is nothing to be said. Many urgent post-war problems will be sadly mishandled unless there is much preparation of this kind. Whatever extravagances some planners may be guilty of, no serious criticism can be levelled against, for example, the attempt to measure as precisely as possible the housing deficiencies to be made good in Great Britain after the war, to estimate the volume of labour, skilled or unskilled, necessary for any rebuilding programme, and to prepare ahead an adequate scheme of training for them. But when economists observe planners brushing impatiently aside or even ignoring altogether the fundamental problems of a growing economy, they may well hesitate to give whole-hearted approval to the more grandiose schemes now receiving so much publicity, even if they have no doctrinaire antipathy to state action as such. But they will be even more shy about aligning themselves with those professed whole-hearted supporters of " private enterprise ", who too often content themselves with general incantations about its virtues. Their public declarations afford no evidence of any understanding of those distortions of private enterprise whereby profit is accumulated, not by producing but by checking production, and no inclination either to initiate or to support any policy for the eradication of this evil. Indeed, as we have seen, some who pay lip service to " private enterprise " propose to destroy its essential foundations. Suspicions are not entirely unfounded that many of them put far too much emphasis on " private " and far too little on " enterprise ". No appeal on behalf of private enterprise can be convincing which fails to include proposals for reversing the unenterprising policies of restriction which have had such far-reaching and damaging consequences in recent years.

32. Nor can the economist have much confidence in the hybrid schemes put out by some disappointed socialists who, having abandoned hope of converting their apathetic fellow countrymen to a full-blooded programme for the nationalisation of the means of production, distribution and exchange, have persuaded themselves that a working compromise is possible by meeting the corporatists half-way and giving them a good deal of what they have been asking for. To put more power into the hands of restrictionists is scarcely the most hopeful method of uprooting the evils for which they have been responsible, and in this uneasy alliance between socialists and corporatists it is over-optimistic to suppose that the socialists will ultimately prevail.

33. If we are to have either higher standards of living or greater economic security, the first essential is more enterprise. In sectors where the State seems likely to be enterprising, the case for State activity is strong ; elsewhere its more important function is to create conditions favourable to its enterprising citizens, and unfavourable to those who wish to check enterprise. A realistic programme must provide for both these requirements. It is of little use to dilate upon the virtues of an expansive economy unless we take effective steps or allow effective steps to be taken for steady expansion of the goods and services which ordinary consumers, finding their incomes rising, would be glad to purchase. *Laissez faire* nowadays has an unpleasant sound about it, which makes it a ready and convenient term of abuse. Many of its practical applications in the past were such as to justify attaching these unpleasant associations to it. We should not, however, forget that its original literal meaning was letting people make things. By the time that so-called *laissez faire* doctrines became popular, there had been a considerable experience of the unhappy consequences of interfering with people who wanted to make things, and there was a natural and healthy revulsion against them. In recent years we have accumulated still more experience of the same kind. The time is ripe for another revulsion of feeling.

CHAPTER XIV

INTERNATIONAL ECONOMIC ADJUSTMENT

(a) INTRODUCTION

1. SOME passing references have already been made to the effects upon international economic relations of efforts to evade the necessity for changes in national economic structures. Many of the causes of international friction in recent years can be found in resistances of this kind, and the international aspects of our general problem therefore deserve closer examination. We shall not indeed attempt anything like an exhaustive analysis of international economic relations during the inter-war period. Our interest is confined to the circumstances in which structural adjustments are needed, the international consequences of resistance to such adjustments and the self-frustrating effects of national policies which fail to take into account their repercussions upon other economies. Even this limited interest would justify a much more elaborate study than is possible here, for in the international no less than in the national field few problems could be discovered which did not in one way or another raise the issue of structural adjustment. With such a wide range of topics deserving attention, we must be content with something like a series of essays, the argument of which will be presented with even less pretence to systematic thoroughness than the argument of earlier chapters.

2. Our general thesis may be briefly recapitulated. If the fruits of increased productive efficiency are to be enjoyed, there must be more or less continuous transfers of resources of production for the expansion of old or the opening up of new fields for employment and investment. To the extent to which these transfers are successfully resisted, the achievement of higher standards of living is postponed, and the risks of insecurity, by reference to which resistance is often defended, are usually increased. The creation of conditions in which transfers will be

less difficult and resistances less likely to be successful should therefore be a major objective of public policy.

3. So far this thesis has been presented in terms applicable to any imaginary single closed economy, unrelated to the rest of the world. No such closed economies now exist, or are likely to exist, except perhaps in some of the scattered remnants of primitive societies still surviving in the distant backwaters of Africa and Central Asia, and it becomes progressively less probable that even these can long remain without effective economic contact with the outside world. In principle, however, no modification of our theme is necessary to cover the more complicated reality presented by normal economies with significant and sometimes very close links with each other. Changes in the conditions of production inside one national economy sometimes demand structural adjustments in other economies. The same urge for security induces resistance to such adjustments, and successful resistance again means sacrifice both of potential improvements in standards of living and of the security so eagerly desired.

4. The obvious fact has already been mentioned [1] that policies designed to obviate the need for awkward readjustments seem at first sight to have unusually good chances of success when they are backed by the power of government, and inconvenient changes can therefore be left for people in other countries to make. Even when there are " attractive " forces operating inside an economy which can absorb the labour and capital ejected as a result of technical change, it is often difficult to allay alarms about the decline of employment in industries where the demand for labour is falling off. But where the " attractive " forces get to work first in foreign countries, and the obvious expanding opportunities for employment are in regions migration to which, even if it were possible, requires adjustment to a different language, different customs and different ways of life, the search for alternative avenues of investment and employment demands more foresight and care than many governments seem willing to display. The existence of the machinery of the State, moreover, offers national groups of producers opportunities which, sometimes without the aid of any formal monopolistic organisation,

[1] Cf. VII, 21, 22.

they have not been slow to seize for making monopolistic obstruction to structural readjustment effective.

(b) International Economic Interdependence

(i) *International Implications of Rising Living Standards*

5. Within the international framework we thus encounter again the familiar rival claims of economic progress and security. Here too we can show that, in the conditions of the modern world, short-cuts to economic security for single states are likely not only to necessitate the sacrifice of progress, but also in no very long run to destroy the security which has been made the immediate objective of policy. Unless the organic relation between the two purposes is more clearly understood than was usual during the inter-war period, the attractive programmes of world economic development now being extensively canvassed may well end in nothing but disillusionment. For example, the governments and authorities represented at the United Nations Conference on Food and Agriculture have announced (on June 3, 1943) their intention to " embody in a formal declaration or agreement the obligation to their respective peoples and to one another henceforth to collaborate in raising levels of nutrition and standards of living of their peoples ". Such declarations can have no useful effect unless it is clearly understood that the governments subscribing to them are thereby undertaking an obligation to make structural adjustments, as defined earlier, in their own national economies.

6. This point can be most easily established by examining specifically the implications of raising standards of living in any selected country, and we shall take China as a convenient illustration. The average standard of living of the Chinese is at present very low, and it is generally agreed that it would be advantageous for the world as a whole to raise it. How is this to be done ? None of the elaborate and detailed answers which might be or have been given to this question will have much practical value unless the following simpler, more elemental facts are understood. A raising of Chinese standards of living implies, is indeed the same thing as, an increase in the volume of Chinese

production. When we say that the Chinese standard of living is low, we mean that they consume very little. If it is to be raised, that means that they will consume more, and they will be unable to consume more unless they produce more. For apart from gifts, the only ways in which the people of any country can increase their consumption are either by increasing the volume of production for their own needs, or by increasing the volume to be sold abroad in exchange for imports. (In a complete statement, the possibility of getting more imports in return for a given volume of exports, an improvement in the terms of trade, should also be considered, but the effects of such improvements upon standards of living would be limited, and their analysis would lead to exactly the same general conclusions as follow from examination of the simpler cases.)

7. It is just conceivable, but in the highest degree improbable, that the Chinese might be able to increase production for their own needs along lines which in no way interfered with existing trade connections with other countries. In other words, their increases in production might be net increases, and not made at the expense of any imports previously purchased elsewhere. Much of their increased production would no doubt be of this kind, for many of the things which they would consume if their living standards were higher could only be made locally. Both history and general reasoning are, however, unfavourable to any belief that increases in home production would not to some extent, and probably to quite a substantial extent, be at the expense of replaced imports. So far as this was necessary, standards could not be raised unless there were some structural adjustments in other economies formerly accustomed to send imports to China.

8. It is equally just conceivable, but equally improbable, that the Chinese might find it possible to raise their standard of living to an appropriate level without increasing in any way their demand for certain classes of imports. For all significant practical purposes, however, we may safely assume that they would wish to purchase from abroad at least for some considerable time a volume of goods and services above their recent customary import level. Indeed, in the aggregate, this increased demand

would probably more than outweigh the decline in demand for imports attributable to the expansion of Chinese industry, but as the increased demand would be for goods of a different type, it would not diminish the necessity for structural adjustments elsewhere. Economies are seldom reluctant to face the adjustments needed to meet increased demands for their exports, so that this aspect of raising Chinese living standards would not at first impose any inconvenient obligations upon other countries. But the Chinese increased demand for imports cannot be made effective unless at the same time, or perhaps a little later, parallel steps are taken to increase the volume of Chinese exports, and in this connection the task of adjustment elsewhere is more difficult and complicated.

9. For a very poor country such as China, moreover, the process of raising living standards must be very slow if reliance has to be placed on none but internal capital resources. The history of the U.S.S.R. shows that, when raw material conditions are favourable, remarkable expansion is possible without external capital, but the strain placed on the inhabitants of the U.S.S.R. was so severe and the actual raising of standards of living there so slow that other countries who lacked the raw material endowment of the U.S.S.R. might well shrink from submitting themselves to a similar ordeal, the necessity for which in any case appears to be excluded if the nations are " henceforth to collaborate in raising standards of living ". If, however, China is to receive foreign capital, on whatever terms, the debt so incurred must in some way be serviced, and again the only effective way of doing this is through an expansion of Chinese exports.

10. On both these counts, therefore, the obligation to raise Chinese living standards cannot be discharged unless other countries are prepared to accept a larger volume of Chinese exports than in the past. It is again just conceivable, but highly improbable, that the goods suitable for this purpose might in no case be competitive with any goods already available for the recipients of Chinese imports. It is, however, much more likely that the acceptance of Chinese imports would necessitate some rearrangement of the existing pattern of production either in the importing countries or in other countries who would find Chinese

xports competing with theirs. Thus the necessity for structural djustment outside China would again arise. On no hypothesis o whose consideration time can usefully be given can this neces- ity be evaded, if the obligation to raise Chinese standards of iving is to be taken seriously. Discussions of international conomic collaboration for raising standards of living will be terile unless this prior condition for success in every conceivable ase is placed in the forefront of any programme of action.

(ii) *The Effects of Industrialisation on Foreign Trade*

11. Nor, it should be added, can these inconveniences be evaded by neglecting our formal obligation to raise standards of living elsewhere. The rate at which they can be raised is by no means entirely dependent on international collaboration. Some countries have both the will and the power to raise their own income levels by their own efforts ; we cannot therefore merely by doing nothing avoid the repercussions of changes in their economies initiated by themselves.

12. Our problem does not indeed arise because of any senti- mental regard for the welfare of the inhabitants of other countries, but directly from the process of industrialisation which in many countries has been pushed rapidly ahead during the war, and is likely to go still further when the war is over. Some of the new productive capacity now being used will no doubt be merely temporary, but a significant part will be permanent, and there will be many further additions to it.

13. These movements present problems of adaptation for all producers who have built up export connections with countries where new industries are being developed. We may conveniently examine the situation from the standpoint of Great Britain, but the standpoints of the United States, of Sweden and Switzerland, of Germany and Czechoslovakia, are not significantly different. To many exporters the trend at first sight seems likely to be harmful, for many of the new industries will concentrate upon producing goods similar to those previously imported. It can, however, be shown that, provided the traditional exporting economies maintain a sufficient degree of flexibility, the trend will often in the long run benefit them. International trade is no

exception to the general rule that it is usually better for everybody if other people become richer.

14. In the nature of things there must be incessant change in the " natural " relationships arising from the comparative advantages of different countries in respect of labour, raw materials, capital and the like, which, despite the vigorous and persistent efforts of governments to remould their countries' economies on other lines, are still the most important factors determining the structure of international trade. " Natural " differences in productive capacity are seldom unchanging differences. Even if we neglect the effects of the discovery of new sources of raw materials, standards of labour efficiency are constantly varying, significant changes occur in accessibility to capital supplies, the process of raising standards of living itself changes relative labour and capital costs in different countries, and technical improvements are also constantly altering the relative advantages of different sources of supply.[1] However " natural " the international division of labour of the nineteenth and early twentieth centuries may have been, it would be quite unnatural to expect that the course of time would make no radical changes in it.

15. Many people still have in their minds a picture of the exchange of foodstuffs and raw materials from the relatively undeveloped overseas countries for the manufactured goods of the more highly industrialised countries of Europe and America as representing the " normal " character of international trade. This picture never precisely fitted the actual facts, and is less likely to do so as time goes on. There was no place in it for the export of coal from England or of foodstuffs from the United States, and, perhaps still more important, there has also always been an important trade in manufactured goods between the highly industrialised countries themselves. In the inter-war period " intra-European trade was conducted mainly among the ten industrial states [*i.e.* the United Kingdom, Germany, France, Belgium-Luxemburg, the Netherlands, Italy, Sweden, Switzerland, Czechoslovakia and Austria]. It was their interdependence rather than the interdependence of industrial and agricultural areas that was really significant." In 1935 the industrial countries of

[1] Cf. A. J. Brown, *Industrialisation and Trade*, pp. 25-9.

Europe consigned 44 per cent. of their exports to each other.
The goods exchanged between the industrial countries of
Europe are chiefly manufactured, though there is also a considerable exchange trade between the industrial countries in such
products as coal, iron ore, potash and foodstuffs." [1] Great
Britain herself in 1928 disposed of 20 per cent. and in 1937 of
17 per cent. of her exports to the other nine highly industrialised
countries mentioned above. Industrialisation has clearly in the
past been no barrier to a thriving trade, for, especially when it is
practised in such a way as to be consistent with a high level of
income, a process of specialisation goes on within the field of
industry itself, each industrialised country finding it convenient
to draw a significant fraction of its industrial requirements from
other countries. The vigour and volume of this trade are, moreover, all the more significant when we recall the pertinacity with
which restrictions were placed upon international trade during the
pre-war decade. Provided that traders in each country realised
the necessity of adapting their production schedules to the
changing requirements of their customers abroad, and were
successful in making the necessary adjustments, advances in
industrialisation did not necessarily contract the volume of their
foreign trade, though inevitably there were important ups and
downs in particular items.

16. How far are we entitled to expect the experience of the
past to repeat itself in connection with post-war industrialisation ?
The process will in fact be based on a wide variety of motives ;
the significance of its consequences for international trade will
largely depend upon whether it is likely or not to raise the income
level of the industrialising country. Decisions about industrialisation, like decisions about most other things, may easily be mistaken, and many industrialising experiments which have been
made, and even persisted in, have not made available, even in the
long run, goods superior either in price or in quality to imports
which might have been obtained if no industrial development had
occurred. But if we look at the world as a whole, the process of
raising standards of living has been to a large extent a process of

[1] *Europe's Trade* (Economic Intelligence Service, League of Nations, 1941), pp.
8, 20.

industrialisation, and discriminating policies of this kind, with due regard to the basic elements upon which productive efficiency must depend, have often made and will in the future continue to make valuable contributions to the improvement of standards of living. The immediate impact upon competing exporters elsewhere may be highly inconvenient. Several British export industries, *e.g.* textiles and footwear, have had abundant experience of this fact. But if industrialisation is accompanied by higher standards of living, there is a general presumption, confirmed by much actual experience, that increases of income will simultaneously provide outlets for other types of export which previously could not be sold in the industrialising country because the people there were too poor to buy them. A rising income level is the same thing as a net addition to the volume of production, and part of this net addition may often conveniently be supplied by foreign producers. Sometimes the new demands thus made effective will be for goods produced by the old export trades, but on higher levels of quality. Sometimes they will be goods of quite a different type, and in that event the adjustment called for in the former exporting countries may seem more difficult, and certainly less easy to predict in detail. But the process of adjustment is not intrinsically impossible, and has in fact often been made.

17. Further industrialisation itself depends upon an adequate supply of capital equipment of various kinds, and this offers further opportunities for counterbalancing any loss of export markets for consumers' goods. This is of course quite a commonplace in the history of international trade, capital goods forming a substantial fraction of the exports of all highly industrialised countries. The comfort to be derived from this fact is sometimes thought to be very slight, because the export of capital goods appears as an almost deliberate attempt to cut the ground from under the feet of other export traders. If Great Britain, for example, sells textile machinery abroad, its use will inevitably cut further into British market outlets for textile goods. In a sense this is true, but if we deplore the fact, we are in effect asking that the structure of production should be permanently crystallised or frozen in its existing form, and that there should be no further

mprovements in standards of living, or at least none which may make it necessary for us to modify any of our habits. This is indeed merely one special and highly important application of the general principle that in the nature of things the problem of production can never be finally solved. It is no less true of production designed for foreign markets than of production to be disposed of at home that every time there is a change which alters the volume of production, our previous solutions of the problem of production must be modified.

18. Are these conclusions to be qualified in any way to meet the not improbable cases where post-war industrialisation may not become the basis for higher living standards ? Some war-time industrialising experiments may, for a variety of reasons, be retained, despite the fact that they are ill-adapted to normal conditions, while population pressure for which no relief can otherwise be found may also seem to impose a necessity for further industrialisation, even if it raises the cost rather than the standard of living. Even here, however, there will be some offset for competing exporters from the increased demand for capital equipment ; the other and more permanent offset will be largely absent, for the increased incomes from which a demand for increased imports might be expected to arise will by hypothesis not be forthcoming. Exporters elsewhere would not, however, necessarily have been better off if no industrialisation had been attempted. Especially when it is designed as a protection against the effects of over-population, it may at least check an otherwise inevitable fall in the standard of living, the consequences of which must have included a declining demand for imports.[1]

19. It is in the interests of everybody that, wherever possible, industrialisation and rising standards of living should proceed side by side. Countries with industrial exports will never be able to control industrialisation elsewhere to ensure that this happy result will inevitably emerge, but so far as their policy is relevant

---

[1] For a more detailed but somewhat speculative examination of the whole of this question cf. A. J. Brown, *Industrialisation and Trade*, pp. 36-38, which comes to the conclusion that " industrialisation in one group of countries — the poorer and more overpopulated ones — is likely to have an expansionary effect on world trade as a whole, while industrialisation in those countries which have become rich while specialising on primary production may well, in itself, tend to produce the opposite effect — for some time, at least ".

to the matter, *e.g.* in connection with international investment they have a limited but useful power to assist industrialisation to move along channels which, assuming reasonable flexibility in their own economies, will help to raise standards of living everywhere.

20. In view of widespread misapprehensions, it should perhaps be added that the industrialisation of backward countries is not necessarily inconsistent with the principle of comparative costs. Those who had become accustomed to a comparative cost situation which justified a large volume of exchange of the simple type described above of food and raw materials for manufactured products, could no doubt easily persuade themselves that a comparison of comparative costs would never justify any modification of this trade structure. But this conclusion was never justified, and even when international trade was largely of this kind, no analysis of the principle which deserved to be taken seriously ever assumed that it was.

21. Our analysis of the reactions of industrialisation upon international trade is indeed far from being merely a piece of deductive reasoning. It could be equally firmly based upon a statistical analysis of the course of trade during the last century. To judge from their bewildered reactions to some of the recent disturbances in apparently secure markets, many would seem to have supposed that they were entirely new things of which the world had never before had any experience. Changes of this kind have, however, been continuous at every stage in the history of international trade. Assured and steady markets are a great advantage to any exporting country, but the countries who have done best out of international trade, and thus been most successful in raising their standards of living, have always adapted their structures of production promptly to changing conditions of supply and demand among their customers and potential competitors. Nor was this experience something peculiar to the conditions of the nineteenth century.

22. Great Britain may again be taken as an illustration here, though any other exporting country would do as well. Some incautious British writers have recently played into the hands of the critics of their country by countenancing the erroneous view

hat during the nineteenth century Great Britain somehow acquired a virtual monopoly of certain export trades, and was thus able in effect to compel the rest of the world to buy what the British thought was good for them. The actual course of events was quite different. The essential reason for the prosperity of British export trade has always been the ability of British traders to supply people in other countries with goods which they were eager to purchase ; when their customers changed their views on what they wanted to buy, corresponding changes were made in the British structure of production, so that customers' requirements could still be satisfied. Even between 1860 and 1910, a period for which popular writers sometimes attribute a remarkable stability to Britain's foreign trade, striking changes were continuously going on in the relative importance of the various items exported and imported. At both the beginning and the end of this period indeed, textile manufactures were the most important British export, with cotton standing well at the head of the list. The country would, however, have been much worse off if other exports had not expanded much more rapidly than textiles, for the proportion of textiles to total exports fell from 62 per cent. in 1860 to 38 per cent. in 1910. The value of chemical exports increased eightfold between 1880 and 1910 (and at the same time chemicals became an important import item), and two entirely new trades, the motor and electrical industries, also made significant contributions to British exports in the latter part of the period. British traders did not relax their efforts to maintain their footing in traditional markets, but far from being satisfied with this, they also seized the opportunities offered for building up entirely new export trades, or for expanding others hitherto of little importance.

23. The history of British trade during the inter-war period offers still more significant illustrations of our thesis. The older export trades were then labouring under unprecedented difficulties, and their decline is a matter of common knowledge. By 1932 the total value of exports had fallen to only 45·6 per cent. of the figure for 1924. It is, however, significant that this decline was very unevenly distributed ; in the subsequent period of qualified recovery a substantial group of relatively new export

trades, some of which had not even been separately recorded in the statistics for 1913, showed that, by maintaining a proper degree of flexibility in the structure of British production and taking care to offer overseas customers what they wanted, it was still possible to find export markets. The industries in which exports displayed a certain amount of resilience included the motor industry, rubber tyres, electrical machinery, gramophones, wireless apparatus, electrical and chemical industries, artificial silk, asbestos, photographic materials and books, and the volume of employment in all these industries also expanded much more rapidly than the size of the working population as a whole. These were all industries, it will be noted, producing goods satisfying the requirements of customers with rising standards of living. By 1937 the value of exports from the industries mentioned was 14 per cent. of the total export value, and exceeded the value of the old staple coal exports. The expansion of these and similar industries did not, of course, go far enough to assure prosperity at a high level for the economy as a whole. But at a time when flexibility was widely believed to be abnormally difficult, if not impossible, their expansion showed both that adaptations in the structure of production were possible, and that their results were beneficial to all parties concerned.[1]

24. There is nothing at all novel in this analysis of the effects of industrialisation upon international trade. Much the same argument will be found in the Report of the Balfour Committee of 1926. The overwhelming importance of the proviso of flexibility in economic structure was not, however, fully appreciated at that time, and this lack of understanding was a major influence checking economic progress and intensifying economic instability, and thus helping to produce the overwhelming wave of restrictions which so much hampered world trade. The trend was widely deplored, but, largely because its fundamental causes were imperfectly understood, little that was effective was done to reverse it.

---

[1] Cf. A. G. B. Fisher, *Some Essential Factors in the Evolution of International Trade*, Manchester Statistical Society, 1943 (reprinted in *The Manchester School*, October 1943), and A. J. Brown, *Industrialisation and World Trade*, pp. 59-62.

(iii) *The Significance of International Trade*

25. Critics who emphasise these points to-day are sometimes charged with ignoring the fact that " the maximisation of international trade is not an end in itself ".[1] Some injudicious shorthand expressions might perhaps be quoted in justification of this charge, but no serious student of the subject has ever supposed that an increase in the volume of international exchange of goods or services was to be regarded as " a good thing " for its own sake, irrespective of its connection with improvements in real income.[2] There is no reason in the nature of things why the structural adjustments which have been shown to be an essential precondition for raising standards of living in any part of the world should invariably demand an increase in either the absolute or the relative importance of international trade, and conditions are not inconceivable in which such adjustments would require that international trade should shrink. Changes in the volume of world production need not be at all closely correlated with changes in the volume of world trade. Thought on this subject has often been confused by failure to distinguish between changes in the absolute volume of foreign trade and changes in its relative importance as compared with the national income. The relative importance of foreign trade for any given economy tends to change from time to time according as it becomes more or less convenient to satisfy consumers' demands by the purchase of home products. The increasing relative importance of tertiary production normally associated, after a certain level has been passed, with further improvements in standards of living itself may tend to diminish the relative importance of international trade, for most (though not all [3]) tertiary products are most conveniently produced close to the spot where they are to be consumed. Such a trend is, however, quite consistent with simultaneous expansion in the absolute volume of foreign trade.

[1] H. W. Arndt, *Economic Lessons of the Nineteen Thirties* (1944), p. 273.

[2] Cf. Edwin Cannan, *The Economic Outlook*, pp. 193-4 : " The economic ideal is not for the nation any more than for the family that it should buy and sell the largest possible quantity of goods. The true statesman desires for his countrymen, just as the sensible parent desires for his children, that they should do the best-paid work of the world."

[3] For some economies certain service items have played an increasingly important part in their balance of payments, and the possibility of this tendency being carried further should not be overlooked.

26. If national income were to rise over a period by 50 per cent. and at the same time the proportion of international trade to national income were to fall from 20 to 15 per cent., the absolute volume of international trade would still have increased by 12½ per cent. Movements in the relative importance of international trade in either direction are not necessarily a matter for either rejoicing or regret, but its historical tendency to increase has undoubtedly so far reflected an international specialisation of production in harmony with the general interests of consumers everywhere. Even if further changes in the technique of production which justify corresponding changes in this pattern of specialisation may require a shrinkage in some types of trade, they are equally likely to demand expansion in other directions.

27. In any event, while statistical estimates of the " importance " of international trade, based upon calculations of the percentage of national income attributable to international trade, have some value, they may also, no matter how carefully they are made, easily give a misleading impression of the differences in the real significance of international trade for different national economies. Even if country A draws 10 per cent. of its national income from international trade, and country B only 5 per cent., international trade is not necessarily on that account more important for A than for B. To determine the relative importance of international trade for any country, we must examine in detail the nature of its imports and exports. If the whole of A's imports were luxury goods, while the whole of B's were staple foodstuffs and essential fuel supplies, international trade would be much more important for B than for A, despite the disparity in the percentages. For A the disappearance of international trade might mean only a negligible decline in its standard of living, for a rearrangement of its productive resources might enable it with only slight loss after a short period of transition to produce for itself many of its former imported luxuries. For B, however, the disappearance of international trade might mean the complete disruption of its normal economic structure, and the necessity for rebuilding it on entirely new lines. No one would think of arguing that, because a modern community devotes a trifling fraction of its total resources to water-supply, water-supply is

therefore unimportant and could safely be dispensed with, or allowed to decay without any counter-measures to check its decline. Water-supply is a first essential for the efficient performance of every other activity, including many which statistically make a much more impressive showing. The analogy is not exact, but in principle the point of view of many who look with equanimity upon the decline of foreign trade is not very different from that of some imaginary critic who despised water-supply.

28. Many writers and politicians to-day are impatient of the restraints apparently imposed by participation in an international economic system, and partly because they fear that their own ideas on internal economic policy may be rejected in deference to such restraints, are encouraged to make an outflanking attack on those who insist that for most economies international trade connections are still of first-rate importance, by arguing that modern technical progress is tending to reduce the margin of comparative cost advantage between different countries in the production of different commodities, and that this fact entitles us to regard the decline of international trade without alarm.[1] Any loss arising from neglect of the principle of comparative cost, it is argued, is negligible in modern conditions of technical efficiency, as compared with the " social " benefits which we may hope to enjoy by cultivating our own garden without much regard to comparative cost considerations. If indeed one is fortunate enough to be wealthy, one is justifiably less meticulously careful in precisely measuring the cost situation in relation to every decision taken, and if tedious trouble can be avoided, " material " sacrifice might be thought well worth while. Waste is always a relative concept, and no criticism of our normal peace-time attitude to it is necessarily implied in the urgent exhortations to avoid it in time of war, when the marginal real value of everything is radically altered. But while it is a great advantage not to have to worry about the marginal shilling, it is also a luxury, and the poor cannot reasonably be urged to dissipate their resources in luxuries. If national policies of relatively wealthy countries are based on this principle, unnecessary poverty is likely to be imposed both on

[1] Cf. H. W. Arndt, *Economic Lessons of the Nineteen Forties* (1944), pp. 272-3.

poorer countries and on the numerous group at home which does not happen to enjoy large incomes. If a wealthy man chooses to run a handicraft establishment as a hobby, and get his own sandals and moccasins made on his own private estate by picturesque artisans, no one is seriously injured, and as the artisans may incidentally benefit, he cannot be fairly criticised for deciding that the aesthetic satisfactions to himself outweigh any monetary disadvantage which his estate may suffer. But if the same man happens instead to cultivate chemical research as a hobby, and, having persuaded his government that the ingenious new products of his chemical enterprises do not really cost so much more than those previously imported as a disinterested observer might suppose, succeeds in getting protective measures applied for their benefit, he may completely ruin the producers of other countries who had innocently supposed that they were performing a useful service by turning out good articles at low prices, and at the same time probably prevent the poorer members of his own community, *i.e.* the great majority of his fellow countrymen, from enjoying the full benefits of rising standards of living. " The majority of the human race are still very poor, and if, in the interests of a supposed stability, a halt is to be called in the process of raising real incomes, it is an issue which should be squarely presented to those who are most affected by it." [1]

29. In any event, the thesis that material progress and higher standards of living may in certain circumstances justify a decline in the relative importance of international trade in no way justifies approval of action for limiting international trade transactions which are at the moment essential for maintaining or raising standards of living, and many of the restrictions imposed during the inter-war period were precisely of this kind. In many countries national incomes were not perceptibly rising during this period, and the thesis that the relative importance of international trade might fall *if* incomes were rising has no relevance to a situation in which incomes are not rising at all. It would be no less foolish to argue that, because the growth of public health services might cause in the future a decline in the relative

---

[1] Lionel Robbins, *The Great Depression*, p. 142.

importance of the private medical practitioner as compared with the importance of more far-reaching preventive measures, we should therefore set about at once to limit the number and the range of activity of private medical practitioners, or that in view of the fact that as the age distribution of the population changed in favour of the older age groups crude death rates were likely to rise, we should therefore approve a programme of large-scale killing as being in harmony with natural trends.

CHAPTER XV

INTERNAIONAL TECONOMIC ADJUSTMENT

(*continued*)

(*c*) THE LESSONS OF THE INTER-WAR PERIOD

(i) *International Division of Labour after 1918*

1. THE problem of international structural adjustments was by no means unknown before the inter-war period. Such adjustments have always been necessary and resistance to them has frequently caused dislocation. For our purposes we may, however, conveniently take as a " normal " starting-point the international division of labour embodied in the structure of international trade in 1914. It was far from perfect, but, broadly speaking, it reflected real differences in the relative productive efficiencies of exporters and importers. There was naturally a certain amount of stickiness in making adjustments to changing conditions, so that the 1914 international division of labour might perhaps be more accurately described as reflecting the differences in relative efficiency of a few years before. It was more important that the factors determining relative efficiency were in constant flux. As they changed, the relative advantages enjoyed by exporters changed too, demanding a continuous rearrangement of the pattern of international division of labour.

2. After 1918, at least two important groups of forces produced or demanded changes of this kind. First, the war itself inevitably upset the " normal " relationships hitherto existing between complementary producers. Either for war purposes or because the war interrupted normal transport routes, many countries had been obliged to undertake for themselves production which formerly they had been content to leave to others. Capacity for food production, for example, had greatly expanded, the memory of war-time shortages naturally encouraging many countries to endeavour to make themselves less dependent on imported supplies. Latin American countries, to take an example

of another kind, were during the war faced with a choice between developing their own manufactures and abandoning any hope of enjoying certain articles formerly easily available to them ; they naturally preferred the former alternative. In response to war demands there were in many industries significant changes in technique which permanently altered the balance of comparative advantage between different producers, and the destruction after the war of customary market connections, as, for example, between the different parts of the Hapsburg Empire, necessitated still further changes in the structure of international trade. Even more drastic changes were needed if reparations were to be paid, and to correspond with the far-reaching changes in international debtor-creditor relationships, arising chiefly from the extensive war loans of the United States and the liquidation of part of Great Britain's overseas investments. The adjustments needed for all these purposes encountered, however, the most stubborn resistance, and the failure to carry them through was a major cause of the subsequent international confusion.

3. On top of all the changes in the structure of international trade which as a result of the war were necessary if trading countries were to get the best results, either in standards of living or in stability of employment, the numerous technical and other basic changes of the inter-war period also demanded a further set of adjustments. Japanese industrial efficiency, for example, was rapidly increasing. The displacement of coal by oil went rapidly ahead. " During the nineteen-twenties productive technique was advancing with marked rapidity in nearly all the primary industries ",[1] and heedless of the decline in the rate of population growth already becoming manifest, some of the agricultural countries whose technical efficiency was also improving, based their policies upon the illusory faith that for their exports the " market is practically unlimited ".[2] Electricity and water-power became much more important. There were, moreover, further significant changes in the international capital market, the United States becoming a large-scale lender. All these tendencies demanded radical changes in the structure of international trade ;

[1] J. W. F. Rowe, *Markets and Men*, p. 196.
[2] *Canterbury (New Zealand) Chamber of Commerce Bulletin*, May 1929.

changes in the allocation to different countries of different types
of employment and of investment were necessary in the interests
of the world economy as a whole.

4. The distinction suggested between the changes due to the
war and those which occurred afterwards, is indeed too simple.
The two groups were intimately connected ; many of the latter
were, moreover, merely a continuation of trends already visible
before 1914, and would have demanded some readjustments even
if there had been no war. Nevertheless the classification has a
peculiar interest just now, because at the end of the present war a
similar combination of problems will confront us. The urgent
demand for war material has greatly increased the pace of
industrialisation in countries like Australia and India. The
drying-up of European supplies has had a similar effect in Latin
America. The probable net effects of the war on capacity for
food production cannot yet be accurately estimated, but in certain
directions, and after the difficulties of the immediate post-war
relief period have been surmounted, there may well be again a
tendency towards relative over-supply. The experience gained
of processes such as dehydration will certainly have some lasting
effect upon the competitive relations between different food-
supplying countries. The changes in industrial technique
directly due to the war are probably more extensive and far-
reaching than those of 1914–18. The invention of Lend-Lease
may happily remove one of the post-1918 causes of maladjustment, and it may be hoped that the world has profited sufficiently
from the experience of the last thirty years to avoid the gratuitous
disruption of ordinary trading connections between areas whose
political status it may be thought proper to change as part of the
peace settlement. The liquidation of Great Britain's overseas
assets has, however, gone much further than it did in 1914–18,
constituting indeed in many British minds *the* great post-war
problem for this country, and whatever new devices may be
invented for post-war international investment, post-war international debtor-creditor relations will certainly differ in quite
important respects from what they were in 1939. We cannot
confidently predict what further technical changes may occur
after the war, but it seems natural to suppose that only then will

be reaped the full fruits of some of the improvements now being developed. If, therefore, with whatever variations the conditions after the present war are likely to be similar to those after the last war, a study of the fundamental reasons why things went wrong then is clearly of immediate practical importance, and something much more than an interesting academic exercise.

5. There were, of course, during the inter-war period numerous changes in the structure of international trade, many of which pointed in the right direction, but the need for reorientation on quite an unprecedented scale was never properly faced. The result was that appearance of universal over-production which seemed such an irrational paradox. Many producers who had irrevocably lost their old competitive advantages struggled hard by protective measures to maintain their former position in their own home markets, and where circumstances seemed favourable also entrenched themselves in such foreign markets as they could control against the inconvenient competition of people like the Japanese. Every country tried to strengthen the industries which it had come to regard as "basic" for its economy, and where new production was organised, it was too often for the most part production of things, such as wheat, for which suppliers in other countries still had, and indeed had sometimes actually increased, their competitive advantages. And there was everywhere a failure to realise the elementary fact that rights to money payments from foreign countries were worthless unless their owners were prepared to allow the entrance into creditor countries of a corresponding volume of the goods and services which debtors were able to offer. This fatal ignorance displayed itself both in the refusal of the United States to modify its commercial policy so as to permit the passive balance of payments on current account necessary for the liquidation of war debts, and which should in the course of time have become normal as a result of its extensive international investment activities, and in the widespread and fantastic belief that fabulous reparation payments could be extracted from Germany without any considerable purchases of German goods.

6. Insensitiveness to the necessity for structural adjustment was not, of course, the only disrupting factor at this time. The

world had also to contend with currency chaos, with ignorance of the principles of credit policy, with the effects of rash attempts to restore the gold standard at exchange parities which often ignored the far-reaching consequences of the war, and with political instability and mutual distrust. In retrospect, at least these subjects have already received widespread attention without in any way attempting to minimise their importance, we are justified here in concentrating our attention mainly on the failure to make the proper structural adjustments, for this aspect of the problem has often been too much neglected.[1] It is a long way from offering a complete explanation of the violent economic fluctuations of the inter-war period. But if our previous analysis is sound, this widespread refusal to face the necessity for readjustment would by itself have sufficed to produce quite a tidy series of depressions; any interest in practical efforts to avoid similar fluctuations in the future, therefore, demands more detailed consideration of this neglected side of the problem.

7. Some observers, looking back over the last twenty-five years, have argued that the structural adjustments then needed were so far-reaching and fundamental in their character that it would in any circumstances have been impossible to carry them through in any thoroughgoing way without measures of direct international control much more far-reaching than anyone at the time had ever dreamt of. We need not pronounce any judgment on this point; what is, however, clear is that no serious attempt to make adjustments on a sufficient scale was ever made. Their necessity was seldom properly understood, and when structural changes were made, as they often were, they were in some countries frequently in the wrong direction. The really astonishing fact is that despite all this confusion there were such solid advances in both productive capacity and in the volume of production. Recovery after the losses of the war was more rapid than anyone could have expected, and even the pressure of

---

[1] It is a serious defect in, for example, Michael Young and Henry N. Bunbury's generally admirable pamphlet, *Will the War Make us Poorer?* (Oxford Pamphlets on Home Affairs, No. H.5, 1943), that it almost completely ignores this issue. " Looking back," it is said, "it is plain that we had not thought out the monetary aspects of our plans for the 1920s " (p. 3). But it is equally plain, and probably more important, that we had not thought out the structural adjustment aspects either.

unemployment which for so long was such a heavy burden in many countries failed to check the long-term trend towards greater productivity and higher average income standards.

8. The full extent of the structural adjustments which should have been taken in hand after the last war was for a time concealed by the flow of international capital. This movement in itself was entirely to the good, but in some of its concrete manifestations it positively increased the magnitude of the maladjustments which it ought to have diminished, and itself demanded further structural changes, which were not forthcoming, to conform to the altered relations between creditor and debtor countries, who could discharge their obligations only if their creditors were prepared to facilitate imports on a sufficient scale.

(ii) *National Policies during the Great Depression*

9. The onset of the Great Depression revealed the imperfections of the foundations upon which international economic activity had been based. Faced with a sudden onrush of unexpected uncertainties, each national economy in succession began feverishly to seek for some provisional safeguards against complete catastrophe. The disease was an international disease, but attention was focused almost exclusively upon its national symptoms. In the circumstances it was not surprising that little attention was paid to the needs of other economies. Such consideration demanded both time and calm deliberation. But problems were urgent and pressing : delay was impossible, and each country felt obliged to initiate independently its own imperfect best. With unemployment rising everywhere to unprecedented heights, each government continued to pay lip-service to the virtues of freer international trade ; but as any independent relaxation of its own restrictions seemed likely to intensify its own short-term difficulties, in practice nothing was done. In effect, each government declared itself prepared to relax trade barriers as soon as its employment situation improved. In the meantime, other means of providing employment had to be used until export trade should revive. In their application, however, these policies often merely exported unemployment to other countries, and thus themselves made the revival of export trade more difficult.

The unemployment which was urgently demanding prior atten
tion was itself in large measure a consequence of trying to preserve
an out-of-date economic structure by methods which impeded
trade with other countries, and as emergency measures often
merely carried this a stage further, the situation rapidly degenerated
into a vicious circle from which no satisfactory escape could
easily be found.

10. In some countries a policy of " insulation " was deliberately and consciously adopted. The inconveniences of fluctuations
apparently generated in other parts of the world economy were
so obvious that prudence seemed to demand an attempt to get
clear as far as possible from these entangling links. Even, for
example, in New Zealand, for whom the ratio between foreign
trade and national income was probably at least as high as anywhere in the world, the Prime Minister, Mr. Savage, explained
that the system of exchange control and import licensing instituted
in December 1938 was a practical expression of an insulation
plan, which he indeed hoped would last for ever, designed to
protect New Zealand from the effects of overseas recessions and
maintain her standard of living.[1]   But even where the word
insulation was never used, most national policies during this
period could accurately have been described by that name, and
there was everywhere a strong tendency to aim at re-establishing
stability by internal policies which paid little attention to their
effects elsewhere. This insensitiveness to the effects of national
policies on other economies was sometimes admitted and even
sincerely regretted, but in difficult times, as was often said, charity
must begin at home. However regrettable the condition of other
economies might be, nothing much could be done about it until
internal problems had been settled. It was indeed pointed out,
with much justice, that it would be foolish to wait passively for
international conditions to improve, that a healthy and virile
economy must itself initiate such measures as were needed to
assure the welfare of its own people. Unfortunately, in thus
legitimately insisting upon the necessity for self-help, the distinction was seldom made between wise internal policies which might
at the same time make a positive contribution to world recovery,

[1] *The Times*, December 8, 1938.

and internal policies which, however well-contrived technically, actually depended for their so-called success upon the speed with which the troubles of the countries which adopted them were unloaded upon others. The most obvious illustration is the widespread practice of competitive exchange depreciation. This offered an attractive temporary way of escape, for those who first seized the opportunity had a chance to expand their export trade at the expense of their rivals. But inevitably others quickly followed the example of the early depreciators and in the end the relative positions of all were little changed.

11. The state of mind of those who sought to shelter their own national economies from the disturbing effects of international fluctuations initiated elsewhere is indeed almost identical with that which within the limits of a national economy aims at the assurance of greater security for the individual. As we have seen, individual or group efforts of the latter kind are likely to be ineffective, unless combined with a full recognition of the necessity for adjustment to other parts of the national economy. The parallel proposition, applied to international economic relations, is still rejected by many people, who, while they do not deny the theoretical advantages of policies which take a wider view than that of any single national economy, nevertheless believe that a significant measure of national economic security can be attained without paying much attention to the international repercussions of national policy, and accordingly relegate problems of international co-ordination to a subordinate place.

12. It is natural enough that our thinking at the present time should still be strongly coloured by our recollections of the Great Depression and the events which followed it. The tasks of the future will not, however, be adequately performed if we think merely of applying more effectively then the techniques which we now think ought to have been used when we had been engulfed in that catastrophe. The most significant lessons of the inter-war period are to be drawn from the events which preceded and indeed caused the Great Depression. Practically all national policies after 1929 or 1930 were salvage policies. The damage had already been done, and apparently little remained but to gather up the fragments with the minimum of loss. The really

important question is, however, What caused the Great Depression? Its causes were very complex, but if the lack of flexibility in the international structure of production deserves a high place in the list, we are more likely to derive useful lessons from a study of this aspect of inter-war policy than from further elaborate analyses of the technical efficiency of the salvage policies which are still fresh in our minds. Economists are quite entitled to continue their studies of the merits of the various national policies with which governments endeavoured to solve the problems of the Great Depression, but from the standpoint of future action much of the discussion may miss the mark. For in the circumstances of the time, the right thing not being within the effective range of choice for national statesmen, it was almost meaningless to enquire whether or not their choice was correct. In the absence of any efficient framework of international economic institutions they had no alternative but to do what, on a longer view, inevitably proved to be the wrong thing. Many of them were no doubt foolish and short-sighted, but it would be equally foolish and short-sighted on our part to enjoy the luxury of criticising them after the event, instead of directing our minds to the much more difficult but much more fruitful task of devising means whereby their successors may be protected from the risk of falling again into such a tragic situation. In the nature of things no absolute protection will be possible. No institutional framework can safeguard us from the follies and frailties of human nature. The new international institutions whose creation is the most urgent task for the post-war world will require for their efficient operation the highest qualities of foresight and restraint, but we can at least try to ensure that in the future harassed national statesmen shall no longer find themselves in a position which obliges them to adopt policies which can scarcely be other than harmful to other economies, and which therefore are almost certain in the end to be self-frustrating and contradictory. We can make no facile assumption that appropriate international institutions either can or will be created, and prudent statesmen will therefore no doubt keep in reserve some insurance devices which may be helpful in protecting their own economies from the worst consequences of failure. But we should be deceiving ourselves if we believed that in that event the statesmen's best endeavours would achieve anything entitled to be dignified by the title of success. It would merely be a matter of degrees of failure.

13. Especially among those who must accept or may even claim some responsibility for national inter-war policy, there is still naturally some reluctance to confess that its whole basis was misconceived, and even amid the chorus of popular approval for wider and more truly international outlooks after the war one often detects tones which suggest excessive readiness to accept discouragements as soon as they show themselves, and to fall back even with some sense of relief upon refined versions of the old national policies. Discouragements we may quite confidently anticipate, but if, whether reluctantly or gladly, we fall back upon national policies, modelled, with whatever refinements or improvements we may invent, on the old lines, we may confidently anticipate unfortunate consequences both for our standards of living and for economic stability.

14. So far as the explanation in terms of structural maladjustment is valid, the instability of the inter-war world economy was the result of producing too much of the wrong things in the wrong places. The reversal of this trend would have necessitated large-scale shifts in employment and in investment. This does not necessarily mean that freedom of migration was an essential condition for world stability, though the sudden imposition of severe restrictions upon the freedom to migrate helped to intensify the difficulties of the situation, and the equally common practice of simultaneously excluding both potential immigrants and the goods of which the same people might have been efficient exporters ran directly counter to the requirements of stable world development. It did, however, mean that many countries ought to have contracted, to a degree much greater than in fact they did, the volume of their economic activity in certain traditional fields, and correspondingly expanded activity elsewhere. Too little attention was paid to the expansion side of the problem, while the contraction side naturally presented itself primarily as a question of unemployment. The easiest way to prevent unemployment, it seemed, was to shut out inconvenient imports and thus to maintain employment at home either by keeping those

R

already employed at work in their old industries, or by expanding in fields of employment whose products had formerly been purchased from abroad. Other economies were thus obliged to shoulder the burdens of their neighbours, and in the end the limited objective of stabilising the volume of employment at home was itself only imperfectly achieved.

(iii) *The Responsibilities of Large and Small States*

15. Criticisms of inter-war policy should not be made with any idea of encouraging the pleasant practice of moral indignation at the selfishness and short-sightedness of a past generation. Their main purpose should be to indicate the results of a widely accepted attitude of mind, which, if it remains unchanged, is likely at the conclusion of the present war to lead us into another economic morass. And for the purposes of a purely objective analysis there is an important distinction to be noted. There was much dispute during the inter-war period as to how far the restrictive devices of various national governments were spontaneously adopted by them and how far they were a reaction to similar steps taken earlier elsewhere. Discussions of this kind are a congenial occupation for anyone naturally predisposed to self-righteousness ; they tend to be sterile, but in any realistic analysis it should nevertheless be insisted that the responsibility for world policy naturally and inevitably rests much more upon the wealthy and powerful economies than upon the small and feeble. Restrictionism, wherever it is practised, usually has some unpleasant consequences for other economies, but if practised by a small economy, the unpleasant consequences may be so limited that for practical purposes it is not worth while making a fuss about it. The same limitations, or even milder limitations, imposed by a wealthy and powerful economy may, however, threaten disruption to the whole of the remaining world economy. Much attention has been paid, especially since the outbreak of war, to the importance in international relations of the element of power, which, for some unaccountable reason, it is often suggested had previously been neglected. Discussion of this point has unfortunately tended too much in the direction merely of suggesting that in the last resort the really important decisions

are likely to be taken by the Great Powers. This indeed has been the normal experience for many years, and no elaborate apparatus of argumentation seems necessary to establish such an obvious point. But in the field of economic policy it is almost irrelevant to establish the thesis that what the Great Powers decide is likely to determine world policy ; the much more significant fact is that if the Great Powers fail to make the right choice, and show no proper respect for the effects of their decisions upon other economies, their efforts will be self-frustrating and world economy as a whole will be plunged into instability. In thinking, therefore, about the need for establishing an international code of good manners in economic relations, we need not, at least at first, worry much about the idiosyncrasies and obstinacies of the smaller states. It is the behaviour of the powerful states which really matters. Aberrations on the part of small countries may inflict damage upon themselves, or even cause some slight repercussions unpleasant for other countries. The task of checking these aberrations is, however, much less important than the task of checking the divergences of the larger countries from the path indicated by the principles of international collaboration, even though in form the magnitude of these divergences may sometimes appear quite small.

16. Both experience and general reasoning indeed justify the conclusion that there is quite a sharp contrast between the degrees of freedom enjoyed by small and large economies to determine for themselves the lines of action to be followed when confronted by radical changes in the conditions of world supply and world demand. A choice can apparently be made between three divergent courses. An economy may attempt to isolate itself from the world market, it may attempt to control movements in the world market for its own benefit, or it may adapt its own economy to the changing requirements of the world market.[1] Small economies have indeed on occasion attempted both the first and the second of these lines of action. The capacity of a small economy for isolation from the rest of the world is, however, so strictly limited, even if it is prepared to submit to a very low standard of living, that this possibility need scarcely be

[1] C. M. Wright, *Economic Adaptation to a Changing World Market*, ch. i.

seriously considered. Even for a large economy the difficulties of isolation would be very great. It demands the greatest diversity and abundance of natural resources, such as few of even the most wealthy economies can command. The United States might do it, for in recent years imports into the United States have sometimes been no more than 5 per cent. of national income. But a large part of this 5 per cent. has an importance for the economy as a whole much greater than a mere statistical statement might suggest, and the disruption of United States exports would have far-reaching repercussions for the rest of the economy. The U.S.S.R. too might do it, but so far the standard of living attained in the U.S.S.R. has been low, and as it rises the U.S.S.R. too will probably find the maintenance of more intimate connections with world markets indispensable for further development. Germany attempted to combine isolation or self-sufficiency with a vigorous policy of intervention in world markets, but experience too taught her that, if her purposes were to be realised, the area under her centralised control had to be greatly widened.

17. The alternatives remain of adaptation to world conditions or control of world conditions. The new techniques of trade regulation, exchange control and the like, offer tempting opportunities to large and powerful economies for exerting pressure which has sometimes been effective to ensure that changes shall be made in the structures of weaker economies for the benefit, in the first instance, of the more powerful. Some of the smaller economies were indeed among the first to resort to these new techniques, and others have not been slow to follow their example, and, despite the fact that their power to influence world trends in their wider aspects is strictly limited, have thus attempted to direct or control the impact of world forces as it affected themselves. Such success as they have so far had has, however, been in large measure due to the fact that their efforts were made at a time when the world still had no experience of the consequences of the whole-hearted and simultaneous application of the new techniques by several powerful economies. The United States never adopted them, and British efforts to adapt them to her own conditions were far from thoroughgoing. If simultaneously all economies were vigorously to apply modern methods of control,

the small economies would have a very thin time. For them the only sensible course is adaptation. " The little countries must emulate David who rejected the hampering armour that Saul pressed upon him and relied on his mobility and quick adaptability." [1]

18. It is possible moreover that, by relying too much on conclusions drawn from observation of the apparent " success " of German policy during the thirties, the powerful economies too may deceive themselves as to the extent of their power to control world conditions. Apart from some useful but limited technical lessons, observation of a quite abnormal period when German policy was to a large extent nowhere seriously opposed can throw little light on what would probably happen if several powerful economies were all trying to do the same thing. David's distrust of Saul's advice was in the event abundantly justified. If each one of the Great Powers were to don a suit of protective armour, much more elaborate and technically complete than the somewhat half-hearted imitations with which some of them were content in the inter-war period, the final result might well be mutual frustration for all of them. For them, too, adaptation to changing world conditions is perhaps the most sensible course.

(iv) *Agricultural Policy*

19. In selecting suitable illustrative examples to indicate the importance of the problem of structural adjustment during the inter-war period, the order of exposition is a matter of some delicacy, if there is any risk that the reader may assume that by placing a country first on our list we thereby mean to imply that its responsibility for the economic disorders of the period was also judged to be greatest. We shall deal in some detail mainly with the policies of the United States and of the United Kingdom, with some further incidental observations upon German policy in subsequent sections ; but we have no such implied judgment in mind, partly because, as we have already seen, the errors which statesmen might have avoided during this period are for our purposes less significant than the errors which the existing international anarchy obliged them to commit. It will, moreover, be

---

[1] C. M. Wright, *op. cit.* p. 243.

convenient to examine agricultural policy in general first, in relation to which many countries, each within the limits of its power,
played a significant and obstructive part.

20. The part played in the Great Depression by the catastrophic fall in the prices of nearly all primary products has often
been interpreted as distinguishing it sharply from its predecessors,
and some observers have even found the main causes of the
depression in this movement. However that may be, the course
of agricultural production after 1918 clearly illustrates the
unfortunate consequences of failure to make prompt adjustments
in the structure of production and of the adoption by individual
states of policies which ignore their consequences for other
economies. For many years before the depression the prices of
primary products had been tending to fall relatively to those of
manufactures. The conditions of production, as a result of the
opening up of new agricultural land and of rapid improvements
in production technique, facilitated a relative fall of costs for
many primary products. Agricultural producers, who for one
reason or another had to carry a burden of high costs, were
naturally the most troubled by the effects of this trend, which
obliged them either to turn to other forms of production or to
seek protection from their governments.

21. The war of 1914–18 left, moreover, a good deal of excess
productive capacity in certain important products, such as
cereals and sugar. In the long run the only satisfactory response
to such a situation would have been a reduction of production
capacity concentrated as far as possible upon high-cost producers.
Instead of this, the experience of the war was often felt to justify
further efforts to attain the self-sufficiency in food production, the
absence of which had caused great inconvenience everywhere
during the war ; in certain directions the number of high-cost
producers was even increased behind the protective barriers which
national governments created or pushed to a higher level. The
long-run effects of this movement were for some time masked
by the industrial prosperity of the world as a whole up to 1929.
So far as this industrial prosperity was firmly based, the agricultural production which satisfied the demands of industrial
producers could not be regarded as excessive ; it too was, how-

ever, in part built upon shaky foundations, the result of ill-judged capital investment which was certain to end later in a slump, so that it merely provided agricultural production with a temporary cushion which in the nature of things was certain to be withdrawn.

22. The war had already encouraged a considerable expansion in the food-producing capacity of overseas countries. Between 1909–13 and 1922–7 the wheat acreage of Canada increased from 10 to 22 million acres, and of Australia from $7\frac{1}{2}$ to 10·4 millions. In New Zealand between 1911 and 1922 dairy herds were doubled. Nor did the expansion of wheat acreage cease with the immediate adjustment to abnormal conditions. The average world acreage (excluding the U.S.S.R., China, Turkey, Persia and Iraq) for 1928–32, 244,400,000 acres, exceeded the 1923–7 average, 225,640,000 acres, by 8·3 per cent.[1] The greater part of this increase occurred in the exporting countries, whose acreage expanded by 10 per cent., but importing countries also made significant contributions. Many European countries were aiming at self-sufficiency in wheat by protecting local high-cost producers, and at the same time some of the overseas countries were also encouraging the cultivation of marginal areas which later experience showed to be unsuitable. The motives lying behind agricultural policy in particular cases were varied and complex, but within the field of agriculture itself the repercussions of one national policy upon another can be illustrated in an instructive way. Looking back at the inter-war economic history of the Danubian region, it is easy now to draw the conclusion that the over-expansion of wheat-growing in Czechoslovakia was a serious blow to the stability of other wheat-producing countries in that area. It should not, however, be forgotten that among the influences inducing Czechoslovakia to follow this line was the British decision in 1929 to lower the tariff on raw sugar while maintaining the duties on refined sugar, and thus to allow British refiners to monopolise the British market. Czechoslovakia had previously sold about half of her sugar exports, equivalent to one-third of her total production, to Great Britain, but after 1929 Czechoslovak sugar exports to Great Britain sank to a negligible

---

[1] International Institute of Agriculture, *Documentation for the Monetary and Economic Conference* (1933), p. 260.

figure, and a strong inducement was thus given to transfer part of the old sugar acreage to cereal production, the wheat acreage in fact increasing from 1·58 millions in 1922–7 to 2·26 millions in 1932–7.[1]

23. For some products, *e.g.* coffee, rubber and to some extent wheat, schemes of " valorisation " and price regulation provided a temporary stability, which, however, gave a further stimulus to the expansion of productive capacity, especially in areas outside the scope of these schemes. The only sensible course for people engaged in some branch of production where they are likely to be permanently undercut by more efficient producers elsewhere is to divert their energies in some other direction. In theory international marketing organisation might facilitate an orderly redirection of this kind, without undue hardship for high-cost producers, but in practice too often they became devices to enable high-cost producers to stay where they were. Structural changes in agriculture to encourage the production of higher class products with a more elastic demand were a good deal discussed, but it was a common criticism of agricultural policy at the time that any action taken for this purpose was quite inadequate.

24. With technical progress going steadily ahead throughout the period, the resistance of the agricultural and primary producing sector of the world economy to the necessity for adjustment made it particularly vulnerable to any signs of a down-turn, whatever its immediate cause. Many felt it unreasonable to discuss agricultural problems in terms of over-production, especially as the recorded increase of output of many commodities could be shown, even if the effects of rising standards of living were left out of account, not to be out of proportion to the increase in the world's population. Such statistical calculations, however, missed the main point. No demand for primary products from the world's population as a whole, and still more no increased potential demand arising from rising standards of living, could

---

[1] This episode is paralleled by one of the minor reactions of the Hawley-Smoot tariff. The fall in wheat prices had induced an expansion of dairying in Canada, and when the Hawley-Smoot tariff restricted the entry of Canadian cream into the United States, Canadian dairy farmers insisted upon the imposition of a prohibitive duty on New Zealand butter (W. K. Hancock, *Survey of British Commonwealth Affairs, Problems of Economic Policy, 1919–1939*, Part I, p. 212 note).

become effective unless the structural changes dictated by changes in conditions of production were expeditiously made. These changes were impeded or were carried through too slowly. Over-production could not sensibly be measured in terms of the consequences of structural changes which were not allowed to occur. In the last resort the only satisfactory world agricultural policy was one based on a recognition of the necessity for shifts in production.

(v) *The Policy of the United States*

25. Certain aspects of United States policy during this period have a special interest for our argument, not only on account of the importance of her own efforts at insulation, but even more because the limitations of the important change of policy initiated in 1934, which deliberately and consciously turned aside from insulation, themselves illustrate with unusual clarity the nature of our problem. Among the most far-reaching consequences of the war of 1914–18 was the transformation of the United States from the status of a debtor country to that of a large-scale creditor. "A net debtor status of approximately $3,700,000,000 in 1914 was transformed into a net creditor status, excluding inter-governmental debts, of the same amount by the end of 1919." [1] In due course this transformation was sure to make necessary parallel structural adjustments in the economy of the United States, in the interests of the people of that country no less than in the interests of the rest of the world. As a debtor country the United States had normally had an active balance of trade, its surplus exports being used to meet overseas debt obligations. In the early stages of transition to creditor status, when new international investments were still being made, no change was needed in the balance of trade, surplus exports being now required for a different purpose, the provision of the goods purchased by borrowers from the United States, and the United States net creditor position in fact increased from $3700 millions at the end of 1919 to $8800 millions at the end of 1930. [2] As time went on, however, the situation was bound to change. As

[1] Hal B. Lary, *The United States in the World Economy*, p. 122.
[2] Hal B. Lary, *op. cit.* p. 123.

more capital was lent abroad, the claims of United States lenders steadily increased. These could in the last resort be met only by a corresponding increase in United States imports of foreign goods and services, and ultimately the new creditor status demanded a parallel transformation of the balance of trade, a surplus of exports being replaced by a surplus of imports. This had been the normal trend as Great Britain became an important international investor,[1] and has also been repeated in other countries who have lent extensively abroad.

26. There was no inherent reason why the adjustment of United States foreign trade to her newly acquired creditor status should have been made precipitately immediately on the conclusion of hostilities. But while it might with advantage have been carried through gradually and almost painlessly over a long period, the immediate pressure being relaxed by a wise policy of foreign investment, two special circumstances soon made it an urgent necessity. Even when the United States was lending heavily abroad, it was at the same time pressing for the repayment of war debt, which ultimately was possible only if the United States had been prepared to receive a larger volume of imports. And partly as a result of the lack of discrimination shown in the details of a foreign investment policy which in general might have been highly advantageous both to the United States and to the rest of the world, the cushion of foreign lending was suddenly removed in the middle of 1928, and there was little inducement for its recovery when the Great Depression made still clearer the uneconomic and extravagant character of much of the lending of previous years. The cessation of capital exports at once deprived foreign countries of the protection hitherto enjoyed against the immediate necessity of paying their interest and dividend liabilities to their creditors in the United States, and there was even some withdrawal of the capital already invested abroad.

---

[1] It is interesting to speculate how far Great Britain's process of adaptation during the nineteenth century was in fact conditioned by the reaction to the Irish famine which was the immediate pretext for the repeal of the Corn Laws in 1846. It would be an ironical circumstance if parallel adjustments in the United States were held up primarily because of the difficulty of discovering some similar tragic disaster which would make it easier to apply effective pressure upon the vested interests of that country.

27. So far, however, from adapting her trade policy to this change in her fortunes, the United States at first moved sharply in exactly the opposite direction. It had both before and during the Great Depression, like most other countries, pursued a policy dictated by its own short-term views of its own immediate interests. The devastating effects of the policies thus adopted, culminating in the Hawley-Smoot Tariff of 1930 and the revaluation of the dollar in 1933, have since been widely recognised in the United States. As Mr. Sumner Welles has put it, " after the last war, at a time when other countries were looking to us for help in their stupendous task of economic and social reconstruction, the United States suddenly became the world's greatest creditor nation, and, incomparably strong economically, struck blows at their war-weakened debt-burdened economic structures that were heavy morally as well as economically. The harmful effects of this policy on the trade, industry and conditions of living of many other foreign countries were immediate. Our high tariff policy reached out to virtually every corner of the earth and brought poverty and despair to innumerable communities." [1] It would indeed be a mistake to suppose that the catastrophic decline in United States imports at this time was entirely attributable to the Hawley-Smoot Tariff. It may be doubted whether any clear-cut distinction can be drawn between the effects of the depression in general and the effects of the new tariff, but if such a distinction were admitted to have some provisional validity, it may be plausibly argued that the restrictive effect of the new duties was relatively far less than that of the depression.[2] Nevertheless attention is rightly directed here to the effects of the tariff, because it symbolises so aptly the typical reactions of this period, when people at once turned in time of trouble to the notion of resisting any necessity for structural adaptation.

28. Experience indeed brought home to United States leaders rather earlier than to the statesmen of other countries the lesson that insulation was a deceptive blind alley. As soon as the Hawley-Smoot Tariff was passed, foreign governments proceeded to

[1] In a speech at the Twenty-eighth National Foreign Trade Convention in New York, October 7, 1941.
[2] Hal B. Lary, *The United States in the World Economy*, pp. 171-2.

retaliate. " Before 1931 closed, fully twenty-five coutnries either had made extensive tariff revisions, had increased specific duties, or had threatened to do so. In almost every important case, the justification advanced was the necessity for fighting the United States with her own weapons." [1] With a uniformly disappointing experience of efforts to reach world-wide agreement for the expansion of world trade upon a basis of equality of treatment, which Mr. Cordell Hull, who became Secretary of State in 1933, firmly believed to be an essential condition for the construction of a stable world order, he decided to experiment with a more modest approach to the problem through a series of bilateral agreements for the lowering of trade barriers, which by preserving the Most Favoured Nation principle would at the same time constitute a programme of general concerted economic collaboration.

29. The Reciprocal Trade Agreements Act of June 1934 accordingly authorised the President of the United States to conclude trade agreements with foreign countries for variations in rates of duty, which, however, were not to exceed 50 per cent. of the existing rates. Such variations were to apply to imports from all countries, except that the President was empowered to exclude any country from Most Favoured Nation treatment " because of its discriminatory treatment of American commerce or because of other acts and policies which in his opinion tend to defeat the purposes " of the Act. From 1935 Germany was uniformly excluded from Most Favoured Nation treatment, and Australia was also for a short time placed on " the black list ", but this power was not as extensively used as a jealous interpretation of the trade policies of other countries might have warranted. Where exchange control or quotas formed an important part of the apparatus of foreign trade policy, strict logic might compel the conclusion that discrimination was an inevitable consequence of their use. But in this matter the United States was not bound by strict logic, and by the use of rather rough-and-ready formulae sought practical compromises which would make possible the conclusion of agreements with countries which practised exchange control or imposed quotas in a way which was not too blatantly discriminatory. There were, how-

[1] A. D. Gayer and C. T. Schmidt, *American Economic Foreign Policy*, pp. 69-70.

ever, limits to this complaisant attitude, and no agreements were concluded with the most whole-hearted exponents of the new techniques of trade regulation. Special provision was also made for the maintenance of the United States' own exclusive agreement with Cuba.

30. The Act itself laid down no precise rules for determining the items in respect of which negotiations with foreign countries might be initiated, but action was usually, though not invariably, guided by the so-called chief or main supplier principle, whereby concessions were limited to goods of which the other signatory to an agreement was already the chief foreign supplier of the United States. This principle, it was argued, was implied in the statutory provision insisting upon the exchange of reciprocal benefits, and its adoption inevitably severely limited the effective significance of the formal maintenance of the Most Favoured Nation principle. With a view, moreover, to further limiting any uncovenanted gains accruing to other countries through the application of this principle, the items in the tariff schedule were sometimes reclassified in a detailed and elaborate way which ensured that benefits for third parties should be reduced to the barest minimum.

31. By September 1939, twenty-one trade agreements had been signed in accordance with the provisions of the Act, eleven of them with Latin American countries. War conditions inevitably restricted the possibility of further action ; the technique has, however, not been abandoned, and by the end of 1943 six more countries had been added to the list, with negotiations still pending with two others. The most important agreement in the series, that with Great Britain, was signed on November 17, 1938.

32. The Trade Agreement Act represented a highly significant turn in United States policy. The question, however, remained, Was the turn sharp enough ? The new policy was based upon the principle of non-discrimination. It was realised that in an imperfect world compromises were unavoidable, but the objective kept steadily in mind was to ensure that to the utmost possible extent the decision as to which foreign country should be a source of supply of imports should be determined by reference to the relative efficiency of production of the competing countries, and

not the condition of the balances of payments with particular countries or the like. The problem which, however, was never quite squarely faced at the time [1] was the extent to which the discriminatory practices condemned by the United States might have been in effect imposed upon other countries by the tariff policy of the United States itself. In some instances this plea may now have the appearance of a rather belated and unconvincing afterthought. " Although the basic disturbance generated by the drastic reduction in dollar payments to a world heavily indebted to the United States could scarcely be over-stated, it would be erroneous to suppose that the various measures taken by foreign countries were directly and consciously prompted in all or most instances by the shortage of dollars." [2] Discrimination appeared to offer short-term advantages which certain economies were eager to grasp, without much reference to anything the United States might have done. The central question, however, still remained, What was the rest of the world to do if any powerful economy insisted upon a policy which, with whatever fluctuations might from time to time occur, placed the rest of the world in a position where chronic passive balances of payment were inevitable ? This question was not always clearly understood at the time, either in the United States or elsewhere. The implications of the question are now widely seen to be fundamental in any consideration of rational post-war international economic policy.

33. The actual results of the trade agreement policy, while perhaps not yet of the first order of importance, have certainly been far from negligible. But leaving aside the limitations imposed by the main supplier principle, and by the fact that duties cannot be reduced by agreement by more than 50 per cent., one further fundamental fact justifies the conclusion that the Trade Agreements Act is not enough. " The primary aims of the Reciprocal

---

[1] Writing in May 1943, Mr. Wayne C. Taylor, Under-Secretary of Commerce, declared that " a world economic structure organised on the basis of equal treatment and with large scope for free enterprise cannot be maintained in the face of such reductions in the supply of dollars as have occurred in our international transactions in the past. . . . Unless dollars are made available with greater regularity than in the past, it would be both unjust and unwise to demand the removal of restraints and controls largely designed to protect the internal economies of other countries against external shock and pressure " (Foreword to Hal B. Lary's *The United States in the World Economy*, published by the United States Department of Commerce, 1943).

[2] Hal B. Lary, *loc. cit.* p. 179.

Trade Agreements Act ", it has been said by one American writer, " are the expansion of our exports through the reciprocal reduction of tariff and other obstacles to trade and the restoration of multilateral trade on the basis of equality of treatment." [1] In other words, reciprocity is interpreted as involving not only reciprocity in the kind of treatment afforded by one party to an agreement to the other, but also reciprocity in the volume of benefits enjoyed in the shape of expanding trade. There is no attempt to enforce an exact balance of advantage. In particular cases United States imports may increase a little more than United States exports. But in other cases this relation may be reversed, and the general objective is an expansion of imports corresponding as nearly as possible to the expansion of exports arising from concessions granted by the other parties to trade agreements. The same writer points out that " examination of the concessions obtained and granted by the United States makes it plain that our exporters have secured considerable benefits from the program ", and explains that the technique of preliminary investigation and public hearings which has been developed makes sure " that concessions received will prove of definite advantage to United States exporters ".[2] But so long as this principle is maintained, the fundamental maladjustment remains unaltered. So far as it goes, it is a good thing that United States imports should increase even if the increase is contingent upon a parallel expansion of United States exports, but if the balance of trade is already chronically out of adjustment, *i.e.* with imports too small as compared with exports, the addition of an equivalent amount to either side of the account leaves the original position of disequilibrium exactly as it was. Leaving aside the possibility of the resumption of foreign lending, which would in any event merely postpone the impact of the problem, the inexorable condition for the establishment of international equilibrium is an expansion of United States imports at a more rapid rate than the expansion of United States exports. The world in general (and the United States is obviously to be included here) needs now a trade policy

---

[1] Alexander Stevenson, " The Reciprocal Trade Agreements Program ", *International Conciliation* (May 1943), p. 400.

[2] Alexander Stevenson, *op. cit.* pp. 401, 403.

whose primary aim will be not the expansion of United States exports, but rather the expansion of her imports. This condition was operative even before the outbreak of the present war. Its urgency will be much increased by the structural changes imposed by the war. To ask for the fulfilment of this condition is, however, the same thing as to ask for structural adjustments in the United States economy of exactly the kind which we have been discussing. Here we have one clear and outstanding illustration of the inevitably disruptive effects of refusal to make these adjustments. Mr. Cordell Hull's courageous and pertinacious efforts to re-establish a world economic order have pointed in the right direction. But the limitations imposed by the legislation under which he has carried on his negotiations have made it impossible to carry them far enough.

(vi) *The Policy of Great Britain*

34. The structural adjustments which were called for in Great Britain after 1918 were more extensive and more difficult than those required in the United States, for, broadly speaking, they were a response to war-time losses of wealth, whereas in the United States the new status was the result of an expansion of wealth. But, as in the United States, the necessity for change was also for a time cloaked by the illusions of the immediate post-war period, and some time elapsed before it was generally realised that the competitive position of many of the traditional British export trades had permanently changed for the worse. When the facts could no longer be ignored, policy was generally directed much more to providing supports for declining industries, such as coal, cotton, and iron and steel, than towards stimulating the more rapid growth of newer industries to take their place. Large-scale unemployment was a constant feature of British economic life during the greater part of this period, and with the onset of the Great Depression the preoccupation with depressed industries and depressed areas became almost an obsession.

35. For Great Britain in depression anything like insulation in the literal sense was obviously impossible. Her trade and investment interests were world-wide, and the direct connections between her own prosperity and that of her customers and debtors

could never be ignored, even by those who were most impatient of international restraints. This obvious fact in large measure accounted for the varied nature of the devices used by British governments during this period. In their efforts to get the best of both worlds, their policy did not readily fall into any of the neat logical categories which were easily elaborated by those who theorised about international economic policy. The frequently repeated protestations of devotion to the principles of a world economic order were sincere enough, but in Great Britain too there was a strong tendency during this period to take decisions without much regard to their effects upon other economies, or, where the reactions of other economies had to be taken into account, to induce or compel them to make adjustments such as would be most convenient for Great Britain herself. The outstanding events were the abandonment of the gold standard in September 1931, the adoption of protection in March 1932, and the Ottawa Agreements of September 1932, which brought to a head earlier tentative movements for the formation of an Empire trading bloc. We have already indicated that for many purposes it is no longer very helpful to enquire whether in the circumstances of the time the decisions taken were either wise or inevitable. It is, however, of great interest to illustrate their damaging effects upon other economies, and the subsequent boomerang effects upon the British economy itself.

36. Whatever the immediate motives for abandoning the gold standard, and whether or not Great Britain could genuinely plead that she had been " driven off " gold, the decision inflicted substantial immediate losses upon other sections of the world economy. All foreign holders of sterling suffered,[1] and the inherent instability of the gold exchange standard as a device for economising the use of gold was at once revealed. Fourteen countries had been compelled to follow the British example by the end of 1931, and during the following year eleven more followed a similar course.

37. In respect of some of these countries indeed the term

[1] One-quarter of the central bank reserve of Greece, for example, was deposited in London. The Bank of France also held sterling assets to the amount of £62 millions, and was obliged to negotiate with the French Government for a Treasury bond to cover the loss involved. H. V. Hodson, *Slump and Recovery, 1929–1937*, pp. 87, 91.

compulsion may sound somewhat exaggerated, for there was some sense of relief in thus being given an opportunity to relax the rigours of a monetary policy which was becoming more and more irksome. An orderly devaluation of the majority of world currencies might at that time have been in the interest of everybody, and it is certainly now impossible to defend the decision in 1925 to re-establish sterling at the pre-war rate of exchange. But in the absence of appropriate international institutions such orderly devaluation was impossible. Particular national authorities cannot fairly be criticised for refusing to delay action on their own account until these institutions had been created, but the unilateral action which alone in the circumstances of the time was possible involved damage and embarrassment for other economies, the subsequent reactions from which moreover to some extent offset the benefits which unilateral action was expected to bring.

38. For a variety of reasons, some of which were not entirely foolish, a number of important economies at first refused to swim with the tide and made vigorous efforts to maintain the original gold values of their currencies. To a significant extent their position was made more difficult by those very benefits which Great Britain and the other countries which decided to follow sterling derived from exchange depreciation. Sterling prices remained unexpectedly stable after the gold standard had been abandoned, but no one could accurately determine how far this stability was dependent upon the steep decline elsewhere where the gold standard was still maintained. There was, therefore, a certain amount of disingenuousness about the plea that the latter could easily avoid their difficulties by abandoning their stubborn resistance and falling into line with sterling. The competitive advantages of depreciation for British exporters may not have been an important motive in determining the final decision, but it was at once realised everywhere that "depreciation of the £ will operate like a varying tariff on imports or a bounty on exports".[1] Other countries naturally thought these advantages of the greatest importance, so that the forces favouring restriction of trade elsewhere were strongly reinforced, with further damaging repercussions upon British exports.

[1] *The Times*, September 28, 1931.

39. However disturbing the immediate consequences of the British abandonment of the gold standard may have been, it could be argued with some plausibility that this was for the world as a whole a movement in the right direction which, in the absence of suitable international institutions, could not have been carried through in a more orderly way. The revolution in British trade policy in the following year was also defended as giving a lead to the rest of the world. It was claimed for the Ottawa Agreements not only that they would facilitate " the flow of trade between the various countries of the Empire ", but also " that by the consequent increase of purchasing power of their peoples the trade of the world will also be stimulated and increased ".[1] But it was manifestly impossible for devices which diverted to some part of the Empire trade which had formerly gone to a foreign country to result in any *net* increase either in purchasing power or in world trade. Foreign countries had no difficulty in recognising the essentially restrictive nature of the Ottawa Agreements, and within the limits of their power reacted by way of retaliatory measures.

40. Already before 1931 Great Britain had taken a few significant steps in the direction of building up a tariff, but she had not hitherto equipped herself with a comprehensive system, embracing both manufactured and agricultural products, a system moreover which, from October 1932, was integrated by means of the Ottawa Agreements with the tariffs of the Dominions and colonies in an intricate preferential system. There had also been some earlier significant essays in imperial preference, but its more whole-hearted acceptance was due to the desire on all sides to get some emergency protection against a world of rapidly declining trade. Dominion producers felt that their only hope was to persuade Great Britain to reserve markets for themselves by shutting out foreign competitors. British producers were not so confident that Dominion and colonial preferences would give them all the market outlets which they needed, but were nevertheless quite grateful for any partial protection which might come their way along the path of imperial preference.

[1] Cmd. 4174, p. 10.

41. British statesmen were not at the time unaware of the risk that the new policy might provoke retaliatory measures elsewhere. " There are two ways ", Mr. Baldwin told the Conference, " in which increased preference can be given — either by lowering barriers among ourselves or by raising them against others. . . . It seems to us that we should endeavour to follow the first rather than the second course. For however great our resources, we cannot isolate ourselves from the world. . . . Let us remember that any action we take here is bound to have its reactions elsewhere." In the event it was, however, for the most part the method which Mr. Baldwin condemned which was adopted. Exclusion, partial or complete, from the British market increased the difficulties of primary producers elsewhere, in Latin America, for example, in South-Eastern Europe and Denmark, and the increased restrictions upon industrial imports imposed additional losses upon Britain's leading industrial competitors. The countries thus affected naturally endeavoured, within the limits of their powers, to protect themselves against the consequences of the change in British policy. Their retaliatory measures seemed to short-sighted observers in Great Britain to justify the precautions which had already been taken. We are in danger of being excluded from world markets, they had argued, and their own decisions having accelerated the trend against which they sought an insurance, they then asked for congratulations upon their foresight.

42. Both political and economic considerations must be taken into account in any final judgment of the Ottawa Agreements. They were widely interpreted as serving notice on non-British countries that no lively British interest was to be expected if severe economic pressure were to be exerted upon them from other quarters ; they thus facilitated German economic and political penetration into South-Eastern Europe and various parts of Latin America. And so far from encouraging or even permitting the rest of the world to follow the Ottawa example, the Ottawa signatories, while firmly insisting upon the " settled principle " laid down in 1910 that " trade agreements between parts of the British Empire are to be considered matters of a domestic character which cannot be regarded as discriminatory

by any foreign power ",[1] were equally firm in insisting that their own Most Favoured Nation rights should be scrupulously observed by foreign Powers. The Ouchy Convention of July 1932, for example, which would have created a similar preferential bloc for Scandinavia and the Low Countries, was in effect vetoed by this insistence.

43. At the time of their signature the Ottawa Agreements were attractive to the participants mainly as an emergency protection in a world of rapidly declining trade. As soon as anything at all resembling normal conditions returned, it became more and more doubtful whether for any one of them the advantages of more effective access to wider world markets would not have been substantially greater. In any event for certain commodities, such as wheat and cocoa, of which the Empire as a whole has an export surplus, even the immediate advantages for preferred producers were likely to be disappointing, inasmuch as the increased competition of foreign producers outside the Empire tended further to depress world prices. At least in Australia this had been realised even at the time of Ottawa, and subsequent more widespread understanding of this dilemma played its part in the modest modifications of the preferential system which were registered in the Anglo-American Trade Agreement of 1938. There was a perennial clash of interests between the British manufacturers who found that Dominion markets for their goods were, as they thought, unduly restricted, and the Dominions who were anxious to build up more " balanced " economies, and it was doubtful whether the growth of harmonious intra-Commonwealth relations would be encouraged by the infusion of hard bargaining introduced both in the Ottawa negotiations and later interpretations of the Agreements. Some British critics felt that foreign countries, whose own record in the matter was far from clear, were not in the strongest position to complain of the abandonment of the Open Door principle in British colonial territories, but this movement in the direction of an exclusive imperialism inevitably provoked criticism from foreigners who had formerly been able to compete on equal terms in these markets.

[1] Cmd. 5369 of 1910, para. 122.

44. With an apparently intractable unemployment problem in some of her most important staple export industries measures for the encouragement of exports naturally occupied a prominent place in British depression policy. But, however natural this might be for an economy to whom a large volume of exports was so overwhelmingly important, it was unfortunate that relatively so little attention was given to exploring the possibilities of new industries, and so much to bolstering up the old. For even when it was effective, such action was almost necessarily at the expense of foreign competitors ; the check thus given to their recovery held out little hope for the restoration of world trade, in which Britain had such a vital interest, on any assured basis. Protectionist propaganda had always insisted upon the usefulness of a tariff as a bargaining weapon to compel concessions to British trade in foreign markets. In a wicked world where everybody was struggling desperately to maintain a share in a contracting volume of trade, the devil, it was widely feared, would inevitably take the hindmost, and any country which had failed to equip itself with a tariff would almost certainly be at the end of the race, a ready prey to devilish machinations. The British Government was accordingly active in using the new weapon which it had forged to conclude a series of bilateral agreements with foreign countries who were in a weak bargaining position inasmuch as their normal exports to the United Kingdom were much in excess of their normal imports. Pressure was thus placed upon Argentina, the Scandinavian and Baltic countries and Poland to increase their purchases of British goods, in some cases particularly of coal, under the threat of a diversion of British demand for their exports to other markets. This naturally intensified competition elsewhere from suppliers who had formerly exported to these markets, so that Britain's gains in the markets where she could insist upon favours were in danger of being offset by losses elsewhere. While the demand from the Scandinavian countries for coal from the North-East and Durham increased, there was more intense competition from German and Polish coal in Mediterranean markets in which British exporters were also interested, so that the benefits for the coal-producing areas in the east of England were offset by losses for South Wales.

45. The varied forms which the widely divergent pulls of competing interests obliged British policy to take were well illustrated by the trading relations with Argentina. A simple application of the straightforward principles of imperial preference, such as would have gratified some of the Dominions, might have been extremely damaging to the Argentine economy. British interests, however, required that Argentina should not be too ruthlessly damaged, as otherwise the difficulty of ensuring the remittance of the earnings of British capital invested in that country would have been much increased. On the other hand, undue tenderness to the interests of Argentine exporters would have provoked opposition from British agriculturalists. The normal balance of trade, therefore, made it possible to hold the threat of more drastic applications of imperial preference in reserve as a weapon to compel the Argentinians to grant British exporters more favourable treatment, and they were encouraged in the belief that it was " natural " to " buy from those who buy from you ". Agreements were concluded which earmarked a large fraction of the sterling proceeds from the British imports from Argentina for the repayment of outstanding debts and further purchases of British goods, the *quid pro quo* for Argentina being a promise not to restrict her exports of meat below the level set by the Ottawa Agreements. Without any formal breach on her part of Most Favoured Nation principles, Great Britain was thus able to compel some of her trading partners to grant her favours which involved a *de facto* departure from those principles. This naturally provoked resentment in the countries against whom discrimination thus came into play, and for a long time helped to make difficult the conclusion of a trade agreement between Argentina and the United States.

46. In other directions also imperial preference was an obstacle in the way of the exchange of concessions which was the common objective of negotiations for trade treaties, for the obligations which both Great Britain and the Dominions had assumed to maintain agreed margins of preference sometimes limited their freedom to agree to tariff reductions for the benefit of other countries, such as on other grounds they might have been prepared to offer. Towards the end of the period, and partly

for political motives, there were, however, some signs in Great Britain of a tendency to reverse the movement in favour of discriminatory bilateral bargains. There were some half-hearted efforts to withstand German penetration in hitherto neglected areas, and, much more important, the Anglo-American Trade Agreement of 1938 marked the first significant reduction in British customs duties since 1932, and a partial reversal of imperial preference itself. This was indeed to some extent merely a recognition of the fact that for certain commodities imperial preference meant very little, the largest nominal reduction being applied to wheat, of which the Empire was necessarily a large net exporter to the rest of the world.

47. Future historians will no doubt long continue to debate the merits and demerits of British depression policy. No final judgment will be attempted here, as it would involve a much more detailed analysis than would be relevant to our immediate purpose. Our interest, here as elsewhere, has been mainly in the inter-actions between contradictory national policies and the consequences of the widespread refusal to facilitate adjustments in national economic structures. Happily not even the most stubborn attitude in the face of this necessity can inside a national economy completely obstruct the path of economic progress, and the current level of income is influenced by many factors other than those with which we have been concerned. The qualified recovery from the depression which subsequently took place occurred, however, in large measure in spite of rather than because of the measures which we have been discussing. The new level to which economic activity was raised in Great Britain was moreover still unsatisfactory. At the peak of the boom in 1937 nearly 10 per cent. of the insured population was still unemployed. There had been a considerable shift of labour away from the depressed export industries, but large-scale unemployment was still mainly concentrated there, thus indicating that the attempt to evade the problem of structural adjustment was still far from successful. Few countries indeed could safely have persuaded themselves in the years immediately before the war that steady foundations had been laid for their economic development. For industrial activity was dominated by defence prepara-

tions which, whether or not they culminated in war, could offer no satisfactory assurance for a more distant future. One vital factor throughout in British development was the disproportionate fall in the prices of foodstuffs and raw materials. Britain as a large importer benefited substantially from this, and the real incomes of employed persons in Great Britain actually increased during the years of the depression. But this was a measure of the advantages to be gained from international division of labour, and not of the success of the new policies which were threatening more and more to impede the fruitful cultivation of that principle.

(vii) *Was the Attack on Trade Barriers Misdirected?*

48. To many adherents of some fashionable modern schools of economic thought our selection of the outstanding points in the economic history of the inter-war period will seem simple and even naïve. We are, they will say, repeating the errors of the participants in the numerous futile international conferences of the period who passed resolutions deploring the growth of trade barriers, but, broadly speaking, achieved nothing. We may indeed agree that " to some extent it is true to say that the disequilibria in international trade were the cause of the trade barriers rather than caused by them and that to deal with the barriers alone would have meant mistaking effect for cause ",[1] and the intention of our argument would have been misconceived if it were supposed to imply a summons to resume the somewhat simple-minded attacks upon trade barriers which produced such disappointing results during the 'twenties and 'thirties. The rock upon which these attacks almost invariably came to grief cannot be removed without a careful probing of the fundamental causes of resistance to reform. Whether any reliance at all can be placed on frontal attacks, they must be supplemented by outflanking attacks which will get closer to the root-causes of the disease.

49. Our critics, however, often go a good deal further than this. In their eagerness to remove trade barriers altogether from the list of fundamental causes, they frequently move to a position which in effect also denies their importance as symptoms. Having,

---

[1] *Commercial Policy in the Inter-war Period : International Proposals and National Policies* (League of Nations, 1942), p. 147.

for reasons which we have already seen to be unconvincing, persuaded themselves that the losses inflicted by impediments to international trade are in the modern world so slight that we need not worry much about them, they are quite prepared to leave them indefinitely as they are, or even to use them as instruments of the internal policies which they approve. This attitude must be rejected without hesitation, as dangerous to the cause both of progress and of stability. In any event trade barriers deserve a prominent place in our story, for whatever the original inducements to impose them, they often became secondary causes of disruption in their own right, and few things illustrate so clearly the stultifying effects of reluctance to face structural change.

50. "There is" indeed "little hope of a better world economic order unless we go beyond the symptoms to the causes of the disease ",[1] but even the fullest acceptance of this thesis still leaves in doubt the real nature of the disease. Whether or not there is any value in general agreements for the moderation of restrictions on international trade, a prudent statesman would certainly insist upon combining them with something else, and it is important to get as clear an idea as possible of the nature of this " something else ". Among the reasons which have been held to justify the current insistence on the value of the nutritional approach to economic policy is the belief that this would provide the essential " something else ", and that people who had become enthusiastic about nutrition would thereby be impelled to take a more lively interest in the trade obstructions which hitherto have often barred their access to good and sufficient food. Whatever validity there may be in this claim, it merely illustrates our more general thesis that the real enemy both of progress and of economic stability is the rigidity of national economic structures, based upon the widespread determination to evade the apparent inconveniences of structural readjustment. The " something else " which is needed must include a variety of devices for loosening up the rigid structures of national economies too timid to make the changes needed if they are to enjoy the benefits of technical progress. In the interests of both national and world welfare, the growing points in modern productive development must be identified and

[1] H. W. Arndt, *Economic Lessons of the Nineteen Thirties* (1944), p. 271.

given careful attention, to ensure not only that growth there is not impeded, but also positively encouraged. From whatever angle problems of international economic relations are approached this requirement confronts us. Those charged with the administration of regular machinery for international consultation and continuous investigation could scarcely do more useful work than to direct the organs under their control to a concrete examination of the implications of industrial expansion and the harmonious coordination of the processes of adaptation in various national economies which such expansion demands.[1]

51. This unfortunately is not the direction in which the thoughts of many of our critics run. They can scarcely formally deny the importance of structural adjustments, and often make some show of paying deference to it. But some of them scarcely attempt to conceal their impatience when the point is pressed,[2] and in their detailed expositions of policy, structural adjustment is relegated to a quite minor position, if not forgotten altogether. The really important thing, they tend to argue, is national monetary and credit policy to ensure " full employment ". For this purpose any country is entitled, it is claimed, to adopt an expansive monetary policy. If other countries were sensible enough to follow suit, all would be well. But unfortunately some countries have other views on these matters, and trade restrictions must therefore be imposed to check the flow of imports which the maintenance of internal purchasing power would otherwise attract, thus upsetting the balance of payments and destroying the monetary equilibrium, the maintenance of which is one of the objectives of the policy adopted. Policies of this kind, however, often reflect that same indifference to the effects of national policy on economic conditions elsewhere the dangerousness of which we have been concerned to demonstrate as among the chief lessons of the economic history of this period. Expansive monetary policies from which trade restrictions are assumed to flow as an inevitable corollary easily become devices for exporting unemployment, and through the repercussions and retaliatory measures

[1] Cf. Eugene Staley, *World Economic Development : Effects on Advanced Industrial Countries* (1944), pp. 198-9.
[2] Cf. E. F. Schumacher, *Export Policy and Full Employment*, p. 9.

which they generate, tend in the long run to be sterile and self-frustrating. The belief in the inevitability of such policies stems directly from failure to examine the problem of structural readjustment with sufficient seriousness.

52. Nobody has ever seriously believed in a preordained natural harmony which makes it inevitable that wisely directed national policies will in no circumstances harm the inhabitants of other countries. There are numerous cases on record where states have successfully carried through policies for their own benefit at the expense of other states. The range within which such self-regarding national policies can hopefully be applied has, however, been much exaggerated in recent years. It would be utopian to hope that in normal circumstances, and much less in the desperate conditions of profound depression, any state would deliberately sacrifice its own economic interests for the benefit of others. But we should not on that account despair of convincing even the hard-boiled politician and business man that self-regarding policies often and inevitably fail to attain even their own limited objectives. We may then hope to avoid a repetition of the worst excesses of the past, and modestly begin to lay the foundations of a stable international order.

53. We must be particularly careful to ensure that in our eagerness to avoid the errors of those who dissipated their energies in the inter-war period in tilting directly at trade barriers we do not repeat other errors of a different and much more serious kind. Among the numerous limitations of the human mind probably none has more unfortunate consequences than that which makes it inevitable that we should discuss economic problems, even when they are organically related and interdependent, in some kind of temporal order. Everything is mixed up with everything else, but we cannot profitably talk about everything at the same time. Unfortunately the choice of order for exposition sometimes has the effect of creating a subconscious impression that the order of importance is identical with it, and therefore that the thing mentioned first should also be dealt with first, other problems being left for later treatment. For example, because it is generally agreed that strenuous efforts must be made after the war to maintain employment at the highest possible level, people

are apt to say that this supreme objective must be achieved first, and then afterwards we can, if we still feel so disposed, get on with the business of lowering trade barriers. According to one recent writer, for example, " the solution of the problem of the trade cycle is an essential precondition of a reintegration of the world economy ".[1] And many go further and urge the prior importance of solving the problem of the trade cycle, and thus ensuring " full employment ", within a single national economy, before any serious attempt is made to integrate it with the world economy as a whole. According to Mr. Chifley, the Australian Minister for Post-War Reconstruction, for example, " the most important contribution we can make to the prosperity and welfare of other countries is to maintain the Australian people in full employment at the highest possible standard of living ".[2]

54. Obviously, however, there are numerous paths along which we may attempt to ensure " full employment " and " the highest possible standard of living ". The implicit assumption that international trade and internal " full employment " policies can safely be handled as independent problems greatly increases the chances that the path chosen will be inconsistent with the maintenance of a high level of employment and rising standards of living in other economies, and will, therefore, by provoking retaliatory measures elsewhere, lead us quickly back to the same confusion and contradiction as marked our feverish efforts to get out of the Great Depression. The degree of interdependence between foreign trade policy and internal employment is not the same everywhere. For Canada it has been argued that " if there is to be no revival of a world market, then the sooner Canadian politicians eat their words on the subject of Full Employment, the better their chance of remaining in politics ".[3] The point might properly be put less forcibly elsewhere, but in varying degrees the fundamental truth is much the same everywhere, and for no economy would the attempt to deal with the two problems in watertight compartments have more fatal results than for Great Britain.

---

[1] H. W. Arndt, *Economic Lessons of the Nineteen Thirties* (1944), p. 275.
[2] Broadcast on May 17, 1943.
[3] Gilbert Jackson, *Facts in the Case : A Manual for Canada's Planners*, p. 25.

55. It is the more remarkable that views such as those we are now criticising should be most popular among those who insist most strongly upon the necessity for a complete break with the past. In effect they are urging us to return to the short-sighted practices which had such disastrous results during the inter-war period. The consequences at that time might have been a little less unhappy if national policies had been technically better devised or internally more consistent, but no improvement of this kind can remove the inherent contradictions between them. If we urge statesmen to-day to concentrate first upon ensuring full employment at home, and to leave problems of international relations aside for the time being, we are in effect asking them to ignore the lessons of history. Many in the past have found satisfaction in deriding the simple-minded who believed that an "invisible hand" would infallibly ensure the welfare of all if individuals were left free to pursue their own self-regarding activities. The belief that we should somehow stumble into a stable world order if each national economy applied itself to the task of ensuring a high level of employment for its own people, leaving international relations to be cared for, if at all, later, could be justified only if we were prepared also to believe in another "invisible hand" much more miraculous and improbable than anything ever attributed to the most simple-minded of our ancestors. The solution of the problem of the trade cycle is not a precondition of a reintegration of the world economy, for unless we are prepared for declines in national living standards which themselves would be a confession of defeatism, we must grapple simultaneously with both problems, and with a proper appreciation of their interrelations.

56. Much of the thought of supporters of the many-sided New Deal indeed illustrates directly the danger of misunderstandings of this fundamental point. It is not easy to reconcile all their ideas in a single consistent body of doctrine, and some New Dealers never lost sight of the importance of international relations for their country. But others were most anxious to do precisely what is now being urged upon us as a duty for every national economy, to ensure first as high a level of employment as possible inside the United States, and only afterwards, if at all,

to pay some attention to the rest of the world. Nor is it at all reassuring to be told that some of the measures they took were ill-suited for their purpose, and that a " full employment " policy would now mean something quite different. Even if this were true, the attractiveness of trade restrictions as an instrument for protecting employment at home is so obvious that it would be dangerously rash to assume that people who had whole-heartedly accepted the principle of the primacy of " full employment " could be trusted never again to be led astray by the errors of the past. It seems unwise to tell the responsible persons in the United States who are now anxious to repair the damage caused by past exclusiveness, in effect, that they are mistaken, that " it may very well be the case that the much-abused American tariff is more of an irritant than a real obstruction to the flow of trade ",[1] and that the effort to integrate United States trade policy with the requirements of a co-ordinated world economy should therefore be abandoned or at least postponed until some indefinitely remote future. The Australian doctrine quoted above might be thought to offer a complete justification for the insensitiveness to the reactions of United States policy upon other economies which the prudent United States statesman, no less than the historian, now so much deplores. Those who to-day are impatient of the apparent restraints which adaptation to world conditions imposes upon them should ask themselves whether it is really wise to provide reasons for maintaining without further modification the Hawley-Smoot tariff.

(viii) *Economic Policy and Political Security*

57. Little has been said here about the political background of the economic strife of the inter-war period. " The increasingly evident dependence of a country's military strength — and of its status as a political Power — on its possession of highly-developed engineering, vehicle, precision instrument, and chemical industries, and on its immunity against the more drastic effects of blockade, has been a factor of steadily increasing importance in the shaping of economic policy ",[2] of which it would be easy to compile a

---

[1] *Economist*, December 4, 1943.
[2] A. J. Brown, *Industrialisation and Trade*, pp. 12-13.

long list of illustrations, drawn from the history of both great and small Powers. Whatever the importance at first attached to work creation in Nazi Germany, rearmament entirely dominated the economic policy of that country in its later stages, and elsewhere too the experience of the war and blockade of 1914–18 was a powerful reinforcement of all the influences favourable to agricultural self-sufficiency. These facts must be given a place in any balanced picture of the inter-war world economy, and there is little need now to emphasise the inter-dependence of rational post-war economic policy and the attainment of a sense of political security more deeply rooted than was possible in many countries prior to 1939. Without attempting any full analysis of the significance of this relationship, two general remarks are relevant here. First, the fact that military security has been put forward as a justification for some particular economic policy is not by itself an adequate reason for believing that military security was the most powerful motive at work, and some of the defences on grounds of military security for some of the worst extravagances of inter-war economic policy arouse a certain justified scepticism. A little ashamed of what they then insisted on being done, some people are now inclined to put forward the plea that everything was justified by the appeal to military security. Much, however, which is now so defended was at the time based on little more than crude protectionist prejudice, of which the appeal to the defence motive is an unconvincing rationalisation.

58. More important is the fact that the relation between political and economic considerations is strictly one of *inter*-dependence, not merely of dependence. The task of statesmen is not first to ensure political security, and then, it might sometimes be thought as a mere afterthought, to elaborate a wise international economic policy. For the effectiveness for their immediate purpose of measures to ensure political security will sometimes depend upon the extent to which they aid the evolution of wise international economic policy. Otherwise they may make more real the very political risks against which they are intended to be an insurance. The case for a wise international economic policy thus rests not only upon the belief that it will assure higher standards of living and greater economic stability, but also upon

the important and indeed essential contributions which it may make to the creation of the favourable psychological and social conditions upon which in the last resort political security must depend. Those who at the present time are naturally preoccupied with the problem of political security should therefore be reminded that the construction of a rational international economic order is not, as some of them sometimes seem to think, an irrelevant distraction from a more immediately pressing purpose. Failure to construct such an order would at the same time greatly increase the difficulties of ensuring political security.

59. We should also make the elementary point that judged by their practical results most of the efforts made before 1939 to use economic policy for purposes of political security were complete failures. Many of the smaller countries excused their agricultural policies on security grounds, but most of them could scarcely have been worse off during the present war if they had never made any such efforts. And the measure of foresight upon which some of the larger countries may now be entitled to congratulate themselves is in fact extremely limited, because in every case defence would have been difficult and perhaps impossible without support from outside. In the most conspicuous case of the moulding of economic policy for purposes of military strength, that of Germany, the ultimate result will be a quite unqualified failure. In the light of the history of the last twenty years a sober realism appears to suggest an approach to the relationship between economic policy and the requirements of political or military security of quite a different kind from that which has recently been popular. It may be true that " so long as countries have reason to fear the recurrence of war, no emphasis on the economic benefits of international trade will induce them to forgo such a measure of economic self-sufficiency as their governments consider feasible and desirable for their military security ",[1] but the historian of the recent past is obliged to add that the utmost measure of self-sufficiency so far considered either feasible or desirable has usually been shown by events to be inadequate or even irrelevant to the purpose in view.

[1] H. W. Arndt, *Economic Lessons of the Nineteen Thirties* (1944), p. 274.

T

CHAPTER XVI

INTERNATIONAL ECONOMIC ADJUSTMENT
(continued)

(d) SOME POINTERS FOR THE FUTURE

1. THE elaboration of a practical programme to deal with the international aspects of our problem would clearly be a more complicated and more delicate task than was the elaboration of a similar programme directed in the main towards the correction of internal maladjustments. The two programmes would indeed necessarily have much in common, and much of what was said earlier in Chapter X might with advantage be recalled here. Anything which makes internal structural adjustment easier is likely at the same time to facilitate international structural adjustment, and few of the suggestions made earlier would be entirely irrelevant, even if one had nothing but the problem of international relations in mind. A more careful examination of some of these suggestions might indeed suggest the wisdom of more extensive international action in fields from which it has hitherto been almost completely absent. Bearing in mind the radical importance of education, for example, and the fruitful analogy between investment in material capital equipment and investment in human capacity, we might speculate on the possibility of adapting the international capital market for investment in human capital, by raising educational standards in backward countries.

2. The elaboration of anything which pretended to be a complete programme would, however, demand a much more detailed and far-ranging discussion of fundamental economic issues than could conveniently be attempted here. We shall therefore conclude our series of essays on international economic adjustment with an analysis of some of the " blind alleys " and " third-rate solutions " which have recently attracted attention, some observations upon the position of Great Britain and the United States in the post-war world, and a modest positive proposal for an international institution of a kind which it is

hoped may not be thought entirely impractical in our very imperfect world. The points to which we shall devote most of our time are not necessarily all matters which on an objective view could be regarded as the most important. A great deal of work has, however, already been done on many of these issues, and no useful purpose would be served merely by recapitulating what others have already said more effectively. So far as possible our attention will be confined to issues which seem in danger of being neglected.

(i) *International Planning*

1. The idea of planning has attracted at least as much attention in discussions of international economic reorganisation as in relation to internal policy, and it will be convenient to deal with it at once, as an analysis of the idea in this context will also give an opportunity for discussing some of the problems peculiar to the international sphere.

2. Much of our earlier discussion of planning [1] is also relevant to planning on an international scale. Here, as within the narrower confines of any single national economy, there is no limit to the advantages to be reaped from more careful forethought, from a more sensitive appreciation of the inevitable relationship between means and ends. Our criticisms of international economic policy in the inter-war period might be summed up by saying that at that time there was far too little of this forethought ; any proposals for reform should aim at making it easier to look ahead, to weigh the consequences of our decisions and to modify our first thoughts in accordance with the results of our investigations.

3. We found, however, that fruitful discussion of planning within a national economy was often made difficult by doubts about the precise meaning of the term, and especially by the failure to distinguish between the State's responsibility for maintaining and reforming the institutional framework within which all decisions affecting economic activity must be taken, and the State itself assuming direct responsibility for such decisions. For all practical purposes no institutional framework of this kind

[1] In Chapter XIII.

now exists for the guidance of international relations. It might therefore have been expected that speculation about international planning would have concerned itself largely with the problem of its construction. On the contrary, however, most international planners, preoccupied as a rule with direct State activity at home, have approached international questions too with the same interest in their minds, and their discussions have largely been in terms of international executive organs, not yet created, but sometimes responsible, it is suggested, for making decisions even more far-reaching than is contemplated for national planning organs.

4. The construction of such organs evidently depends upon the consent of national governments, and as there is still little evidence that many of them are prepared to abandon their formal right to the last word on vital issues, the discussion of international instrumentalities which assume a state of affairs other than that which actually exists tends to become academic and to lose touch with realities, and the crucial questions, who is to do the planning, and how are national authorities to be persuaded to submit to the instructions of the planning organ, are too often left unanswered, and sometimes scarcely even discussed.

5. If planning were to be interpreted in the strict sense implied in *Planwirtschaft*, it would mean the application to the world as a whole, or to a very large part of it, of a centralised control of production comparable with that which many socialists regard as necessary for national economies. Some writers have been prepared to go to these lengths ; " there must be ", it has been said, " a central organisation to consider and to decide where it is in the interest of the world as a whole that production of various commodities and their transformation into manufactured products should take place ".[1] Whether such a proposal is theoretically desirable or not, even the most cursory examination makes it clear that there is not the slightest chance of any such full-blooded collectivist scheme coming into operation within any period of time which it is worth while to consider, and most writers on this subject have therefore been content with something not quite so far-reaching. Sometimes it is proposed that some international organisation should take upon itself responsibility for allocating

[1] F. E. Lawley, *The Growth of Collective Economy*, vol. ii, p. 374.

the world's capital supply, or more frequently those parts of it which are available for foreign investment, among the many competing claimants who would like to have access to them. It is often proposed that the production of individual key commodities should be controlled by a specialised international organ, with power to allocate quotas and perhaps to control marketing, and as both reflection and experience suggest that the results would not be very satisfactory if any number of such organs, controlling different commodities, were to get to work without any regard for each other's interests or policies, the suggestion is sometimes added that a super-organ should undertake the responsibility of co-ordination. If complete control of the production of all important commodities seems quite outside the range of possibility, some have, nevertheless, thought it possible that, with a view to realising higher standards of food consumption more in accord with the requirements of modern nutritional science, some central organisation might prescribe for different countries the volume and character of the crops to be produced. From other quarters comes the idea of allocating export markets among the different countries whose producers are interested in export trade. The sponsors of the World Trade Alliance have suggested that the producers of the world's chief export commodities should form product committees to fix prices and agree on the quantities which each national group should export, with a world council set up by governments to supervise the agreements.[1]

6. Much that goes by the name of planning in this sphere is, however, much less pretentious than anything so far mentioned. Many supporters of planning appear not to understand fully the profound difference between the " considering " and the " deciding", for which the author quoted above wished a central organisation to be responsible, and expressions of approval for a general co-ordination of national policies are therefore often quoted by them as indicating also approval of planning in the stricter sense. If the more modest proposals to be outlined later are made more acceptable by being described as proposals to

---

[1] Memorandum by Sir Samuel Turner on the World Trade Alliance in Action, March 1943.

create organs of international planning, we may agree to use the term, but we should not forget that in so doing we have radically changed its meaning.

7. It is often made a point in favour of many of the proposals described above that their adoption would make competition unnecessary. This view is, however, based on an illusion. There is no reason why bargaining carried on in the privacy of a board-room or a council chamber should be described by a name different from that given to the processes of the market-place. Nor will a change of name necessarily carry with it any change in the relations of competing producers. Two or more producers who have goods to sell in foreign markets are by that very fact necessarily and inevitably in a competitive relation with each other. In the past it has normally been left to the foreign con-sumer to decide between them, and producers have competed in the endeavour to win his approval. Even when international cartels limited the freedom of consumers' choice by agreements for the allocation of markets, competition between producers did not cease, but merely took another and sometimes more intense form. An international executive organ might further limit consumers' freedom, but so long as someone has to choose between the producers who wish to cultivate a market, there must be competition between them.

8. The same questions by reference to which we asked earlier that any proposals for planning should be judged are equally relevant in the international field. First, what does the plan propose to do ? Secondly, how does it propose to do it ? What principles will it apply in making decisions ? And will it have sufficient regard for the necessity for continuous change and adaptation ? And, finally, will instruments be available for executing the plan ?

9. The purposes of international plans are usually set forth in the most general terms, with a show of appropriate deference to rising standards of living everywhere and the maintenance of economic stability. The most important concealed disagreement which lies behind the apparent unanimity with which these purposes are accepted arises from the implicit belief of many supporters of international planning that somehow or other they

will succeed in realising all the cherished purposes of their own national economies. Sometimes this belief is not merely implicit, for, as we shall see later, among the grounds upon which the idea of international planning appeals most strongly to some of the members of powerful economies is the belief that thereby they will much more easily impose their will upon weaker economies.

10. The second question, What principles do international planners propose to apply in making their decisions ? is still more important. According to what criteria will they distribute the capital available for foreign investment, or decide how much of X should be grown in one country and how much in another, or how much of Y the exporters of Ruritania should be allowed to sell in foreign markets, and how much should be reserved for the exporters of Utopia ? The answers given to such questions are usually no less vague in the international than in the national sphere. Especially in relation to international investment the criterion of profitability has been as much derided as in the national sphere, but it is usually impossible to get any clear idea of what is to take its place. In the absence of any objective standard of comparison, it is, however, difficult to see how decisions about international investment can be other than arbitrary. The number of capital projects for which a plausible case could be made out is almost literally infinite. The volume of capital needed for even a fraction of them greatly exceeds the most optimistic estimate of what is likely for many years to be available. We must somehow choose between them. We must compare the benefits likely to accrue from constructing new railways in China with those of improving the navigation of the Danube, we must choose between the claims of many backward and over-populated areas each of which needs capital for industrialisation. International " plans " seldom reveal the criteria according to which such decisions are to be made.

11. At first sight the allocation of production or expert quotas might look a little easier, for in one way or another a good deal of experience of these things has been accumulated, and we therefore have precedents to guide us. International cartels have experimented extensively in the allocation of markets, the international control of the output of key raw materials is no new

thing, and the new techniques of trade control developed in recent years have obliged most governments to hammer out some kind of principle for allocating import quotas. The experience thus gained has, however, revealed very clearly the immense difficulties of the problem, and the principles so far applied have almost invariably illustrated the great power of the forces which aim at ensuring that existing structures of production shall not be disturbed. In other words, planning has so far normally meant in practice decisions based upon principles exactly the opposite of those which we have argued to be fundamental for both economic progress and economic stability. Import quotas have in the first instance been based upon the experience of some earlier period. Raw material control schemes have tended to preserve the rights of existing producers. Some uneasy modifications have sometimes been introduced in the course of time, but it has been a slow and difficult business, and the tendency to preserve and crystallise the *status quo* has always been strong. There is now general agreement that international raw material controls are to be judged by their effectiveness in facilitating the smooth adjustment of production so that low-cost producers will expand and high-cost producers will be forced to undertake activities elsewhere, and most current discussions of this question hopefully assume that this principle will be more faithfully observed in the future than it has been in the past. There are no doubt some good reasons of another kind for approving international raw material controls, and as they are more or less certain to play an important part in the post-war world, we must in any event try to make the best of them. It would, however, indicate a dangerous propensity for wishful thinking to conceal one's fears that it may not be found possible to keep these powerful instruments under control, and that under the guise of an " international plan " we may unwittingly impose upon ourselves machinery which will mean stagnation and decay.[1]

12. The further consideration of these issues brings us at

---

[1] The frequent exhortations to take the international Wheat Agreement of June 1942 as a model for imitation elsewhere are not very encouraging from this point of view, as no arrangements are made therein for discouraging high-cost production, nor is there any provision for the periodical reallocation of quotas in favour of predominantly low-cost countries.

once face to face with our third question, What instruments will be available for the execution of international plans ? In this connection two main currents of thought call for attention. The same process of reasoning which has made the idea of " consumer representation " in national economic control agencies fashionable [1] has also led many to believe that the same device might be used to check at least the more obvious defects revealed in the operation of the inter-war commodity controls. It may be agreed that in an imperfect world it may be worth while experimenting with something of this kind, but consumers' representation must for the purposes immediately in view mean the inclusion of government representatives on the governing bodies of controls ; governments have not yet so completely freed themselves from the influence of the specious pleas in favour of " stability " put forward by producer interests as to justify any confident expectation that their defence of the consumer would be so effective as the stimulating influence of competing producers prepared to offer goods of satisfactory quality at prices lower than those which established interests found to be comfortable.[2]

13. The second current of thought introduces issues of wider significance. Inevitably the influence of the more powerful economies in world affairs will always be very great, and no one with any sense of realism would in this connection be disposed to dissipate his energies by kicking against the pricks. It is, however, one thing to admit the inevitable consequences of wide divergences of economic strength ; it is quite another thing to grant these divergences formal recognition and status of such a kind as will immensely strengthen the more powerful economies and relegate the smaller and weaker to the position of mere pawns to be more or less gently shifted about for the convenience of their more powerful collaborators. This is in effect what some international economic plans would threaten to do. Just as planning inside an economy may easily become an instrument for establishing more securely the influence of groups already

---

[1] Cf. *supra*, XIII, 24.

[2] The position is particularly unsatisfactory in cases like the Wheat Agreement, where the main consumer interest is represented by Great Britain as a large importer, and the British Government's attitude is inevitably affected by consideration for the interests of its own home producers.

dominant there, so in the international sphere planning may be attractive as a means for ensuring that the policies of the smaller economies are adapted to suit the convenience of the larger.

14. Any attempt to interpret the half-conscious motives of human action would lead us into fields where even the most confident psychologist might hesitate to tread with assurance. It cannot, however, be doubted that among the influences which have made the idea of planning so attractive to many people the ordinary normal human lust for power deserves an important place. It is so often obviously apparent that other people are foolishly stupid, and few of us are quite free from the temptation of supposing that the affairs of other people would be better managed if we had control of them. This human frailty plays a significant part in thought on the planning of national economies, but it is by no means absent from the international sphere. Nor is the fundamental idea of imperialism, the notion that other people would be better off if they allowed themselves to be controlled by us, confined to those who are popularly described as imperialists, for similar ambitions are to be found among many thinkers on the Left. Some of the plans now current for the development of backward areas, such as South-Eastern Europe, are no doubt in part motivated by a sincere regard for the welfare of the inhabitants of those countries. But with this is often combined a belief that if they are wise they will be content to do what the planners tell them, and sometimes the incidental benefits of an assured demand for the capital goods of the more advanced countries looms so large in the discussion that it is not an unfair caricature to describe the plans as primarily a means for assuring stability to these economies, any benefits accruing to the countries to be planned being for the most part purely incidental.

15. These tendencies have not entirely escaped the notice of the leaders of thought in the smaller economies. Many of them are ardent devotees of the current fashionable planning philosophy, but on second thoughts they may well be a little doubtful whether planning in practice, under the domination of the Great Powers, will give quite the attractive results for which they have been hoping, and sometimes even as they are fascinated in contemplation of the mighty engine to which the climate of contemporary

opinion is so favourable they shrink back in some alarm from committing themselves too whole-heartedly to decisions which may shortly place them in a position resembling that of guinea-pigs subjecting themselves to interesting experiments devised by others.[1] Their natural fears will be carried too far if they encourage again the cultivation of policies of narrow economic nationalism. No state, small or great, can expect always to get its own way. But while the small states must be firmly urged to submit themselves to some necessary adaptations in the interests of the world as a whole, they may rightly think that the interests of the world as a whole are not always precisely identical with the interests of the large Powers, and that adaptations required in the interests of the world economy may be quite different from those which the large Powers would like to impose.

16. Some of the current sentiment in favour of international planning is indeed based on little more than impatience with the inescapable fact that the world is a very complicated place. With sixty-odd nominally independent centres of authority, the difficulties of getting agreement on anything more than the vaguest and most general aspirations are obvious, and to many it seems an attractive short-cut to simplify the position by placing the final responsibility for decisions more or less formally in the hands of representatives of the much smaller number of large Powers. While such a decision might change a little the way in which the world's complications were presented, it would not essentially

[1] Professor Zweig is careful to remind his readers that " national sovereignty may be regarded as a mere superstition by powerful nations whose interests — owing to the weight of their power — are safe in international arrangements, but it is looked upon differently by small nations, whose interests in international arrangements are often overlooked " (*The Planting of Free Societies*, p. 110). It is plausible to suppose that in the decision to place pure relief measures in the forefront of the programme of U.N.R.R.A. and to relegate rehabilitation and reconstruction to a quite subordinate place, some part was played by the reflections of the representatives of some of the smaller states, who may have felt that, despite their natural anxiety to get as much outside assistance as possible, the risks of placing the whole of their future development in the hands of authorities on which they themselves could hope to exert little influence were too great to be faced. Many economists must from time to time have sympathised with Professor Cannan's feelings when he confessed that, even when he felt bound to oppose some particular proposal for the extension of conscious organisation, he often had " a sort of desire that opposition may fail because the experiment will be so interesting and afford matter for economic lectures " (*The Economic Outlook*, pp. 281-2). Such feelings should, however, perhaps be held in check if the experiments are to be made only in economies other than one's own.

alter either their character or their range. The world is indeed a complicated place, and even superficial reflection upon its complications justifies some doubts about the applicability of the planning technique, whatever its merits or demerits elsewhere, to the world as a whole. The sketchy character of most of the plans thus far disclosed may indeed be explicable in part in terms of a half-conscious realisation of this fact.

17. To descend to a more pedestrian level, the problem of personnel which we have already seen is likely to be acute for a national planning authority, is even more serious in the international field. If we rightly entertain some doubts whether the " new types of men and women " said to be required to handle the new national tasks proposed will be available in sufficient numbers and in sufficient time to prevent so-called plans from breaking down into a mixture of prohibitions of productive activity and a number of purely *ad hoc* arbitrary and uncorrelated positive decisions, similar doubts become quite overwhelming when we reflect upon the probable personnel requirements of an international plan. The League of Nations and the International Labour Office have indeed every reason to congratulate themselves upon their high degree of success in laying the foundations of a genuine international civil service. But they left many problems still unsolved ; the scope of the work they undertook was much narrower than is now contemplated by some international planners, and though it raised some delicate issues, it was relatively simple as compared with those which an executive international planning authority would have to face. The number of competent international civil servants who emerged during the inter-war period was moreover quite small, and fell far below the level needed to put some of the current ideas of planning into operation. Even for the much more modest advisory bodies whose functions we shall discuss later, the problem of personnel will be serious. On every occasion when the creation of an international organ has been discussed in recent years, somebody quite rightly and properly makes the point that its administrators must be men or women of wide experience and first-rate ability. It is, unfortunately, to be feared that there may not be enough of such people to go round. In these circumstances we should clearly be

well advised to refrain from adding unnecessarily to the claims made on the services of the limited number of people available. It is indeed by no means certain that even the Great Powers by themselves will agree upon any formal international economic plan of far-reaching scope. We should be getting the worst of both worlds if, by establishing a few international executive organs to deal with problems of minor importance, we allowed too many competent people to be diverted to their service, until no one was left to undertake the more fundamental long-run tasks of investigation and advice.

18. As in the parallel case of national planning, so here it should be made clear that scepticism about *Planwirtschaft* is by no means inconsistent with the warmest approval of every effort to ensure that the work of international post-war reconstruction shall be based upon the firmest possible foundation of knowledge and timely preparation. The efficient functioning of such a body as U.N.R.R.A., for example, will be quite impossible without planning in this sense, and the same principle has even greater importance for any reconstruction activities which pass beyond the immediate requirements of relief. And our approval is even more emphatic of every effort to construct such a framework of institutions as will be a safeguard against the recurrence of the international anarchy of the past. Evolution in this direction may be quite soberly described as a literally essential condition for both national and international progress and stability. One powerful reason for discouraging further speculation about some of the further ranging ideas of international " planning " is that they so easily become red herrings to distract attention from what is at once more easily attainable and also more urgently necessary.

(ii) *Economic Regionalism*

1. It is to some extent in half-conscious recognition of the difficulties just outlined that there has recently been a widespread revival of interest in the idea of reordering economic policy on the basis of regional groupings. In one form or another this idea has a long history, of which the German *Lebensraum* theory has been the most systematic and influential illustration. In many of its forms economic considerations have indeed played

only a subordinate part, and the attempt to apply the idea
systematically to the whole world has sometimes been rather in
the nature of an afterthought, the main interest being in some
particular region where for some special reason political or
economic integration has seemed peculiarly desirable. A similar
complex of ideas has also sometimes been presented in a framework which cannot accurately be described as regional. The
British Commonwealth, for example, is not a geographical
region, but it has sometimes been urged that it should evolve a
common economic policy along lines similar to those approved
by the regionalists, and other groupings of a similar kind have
also been suggested on the basis of a common ideology or other
common interests.

2. Experience has abundantly demonstrated the limitations
and disappointments of national economic policies, whether
autarkic or not, and the practical difficulties in the way of an
orderly policy which will embrace the whole world are equally
obvious. To many therefore it has seemed more realistic to
tackle the task of building up a more stable international order
piecemeal, with the formation of regional or similar blocs as the
first step. Would it not be wise, they ask, in the present state of
world public opinion, to abandon any hope of early agreement
on a world-wide basis, proceeding in the meantime with more
modest projects which would require agreement among only a
small number of states ?

3. Regionalism has become a popular catchword in current
discussions of the post-war world, but the purposes which those
who favour the idea have in mind are so varied and sometimes
so divergent, and the principles implied as bases for drawing the
boundaries of regional or for determining the membership of
non-regional blocs have usually been expounded with so little
precision, that it is a matter of great difficulty to determine what
value, if any, the regional idea, as such, has.

4. The fact that a regional bloc has been proposed as the
solution of a political problem does not, of course, by itself
justify any conclusion about its merits or demerits. But partly
because it is now so much the fashion even in quarters where there
is no profound understanding of economic problems to believe

that every political solution must also have its economic justification, the political sponsors of such projects are apt to attempt to strengthen their case by building up an economic argument to support the conclusion already arrived at on purely political grounds. If one has no very clear ideas of the conditions which justify close economic association, this is not a very difficult matter, as there are few groups of countries between whose members no common economic interest of any kind could be discovered, so that some kind of superficially plausible case can usually be built up to justify any grouping which may happen to be attractive for other reasons. The political decision is usually made first, and the alleged economic reasons are little more than afterthoughts.

5. Few people in these days are likely to make the mistake of underrating the closeness of the connection between politics and economics, and many are more likely to make the opposite error of exaggerating its importance. But while these two aspects of human life in society can seldom be sharply differentiated, it remains both true and important that a regional grouping may be highly satisfactory for entirely admirable political purposes without any justification for the parallel assumption that specially close association in economic policy would be particularly advantageous for its members. The British Commonwealth, for example, has developed by a long historical process into a political association of the highest value both for its members and for the world as a whole. It by no means follows, however, as has often been hastily assumed, that a similarly close association in economic policy would be equally advantageous.

6. For these reasons it is not a very profitable way of spending one's time to attempt to analyse or correlate the numerous and often contradictory *ad hoc* economic justifications which have been put forward for the numerous regional proposals of recent years. An economic study of regionalism might more profitably begin at the other end by enquiring what considerations should be given most weight in drawing ideal boundaries for an ideal state. This is far from being a merely academic exercise, for though no actual state or grouping of states has ever been constructed on such principles, and regional grouping seldom

implies the complete integration of its members in a single unit, any rational argument adduced in favour of such a grouping must be in conformity with one or other of the principles revealed by such an analysis.

7. We are not concerned here with the economic problems, important as they are, which arise in finding the most convenient boundary-line between two states about whose separate existence there is no serious question. A badly drawn boundary may inflict serious economic loss on the inhabitants on either side of it, but the issues raised are different from those which arise when we are contemplating a closer association between two or more states which is intended to diminish the economic significance of the boundaries separating them.

8. The ordinary classification of economic problems under the headings of labour, capital, money and trade provides also a useful starting-point for examining the economic influences which might make a close regional association advantageous. Political boundaries affect economic welfare by their influence upon the movements of men, of capital and of goods and services, and regional arrangements might facilitate such beneficial movements as would otherwise be impossible. After discussing these issues something should also be said about the pooling of responsibilities for social policy, and the confusion which may result if the authorities in independent states attempt to promote developments which are mutually inconsistent.

9. From a practical point of view little can usefully be said about the relations between regional organisation and migration. Many countries to-day rate very high their right to control the entry of foreign immigrants, and show little disposition to abandon or even to qualify it. Nor is it essential to a regional economic agreement that it should provide for anything approximating to complete freedom of migration within its boundaries. In the present state of public opinion a consideration of migration merely reinforces the obvious truth that close association will be easiest to arrange between states whose citizens are more or less on the same level of culture and standard of living. But this does not carry us very far, for any part which the desire to promote migration may play in strengthening the regionalist sentiment is

usually unimportant as compared with the other factors to be discussed later. In connection with some of the proposals for regional groupings in Europe it has been urged that freedom of migration would ease the pressure of over-population in the over-crowded countries of Europe, but this suggestion comes with a rather bad grace from the citizens of countries outside which do not propose themselves to make any direct contribution to the solution of this problem.

10. One useful general conclusion, to which attention should be directed, though it has no special relevance to regionalism, is that the best method of mitigating any disabilities imposed by one state upon another by refusing to permit the immigration of its citizens is to adopt the most liberal policy in relation to the trade of the other country. There may be excellent social reasons for refusing to receive the people of another country inside one's own territories ; a case can be made for excluding their goods, but no justification can be found for a policy which does both.

11. In the quieter times of the nineteenth and early twentieth centuries the flow of capital from one country to another often ran a little more smoothly than the flow of people, but in recent years both sentiment and institutions have more and more favoured, and sometimes compelled, the treatment of capital supply upon a strictly nationalist basis. It seems likely that for a considerable period after the war exchange controls in many countries will subject to a fairly strict check any outward flow of capital. A regional organisation might mitigate the cramping effects of these controls in one of two ways. An association between a rich country with abundant supplies of capital and a poor country whose development was retarded by shortage of capital might be advantageous to both. The connection between Great Britain and some of her colonies is an illustration, and any reservations about the wisdom of such developments, from the standpoint of the interests of a wider stable world order, arise mainly because in practice such investment is often supposed to justify more or less exclusive trading connections. Regionalism in relation to capital supply has, however, received more attention from those who observe the difficulty of getting efficiency in international capital investment which has to adapt itself to the

U

varied and sometimes conflicting policies of neighbouring national states, and who accordingly propose groupings of poor states, for example in South-Eastern Europe, all of whom need capital for development, but each one of which is unlikely, by itself, to make a very attractive showing in the eyes of potential lenders. It is frequently pointed out that in the United States the " sovereignty " of seven members of the Union had to be circumvented to get the Tennessee Valley Authority working properly, and it is proposed that this should be taken as a model for ignoring or by-passing other national sovereignties in other backward regions in the interests of the co-ordinated development of the whole area.

12. There is clearly a strong case for taking precautions to ensure that the kind of industrial development which investment in Yugoslavia, say, would promote is not wastefully duplicated by allowing much the same thing to be done in Greece or Hungary. The T.V.A. analogy, however, is often pushed much further than the facts of the case warrant, for the circumventing of sovereignties, which was the condition of its success, was made possible only by the prior existence of the federal authority, with great power and enormous financial resources. Nothing comparable to the federal authority yet exists in any areas where similar co-ordinated investment activities now seem attractive, and if something of the kind were to be set up, it would lack financial strength, unless it were actually controlled by the outside suppliers of capital, involving a situation of dependence for the poor members of the regional grouping which they might wisely be reluctant to accept. Within limits, however, the regional concept presented in this form may well turn out to be fruitful. The main mental reservations about according it wholehearted support again arise because it is so often assumed that special and exclusive trading connections are necessarily implied in this case too.

13. There are some obvious advantages in having a common monetary policy, or even a common currency, but most important issues which arise in this connection are more conveniently treated as part of the wider problem of avoiding national economic policies which are inherently incompatible.

14. So far indeed we cannot pretend to have thrown much light upon the question, If a regional association is to be formed, upon what principles should its members be selected and its boundaries drawn ? We get a little closer to this question in examining the trade aspects of regionalism, and, as the factor which in the last resort most directly determines the volume and character of trade, the influences of natural resources. Regional groupings are usually defended on the ground that they will stimulate a more lively interchange of goods and services within the region, the advantages of a common monetary policy assuring stable exchange rates are most obvious for countries who are important trading partners, and the payment of interest on foreign investments is also dependent on the existence of suitable trade outlets. This aspect of regionalism has naturally already attracted much attention. Several principles of selection have been given at least implicit approval, but unfortunately the two most important, the principle of homogeneity and the principle of complementarity or potential self-sufficiency, lead to diametrically opposed conclusions.

15. The value of homogeneity as a basis of classification for analytical purposes is clear enough. Both the economic historian and the economic geographer will find it convenient in studying European development to distinguish between the industrial west and the agricultural east. A convenient basis for analysis is not, however, necessarily an equally convenient basis for long-term economic policy, and much less for day-to-day administrative decisions. The boundaries of the regions indicated by the principle of homogeneity may be quite clear and distinct, though this is not very probable, but if, as will often happen, for most important practical purposes the interrelations between the regions are at least as important as their internal relations, those responsible for economic policy must pay at least as much attention to external as to internal problems, and the attractiveness of the regional idea, which was expected to facilitate concentration on internal questions, disappears.

16. The obvious and important common interests between the various countries of Eastern and Central Europe, for example, despite some wide divergences between their social structures,

historical backgrounds and general outlooks, justify us in regarding this as being for many important purposes a homogeneous area.   They are nearly all poor countries, mainly engaged in peasant agriculture, faced with difficult problems arising from rapid population increase, and at a competitive disadvantage for their traditional staple exports as compared with overseas producers.   Cut up into a number of independent states, the area as a whole has a credit standing inadequate to justify the importation of foreign capital on a scale sufficient to make the structural adjustments in its economy which are needed if more adequate standards of living are to become available for its inhabitants. We have already mentioned the advantages to be anticipated from a co-ordinated investment policy for such an area, the benefits of each specific item in which would not be liable to be destroyed by obstructive action in some other part of the region.   But if a regional policy means, as is often implied, or would easily turn out to be the case in practice, comparative neglect of the economic links between this region and the world outside, even the highest degree of homogeneity would not warrant the conclusion that the interests of the area would be best served by regionalism. The very fact of capital deficiency itself shows the overwhelming importance of cultivating the closest associations with the rest of the world, and in ordinary trade matters too its connections with other areas, whether close at hand or geographically remote, are such important factors that any serious neglect of them might easily make almost useless the most carefully contrived internal policy.

17. There are probably few people who would in set terms deny the force of this argument.   Whenever the point is raised we are usually given assurances that connections with the outside world are not to be neglected.   But a careful examination of such details of concrete schemes as are available often shows the risk of neglecting outside connections to be a real one, and the assurances offered to be merely formal.   It is to be feared that regionalism, particularly on the continent of Europe, is sometimes attractive to its sponsors who live elsewhere, just because it seems to offer them a hopeful chance of getting clear of inconvenient responsibilities.   The inhabitants of these areas are awkward

customers. They seem always to be causing trouble. If only we could start them off on the right path, it seems sometimes to be suggested, and persuade (or even compel) them to get together and run their regional affairs better, we could then wash our hands of any further responsibility for them.

18. Regional organisation has also been strongly urged for such areas to increase the bargaining strength of its exporters, who in the past have often found themselves in a weak position in competition with overseas producers. Any advantage to be gained in this way is, however, unlikely to be very substantial. The fundamental weakness of their position is the paucity of adequate export outlets (which before the war made them easy victims for German policy) and their unfavourable cost situation. Chronically weak sellers may get slightly better terms if they act together than if they compete separately, but so long as they remain chronically weak their position cannot be very happy. If better export outlets were available, — and this depends very much on the policies of countries outside the region, — their position would be substantially improved without taking the trouble to build up a regional organisation.

19. Appeal has also been made to the principle of homogeneity as the basis for a close economic association between countries with more or less uniform standards of living. The psychological barriers are certain to be less difficult to surmount in such cases, if a regional association is already thought desirable on other grounds, but uniformity in standards of living has certainly not always been a feature, either of the countries which are already so large as in themselves to constitute a single region, or of the economic blocs which have been hesitatingly formed in the past. The contrast between the standard of living of California and of some of the southern states of the United States is almost as sharp as any to be found in Europe, and whatever advantages the British Commonwealth may enjoy for the elaboration of a common economic policy, uniformity in standards of living is certainly, if the colonies and India are to be included, not one of them. These groupings indeed are the results of long historical processes, and were not consciously or deliberately constructed as instruments of economic policy, so that the

importance of homogeneity of this kind may be greater in the future if there is a strong movement in favour of regionalism.

20. Much of the speculation about regional economic blocs has, however, probably been much more influenced by the principle of complementarity or potential self-sufficiency. In some instances the appeal to this principle is quite deliberate and has a clearly defined political and military objective. Nazi policy aimed at a reduction to the barest minimum of the dependence of the German economy upon imports of essential materials, and as even with the most strenuous efforts to replace imports by substitute materials produced at home, a considerable measure of such dependence remained, it was further directed towards building up a Greater German economic bloc, whose policy was under German control, and the resources of whose subordinate members in varying degrees supplemented the deficiencies of Germany. Elsewhere policy has not always been guided by such deliberate and conscious thought, but has been affected by the timidities of people who shrink from the complexities and complications which arise when normal life appears to depend upon maintaining a proper and constantly varying balance in their relations with many countries outside. More forceful characters are less alarmed by these complexities, but having committed themselves to a form of policy at home whose success depends upon gaining the approval or support of other countries, they direct their energies to cajoling or coercing such other countries as seem most convenient for their purpose, and observe with little more than a show of regret the decline of their economic connections with other areas less amenable to such treatment. Even the former group realises that life would be very hard without trade with other countries, and for the success of the plans of the latter trading connections are necessary such as will assure an adequate volume of essential imports. A compromise is therefore sought by linking together a number of countries whose relations it is hoped will not be too complicated to be manageable, but with sufficiently varied resources to reduce to a minimum any risk of serious loss arising from the neglect of trade connections in other directions.

21. Whatever precautions may be taken to ensure a wide

range of natural resources, self-sufficiency still has little meaning, however, apart from some judgment of the standard of production and consumption at which it is thought proper to aim, and the degree of self-sufficiency which can be attained in any region can never be estimated absolutely without reference to this standard. The U.S.S.R., which has an abnormally low ratio of foreign trade to national income, has also a low average income level. It happens also to have extensive and varied natural resources through the development of which its income level will certainly be further substantially raised. But probably if the U.S.S.R. were to attain an average income level comparable with that of other more advanced industrial countries, its maintenance would be found to depend upon a considerable modification of its former self-sufficiency.

22. If a large proportion of the trade of the countries within any given region were already being carried on between themselves, it would not follow that the formation of a regional bloc would be the most appropriate means for further improving their economic standards. The existing trade structure may correspond very well to existing requirements and existing income levels. But if income levels are to be raised, existing requirements must change, and it may well be that the necessary modifications will more easily be made, with advantage for all parts of the region, by pressing for closer economic relations with countries outside the region. In any event, it seems a curious assumption that progress can only be made by persuading people who already trade extensively with us to trade still more extensively. There is always a risk of satiation, and ordinary commercial prudence seems to suggest that better results would often follow attempts to persuade customers who had not previously bought much from us to give our goods a trial.

23. A concrete examination of complementary resources in any given case involves elaborate statistical enquiries to which investigators have already devoted much time and attention. A brief summary of the results is not easy, but it is not unfair to say that invariably, unless quite irrational sacrifices of standards of living are contemplated, it is found that some substantial outside trading connections always remain essential for even the

most carefully designed region or group of countries. That independence of external conditions which many are so eager to establish still eludes our search even when we widen the boundaries of the unit for whose independence we are working, until it becomes clear that it can be attained only if our policy embraces the whole world. And as some of the countries whom the economic geographer might like to include in his ideal region will very likely refuse to play, any actual region will probably fall still further short of the objective in view. In building up new intra-regional connections, moreover, there is also a risk that old connections which have hitherto proved quite satisfactory will have to be sacrificed, so that the volume of net losses arising from the new type of organisation will be still further enlarged.

24. Many regionalists may, however, quite honestly and reasonably complain that all this seriously misconceives their intentions. They have no thought of working for an unrealisable insulation from world conditions, and fully realise the futility of such attempts. But, as they insist, we live in a wicked world where, if we wait until every country, or even all the more important countries, have agreed to a rational policy, nothing will ever be done. We must take care not to allow the best to become the enemy of the good, and accepting the world as we find it, we should for the time being be satisfied with such partial improvements as we may be able to arrange on a scale less pretentious and far-reaching than the whole world. Ideas of this kind were in the minds of those who before the war favoured the formation of a so-called low tariff club. The Most Favoured Nation principle, whose original purpose had been the extension on the widest possible scale of the benefits of any relaxation of restrictive trade policies, had in practice often seemed to have precisely the opposite effect. For the knowledge that any " concession " granted to one country would have to be automatically extended to others was often a powerful deterrent preventing any significant change in tariff policy. It was, therefore, thought that practical measures for the moderation of trade restrictions might be made more acceptable if partial relaxations were permitted, accruing only for the benefit of certain specified partners. The absolution which the members of the British Commonwealth

of Nations insisted upon claiming, in regard to their relations with each other, from the general obligations of the M.F.N. principle, would have been in accordance with this proposal, if they had in fact refrained from raising tariffs against other countries and had contented themselves with lowering tariffs as between themselves.

25. It has sometimes been argued that suggestions of this kind deserve serious consideration because their acceptance might provide the first step towards a wider extension of freer trading conditions everywhere. The more substantial, however, the relaxation of trade barriers may have been in the first instance, the more difficult it becomes to conceive of the later admission of important partners into the preferential system. From the standpoint of the immediate interests of its members, the essential purpose of such a system is to create privileges, and membership must inevitably lose its attractiveness the larger the number of states sharing the privileges. Production schedules are sensibly and inevitably based upon estimates of current marketing prospects, and producers in privileged countries who had been encouraged by the probability of assured markets within the preferential bloc could not be expected to regard with equanimity such a radical change in trading conditions as the admission of new partners would involve. It is to be feared that in real life the formation of such blocs would hamper rather than aid the further relaxation of trade restrictions in relation to areas outside. The experience of the British Commonwealth suggests, moreover, that it is much easier to talk about a preferential arrangement to be implemented exclusively by lowering barriers inside the bloc than it is to give this idea a concrete shape. When it comes to a matter of hard bargaining and negotiation, good resolutions are too easily forgotten. If the minds of the parties concerned were genuinely prepared for a renunciation of the right to raise barriers against non-members, the climate of opinion would be at least equally favourable for negotiations covering a still wider area. If their minds are not so prepared, any hopes of the climate becoming more favourable later may be rendered illusory by the influence of the new vested interests which will grow up inside the new sheltered positions.

26. If human beings could be treated as purely passive units at the disposal of governmental policy, there would be a strong case from the standpoint of social welfare for the organisation of policy on the widest possible geographical basis, for the opportunities would then be expanded for that redistribution of income which is the essential purpose of social insurance measures. Human beings are not, however, at all like this, and while they may be prepared with some reluctance to approve of redistribution for the benefit of their fellow citizens with whom they share a strong sense of kinship and common interests, their willingness to submit to income redistribution for the benefit of the citizens of other countries cannot in the present state of world opinion be rated at all high. Even in proposals for regional blocs which are otherwise taken very seriously, provision for common social insurance services does not usually play any important part.

27. The position in relation to policies of " full employment " is, however, very different, and some of the current regionalist sentiment is much influenced by the desire to ensure that the expected beneficial effects of an expansive monetary policy for any given national economy will not be offset by other countries refusing to fall into line. Or the same intention may be expressed positively in terms of a desire to insulate an area from the risks of world depression. The ideal thing, in the view of those who are influenced by these ideas, would be a thoroughly co-ordinated " expansionist " policy covering the whole world, but as this is felt not to be very likely, and the possibilities of insulation for most single economies are strictly limited, they fall back on the notion of co-ordinating expansionism among such states as may for other reasons be disposed to work together. This policy is frequently presented in a framework of " planning ". A little reflection easily reveals the limitations of planning which has to be confined to a single national economy. Stability seems to be threatened by unpredictable changes in economies outside with whom links must be maintained, and planners are therefore apt too hopefully to imagine that their task would be easier if the area in which they were allowed to operate could be expanded.

28. We have already seen some reason to doubt whether expansionism is not interpreted by the members of this school too

narrowly, and too exclusively in terms of one particular technique. A genuine expansionism would no doubt have a place for some of the technical devices which they favour, but it also demands the flexibility of economic structure which the precautionary measures *vis-à-vis* the rest of the world contemplated by the regional expansionists are often in practice designed to delay or even, as they hope, to render unnecessary. In an imperfect world regional agreements in this sphere are not to be ruled out altogether, but they should be clearly recognised as third-rate solutions, and the utmost care should be taken that in our eagerness to elaborate their details we should not find ourselves in effect sabotaging efforts to make arrangements on a wider scale which, even if they were only partly successful, would bring us still more substantial benefits.

29. In any hypothetical regional bloc it is usually not very difficult to identify the countries who should form its nucleus, but for various reasons, at which we have already hinted, the selection of the countries or areas to round off the bloc is a matter of great difficulty. An extension in one direction may seem appropriate from the standpoint of one or two essential raw materials, but new trading connections with other areas beyond will inevitably be introduced, so that on balance the " independence " of the region may be in no way increased. Nor can it be argued that decisions in regard to the areas on the periphery of a regional bloc have little practical importance. They may on the contrary be absolutely vital for the future determination of policy.

30. Thinking on this subject has been far too much influenced by the ancient and convenient geographical tradition of dividing the world into continents. It is no doubt natural that the future organisation of the continent of Europe should be a matter of widespread and general concern. But when we are invited to consider the economic interests in relation to which Europe could conveniently be treated as a unit, we are obliged to reply that, with the exception of inland transport, rail, road, river and canal, they are very hard to find. If we took the several countries of Europe one by one, we should find that, even for those whose European connections were most vital, there are also extra-European connections of no less importance. The relations

between the areas on either side of the Mediterranean are at leas
for some purposes as close as the relations of France, Spain an
Italy with the rest of Europe. The countries on the Wester
European seaboard look across the Atlantic and to the other sid
of the world with at least as lively an interest as they look at thei
continental neighbours, and the interests of some countries i
South-Eastern Europe shade imperceptibly into the interests o
the Middle East. A regional European organisation might offe
each one of the European countries advantages in one directio
or another, but the advantages of a wider organisation woul
be at least as great, and for some countries even greater.

31. The defects of regional solutions would naturally not b
the same for all countries or all areas, but in relation to nearl
every aspect of the problem there are few countries for which th
economic distortions necessary to fit into a geographical regiona
framework would be so serious and so damaging as for Grea
Britain. The economic relations of Great Britain with all part
of the world are so intimate and complex that any attemp
gradually to disentangle herself from any one set in the interest
of a closer association elsewhere would almost certainly be harm
ful both to Great Britain and to the world as a whole.

32. We are not here arguing for a complete rejection o
doctrinaire grounds of the regional approach. Post-war problem
will be so complex that we shall certainly be obliged for a tim
to work with admittedly imperfect instruments. But the arbi
trariness which inevitably enters in making our first decisio
about membership of a bloc is not a very hopeful augury fo
any benefits to be expected from this technique. A wise ma
will not neglect protection in case more far-reaching arrangement
go wrong or are found to be impossible. Regionalism to-day is
however, it may be suspected, sometimes an expression of funda
mental defeatism. Commended to our notice as a useful way o
escape if wider plans have to be dropped, it too readily assumes
form which makes it quite certain that the wider plans will hav
to be rejected. A wise man will not commit himself to pre
cautionary insurance devices of this kind.

33. Part of the appeal which regional solutions have for som
logical minds is based no doubt upon the fact that they can be pre

ented in a neat and tidy form. We tend to feel that we have got
omething done when we have rounded off a convenient geo-
raphical area and called it a region. But the logic of this reason-
ig is incomplete. The demarcation of a region is not even the
rst step in finding a genuine solution for any difficult problem.
.verything still remains to be done, and especially when we bear
i mind that there must also be some machinery for dealing with
he relations between regions, we may well conclude that the
ffort necessary to create regional organisations is likely to be
lisproportionate to any benefits they are likely to bring.

iii) *The Lend-Lease Principle*

1. The " act to promote the defense of the United States ",
pproved by the President on March 11, 1941, introduced a
undamentally new element into the relations between Great
3ritain and the United States. It has also been widely assumed
hat it created a new instrument of international economic policy,
apable of fruitful application to the difficult problems of the
ost-war period, and representing a radical and highly desirable
oreak with the practice of the past. Before we can pronounce
udgment upon the validity of the claims thus made on behalf of
end-lease, we must, however, first ascertain exactly what the
ohrase means. In some quarters appeals have been made to this
orinciple as if it were a kind of *deus ex machina*, providing a solu-
.ion for every insoluble riddle. We may see its significance in a
nore correct perspective by recalling the purpose for which it
was originally invented.

2. President Roosevelt's intentions were first announced at a
press conference on December 17, 1940. " If your neighbour's
house is on fire," he said, " you do not open negotiations to sell
him your hose-pipe. You lend it to him, and he returns it to you
afterwards, and pays you for any damage done to it." Let the
same be done, he advised, with our armaments. He added that
he was trying to " eliminate the silly-fool dollar sign ". " We
would leave out the dollar mark in the transactions," he said,
" whether it dealt with guns, planes or merchant ships, substituting a gentleman's agreement to pay in kind."

3. A system of deliveries based on the principles suggested by

these picturesque analogies was obviously most easily applicable to munitions, in the narrow sense of the word, though there is no reason to suppose that, in the mind of the President, the principle was at any time limited in this way. In relation to munitions it was reasonable also to expect that the problem of ultimate repayment would present no serious difficulties. Many of the " hose-pipes " useful in twentieth-century warfare are such that the supplier would be unlikely to insist upon their return at the end of the war, at least in quantities comparable with the original deliveries. It was therefore not unduly rash to assume that at the end of the war the United States Government would in effect, say, " You have accepted a gentleman's obligation to return to us X million shells, Y thousand anti-aircraft guns, Z thousand searchlights and so on. Happier conditions now prevail and our supplies of these things at home are already more than enough to cover all our reasonable requirements. You are therefore released from your obligation ", and in this way the whole transaction would be wound up in a mutually satisfactory manner.

4. In the Act which later embodied the President's idea, however, the range of articles to be covered was immensely widened, as was indeed both logically and practically inevitable as soon as the idea itself was accepted. The " defense articles ", the disposition of which the Act placed in the hands of the President, were so widely defined (in section 2(b) of the Act) that it was difficult to think of anything whose transfer was formally excluded from its operations. At first sight, repayment " in kind " of food and industrial raw materials, useful for peace-time purposes, might seem quite possible on a scale much more extensive than the similar repayment of munitions. But while some goods supplied under lend-lease might be in short supply in the United States after the war, and imports of these would therefore be gratefully received in repayment of lend-lease deliveries, many of the goods so delivered would certainly already be available there in such abundant quantities that further importations would serve no very useful purpose. Again, the principle of repayment " in kind " might well mean in practice that a large proportion of the deliveries were never paid for at all in any material form.

5. In his Address to Congress on January 6, 1941, however, he President had already extended considerably the range of goods which might later be an acceptable *quid pro quo* for lend-lease deliveries. " For what we send abroad ", he said, " we shall be repaid within a reasonable time after the close of hostilities in similar materials, or, at our own option, in other goods which they can produce and which we need ", and the Lend-Lease Act extended the interpretation still further. Section 3(a) authorised the President " to sell, transfer title, exchange, lease, lend, or otherwise dispose of, to the government of any country whose defense the President deems vital to the defense of the United States, any defense article ", and section 3(b) provided that the terms and conditions upon which such aid was given " shall be those which the President deems satisfactory, and the benefit to the United States may be payment or repayment in kind or property, or any other direct or indirect benefit which the President deems satisfactory ".

6. The White Paper of February 24, 1942, " on the Principles applying to Mutual Aid in the Prosecution of the War against Aggression ", throws some further light upon the proper interpretation of the lend-lease principle. It deferred " the final determination of the terms and conditions upon which the Government of the United Kingdom receives such aid and of the benefits to be received by the United States of America in return therefor ", but also affirmed (in Article 5) that " the Government of the United Kingdom will return to the United States of America at the end of the present emergency, as determined by the President, such defence articles transferred under this Agreement as shall not have been destroyed, lost or consumed, and as shall be determined by the President to be useful in the defence of the United States of America, or of the Western Hemisphere or to be otherwise of use to the United States ", and for the final settlement provided in Article 7 that " the terms and conditions thereof shall be such as not to burden commerce between the two countries, but to promote mutually advantageous economic relations between them and the betterment of world-wide economic relations ".

7. There have been some further modifications inserted in

subsequent renewals of the Act, but the account we have give of the development of thought in its early stages provides a adequate background for examining the view that lend-lease is new and revolutionary instrument of international economi policy whose use may help us to evade the troubles of the post war period.

8. Essentially the Lend-Lease Act was an agreement to deliver at the absolute discretion of the President and on the ground tha such deliveries were vitally necessary in the interests of the Unite States itself, goods so urgently needed in an emergency by anothe country that the determination of the terms upon which deliverie were accepted was necessarily deferred until a later date. The obligations incurred by the beneficiaries of lend-lease are lef almost entirely without precise definition, but they are quite real and the distinction between lend-lease goods and gifts is quite clear.

9. It is worth while to remark, moreover, that while the Presi-dent's phrase about " eliminating the silly-fool dollar sign " wa: a vivid metaphor and served a useful purpose, it was at best stil only a metaphor. In fact the dollar sign has not disappeared, no: in the nature of things could it do so. It has merely changed it: position, being transferred from the accounts of the beneficiaries of lend-lease to the accounts of the United States Governmen and ultimately of the United States citizens who by loan or tax provide the money to pay for the goods. The goods have to be paid for by someone, and this hard fact cannot be evaded simply by wishing financial problems away.

10. The goods to be supplied through the channels of U.N.R.R.A. to the liberated countries, and paid for by the contributions of the United Nations to the funds of that organisa-tion, might be regarded as being in the lend-lease tradition. It would, however, be misleading so to describe them, for these transactions are entirely free from any element of either lending or leasing, the contributions to the funds of U.N.R.R.A. being clearly and unequivocally gifts.

11. The idea in the minds of those who believe that lend-lease can be adapted to the requirements of a world at peace seems to be something as follows. The general economic development

of the world will be seriously retarded unless there is a revival of the stream of international lending. Such investment has been a powerful instrument of economic progress throughout the last century or more, but some of the results of earlier international capital movements have not been entirely happy, for either the borrower or the lender, and their direction and volume, it is argued, were sometimes unduly influenced by the attention paid to the size and certainty of the income likely to be enjoyed by the lenders by way of interest or dividends. This preoccupation sometimes unduly limited the volume of capital made available abroad, and sometimes diverted it into channels which in the long run were found to be undesirable. Would it therefore be possible, it is asked, to arrange future international capital movements so that, instead of being determined by the expectation of a direct income return, they should depend rather upon the more justifiable expectation that indirect benefits would accrue which would make the investment worth while? These benefits might appear in the shape of improved opportunities for ordinary trade, after, for example, the provision of improved transport facilities in Brazil or the Balkans had made the exploitation of the mineral resources of these countries profitable, and higher local standards of living therefore called for additional ordinary exports from the country which had provided the capital for their development. Or the lenders might be satisfied with immaterial gains, the satisfaction to be gained from the contemplation of social betterment in other countries, or the assurance that the maintenance of social stability would provide a firm foundation for international peace. And as it seems unlikely that private investors would in the ordinary course of events be much influenced by the prospect of such indirect gains (though private individuals have often been more generous than their governments in their treatment of the citizens of foreign countries), and the State is also in a position to take longer views than the private citizen (though historically State policy has often been much more short-sighted than the policy of its more prudent citizens), it is further suggested that the provision and acceptance of capital on such terms is a responsibility which in the future governments may properly be expected to assume.

12. The allocation of capital in accordance with estimates of various indirect benefits, material or immaterial, rather than the direct financial return which it is expected to produce, is already a well-established practice, and a considerable economic literature deals with the wide variety of motives which help to determine the investor's choice, with the conditions under which undue attention to narrowly financial considerations is likely either to encourage or check investment, the net social benefit from which does not correspond to the net private benefit accruing to the investor, and with the institutional or other devices likely to be useful in correcting such divergences. In many such cases the individual investor, less indifferent to financial considerations than those immediately interested in arranging the capital transfer, has been induced to put up the necessary funds by guaranteeing him a regular return, corresponding fairly closely to the current market rate, and ultimately payable not out of any income arising directly from the investment itself, but by the taxpayer of the country where the investment has been made. French loans for military purposes to Russia before 1914 and later to the members of the Little Entente are illustrations of this procedure, and it is worth noting that in the case of Russia default occurred when the government of the U.S.S.R. decided that the conditions upon which French aid had been given were intolerable and therefore had to be repudiated. The interest on money borrowed by the governments of " new " countries for such purposes as railway construction has also often in part been paid out of taxation, when the earnings of the railways proved insufficient to cover all the liabilities which had to be met. The borrowing government estimated the indirect benefits from such investments sufficiently highly to accept the inconvenience of raising additional taxes to meet any deficit, and the lender was again safeguarded by a government guarantee.

13. An additional guarantee might be given by the government of the lending country, in cases where it attached great importance to the indirect benefits, political or otherwise, likely to follow the granting of a loan, but private lenders took an unfavourable view of the creditworthiness of the borrower. In the event of default the claims of investors would then be met, in the last resort, from

funds provided by the taxpayers in the lending country.

14. Those who contemplate the incorporation of lend-lease in the normal practice of states envisage this process being carried one stage further. Instead of the government of the lending country safeguarding the interests of lenders by guaranteeing to meet their claims in the event of an unexpected default, a lend-lease borrower would from the beginning be formally absolved, either in part or in whole, from any obligation to provide regular funds from which the interest due to lenders would be paid.

15. An analogy of a different kind, which is perhaps closer than anything quoted above, may be seen in the activities of investors in, for example, colonial areas, who are prepared to risk financial loss on the money invested, if they can expect incidental profits from an expansion of either export or import trade. Returns of this indirect kind are one of the obvious well-recognised benefits which have made foreign investment attractive, and they explain in part the intensity of the conflicts over the maintenance of the Open Door in territories such as China or Morocco. In the view of one American writer before the war, " between 30 and 40 per cent. of British exports to Argentina are sold on the basis of what the English term the ' loyalty ' of British investment interests to British goods ". This claim was perhaps exaggerated, but the disappointment of the British holder of Argentine railway shares, when his company failed to provide the expected dividends, was nevertheless to some extent offset by the consolation which those who had originally planned his investment derived from the knowledge that they were making good money from the sale of locomotives or rolling stock to the company, or of other goods the demand for which had been indirectly stimulated through the existence of a British railway in Argentina. In these cases, of course, the investor had no guarantee, and partly because his expectations were frequently thus disappointed, international lending has declined in recent years.

16. In the last resort any decision as to the possibility of extending the lend-lease principle on the lines suggested must be left to the discretion of those cast for the role of chief post-war lend-leaser. This means for the most part the United States, though other countries are not precluded from participating. No one

outside the United States can safely prejudge the views of United States citizens on such matters, and the idea of cutting the Gordian knot of the chronic United States active balance of payments by writing off the balance from time to time has been seriously discussed by some of them, while some of the Latin American activities of the Export-Import Bank appear to conform approximately to what the supporters of permanent lend-lease have in mind. If the United States decides in favour of a generous interpretation of the requirements of the relief period, there will certainly be no disposition to criticise in any other part of the world. Before, however, according even a theoretical approval to the idea of extending the lend-lease principle still further than this, certain general considerations should be taken into account, which suggest doubts about both the practicability and the desirability of such an extension.

17. The first consideration indeed leaves it quite doubtful whether it is not misleading to attempt to describe the war-time and the hypothetical peace-time procedure by the same name. Lend-lease deliveries are made during war with the one purpose overriding all others that the war should be won with the least possible delay, and on scarcely any other condition is it conceivable that the conditions which the beneficiaries are expected to fulfil should be left undetermined for such a long time. There could not be the same sense of urgency about peace-time deliveries, the supplier would therefore probably be unwilling to postpone the precise determination of conditions, and the beneficiary would be equally anxious to know what obligations he was incurring.

18. There is indeed no obvious means whereby the President can compel any important beneficiary of lend-lease at the present time to comply with conditions which the beneficiary may dislike. The final settlement must be a matter of negotiation, and during the war emergency it may be assumed that the United States would not contemplate the withdrawal of any assistance which it was in its power to grant and which it regarded as essential for the speedy achievement of victory. In times of peace failure to comply with any conditions which the United States thought it proper to impose might effectually prevent any further assistance

by way of lend-lease or otherwise.

19. Essentially a peace-time lend-lease programme would mean an agreement to deliver, at the absolute discretion of the President of the United States for the time being, goods (mainly, though not necessarily exclusively capital goods) which for a variety of reasons were thought likely to provide permanent economic benefits for the countries receiving them, and which would at the same time ensure indirect benefits for the United States, either in the shape of better opportunities for trade, or of concessions in political or economic policy which would not otherwise have been made.

20. The experience we have had during the war of the suspicions of the misuse of lend-lease deliveries aroused in the minds of jealous competitors should have been sufficient to demonstrate the very great difficulties in the way of incorporating lend-lease in the normal life of international society. United States complaints that lend-lease goods were being re-exported, either directly or indirectly, by British manufacturers who wished to protect their competitive position against their United States rivals were no doubt ill-founded or sometimes positively malicious, but they indicated a quite genuine problem for which under peace-time conditions there is no obvious remedy. United States manufacturers would then naturally object to materials despatched under lend-lease conditions being used, directly or indirectly, in the export trade of the beneficiary country, in competition with United States producers either in markets in third countries or even in the United States itself. Any attempt to confine lend-lease deliveries to goods in connection with which no such complications could possibly arise would restrict their range within very narrow limits.

21. There is, however, another and even more important objection. Exports for which the recipients are excused from any obligation to pay are in principle the same thing as exports subsidised to the extent of 100 per cent., and export subsidies much smaller than this have normally, and for obvious reasons, been regarded by competing exporters in other countries as hostile acts to which they were entitled to expect their governments to put up a vigorous resistance. At the present time traders else-

where have no reason to resent United States lend-lease deliveries to either their own or to other countries, because it is quite impossible for them to contemplate any competitive activity, while their own products are being purchased as extensively as blockade and other limitations permit. But even now there are fears lest lend-lease deliveries should establish the United States position in markets, such as those of Latin America, to which British traders would like to return after the war, and some apprehensions have been expressed in the Dominions at the opportunities which lend-lease affords to United States producers to entrench themselves in markets in Great Britain and perhaps elsewhere from which Dominion producers do not like to feel themselves excluded. After the war these and similar fears would revive and become much more intense if the attempt were made to adapt lend-lease to peace-time conditions. Other countries for which it will be a matter of urgent importance to seek new export outlets would be unlikely to accept without protest the competition of United States goods with a 100 per cent. export subsidy attached, and in circumstances which would make possible discrimination on an unprecedented scale. The attitude of producers in other countries to any British or other exports subsidised in a similar way would naturally be the same. If the United States acquired a taste for discrimination, that very wealth and power which to some seem to mark it out as the most likely lend-leaser would make it a comparatively easy matter for it to press discrimination at its discretion, without any crippling cost to itself, and without much consideration for the interests of other countries.

22. If it were thought possible to make lend-lease a permanent feature of international relations, it is interesting to speculate upon the position which might arise at a later more normal period, when other countries might feel able to join the ranks of the lend-leasers. The practical necessity for determining the *quid pro quo*, whether material or otherwise, for lend-lease deliveries before the movement of goods was actually authorised would place in the hands of the United States authorities, if that country was the lend-leaser, powers over the policies of other countries much more extensive than have ever before been exercised in times of

peace. But in proportion to the lend-lease supplies which they could make available, the powers of other lend-leasing countries would be no less great, and some analogies might be noted here with the effects of German pre-war policy in the Balkans. A powerful and wealthy country which decided whole-heartedly to adopt the lend-lease principle without considering the costs imposed upon itself would have at its disposal an instrument of unequalled power for the pursuit of imperialist aims. Its rulers would be in a position in effect to dictate the policies of any countries which wished to continue the receipt of lend-lease goods. If several countries were equally whole-hearted in the pursuit of such a policy, there would be little prospect of orderly international development, and a high probability of international friction likely to be a serious danger to international peace.

23. Such a picture of competitive lend-leasing may seem so fantastic as not to warrant any waste of time in contemplating it. But lend-lease has in some quarters become such a magic catchword for solving all post-war economic difficulties that it is worth while taking some trouble to show up its illusory foundations. It is another blind alley, to be condemned because it distracts attention from the much more difficult problem which cannot safely be evaded of devising orderly means for the mutual adaptation of national economic structures to the requirements of an ever-changing world.

(iv) *British Post-War Policy*

1. Even if they approve of the general character of our analysis of the course of international economic relations during the last generation, some people may be a little impatient because they feel that it is not obviously and immediately relevant to the issues upon which governments everywhere will shortly be obliged to define their attitude. As an abstract general statement, they may feel inclined to say, this is all very well, but in these difficult times our interest is inevitably concentrated upon the future of our own country. Its post-war conditions seem likely to be so peculiar that general principles, worked out without special reference to them, may be quite inapplicable. An analysis of the conditions of material progress may on a short-sighted view seem somewhat

academic when our first task is to repair a shattered, or at least a seriously strained economic organisation. But, as we endeavoured to show in the first part of this study, disruption by war increases rather than diminishes the urgency of the need for flexibility in our national economic structures. Whatever institutional innovations may be approved for the difficult times to come immediately after the war, the results will be unsatisfactory unless this prior necessity is constantly kept in mind. Similarly in the international sphere, we shall make no attempt to work out a detailed programme of action for the transitional period from war to peace. But whatever is done then will prove equally unsatisfactory unless, with a full appreciation of the implications of inevitable interdependence, national economies abandon the idea that somehow they will always be able to get their own way.

2. English readers in particular are by now quite familiar with the peculiar British post-war problem of a maladjusted balance of payments, and some of them may even sometimes forget that several other economies will also have to face a problem of the same kind of no less difficulty. Before the war a considerable part of Great Britain's real income accrued as a result of investments, interest or dividend payments giving residents in Great Britain the right to draw income from abroad, or of the sale to foreigners of shipping, banking, insurance and other services. These rights to income from abroad made possible the purchase of large quantities of food and raw materials from overseas. As a result of the war a large part of this investment income has disappeared, or been transferred to other owners, and at the best income from the sale of services to non-British buyers will also probably for a considerable period be below the pre-war level. A precise quantitative estimate of the effects of these changes is not easy ; it is now commonly believed that if after the war the volume of essential imports necessary to protect British standards of living against serious decline is to be paid for, the volume of exports will have to be increased by at least 50 per cent. and perhaps more above the pre-war level, and on any hypothesis the gap to be filled will be very large. Nor are these losses all that we have to take into account. During the war many countries, the Dominions and Latin America, for example,

have been building up large blocked sterling balances, estimated in 1943 to exceed £1000 millions,[1] with a marked tendency to further increase, and upon which they will be anxious to draw after the war. Lend-lease liabilities are uncertain, and some people also fear that British residents may be anxious to transfer part of their capital to other countries. Finally, reconstruction requirements may for some time tend to raise British demand for certain imports above the pre-war level. All these factors in combination will create demands for foreign currency, and in particular for dollars, far in excess of the amounts likely to be available from an export trade which itself may have considerable difficulty in re-establishing itself in old markets or in finding a footing in new ones. If nothing is done about it, the exchange value of sterling may fall to an embarrassingly low level, and the British standard of living be seriously impaired.

3. Within the wide range of conceivable responses to such a situation two sharply contrasted types of policy, each of which might itself be applied in a wide variety of ways, may be distinguished. On the one hand, British policy might be directed primarily towards such an allocation of productive resources after the war as to ensure the highest possible efficiency in production, whether for the home or for export markets, and the highest degree of capacity and willingness to supply consumers with what they want. The application of this principle in a new set of circumstances may demand some sharp breaks with custom and precedent, but in the principle itself there is nothing novel or revolutionary, for, stated in general terms, it not only accurately describes the foundations upon which most successful trade in the past has been based, but is also a natural reflection of " the initiative, boldness and enterprise of our industrialists, scientists and technicians, and the adaptability of our workpeople ", which have been described [2] as the most important fact standing out in the industrial history of Great Britain during the war. Some, however, on the other hand, believing that " the fact that we are by far the best consumer market puts the ace of trumps in our

[1] *Economist*, August 7, 1943.
[2] By Sir John Anderson, Chancellor of the Exchequer, in the Budget speech of April 25, 1944.

hand " [1], tend to take the view that it will be possible after the war to compel weak sellers in other countries to supply adequate quantities of the goods Great Britain will then need, accepting in return not, as they were in the habit of doing before the war, the right to purchase goods at their own discretion, but rights only to purchase goods in Great Britain, and even perhaps only goods selected under varying degrees of influence by the British authorities. Great Britain's power to act in this way would, in the view of some, be based not only on the bargaining strength arising from her very large importing capacity, but also on the alleged bargaining strength of a large-scale international debtor with a liability for a large accumulation of blocked sterling balances. If Great Britain should have any temporary difficulty in supplying the goods which the partners to these transactions may want, they would be expected to allow their sterling claims to accumulate until such time as they had been persuaded or compelled to change their preferences or until Great Britain found it more convenient to supply their needs.

4. This at first sight singular arrangement is *prima facie* unlikely to be very attractive to other countries. It reflects in the international sphere the same indifference to the principle of allowing consumers to get what they want which we have already noted in some current proposals for internal post-war reconstruction, and is indeed essentially an adaptation to British circumstances of the technique elaborated before the war by Dr. Schacht. One current of thought which much favoured the acceptance of Dr. Schacht's technique was the simple-minded belief, which had a wide currency in Great Britain as well as in other countries, especially during the depression period, that it was somehow " right " and rational that each country should aim at inducing or compelling its citizens to buy from the countries which were buying its exports, and that exports and imports should therefore as nearly as possible balance between each pair of countries. There is no reason why in suitable circumstances we should not be prepared to take lessons from Dr. Schacht, but bearing in mind the resentment and suspicion provoked by his pre-war policy, we

---

[1] Captain C. Waterhouse, Parliamentary Secretary to the Board of Trade, in a speech reported in the *Manchester Guardian*, April 19, 1943.

should, before deciding to imitate it too whole-heartedly, enquire whether the peculiar conditions under which it operated are likely to be repeated.

5. Leaving political considerations aside, there has been a good deal of controversy about the economic effects, short and long run, of Germany's pre-war trade policy upon her satellite partners. In general they appear not to have liked the policy very much, despite some incidental gains for themselves ; nor was this dislike based purely on fears of its political implications. They all resisted German infiltration so far as it was in their power to do so, and the resounding success which the Schachtian technique enjoyed for some years was in part the same kind of success which normally attends any sudden onslaught upon people who are not expecting attack. As the countries upon whom the technique had been sprung rather suddenly were able to review more carefully the possibilities open to them, they began by cultivating other outlets to devise measures of relief which might in the course of time have freed them from complete dependence on the German market, and to that extent destroyed the advantages enjoyed by the Germans through their short-term power to impose bilateral bargains. Despite their poverty they were prepared to subsidise by a variety of means exports to markets other than Germany, and had some measure of success in these efforts. It was no doubt only a minor contributory cause influencing German policy immediately before the war, but nevertheless a significant cause, that the Germans, realising that purely Schachtian measures might become more and more ineffective as time went on, felt themselves obliged to reinforce them by something more direct, and to bring under direct military control even countries where their economic influence had been greatest.

6. In any event the countries from which the Germans were anxious to draw supplies were dependent upon quite a small number of staple products, which were in a state of chronic over-supply. They were almost completely cut off from alternative outlets, for other big markets, such as the British and American, were for the most part not interested, and steadily refused to take any steps to diminish the complete dependence of the sellers

concerned upon German buyers. The countries concerned were
for the most part very poor, without any capital resources worth
mentioning of their own, and however much they may have
desired to diversify their economies and thus strengthen their
bargaining strength, lacked the capital needed for such adjustments, and were unable to draw enough for their purposes from
foreign capital markets. Their diversifying activities were thus
largely confined to those which the Germans desired, and in
these circumstances the changes in production which occurred
were not designed to loosen the German grip.

7. In more general terms we may say that German "success"
was largely a result of the fact that they were the only important
party operating in this field. So long as it could safely be assumed that the other powerful economies would not play the same
game, or would play it only in a half-hearted way, the Germans
had a clear run, and were able more or less to get their own way.
There is an interesting parallel here with the experience of
exchange depreciation. The first depreciators for a time reaped
substantial benefits, but as soon as the device was more widely
adopted, its efficacy disappeared, and if everyone were to try it
at the same time, the net results for everyone would probably be
bad. It takes much longer to devise effective counter-measures
to the Schachtian trade technique, for they demand far-reaching
changes of policy much more fundamental than the simple method
of depreciating one's exchange rate. The difference is, however,
only one of degree, and probably when everyone was playing the
Schachtian game, everyone would also be losing.

8. Is there any reason for supposing that after the war Great
Britain will be in such a favourable position as to be able to draw
to herself all the imports she would like by adaptations or variations of the Schachtian technique? There are certainly some
obvious embarrassments attending any suggestion that the technique should be applied to Europe. For described in its simplest
terms it means that Great Britain would attempt to earmark for
herself an undue proportion of essential commodities which by
general admission will after the war be in short supply in relation
to the needs of the world as a whole. It might be argued, as it
was by Germany, that some of the exports thus earmarked would

not, in the absence of such arrangements, be exported, or even produced at all. It is difficult, however, to believe that there could be any careful limitation of the technique to such cases ; the German claim was at least plausible because the Germans were buying things which otherwise threatened to glut the market. Great Britain, on the contrary, would be proposing to buy things which were scarce, and the only ground discoverable for such a claim in our favour would be that this country had long enjoyed a standard of living a good deal higher than that of most other countries, and was accordingly entitled to the maintenance of this privileged position. Such a claim would not be very convincing to the rest of Europe, and the British might well hesitate to press it, even in the most carefully guarded terms, when they reflected upon the obvious fact that many other European countries had suffered much heavier losses in consequence of the war, without any more direct responsibility for their unhappy situation than could fairly be imputed to Great Britain.

9. The position of the Dominions is in certain respects different. At the time of the Ottawa Conference they set great store upon the enjoyment of privileges in the British market, and their eagerness for reciprocal preferences was considerably greater than the eagerness of Great Britain. Experience has, however, taught them that the British market was not enough. " It was already clear before the war that Empire markets, wide as they are, were too narrow for Canadian wheat, for Australian wool, and were becoming almost too confined for New Zealand and Australian dairy produce or for Empire meat. In the post-war years the development of Dominion manufacturing will make the negotiation of reciprocal preferences a formidable problem." [1] Other outlets are no less vital for the economic welfare of the Dominions, and they may hesitate to give a favourable response to invitations from Great Britain to grant British manufacturers further privileges as a *quid pro quo* for the maintenance of British markets which in any event will be unable to absorb all that the Dominions have to offer to the world. One of the main attractions, moreover, of membership of the pre-war sterling bloc was that it in no way interfered with the right of its members to use their sterling

[1] F. L. McDougall, in an address to the Royal Society of Arts, April 1, 1941.

balances in the ways and for the purposes which seemed most suitable to the peoples of the countries which accumulated them. This attraction would be gravely impaired if sterling balances could be used only in Great Britain itself or at the discretion of the British authorities. The Australian or the South African authorities may sometimes take wrong-headed views of the purposes to which it is proper to apply their sterling balances, but there is no obvious reason why they should agree that the British authorities were in a better position to make such decisions for them. Nor are any of the Dominions in the same weak position for diversifying their economies as were most of Germany's satellite partners. Their average income levels are high, and their own capital resources already considerable and capable of rapid growth. The industrialisation which had already gone a considerable way before the war has been much accelerated by it, and while some war-time industrial extensions will no doubt be abandoned, there is no reason to suppose that the trend as a whole will be reversed. Any hopes entertained by Great Britain that by offering steady markets for primary products, a considerable proportion of which must in any event be disposed of elsewhere, in return for supplies of British manufactured goods which in many instances the Dominions are anxious and in some instances also now well equipped to produce, the Dominions may be induced to bind themselves for any long period to the acceptance of a British Schachtian plan, are likely to be illusory.

10. Many of the Latin American states are poorer than the Dominions, and therefore still unable to mobilise any considerable capital resources of their own, but on the other hand they have the active interest of the United States already engaged on their behalf. The process of industrialisation has already gone far, especially in Brazil, Mexico and Chile, and the United States has shown a practical willingness to assist this process in the most effective way, by the provision of capital. Any attempt to obstruct this process could only provoke the resentment and perhaps the hostility of both the Latin American states and the United States herself.

11. There can be no serious question of compelling the United States to send imports to Great Britain in return for British exports

which United States buyers do not particularly want to have. The attitude of the United States to such a general policy to be applied elsewhere is, however, a factor of first-rate importance. Discrimination is a slippery term, for which it is not easy to discover any precise watertight definition which would apply in all conceivable circumstances. We should not, however, on that account hastily assume that the term has no meaning whatever. In many cases it is perfectly easy to recognise it when we see it, and the policy here being analysed is in this obvious sense discriminatory, because the opportunities of exporters in other countries to offer purchasers in the countries bound by agreements with Great Britain goods which they would be free to accept or reject after comparison with what Great Britain was able to offer would be in varying degree seriously restricted. United States opinion and policy have for some time been strongly opposed to discrimination of this kind, though, as is usual in such cases, it is not difficult to pick some holes in her practice which convict her of a certain inconsistency. The United States aversion to discriminatory policies is no doubt in large measure based upon a shrewd appreciation of her own national interests, but, what is very much more important from the standpoint of the world economy as a whole, it is very much in the interest of other countries, and in particular of Great Britain, that she should not be cured of what some people in Great Britain are inclined to regard as her prejudices on this subject.

12. To point out that even the most refined and humane British revised version of Schachtianism would almost certainly fail unfortunately does not carry us very far towards a solution of Britain's post-war difficulties. There is now fairly general agreement that some kind of exchange control, such as provides an opportunity for these discriminatory practices, is not for some time after the war to be avoided in Great Britain and many other war-scarred economies. On the most optimistic hypothesis, a considerable time must elapse before even the outline of a new set of normal world trading relations becomes dimly visible, and something more than a rough guess becomes possible at exchange rates which have a reasonable prospect of being maintained. In the meantime controls must continue to be imposed as a protec-

tion against the risks of monetary and exchange disorder. This at least is the general expectation inside most of these economies, and there is also a considerable measure of understanding elsewhere of the peculiar circumstances which probably make these decisions inevitable.

13. The same facts which make it so difficult to fit Great Britain into any far-reaching regional organisation of the world also make it an evident interest of that country to free its currency without undue delay from transitional restrictions. Among the outstanding characteristics of sterling which in the past made membership of the sterling bloc attractive to many economies was the freedom which its owners enjoyed to use it according to their own judgment. It is a British interest that this characteristic of its currency should be restored as soon as possible. In particular, the prospects for a revival on any substantial scale of British overseas earnings from the sale of services would thereby be considerably enhanced. A fundamental problem for the postwar period will be the devising of means which, while protecting sterling from the immediate dangers which a precipitate return to ordinary standards of convertibility would involve, will not place impediments in the way of the later realisation of this objective. Nor will the resolution of the practical dilemma confronting Great Britain in this connection depend entirely upon the decisions of her own statesmen, important as they must obviously be. The British exchange problem is essentially also an international problem.

14. A still more fundamental problem, however, and one moreover whose solution is ultimately essential for the resolution of these exchange difficulties, is that of the post-war structure of the British economy, in the sense in which we have been using that term. There is some danger that preoccupation with apparently more immediate and pressing concerns may induce some to neglect the elementary fact that in the last resort the prosperity and security of the British economy depend upon its capacity for efficient production. The hope is not unreasonable that the war itself may have changed in certain respects for the better the competitive position of some sectors of the British economy, and it is certainly important that any such possibilities should be

explored and utilised to the full. The balance of payments problem is perhaps too narrowly conceived if it is thought of as requiring a solution only by an expansion of exports or by the exclusion by protective devices of imports for which the British producer is at a competitive disadvantage. If only a part of the claims made of improvements in the efficiency of British agriculture during the war is justified, it should be possible to effect some diminution in the volume of British imports without any deviation from the strict principles of comparative cost, though one would trust these claims more if more of those who make them were to display confidence in their judgment by a greater willingness to dispense with protectionist props.

15. We have referred earlier to the potential effects of war-time research upon productive efficiency. They have naturally enough been most publicised in the United States, but there is no reason to suppose that other economies also may not benefit from them. The full realisation of these opportunities will, however, be impossible unless the traditional prejudices are abandoned which induced so many during the inter-war period to concentrate their thoughts almost exclusively on the rehabilitation of old and declining industries. For Great Britain, even more than for most other economies, a statesmanlike post-war policy will think much more than in the past in terms of the stimulation and encouragement of new types of productive activity.

(v) *International Economic Relations and Social Insurance*

1. Such lively interest has been displayed, both in Great Britain and elsewhere, in the place of social insurance in post-war economic policy that some discussion of its international implications follows naturally our discussion of British post-war policy. Misunderstandings of this matter have given rise to some criticism in the United States, where it has sometimes appeared that certain countries were in effect asking for something like specially favourable treatment for themselves after the war, while at the same time announcing their intention to put expensive social insurance schemes into operation. If you can afford these luxuries, the critics have been inclined to say, surely the claim that without external support you cannot stand on your own feet

Y

after the war cannot be justified. Some inaccurate presentations of the case for social insurance may have provided some colour of justification for these reproaches. A more careful analysis would, however, show, especially on certain reasonable suppositions affecting the method of financing social insurance, that it was perhaps the one field where any country was entitled to follow its own path without any fear of imposing inconveniences elsewhere.

2. Before attempting to meet these misunderstandings we should, however, first direct our attention to the confusion of thought sometimes caused by the continued use of the term insurance. Insurance against risks such as fire, death, shipwreck and other actuarially calculable hazards has long been well known. Those who are subject to such risks pay agreed sums into a common fund, which is drawn on from time to time by the individuals for whom the risks have become realised events. Why not, it is natural to ask, apply a similar principle, say, to unemployment? Before there was any highly developed State machinery for dealing with the problem, the funds of bodies such as trade unions for the relief of their unemployed members in some respects conformed to the principles of insurance, despite the great and probably insuperable difficulty of calculating unemployment risks actuarially, and it was natural to carry over this term when trade union funds were supplemented or replaced by more extensive government schemes.

3. As soon, however, as we agree that " there is no longer a claim of the individual citizen to share in national insurance and yet to stand outside it, keeping the advantage of his individual lower risk whether of unemployment or of disease or accident ",[1] *i.e.* we insist that contributions to so-called insurance funds shall no longer be graded in conformity with the varying degrees of risk run by individual contributors, the provision of social services becomes essentially an instrument for the redistribution of national income, and in all countries the finance of such schemes has to an increasing extent been met out of general taxation.

4. There may in certain cases be sound reasons for maintain-

[1] *Social Insurance and Allied Services* (Cmd. 6404, 1942), p. 13.

ing the insurance façade. In Great Britain it has been claimed that "the insured persons themselves can pay and like to pay, and would rather pay than not do so. It is felt, and rightly felt, that contribution irrespective of means is the strongest ground for repudiating a means test",[1] while it also appears to remove the stigma of unemployment. Unfortunately excessive deference to this prejudice, especially when it takes the form of insisting upon the maintenance of the old-style employers' contributions to insurance funds, has made difficult any proper understanding of the effects of social insurance upon international competitive relations, and misunderstanding of this point has had unfortunate consequences both at home and abroad.

5. First, taking for granted the urgent necessity to maintain British exports after the war at as high a level as possible, it is argued at home that the additional burden imposed by increasing employers' contributions to insurance funds will raise the costs of exporters, and therefore so handicap them in competition with producers in other countries that the volume of exports needed to maintain a reasonable standard of living will be impossible. To this the reply has sometimes been made that we can easily find compensation for any apparent competitive disadvantage in a slight adjustment in our exchange rate, so small that other countries would scarcely notice it, and to which, therefore, they would raise no objection. "In fixing the post-war foreign exchange value", it has been argued, "the effect of the increased employers' contribution would be automatically taken into account, quite irrespective of whether the monetary authorities expressly desire to do so or not", and Ricardo has been quoted in support of the view that the effect upon competitive capacity in export markets of any cause which operated generally upon all prices would be negligible.[2] We may, however, be somewhat sceptical both of the extent to which foreign countries would be willing to allow us, without any risk of reprisals, to depreciate our currency for our own convenience, and of the permanence of the effects of depreciation; and while admitting the difficulties

---

[1] *Op. cit.* p. 108.
[2] N. Kaldor, "The Beveridge Report: The Financial Burden", *Economic Journal*, April 1943, p. 27.

of precisely measuring equilibrium exchange rates, we may fear that other countries will not be willing to allow all the measuring to be done by us. Whether or not the arguments quoted above are sound, they are rather subtle for the suspicious foreigner, and it would therefore seem better to cut at the root of the whole objection, and destroy any necessity for subtleties, by making the method of financing social insurance conform as closely as possible to the pattern of a straightforward income redistribution scheme, with the minimum opportunity left for those who wish to evade redistribution by passing on the burden of their contribution to someone else.

6. Many indeed have argued that the proper moral to be drawn from a consideration of the effects of social insurance upon international competitive relations is the necessity of inducing or compelling other countries to adopt a similar policy, so that all will start off from the same cost level. As it is obviously not a very practical idea to think of persuading the whole world to come into line, they sometimes add that, if a sufficient number of countries were found to be following similar policies, they might with advantage form some kind of economic or trading bloc which would more or less cut itself off from the rest of the world, also not a very hopeful line if, as would probably happen, the rest of the world happened to include countries producing things which the inhabitants of the bloc were very anxious to buy. In any event, attractive for us as is at first sight the idea of persuading other people to install social services on something like the scale which we think proper, it may not be quite so attractive to other people. The problem used to be discussed mainly in relation to Japanese competition, but if, as was largely true, the raising of Japanese standards of living was dependent upon Japanese success in finding new export markets for their manufactured goods, it was not very convincing to the Japanese to suggest that they should raise their costs of production with the avowed object (which was certainly present in the minds of those who made the suggestion) of enabling us to sell more cheaply than the Japanese then could do. For the Japanese would not then have got their new export outlets, and therefore would have been unable to raise their standards of living. This does not mean that there is any

objection to all countries, or as many countries as possible, taking a more liberal view of what they might do in the way of social services, but they cannot reasonably be expected to do this merely for our convenience. Whatever may be the post-war economic position of Japan, precisely the same problem will face us again if we take at all seriously the idea of raising standards of living in China, India or other hitherto undeveloped countries.

7. The problem, however, assumes a different aspect if we think of social insurance as primarily a method of income redistribution. For it is not at first sight clear why such redistribution should have any effect at all upon costs of production. It seems to, and often does, have such an effect, because people who find that they are obliged to make certain payments from which hitherto they have been free, often try to discover some way of getting their money back or " of passing the burden on ". If, however, as is now increasingly true, it is the intention of the legislature that some at least of the contributors to social insurance funds should, for the benefit of those who will later be beneficiaries, be content with smaller incomes, this intention is more likely to be realised if contributions are required in such forms as will make the process of " passing on " most difficult. Direct income taxation comes nearest to satisfying this requirement, though it cannot be claimed that it never is or can be passed on.

8. If social insurance is thus interpreted as an instrument for income redistribution, the issue with which we are here concerned can best be presented in terms of the following question : Do those members of the community who have adequate incomes regard the misfortunes of others who from time to time may lose the whole or part of their incomes so seriously as to permit a partial income redistribution for the benefit of the less fortunate, without reacting by refusing to perform their functions in the economy in the same efficient way as in the past ? The extent to which a community can " afford " a redistribution of income for this, or indeed for any purpose, is best measured in terms of this willingness. The issue ought to be faced in such terms instead of being wrapped up in apparently impersonal discussions of " costs ".

9. Whatever differences in willingness there may be from time

to time or from country to country, such redistribution will, as we have already seen,[1] obviously be easier if the country concerned has already attained a high average income level. It is no accident that, with some exceptions, social insurance has already been pushed furthest in countries with high average incomes. Some very poor countries, such as Poland, which attempted elaborate social service experiments, found the burden too heavy for them, and the machinery tended to break down. The wealthier countries can " afford " social insurance schemes, because there is a wider field in them for income redistribution. There is not much sense in asking whether social service costs are a burden upon us in competition, say, with China, because the fact that our standards of living are already much higher than those of the Chinese shows both that we are already on the average more efficient than they, and that our economy has a sufficiently wide margin at its disposal to carry the so-called burden without any real inconvenience.

10. There are, moreover, some benefits of considerable importance for productive efficiency to be expected from wise social service expenditure. It is not mere speculation but actual experience which justifies the view that the benefits to health, confidence, education and general well-being which ought to follow, and often have followed, from a well-ordered system of social service benefits may make such systems genuinely paying propositions to the economy as a whole, even on the narrowest basis of profit and loss. But some of the benefits may take a considerable time in showing themselves in any easily recognisable form, so that it would be unsafe to press the point too far.

11. Our general argument may sound less convincing if, instead of talking about competition between two economies as a whole, we think more concretely of competition between specific industries. The lesson to be drawn even in these cases is not, however, that social service costs are an intolerable burden. It points rather in the same direction as much of our previous argument, towards the advisability of keeping our economy flexible and of thus being prepared from time to time to substitute newer types of work and investment in which we have competitive

[1] Cf. *supra*, X, 12.

advantages for the older staple types which poorer countries will inevitably develop in competition with us. If those who before the war were troubled by social service costs in certain industries found that Japanese competition, unhampered by these costs, was beating them, that was an indication, not of the foolishness of social services, but of the advisability of shifting some of our productive resources rather more rapidly than we did into other lines more suitable for our capacity. The same thing will be true in the future. If we are unduly conservative and direct all our energies to preserving the old export trades, we shall almost certainly fail, but if those responsible for the failure attempt to place the blame upon social service costs, they will be wrong ; the real mistake will be in having concentrated too much on the wrong kind of export.

12. If we are afraid that the Americans will beat us in export markets after the war because they will not be called upon to pay so much as we for social services, we are really saying that we do not think that the section of our population which receives incomes above the average will go on performing their economic functions efficiently if they observe that people engaged in similar activities in America are not being required to submit to such drastic income redistribution. The inducements to continue the performance of their functions (and that is the real meaning of costs of production) being in their view inadequate, they will go on strike, or at least go slow, and perhaps transfer their activities to America or some other country believed to be more attractive. It would be a great advantage in discussing the whole problem if people who were afflicted by these fears would express themselves in such terms as these, for this is what they really mean.

13. If, then, social insurance is clearly recognised to be a method for achieving a socially desirable end by means of income redistribution, it can be seen to be one of the rather rare cases where each national economy can decide for itself what it wants to do without much concern for what other economies may think it proper to do. Foreign critics of the Beveridge Report may therefore be reminded that, provided the implementation of the reforms there recommended is not assumed to be a ground for seeking

privileges in international economic relations, it is entirely a matter for the British people themselves to decide how far they are willing to move along the path of income redistribution. Others may hesitate to go so far, but they have no valid ground for criticising any different decision which the British people may care to make.

14. The same line of reasoning should help us to view in proper perspective some of the proposals for so-called international social security which have recently attracted much attention. The experience of one country in this field may well be of great value to other countries, but international social security which means nothing more than as high a degree of uniformity as may be possible between the social insurance schemes of different national states can scarcely arouse any lively enthusiasm. It may be a good thing for the citizens of X to redistribute their national income so as to lighten the burdens upon the lower income groups. It may also be appropriate for the governments of Y and Z to explain to the government of X the most convenient method of doing this, as revealed by their own experience. But the service rendered by such advice is not at the best very substantial, if it is not backed by any willingness to subscribe to the funds raised in X for social insurance purposes. If at the same time the governments of Y and Z are in other spheres pursuing policies which, whether so intended or not, inevitably retard the economic development of X and keep its average income level low, there are no grounds upon which the citizens of Y and Z can congratulate themselves upon their devotion to the cause of social security on a world-wide scale. There is some risk that, by neglecting the international implications of the other aspects of national policy which excite them less, some devotees of social security may place themselves in precisely this indefensible position.

(vi) *Post-War Policy in the United States*

1. In our historical sketch of the inter-war period we insisted that there was no justification for imputing any priority in responsibility to any of the powerful economies concerned : all played their part at that time in intensifying the economic difficulties of

each other and of the rest of the world, and any objective analysis of the relative economic power of these states before 1939 would lead us to a similar conclusion. The position after the war will, however, undoubtedly be different. The shift of power in favour of the United States which is now going on rests in certain respects upon factors which may be expected to be merely temporary, but much of it will be permanent : any objective analysis of the prospects of the post-war period shows the future course of United States economic policy to be the single factor of greatest importance for the economic welfare and stability of every other part of the world economy. Experience has shown the people of the United States to be unfailing in their generosity, and of this the substantial contribution voted for the work of U.N.R.R.A. is the latest striking evidence. Many cautious citizens of that country have, however, rightly indicated their unwillingness to be cast by the rest of the world in the role of a perpetual Santa Claus, and the sound instinct which persuades them that permanent reconstruction must be based on a foundation of normal international relations, and not upon one-sided generosity, is entirely in accord with the feeling of the citizens of other countries who, while grateful for United States assistance in times of emergency, also feel the restoration of normal economic relations alone to be consistent with their national and individual self-respect. It remains to enquire into the probable content of " normal economic relations " as interpreted by the Government and people of the United States.

2. Only a citizen of the United States could safely do more than make a few general observations upon this theme. There are two angles from which United States post-war policy will have the most lively interest for the rest of the world. In the first place, it is a matter of the greatest importance that that country should be as prosperous as possible. The very complexity of its efficient industrial structure may make it in certain respects more susceptible to the influences which generate fluctuations in highly developed economies, but while some people may in the past have persuaded themselves that they could snatch benefits from the economic misfortunes of other countries, anyone who to-day thought of depression in the United States as affording such an opportunity

would be incredibly stupid and short-sighted. It is difficult to think of any time in history when the prosperity and stability of a single national economy was such a direct and dominant interest for all other economies as United States prosperity and stability will be after the war.

3. The significance of this point has so far usually been most emphasised by those who are preoccupied with harnessing the trade cycle. The risks of violent fluctuations in the general level of prices in the United States are examined with almost as much anxiety outside that country as within it, for even those who are most confident of their ability to maintain stability in an economy "insulated" from external influences know well that their task will be made much more difficult by violent instability in the United States.

4. The historical course of economic development is often conveniently visualised as a combination of cyclical fluctuations and secular trends. It is a direct interest of the rest of the world that cyclical fluctuations within the United States economy should be kept under control, but of even greater significance is the expeditious adjustment of the United States economy to the long-term changes involved in attaining higher standards of living. For when the rest of the world asks the United States to adjust its economy to the requirements of its new world creditor status, it is in effect asking it to seize as promptly as possible the opportunities available for increased income. And, if our earlier argument was correct, by so doing the United States will also mitigate the risks of cyclical fluctuations. Structural adaptation for the United States means on the whole transfers from less highly paid to more highly paid work. It would be an ironical circumstance if in the last resort the most serious threat to the stability of the world economy were to arise from the refusal of that sector in it which rightly has been most proud of its success in organising conditions favourable to the material advancement of its own people to permit this process to be carried any further.

5. The various channels through which United States economic policy will have its impact on the rest of the world all converge to show their combined effects in its balance of payments. A balance of payments which ensured an adequate supply of dollars

for the rest of the world would be the most important United States contribution to the stability of the world economy. So far as this depends on decisions made in the United States, there are five main methods whereby dollars become available : the purchase of goods from foreigners, the purchase of services from foreigners, the payment of interest or dividends to foreigners, loans and gifts. Nothing need be said about the third item, as past transactions have already determined a limit beyond which it cannot go in the near future. Gifts for some specific purposes have played some part in the past, and will have some importance for immediate post-war relief, but our discussion of lend-lease suggested that it was neither likely nor desirable that gifts or near-gifts organised on a new basis should become a significant permanent feature of international economic relations.

6. The problem of dollar supplies from the purchase of imports is at first sight primarily a tariff problem. We have already discussed the general effects of the unwillingness of the United States to make the structural changes in its economy needed to permit the full enjoyment by that country of the fruits of its new world creditor status. The most obvious direct method of relieving this situation would be such a reform of the United States tariff as would permit a relative increase in the volume of its imports. There are indeed few countries whose citizens can afford to cast any scornful reproaches upon the United States for its reluctance to face this issue, for essentially the same influences have been at work everywhere. Recriminations about the relative heights of tariff barriers are seldom very helpful, and in any event on a realistic view are almost irrelevant to this issue. The important thing is much less the average percentage level of a country's tariff than the effective significance of its trade restrictions, whether nominally mild or severe, in impeding the continuous adaptation of the world economy to continuously changing conditions of production. Judged by this test, the responsibility for stability throughout the world of those who control the United States tariff cannot easily be exaggerated.

7. The economist as such has no particular competence for venturing into the field of prophecy and attempting to forecast the future course of United States tariff policy. That is a matter

which can properly be left to the politician. There have, however, been some aspects of recent discussions of this problem upon which the economist may offer some observations. In face of the obvious political difficulties which arise in any country when radical changes in tariffs are proposed, and at the same time bearing in mind the importance of increasing United States imports more rapidly than United States exports, some, whose preoccupations are mainly with problems in other spheres, have thought that relief might be obtained by fitting into a general scheme of world political security provision for the accumulation by the United States of large stock-piles of essential strategically important raw materials. In real life it usually happens that the solution of difficult problems has to be sought by working simultaneously along a number of lines, and the economist would not reject the assistance which the adoption of this proposal might afford. But he would still be entitled to insist that it was not a radical measure, in the true sense of the term, and would feel it a matter for regret if the interest aroused by it were to divert attention from the necessity for genuine structural changes, the urgency of which would merely be postponed and not destroyed by such measures.

8. There are, however, other issues of a more fundamental character the consideration of which has suggested to some recent writers that the relevance of the United States tariff has been much exaggerated. Many, both in Great Britain and the United States, who have enthusiastically embraced the current doctrines which emphasise the value of expansive credit policies for ensuring a continuous high level of general activity, have been carried so far by their enthusiasm as to believe that such policies would by themselves automatically adjust the United States balance of payments without any necessity for significant tariff changes. In the United States such optimism affords comfort particularly to those who despair in the face of political opposition of ever being able to do anything about the tariff, and they persuade themselves that a high level of activity would generate such a flood of additional import demand that foreign goods would surge into the country in sufficient volume to provide a supply of dollars adequate for the requirements of the rest of the world, and of such

a kind as would not unduly provoke the opposition of high protectionists.

9. On the British side, members of the same school, who have attempted to measure the probable effects of concrete tariff reductions upon the demand for specific British export items, have tended to conclude that the elasticity of demand will not be sufficient completely to fill the probable gap between the credit and the debit items in the United States balance of payments, and are accordingly ready to play into the hands of the faint-hearted Americans by assuring them that it really does not matter very much whether their tariff is lowered or not.

10. We have already indicated with, it is hoped, sufficient clearness the great importance which is rightly attached to the maintenance of high levels of general activity, but it would be disastrous if in our preoccupation with this objective, often wrongly supposed to be a novel aim for public policy, we were to underrate the at least equally great importance to be attached to continuous adjustments in the structure of national economies to changes in conditions of production in the world at large. Tariffs are a powerful though not the only obstruction in the way of these adjustments, and the tariff of a large and powerful economy is disproportionately much more effective for obstruction than the combined tariffs of even a large number of small economies. If in a spirit of defeatism we are tempted to write off the American tariff as a factor of little significance, we condemn ourselves and the rest of the world, including the United States, to a lower level of production and real income than our technical skill and scientific knowledge would justify us in expecting. The stimulus to imports arising from a high level of activity in the United States would no doubt be valuable even without any modification of its tariff, but an examination of the history of the inter-war period warns us against exaggerating its strength.[1] The rest of the world will be entitled to rejoice if the state of internal activity in the United States strengthens its demand for its traditional imports, but it would be an illusion to suppose that this by itself will solve the problem of adequate dollar supply.

11. When great issues are involved affecting the interests of

[1] Hal B. Lary, *The United States in the World Economy*, pp. 14-15.

two powerful states each of whom has in the past in varying ways been accustomed to getting its own way, it is inevitably a ticklish business even to get provisional agreement about the facts of a post-war balance of payments situation in which both parties are intimately concerned, and demanding, in the view of many, drastic changes of policy on either side. In any case many of the facts are necessarily highly speculative. The British are naturally suspected in the United States of exaggerating their difficulties, and any figures which they tentatively put forward, other people will be likely to discount. Human nature being what it is, it would be imprudent to reject outright the possibility of such exaggeration. But, on the other side, it is equally possible for people, feeling themselves uncomfortably pressed to grapple with the thorny political tariff problem, which promises them plenty of kicks but very few ha'pence, to exaggerate the importance of mitigating elements which they feel may excuse them from embarking upon such a perilous undertaking. Europeans may too easily neglect the importance of the services they can sell to travellers from the United States, but while this item may be substantial, it seems optimistic to suppose that it can have the importance which some people in that country would like to suppose. Nor will a judicious estimate of future trends entirely ignore the possibility of movements in United States costs damping down the outward flow of her exports. This would be a doubtful blessing for a world eager to use capital equipment from the United States to accelerate the reconstruction of its war-scarred economies, but there might be some compensating benefits in a relaxation of the pressure to get adequate supplies of dollars. This too, however, is not a factor upon which one can count with any certainty. The only safe course is to face the ultimate necessity for structural adjustments, and to prepare to make them in an orderly manner.

12. The inherent defect, however, which makes so many of these calculations sterile is that almost inevitably they tend to be based upon a static view of economic conditions. We can scarcely get any clear picture of, for example, the elasticity of United States demand for imports from another country except in terms of the goods which have already been imported in considerable volume

in the past. But while a considerable measure of continuity in economic relations is always to be expected, and calculations based on past experience must have a place in estimating the future course of events, the peculiarities of post-war problems arise very largely precisely from the fact that in certain respects continuity has been sharply broken. Many of Great Britain's exports will be the same in the future as in the past, and the United States will continue the importation in greater or less volume of many of the same goods as she formerly purchased from abroad. But the effect of changes of policy upon the movement of many such goods as these will be, or should be, less significant than its effect upon the movement of goods which have hitherto been relatively unimportant in United States foreign trade.

13. There remains to be considered the possibility of solving the problem, whether partially or wholly, by way of foreign investments. The revival of international investment on any substantial scale will certainly depend very much on decisions made in the United States, so that, apart from the special problem of the post-war United States balance of payments, this is a convenient place for adding some more general observations upon the wider issue. Foreign investment, perhaps even more than tariff policy, is clearly a matter for the people of the United States to decide for themselves. The rest of the world has no power to compel either the United States Government or any individual citizen of that country to lend money if there is no will to do so.

14. Any attempt to fit practice into a clearly defined logical framework may not, however, be very helpful in this connection. If there is any post-war international investment by the United States, it is not likely to take a neat logical shape. It has been widely assumed on both sides of the Atlantic that previous unfortunate experience of the unreliability of foreign debtors has completely cured the private investor in the United States of any propensity to dabble further in that stormy field. But while the burnt child may justly dread the fire, he does not, as he grows up, cease to make experiments with the sources of heat and light. British investment, too, in some of its early experiments, had similar unfortunate experiences, which did not, however, deter the British lender from trying again. Sometimes indeed it seems

reasonable to convict some of those who say that private international investment will never revive in the United States of wishful thinking. They dislike " unplanned " activity of this kind, and therefore try to persuade themselves that it can never happen again. Some go so far as to talk as if private international investment were in itself undesirable, and definite steps should therefore be taken to discourage it.

15. A still more defeatist view goes much further than this, maintaining that international investment in the past has on the whole been unprofitable for the investor. It has helped to develop the resources of borrowing countries, but lenders, it is argued, have got very little directly out of it. This view is often made the basis for claims that plans for international investment in the future must be examined on new lines, more or less on the lend-lease model. Lenders should be discouraged from expecting any direct financial return, and place their reliance instead on the indirect benefits flowing from the general development of productive resources elsewhere. It is the more curious that such views as these have been most strongly expressed in Great Britain, the economy upon which international lending has in the past conferred the greatest benefits. It might have been supposed that that very preoccupation with the post-war balance of payments, a problem which arises most directly from the disappearance of the income formerly drawn from foreign investments, should have been a sufficient safeguard against this error. It is, of course, true that much international lending has been unprofitable. But so has much home investment. Even if it could be shown that losses had been so great as to reduce the average net return much below the average return on home investments, it would not follow that lenders as a whole would have done better to keep out of the foreign field, for the profitability of home investment was in many instances itself dependent on the developments fostered by foreign investment.

16. Many who dislike " State interference " are, however, equally unrealistic in assuming that all international investment must be cast in the pattern which they happen to prefer. A more cautious view, justified both by past experience and by an examination of current trends in thought and practice, would not

reject as impossible the revival of international lending on a scale sufficient to be significant, and would also expect the international capital market of the future to be in the highest degree heterogeneous, with scope in proportions which themselves would be constantly varying for private and State loans as well as for many varieties of intermediate compromises.

17. As is often wisely pointed out, international lending can by itself offer no final solution for a balance of payments disequilibrium. It may indeed make the disequilibrium worse at a later date if nothing is done to prepare for the structural changes needed if the subsequent remittance of interest and dividends is not to cause trouble. It does, however, prolong the period during which these adjustments have to be made. It provides a breathing-space, which, like other breathing-spaces, may have disastrous consequences if it merely encourages inaction, but may also, if wisely used, provide an opportunity for carrying through in an orderly way a programme which might seem quite impossible if it had to be undertaken in a hurry.

18. It has also sometimes been suggested that in estimating the prospects for a revival of international lending more attention must in future be paid to the willingness of potential borrowers to submit themselves to the inconveniences of debtor status. Even if capital is offered to them, it is sometimes argued, they may refuse it and prefer to rely entirely on their own resources. The inconveniences in question have on occasion been very serious, but as time passes the reactions to them may become a little blurred. To a considerable extent they were the result of the clash between obligations fixed in terms of money and wide fluctuations in the overseas returns from staple exports. Equity investments, the return from which is likely to vary more or less with the general prosperity of the economy where the investment has been made, has usually been less troublesome from this point of view than government loans which normally carry a fixed interest obligation, though they have some complications of their own if there is felt to be any risk of political pressure in the interests of foreign capitalists. In general, however, the larger the infusion of the equity principle in international lending, the more smoothly it is likely to work. The difficulties in the way of

adapting government borrowing to this principle are great, though probably not quite insuperable, and this is an additional reason for favouring the eclectic view which we have already defended of the most appropriate form for the international capital market of the future.

19. It is a strictly elementary point, but one which seems to require constant repetition, that such problems as are raised by repayment of capital are quite different from, and normally much less important than those raised by the remittance of interest and dividends. It is in no way paradoxical to insist that formal arrangements to ensure the repayment of capital are merely a matter of convenience and not at all of principle. The important thing is that the investment should be a good one. If that condition is satisfied, the home investor does not usually worry about getting his money back, for in case of need he can always find a buyer for such of his capital assets as he may wish to dispose of. The shareholders of a prosperous company would indeed be both astonished and embarrassed if the company insisted on redeeming its shares at their face value. The position of the international lender is in principle the same. The more speculative character of a distant and imperfectly known market may induce him to insist on some more formal guarantee, and the obligation to make amortisation payments may be justified on this ground. Their essential function, however, is to ensure that a market is maintained in the securities concerned. If a market is maintained, there is, strictly speaking, no necessity ever to consider the repayment of capital.

20. The relation between foreign investment and the movements of trade is normally most conveniently thought of as involving a flow of goods subsequent to the negotiation of a loan or investment. The role of the United States in the international capital market after the war must, however, to some extent be interpreted along different lines. In this case it is expected that in any event there will be an excess of exports over imports. This comes first in order of time, and the purpose of the investment is to finance an export surplus which has preceded it. From this follows the important conclusion that United States loans would not be effective for closing the gap in the balance of payments if they were granted on the condition, either explicit or implicit, that

the proceeds would be spent by the borrowers on additional American goods. For this would mean that the excess of exports which by hypothesis creates the problem calling for solution would be increased by exactly the same amount as the increase in the supply of dollars made available for the rest of the world.

(vii) *The Place of the Vanquished in a World Economic System*

1. Even the sketchiest commentary on post-war international economic policy would be lamentably defective if it passed over in complete silence the position of our present enemies. Our formal commitments in this respect have been made perfectly plain. The signatories of the Atlantic Charter have affirmed their intention to " endeavour, with due respect for existing obligations, to further enjoyment by all States, great or small, victor or vanquished, of access, on equal terms, to the trade and to the raw materials of the world which are needed for their economic prosperity ", and their " desire to bring about the fullest collaboration between all nations in the economic field, with the object of securing for all improved labour standards, economic advancement, and social security ". The governments and authorities represented at the United Nations Conference on Food and Agriculture again affirmed " their determination to achieve freedom from want for all people in all lands ", and " to promote the full and most advantageous employment of their own and all other people ".

2. These affirmations of principle are indeed far from precise, but on one point at least they are quite clear, — the intention to refrain from any distinction between enemies and non-enemies. This is in sharp contrast to the practice of the years immediately succeeding the war of 1914–18, though it can occasion little surprise that, under the influence of the emotions and passions which a prolonged and savage war inevitably and naturally arouses, strong currents of feeling should, as the war nears its end, show themselves favourable not only to a revival of this practice, but to its application in a much more severe and intensified form, and even when direct measures of far-reaching severity are not under consideration, there is a strong tendency to edge away from the implications of the statements quoted above. In many of the

post-war proposals made for certain specific areas, for example, little or no scope is left for German or Japanese trade. The reference in Article VII of the Mutual Aid Agreement to " agreed action, open to participation by all other countries of the like mind " has tempted some to dally with the quibble that our present enemies are obviously not " of like mind ", and that we may therefore with a clear conscience discriminate against them, while the widespread confusion of thought which assumes that effective disarmament will be impossible unless some more or less direct control is imposed upon the productive capacity of the disarmed powers has also encouraged the view that we are faced with an awkward dilemma here, and that, much as we should like to ensure economic prosperity to our former enemies, the over-riding obligation to ensure the peace of the world by disarming them may make it impossible for us to gratify our desires. All this is natural enough, but the disastrous consequences of short-sighted policy will in no way be mitigated merely because the policy happens to be based on natural emotions.

3. The world has learnt something from the disappointments which attended the effort after the last war to collect reparations on an astronomical scale, but some recent discussions of the subject suggest that it has not yet learnt enough. The line of argument which is now often followed seems to suggest that the real error was to insist on payment of reparations in money. Reparations in goods, it is argued, stand on quite a different footing. The real trouble after 1918 arose, however, just because most of the countries, which insisted on reparation claims, were not, with a few trifling exceptions, prepared to accept them in the only form, *i.e.* goods, in which ultimately they were receivable. It made no substantial difference whether the liabilities were expressed in terms of money or in terms of goods.

4. The real objection to reparations was the fear, often greatly exaggerated, that their receipt would disrupt the normal working of the economies of the recipient countries, and this objection would not be met by proposing to substitute direct transfers of goods. It may be that in the conditions of Europe after this war there will be more scope than was thought possible or desirable after 1918 for the direct utilisation of German productive capacity

for the rehabilitation of war-devastated areas. But it would be unwise to exaggerate the importance of this. And the idea which attracts some short-sighted people of applying to Germany techniques similar to those whereby she has plundered her victims, either by forced labour or by exchange and currency control, would destroy any hope of building a new civilised world order.

5. The lessons of the inter-war period on this subject are indeed quite clear. They show that policy which, whether intentionally or not, makes defeated enemies unprosperous is contrary to the interests of the victors themselves. We need not stress here the difficulties which such a policy of discrimination would put in the way of any serious attempt to build up a stable political world order. Both as a market and as a source of valuable supplies of goods and services our enemies will have an importance no less than that of any other area of comparable wealth and productive capacity. If we were to carve out from, say, the United States, Great Britain and France an area with productive capacity of similar volume to that of Germany, Italy, Japan and their satellite allies, and decide to impose some kind of economic ostracism or segregation upon it, everyone would at once see that the results for the rest of the world would be disastrous. No such proposal would receive even a minute's serious consideration. Ostracism or segregation imposed upon a similar area with whose inhabitants we happened to have been at war would not at once appear so absurd, but for the world economy as a whole it would equally be an act of self-mutilation.

6. The details of the post-war economic situation of the enemy countries are even more difficult to predict than of the United Nations. In particular we cannot foresee what kind of policy such governments as they may be able to set up will wish to pursue. It is widely assumed, though usually without offering any grounds for the belief, that the government of a defeated Germany will be anxious to pursue exactly the same economic policy as Hitler followed, and that we must therefore assume as a permanent factor in the world situation at least one powerful nation bent on the fullest use of the techniques of trade control first elaborated by Dr. Schacht. There is, however, no evidence upon which a confident prediction on this matter could be based,

and at least the possibility should not be lightly rejected that experience of the practical effects of this policy may cause such disillusionment and revulsion of feeling after the war that the defeated countries themselves may be the most eager to turn to something else. In any event it cannot be doubted that the policies pursued by the United Nations themselves will be a highly relevant factor influencing our enemies' views on these questions.

7. The thing which it is above all most important to avoid immediately on the conclusion of hostilities is a period during which over-strained and exhausted productive machines are allowed to run down still further and perhaps come to a complete standstill. The psychological and economic consequences of such a period would from a long-run point of view be almost as serious as the direct consequences of the war itself. Recovery from the war of 1914–18 was made much more difficult by imposing on top of it the problem of recovery from the immediate post-war chaos. Any efforts we make to protect the organisation of production in Europe from complete disruption after the war should embrace Germany and the other ex-enemy countries no less than the United Nations. And in the long run the best interests of all will be served by reducing any period during which economic disabilities may be imposed upon the defeated enemies to the shortest possible time. Emotions and passions have been roused and tempers frayed by the war, but it would be disastrous if, in deference to natural human feelings, we delayed too long the appeal to a longer sighted reason, of whose ultimate revival at some time or other we can be confident.

(viii) *An International Institutional Framework*

1. The most pressing lesson suggested by the economic clashes and frustrations of the inter-war period is the urgent necessity for some kind of institutional framework within which national states are still free to make their own decisions, but subject to the influence of something resembling the institutional hedges which inside a national state keep the free individual more or less on the right road. By constructing such a framework we might hope to ensure that the architects of national policy were protected from finding themselves in a position where they were obliged to

make short-sighted decisions apparently in their own national interest which nevertheless, because they failed to take proper account of their repercussions elsewhere, were almost certain to be self-frustrating and abortive.

2. A full discussion of this question would raise all the thorny and ticklish issues of national sovereignty hitherto found so intractable. The economic aspects of large-scale federations have already received much serious consideration, but even if such proposals are not ruled out as altogether impractical, it seems more useful, in the concluding stage of our argument, to confine our attention to ideas which do not involve such far-reaching and revolutionary changes in international practice. And, we might add, even if large-scale federations were established on a much more ample scale than at present seems probable, the idea elaborated below would still be relevant, for unless federation were pushed so far as to embrace practically the whole world, the problem of co-ordinating the policies of the federations would remain.

3. The technique which we wish to submit for consideration might be illustrated from any sector in the field of international economic policy. We select for this purpose the problem of the co-ordination of commercial policies. It is not implied that this is the first or even the most important field where such treatment would be useful, but an examination of its possibilities follows naturally from the analysis of our main problem, the disruptive consequences of resistance to structural adjustment. Similar ideas could be easily adapted for use in other sectors of international economic policy.[1] But whatever the ultimate importance to be attached to aberrations of trade policy, their potentialities for disrupting the orderly working of a world economic system are obviously great. The establishment of order in this field alone would therefore be an important forward step. Nor do we have in mind here any proposal for " a return to free trade ". In discussions of post-war trade policy, hostile voices are frequently raised to inform us that " a return to free trade is impossible ".

---

[1] For a discussion mainly in terms of the problems to be handled by the Permanent Organisation for Food and Agriculture see *Political Science Quarterly*, March 1944, " International Institutions in a World of Sovereign States ".

No one has, however, seriously defended the contrary proposition, and its continued reiteration therefore makes no useful contribution to the existing sum of human knowledge. But taking the world as it is, we may still usefully examine the possibilities of an international institution the acceptance of which might provide the *minimum* foundations needed for such a co-ordination of national trade policies as would make it less easy for countries to get stupidly in each other's way.

4. We have already described in sufficient detail the vicious circle generated by the independent efforts of national states to ensure benefits for themselves, or more often to protect themselves from losses, by restricting their trade with other countries. In the light of these depressing experiences, is it too much to ask of governments in the post-war world that they should agree to allow a suitable international organisation to undertake a continuous and detailed survey of their trade policies, to report to this organisation any contemplated changes of policy (including trade agreements, which would be submitted jointly by the parties to the agreement), with a reasoned statement of the purposes for such changes, and of the grounds for believing that the proposed changes would in fact achieve their purposes, and to postpone putting changes into operation until some agreed period of time had elapsed, sufficient to give the organisation an opportunity to comment upon them ? Hitherto in practice sovereign rights have tended to mean not only an insistence on being allowed to make one's own decisions but also a considerable sensitiveness at even an expression of opinion on such decisions by the authorities of other countries. Though no doubt in unofficial communications the representatives of sovereign states allow themselves a considerable freedom and candour of expression, these characteristics are usually absent from public diplomatic documents, and the documents of international organisations have also usually been watered down in deference to the same tradition. It should not be utopian to hope that we might abandon this excessive sensitiveness, at least to the extent of not resenting, or even of welcoming clear and reasoned statements by an international authority of the effects upon other countries of the trade policies which we were pursuing or proposing to pursue. In this

connection the lead must clearly be given by the larger and more powerful states, who should apply themselves to the task of convincing their more nationalistically-minded citizens that their prejudices against " the idea that any international body was to be permitted to pry into our concerns " [1] should be modified at least when there was abundant evidence to show that " our concerns " were also other people's concerns.

5. The question of the detailed constitution of such an international organisation is not a matter of first-rate importance, nor one upon which we need here elaborate at any great length. The machinery already in existence of the financial and economic sections of the League of Nations is an obvious analogy, but the principles involved would not be radically different if it were preferred to construct something entirely new. In any event the organisation would need to be much more extensive than that so far developed by the League, and it would have to be freed from the constant threat of niggling economies which frequently hampered the efficiency of the League. For the task contemplated is nothing less than a continuous detailed survey of every country in the world, and vast as is the information collected by the League which has relevance for this purpose, it is still quite inadequate. Nor would it be sufficient to rely upon official or other published data, which would everywhere need to be supplemented by skilled and independent investigation on the spot. Although, especially in dealing with any specific proposal, provision should be made for associating with the work of the organisation representatives of the state or states immediately concerned, whose business it would be to present their government's case, the work of investigation and report should be in the hands of full-time members of the staff of the organisation, who would be servants of the international body and not servants of national governments. Especially for commenting upon the purposes justifying changes in trade policy, the staff should include men of wide experience and varied background, and should not be exclusively economists, in the ordinary sense of that word. The purposes in mind are by no means always

[1] Sir Harry Lindsay, formerly Under-Secretary to the Bengal Government, *Manchester Guardian*, July 30, 1943.

economic purposes, and some people might fear that economists would be too unsympathetic in assessing the importance of non-economic objectives. Whether the decision to issue reports should rest with the controlling organ whose members would presumably be representatives of the states which had set up the international authority, is a question to be determined after weighing the advantages to be gained from the association of their names with the published reports against the disadvantages of delay if business had to be held up for a body which could meet only at infrequent intervals.

6. Such an organisation should be in a position, if the governments concerned agreed to defer the imposition of changes in trade policy, to comment with little delay (always provided there was an adequate staff for the purpose) upon any changes which it was proposed to make. Governments should then still be formally free to ignore these comments, or to modify their proposals in accordance with them ; but if they were published, as they should be, it might be hoped, especially as the experience of the organisation became more extensive and impressive, that there would be increasing reluctance to adopt an attitude of continuous defiance. It would, of course, be all to the good if governments would assume obligations more onerous and far-reaching than this, undertaking perhaps to observe a code, as detailed as it was found convenient to elaborate, of international good behaviour in their trade policies, but for the moment we are confining our attention strictly to the *minimum* requirements, which would make the least formal demands upon the susceptibilities of suspicious national states.

7. The efficiency of the organisation would obviously be increased if at the same time governments were themselves to set up machinery for a similar continuous survey of economic trends, from the standpoints of the interests of their own countries. They might well feel the existence of such machinery to be an important if not an indispensable aid in their own relations with the international organ, and the detailed structure of the international staff would itself be affected if corresponding national staffs were in existence and satisfactory relations with them could be established.

8. The proposed authority should not confine itself to examining complaints made by governments. On the contrary, it should make its own independent investigations even when no formal representations had been made. Nor should it wait for changes in trade policy to be proposed. It should have the right to make suggestions upon its own initiative, if policies already in force appeared to it to be having consequences to which it was proper that attention should be drawn.

9. Trade policy in this context must clearly be interpreted in the widest possible sense to include not only tariff changes, but also all the other methods now so widely used to influence the direction of trade. If properly organised and administered, the machinery proposed should have the further advantage of making it possible to direct attention to the numerous cases where changes in trade policy are closely connected with conflicts in policy affecting other parts of the economic field, *e.g.* currency and credit, migration, capital investment, production, etc. It should be open to the international authority to examine clashes between policies in these various directions, to suggest perhaps to a complaining state that the effects of some variation in trade policy might be mitigated by some other change, not in trade policy but in some other sector of general economic policy. The variety of possible interrelations and interactions is practically infinite — the most obvious illustration which at once comes to mind is the connection between migration restrictions and trade restrictions — and the authority of the international organ to make observations and comments upon them should not be limited by any narrow interpretation of its terms of reference.

10. It is likely to be objected that governments would often feel reluctant to announce beforehand their intentions to vary trade policy. There are many practical (and some good) reasons why traders should not be given too long notice of proposed tariff changes, and it would be obviously impossible to announce to the world beforehand an intention to vary the external value of a national currency. To meet such difficulties variants in procedure might, however, be worked out to suit the varying character of the proposals likely to be made. The Tripartite Monetary Agreement, for example, contemplated giving notice to other interested

governments, though not to the general public, of intention to vary exchange rates ; in other cases the imposition of retrospective duties might be a sufficient safeguard. The important thing is to discourage the habits of thought and action which in the past created situations where governments felt themselves obliged to enforce without delay rough-and-ready solutions. The objective to be aimed at would be realised when governments felt that, instead of saying " We must do this, whatever other countries may think about it ", they were able to approach the international authority and say, " This is our problem. What do you suggest would be the best thing to do about it ? " The need for swift action is naturally most keenly felt in times of crises, and many important decisions will have to be made immediately after the war which could not be deferred until the approval of the authority suggested had been announced. We have, however, indicated the dangers likely to arise if our thinking about post-war policy is unduly dominated by our recollection of our feverish efforts to struggle against the post-war depression. In the course of time it would be reasonable to expect that the work of the proposed international authority would be a powerful influence in preventing the re-emergence of a state of affairs in which governments felt that they had no alternative but to initiate hasty and even panic measures to ward off the effects of a catastrophic depression.

11. National tariff commissions and similar bodies should also form the habit of working in close collaboration with the international authority, and indeed governments might even be prepared to agree formally to impose upon themselves the duty of making such collaboration possible. In time, instead of working out changes in policy independently of the international authority and then submitting them later for comment, governments might even form the habit of informal consultation at an early date, so that the international authority might ultimately become an important medium for negotiating trade and other agreements.

12. A proposal of this kind is likely to be criticised from two contradictory angles. To many of those who have wider and more far-reaching plans for post-war economic reconstruction the proposal will seem disappointingly moderate and restrained,

for they often seriously contemplate a degree of international control going much further than has here been envisaged. On the other hand, another school, which has little faith in international restraints of any kind, will be eager to brush these old-fashioned proposals aside and to proceed vigorously with a programme of internal reconstruction, and will find some support from others who dislike international organisation in its true sense in even the mildest form. The ideas of this school are usually associated with an overweening pride which grossly exaggerates the capacity of the economy whose internal development is being planned to impose its will on other economies. International discipline of even a mild kind is repugnant to these people, because they believe that by other means other weaker economies may be compelled to do what they want. This is a dangerous illusion, and likely to bring disaster upon those who cherish it.

13. Those who would like a more rigid and sterner discipline may be reminded, on the other hand, that it is of little use drawing up neat plans for an entirely imaginary world. It would no doubt be convenient if every nation, or even only a significant proportion of the more important nations, were suddenly to become convinced of the wisdom of far-reaching international controls of national policy. At a time, moreover, when customary ideas have been so severely shaken as to-day, there may be an increased chance of radical solutions finding acceptance. There is, however, a limit beyond which this confidence cannot be safely pushed. There are few signs so far of any willingness on the part of the main governments of the world to go much further than the present proposal. If they could be induced even to go so far, we should have gone a long way. Provided that they co-operated effectively in enabling the international organisation to build up the foundation of knowledge necessary for the efficient performance of its tasks, it might easily become an instrument capable of doing more important and fundamental work.

14. Formal adherence by every sovereign state would not be an essential condition for the effective life of this organisation. There are no technical reasons to prevent it from operating even if its membership were quite small, though it could not be

regarded as an international instrument of any great importance unless membership covered a considerable number especially of the larger and more powerful states.

15. Such a suggestion put forward in a book where "planners" have already been criticised for their failure to announce the principles whereby their future decisions are to be guided can scarcely ignore the obvious criticism that little light has been thrown here upon the principles which would guide the formation of opinion by the proposed international organisation. The criticism is not entirely unjust, but two points should be taken into account before it is pressed too hard. If it should be found possible at the same time to elaborate an international code which had a fair chance of acceptance by a significant number of national states, that would be all to the good. It should not, however, be too readily supposed that international collaboration necessarily means that every country must do the same thing, expand credit at the same rate, reduce tariffs by the same proportion, or establish uniform labour conditions. Such formal uniformity would often be of little value, for the complexities of international economic relations frequently arise from quite legitimate variations in national policies, which have their roots in corresponding variations in historical and geographical backgrounds. Secondly, the task of a critical commentator, though it would no doubt be made easier by the prior acceptance of a body of agreed general principles, would not be entirely impossible in its absence, for his attention would in any event be directed mainly to forecasting the consequences for other economies of decisions made by any particular economy. In this respect his work would be entirely different from that of the "planner", who must, from the very nature of his office, choose between alternative courses of action. Nor is the difficulty which arises here peculiar to the particular type of international organisation now under discussion. It presents itself at once as soon as any concrete proposal of any kind is put forward for an effective international agency. One reason for scepticism about some of the more elaborate general proposals which have been made, whether they visualise genuine international collaboration or the substitute type which contemplates a hegemony exercised by one or more of the Great

Powers, is precisely the same absence of information about the criteria according to which the administrators of such agencies are to make their decisions.

(ix) *Conclusion*

1. The problems of post-war international economic policy are bewildering in their complexity, and our exposition has sadly neglected many of their aspects which are of the utmost importance. No simple solution is indeed likely to be found, for the complexities are not the result of the evil machinations of either wicked or clever men, but are inherent in the nature of things. In the last resort, however, many of the difficulties will be found to have their roots in one simple social and psychological phenomenon, the difficulty involved in a full realisation of the responsibilities and limitations of adult status. Many parents will recall an early stage in the life of their small children when they were firmly convinced that the activities of everyone with whom they came into contact ought, in a rational world, to be moulded in accordance with their own convenience. Most people leave this stage behind as they grow older ; they realise that the world is not like that, and that they must therefore in various ways adapt their modes of living and thinking to the needs and even to the prejudices of other people. In a profound sense it is true that one's success in becoming a genuinely civilised being and a useful member of society depends on the degree in which one gets clear from these childish illusions.

2. The necessity for adaptation to wider social needs and purposes is obvious within a society, even if it sometimes provokes irritation and resentment. But within the widest social framework of which we have experience, where the units appear not as individual men and women but as national states, the process of growing up has unfortunately not yet gone very far. Autarky, in its literal sense of self-sufficiency, is now somewhat discredited, after the unhappy experiences which the world has had of the consequences of German and Japanese efforts to attain it, and even those whose post-war policies appear to have more than a tinge of autarky in them, usually hasten, however unconvincingly, to reassure us on this point. But many are still much attracted by

the illusory goal of autarchy, the power to control one's own destiny and, consciously or unconsciously, mould their ideas about post-war policy on the comfortable hypothesis that somehow or other the governments and peoples of other nations can be persuaded or, in the last resort, compelled to adapt themselves to the requirements of others, rather than insist upon having their own way.[1]   Few now would go so far as Goering, who told the International Chamber of Commerce in Berlin in July 1937 that " the condition of dependence upon the greater or lesser goodwill of foreign Powers is for a self-conscious people that has the desire to live simply intolerable ", but even when lip-service is paid to the idea of international interdependence, too many people still cherish a secret hope that while interdependence may demand changes from others, they may be excused from any obligation to make awkward adjustments.

3. The whole argument of this book might be summed up as an attempt to establish the impossibility of such autarchy. Whether we like it or not, " the condition of dependence upon the greater or lesser goodwill of foreign Powers " is the inevitable fate of all of us, whether we are members of a large and powerful state or of a more modest small nation. The hard fact is that we live in a world where, in part at least, our fate depends inexorably on what other people do. Unless we are willing, in preparing our own policies, to take into account their reactions upon other economies, other economies will be equally unmindful of the reactions of their policies upon us, and the last state of all is likely to be a good deal worse than the first. No great nation, it was argued in Germany, " is either free, or independent, or sovereign, so long as it is dependent upon the foreigner from the economic standpoint ". The beginning of wisdom in modern international economic life is to realise that in this sense no nation, great or small, can be free, independent or sovereign. We are not asking of national statesmen any conversion to a fantastic altruism, but merely that they should show in their attitude towards international relations, as already most of them do in relation to internal policy, that they have grown up, and no longer cherish childish illusions.

---

[1] Cf. A. G. B. Fisher, *Economic Self-Sufficiency*, pp. 3-5.

4. For obvious reasons this lesson is hardest to learn for the statesmen of the most powerful states, whose habits of thought are based on a past experience which encourages the belief that within fairly wide limits they will normally be able to get their own way. It is they who are therefore most likely to be tempted by illusions of omnipotence, such as are much encouraged at the present time by popular discussions which lay such emphasis, and within limits, justified emphasis, upon the post-war responsibilities of the three or four Great Powers. The fact of interdependence indeed in no way justifies mere passivity on the part of anyone. Someone must take the lead, and the most obvious " leaders " are those who have the greatest power. But there are many ways of taking a lead, and if the Great Powers show an inadequate appreciation of the part to be played by their smaller and weaker neighbours, the evil consequences for the world as a whole will not be restrained outside their own borders. Properly interpreted, there is no question here of the " rights " of small states ; it is primarily a question of facing the world as it actually is.

5. In varying ways the illusion of omnipotence is a temptation for all the Great Powers. The position of Great Britain is, however, probably more complicated and delicate than that of her great partners. Great Britain has long occupied a dominating position in the world, which, partly because it has been filled with discretion and restraint, has enabled her during the last century, broadly speaking, to get her own way. There is no reason to suppose that discretion and restraint will fail to mark her future policy, but in the meantime fundamental changes have occurred in the relative distribution of power throughout the world which make it unlikely that even the utmost discretion and restraint in the future will enable her to enjoy all the same happy advantages as have been her custom hitherto. The intellectual revolution involved in the adaptation of deeply rooted habits of thought which thus becomes necessary for the British people is perhaps the most difficult experience which any people could be asked to face. But unless the adaptation is made, the prospects for the future are most disturbing.

6. The content of any illusions of omnipotence which people in the United States or the U.S.S.R. may be disposed to cherish

will naturally not be quite the same as those which still attract some in Great Britain. The absolute power of these states is still markedly on the up-grade, and short-sighted enthusiasm may encourage the belief that nothing is impossible for them. But a wise statesman in even the most powerful state will constantly remind himself that in the long run he will never be able to get exactly what he wants. At the worst, the smaller states have a considerable capacity for obstruction ; at the best, there may flow from their active and willing collaboration contributions to orderly world development which are literally indispensable.

7. One important characteristic of adult status which requires special emphasis is the realisation that in the nature of things we can never have absolute certainties or absolute guarantees. There are some inexorable risks which we cannot evade. It is natural enough that recent experience of a stormy and uncertain world should have created everywhere a wistful longing for certainties. Some manifestations of this spirit have been subjected to analysis in the course of our argument. Its influence, however, goes much deeper than anything with which it has been relevant for us to deal. We are disappointed when other states refuse to enter into firm commitments binding themselves to action of a precise kind in some hypothetical future situation. And at the same time the same hankering after certainties makes us eager to keep our own hands quite untied so that we shall be perfectly free to do as we please. All this is in a quite literal sense childish, and it is none the less childish when it is wrapped up in the pomposities of diplomatic verbiage. We cannot reasonably reproach a child for acting according to his nature. At least he has the capacity to learn from experience. The human race cannot expect a favourable verdict from history if in this respect it shows itself less capable than a child.

INDEX

THE END

Printed in Great Britain by R. & R. CLARK, LIMITED, *Edinburgh.*

Date Due

MR 12 '48			
MAY 1 8 '50			
MAY 2 2 '53			
⑬			